They Spoke French

A book about

French Heritage in Minnesota

A Minnesota History Educational Project sponsored by the
French-American Heritage Foundation of Minnesota

Compiled by Mark Labine
Third Edition (March, 2018)

Picture on page by Albert Bierstadt (1830-1902) (Public Domain)

Self Published by the
French-American Heritage Foundation.

First & Second Edition
ISBN-13: 978-1522719830
ISBN-10: 1522719830

Third Edition
ISBN-13: 978-1986542500
ISBN-10: 1986542505
BISAC: History/United States/State & Local/Midwest

Table of Contents

Many thanks to the following persons who helped contribute to the writing and publishing of this book:

Greg Brick Ph.D. is a Research Analyst with the Minnesota Department of Natural Resources. His first book, Iowa Underground: A Guide to the State's Subterranean Treasures, was published in 2004. His latest book, Subterranean Twin Cities, published by the University of Minnesota Press in 2009, won an award from the local chapter of the American Institute of Architects. His doctoral research focused on fur-trade era French saltpeter caves.

Jerry Foley is a member of the French-American Heritage Foundation Board of Directors and in his retirement years, Jerry has been an avid student of Canadian history and genealogy. He authored *Minnesota, Eh? A Foley/Perras Family History*. With a Canadian cousin, he created a genealogy of the family of George Fallu, his great-great-grandfather and the first mayor of Nouvelle, Quebec.

Pierre Girard is a member of the French-American Heritage Foundation Board of Directors. Pierre's grandparents immigrated to Wisconsin from the Trois-Rivières area of Quebec. He was raised in an ethnic home and appreciates his heritage. Through his involvement with La Société Canadienne Française, Les Canadiens Errants and trips to Canada and France, he has thoroughly explored that heritage. Now in retirement, he is a volunteer at the Minneapolis City Hall where he gives building tours and plays concerts on the City Hall Tower chime.

Mark Labine is the President of the French-American Heritage Foundation and a longtime lover of history, especially his French-Canadian and Acadian family history. Mark has written a number of books on his ancestors for both his paternal (French) and maternal (English) family lines. His ancestors were early settlers in St. Paul and helped build the original St. Paul Chapel. He was raised on a farm in Minnesota that his French-Canadian Great Grandparents established as pioneers in 1879. He is an attorney and judicial officer for the Hennepin County District Court.

Rev. Jules O. Omalanga is a French Speaking ordained Roman Catholic priest. He worked for the Archdiocese of Kinshasa in the Democratic Republic of Congo. He worked as an Associate Pastor, Pastor, and Procurer of the Archdiocese. He immigrated to the USA in 2003. He was assigned by the Archdiocese of St. Paul and Minneapolis as Hospital Chaplain at Hennepin County Medical Center, North Memorial Medical Center, Parochial Administrator of the Church of St. Leonard's of Port Maurice, and Pastor of the Church of St. Philip's. Currently he is Hospital Chaplain at Fairview Hospital at the University of Minnesota, and Chaplain for the Francophone African Catholic Community located at the Church of St. Boniface in Northeast Minneapolis, MN.

Jane Skinner Peck lived in France at the age of 19, and has returned many times for further study; absorbing the language and culture into her life and work. As a dance historian, choreographer, and professor of dance Jane has researched and performed the dances and cultures of many French cultures: 18th c. Versailles, Quebec, Red River Metis, Haiti, West Africa. She directs her company, Dance Revels Moving History, in many of these performances and teaches workshops across the Midwest. She has been an adjunct faculty member at Winona State University Department of Theater and Dance since 2011.

Jacqueline Regis is a Hennepin County District Court Judge and a board member of the Alliance Francaise of Minnesota. She is a former Assistant Attorney General, and president of Minnesota Women's Lawyers. She was born and raised in Les Cayes, Haiti. Jacqueline has been a featured speaker at a number of events talking about her French Speaking Haitian culture.

John Schade is a Librarian at the Minnesota Genealogical Library. John is the former president of the Minnesota Genealogical Society and an expert in French-Canadian Genealogical Research.

Also special thanks to members of the Board of Directors of the French-American Heritage Foundation, and especially, Dick Bernard, Dustin Dufault, Pierre Girard, Carole Mayers, Mark Petty, Marie Trepanier and Corey LeVasseur for their contributions to this project. Also, special thanks to Judy Labine for her grammatical editing of the book, and David Thofern for his professional advice on the design and layout of book and Fred Johnson for his review and comment on the book's historical accuracy.

"The Mapmaker"
Painting by Robert Perrizo

Robert Perrizo is a French-American Heritage Foundation board member and an artist and storyteller in the historical spirit of Howard Pyle, Frederic Remington, N.C. Wyeth and Charlie Russell. He is a descendant of one of Canada's first French settlers, Jean Dalpe de Parisot. He brings to life the epic 1610-1840 saga of the French voyageurs who defined the northern tier of North America more than a century before other Europeans arrived. He has graciously agreed to allow the French-American Heritage Foundation to use his paintings throughout the book to help illustrate the French Heritage in Minnesota.

French-American Heritage Foundation of Minnesota

Mission: To preserve and promote the French-American Heritage in Minnesota
through education and community events

This book includes many pictures and images. It is the belief of the Foundation that all images being used in this book belong in the public domain. The Foundation has not used any pictures that have a name printed on the picture or that were clearly stated to be protected by copyright. When the name of the author is known, the name of the author is identified. It is the Foundation's intent that the use of pictures and photos used in this book either are in the public domain or would fall under the fair use doctrine which is allowed by the United States copyright law. No provisions of any copyright held by any other person were knowingly violated. If anyone reading this book believes that the Foundation has violated the principal of fair use of a photo or picture, please let the Foundation know at the email address included in their website and the picture or photo will be removed immediately.

Cover Picture

The cover picture is titled "The Falls of St. Anthony" and painted by Albert Bierstadt (1830-1902). The falls have a strong connection to French Heritage in Minnesota since they are associated with French speaking Father Louis Hennepin and his discovery of the Falls in 1680. He later publicized his discovery of the Falls to the world in his books titled *Description de la Louisiane* (Paris, 1683), *Nouvelle découverte d'un très grand pays situé dans l'Amérique entre le Nouveau-Mexique et la mer glaciale* (Utrecht, 1697), and *Nouveau voyage d'un pays plus grand que l'Europe* (Utrecht, 1698).

The picture on the back of the book is a picture by Frances Anne Hopkins, titled "Voyageurs at Dawn" painted in 1871. The original is currently owned by the Library and Archives of Canada.

Preface
The Influence of the French-Canadians on the U.S. Midwest
By Pierre Girard

Lac qui Parle, Marquette, Nicollet, Eau Claire, Prairie du Chien, LaSalle, Little Canada, Faribault, Bottineau Blvd., Centreville, Lac Courte Oreilles, Duluth, Radisson, Roseau, Baudette; and the list goes on and on. Such is the legacy left by the French and subsequently by the descendants of the Canadians of French ancestry.

One has to travel only short distances around the Midwest section of the United States to encounter the influence of French-Canadians. There are cities and towns and rivers and prairies, too numerous to mention, with names given to them by the early French explorers, voyageurs and immigrants from eastern Canada. Like most immigrants, they settled together in areas and gave those locations names in their native language. They established institutions like schools and churches; Ste. Genevieve, St. Louis King of France. Our Lady of Lourdes, Notre Dame du Chutes. French was spoken at Mass and taught in the schools until the state established English as the language to be used in the schools. To counter the change, French continued to be the language spoken in the home. Business in the smaller towns was frequently conducted in French and societies such as St. Jean Baptiste, allowed members the comfort of continuing to speak their native tongue.

The first Europeans to enter the Midwest states of Minnesota, Wisconsin, Iowa, the Dakotas, and Michigan were from "New France" in Canada. Chippewa Falls, Wisconsin was founded by Jean Brunet, St. Paul Minnesota by Pierre Parrent, often called "Pig's Eye Parrent." Pierre Bottineau was one of the founders of Minneapolis and several smaller towns all the way to the Red River Valley. Thus, the state of Minnesota is the only state to have its motto in French:" L' etoile du Nord" and the city of Minneapolis has as its motto "En Avant."

In the beginning, it was the voyageurs and the missionary priests who were traveling about the land. Then, there began the influx of settlers to the land. They came down mainly from the Quebec area of Canada. There were farmers, loggers and tradesmen of all types. They began to establish farming towns all over the Midwest and many resided in the cities. They brought with them their language, culture and religion. Unlike many of the emigrants from Quebec to New England, these people were here to stay. They raised large families, continued to cook soupe aux pois, bake tourtiere, speak French, and practice their Catholic faith. Large beautiful churches were built with schools attached. Quebec customs continued and life went on. As generation after generation was born, the influence of the Quebec heritage waned. For several years Quebec seemed a faraway land that grandpa and grandma came from. Newer generations spoke less French. But still, the names of the towns, rivers, churches, and prairies surround us and remind us from whence we came.

Now a new age is upon us. Canada is the United States' biggest trading partner. Quebec is Minnesota's biggest trading partner. Technology has brought us all closer together. Family groups are forming in Quebec, and now we can once again be a part of our Canadian family. Now, with improved roadways, dependable automobiles, and easy access to great communication methods, travel and access to family in Quebec is no longer and issue. Interest in our heritage is rising. Understanding our heritage brings appreciation to who we are and how we got here.

This is something I noticed while visiting cemeteries in the towns along the Chemin du Roi-standing in the graveyards and observing the grave stones reminded me of visiting the cemeteries in Chippewa Falls, Faribault, Minneapolis Pioneer Cemetery, Centreville, Minnesota and Little Canada, Minnesota (a St. Paul suburb). Many of the names in the Quebec cemeteries are also in our cemeteries! It is a feeling of "home."

Many of us in the U.S. were raised with the customs of our Quebec ancestors. Tourtiere, soupe aux pois, Easter water, patriarchal New Year's blessing, Reveillon and "Prendre un p'tit coup c'est agreable" are all great memories for so many of us. In the Twin Cities of Minneapolis/St. Paul there has been a renewed interest in our heritage. Two new "French" groups have formed in the last two years. One is an "all things French" group that seeks to encourage all the local French groups to celebrate their heritage. That entity, French-American Heritage Foundation, works with the Alliance Francais, Les Survivants, local African-American cultures from French speaking countries, and French speaking Caribbean cultures. We also want to involve the French restaurants in our area, of which there are many, in celebrating the culture. Les Survivants is strictly a Quebec Canadian-French group which strives to reconnect Minnesota French-Canadians to their Quebec culture both past and present.

Recently, a journalist from France came to Minneapolis to produce a documentary on what is left of the French influence in the Midwestern section of the United States. She discovered that so much of the culture of the Canadian-French remains in this area that she has had to limit her program to just Minnesota. Over 400,000 Minnesotans claim to have French-Canadian heritage. Many of us still alive had parents who spoke French before they entered school. We heard our older relatives speaking French at family gatherings and singing the old Quebec songs.

For many of us "Je me souviens"…is still a reality.

Chapter One
Foreword
By Jerry Foley

French-Americans, also called Franco-Americans, are Americans who identify themselves to be of French or French-Canadian descent. According to the 2000 U.S. Census, about 11.8 million U.S. residents are of French or French-Canadian descent, and about two million speak French at home.[1] An additional 450,000 United States residents speak a French-based Creole language according to the 2000 census. In Minnesota, in the 1980 U.S. Census, 321,087 people reported they had French ancestors. At the time, this was 7.9 per cent of the total population of Minnesota.[2]

Although citizens of French descent make up a healthy percentage of the American population, they are arguably less visible than other similarly sized ethnic groups. There are several possible explanations why this is true.

First, a high level of cultural assimilation occurred among Huguenot (French Protestant) settlers who escaped religious persecution in France by heading to New France or the American colonies. Most Americans do not know that Alexander Hamilton's mother was a French Huguenot, John Jay was a descendant of French Huguenots, President James Garfield's mother was a French Huguenot, Paul Revere and Davy Crockett's ancestors[3] were French Huguenots, or that George Washington's great-great-great grandfather, Nicolas Martiau, was a French Huguenot from Ile de Re, France, who arrived at Virginia in 1620. A number of French Huguenots escaped to Germany and immigrated to the United States from Germany before settling in Minnesota. Many of these people do not even know they have Huguenot ancestors.

Second, the French-Canadians and Indians were now a conquered people, generally disliked by the New Englanders and New Yorkers who for years had fought against them. At first the French-Canadians resisted Americanization more than other ethnic groups, carrying a sense of pride as it related to their religion, language and heritage, but they faced discrimination for this. When French-Canadians migrated to New England to work in the forests and textile mills, many were unwelcomed and hired for the lowest paying jobs.[4]

When Minnesota land east of the Mississippi was first opened to settlers in 1837[5], Yankees and Yorkers rushed in and brought their prejudices with them. New England Yankees with

---

[1] Shin, Hyon B. and Bruno, Rosalind, *Language Use and English-Speaking Ability*, 2000 U.S. Census (October 2003).

[2] Information from the 1980 U.S. Census. A summary of the census results can be found on the French in America Calendar, 1989.

[3] The earliest known paternal ancestor of Davy Crockett was Gabriel Gustave de Crocketagne, whose son Antoine de Saussure Peronette de Crocketagne was given a commission in the Household Troops under French King Louis XIV. Antoine married Louise de Saix and immigrated to Ireland with her, changing the family name to Crockett (Lofaro, Michael A (December 2010). "David "Davy" Crockett" *Tennessee Encyclopedia of History and Culture*. Retrieved 24 January 2013).

[4] Levine, Ben, *Waking Up French...! Réveil*, documentary presented at Universite de La Sorbonne, Paris, France (January 30, 2006).

[5] The 1837 Treaty signed July 29, 1837, at present-day Mendota, MN (then called St. Peter or St. Pierre) between the Ojibwe and Dakota and the U.S. Government, ceded Indian Land between the Mississippi River and the St. Croix to the United States. This treaty is also known as the 1837 Treaty of St. Peters and sometimes referred to as the Dodge Treaty.

a strong Puritan influence, including most of the business owners and professionals, played a vigorous role in founding Minnesota.[6] James Mason Goodhue, the first newspaper publisher in the state, proudly wrote that "Minnesota is destined to become the New England of the West."[7] American literature written from the 1830s to the 1860s frequently referred to the French with adjectives like "lazy" or "drunk" and with pejorative names like "Canucks" or "Frogs."

For a time, the French-Canadians avoided assimilation by forming "Little Canada's" that were predominately French and Catholic. In the 1920s, however, the Ku Klux Klan became a strong organization across the nation and in New England, where the Klansmen had a strong prejudice for Catholics and French, who were often recognized for their blood ties with the Indians and thought to jeopardize the Anglo-Saxon race. America's involvement in the First World war (1917–1918) and conflict with Germany and its allies, produced a wave of suspicion, fear and hatred against German Americans and anyone else perceived as less than truly American. Stirring up fears and reactions that had been building for decades, these wartime emotions flared in the 1920s when a wave of immigrants, many catholic and Jews, led to a nationwide resurgence of the Ku Klux Klan. Such hatred fostered the growth of the Klan in Minnesota which, with an attitude of supremacy, claimed over 100,000 members in the state and identified the values of Protestantism needing protection from groups such as Catholics and Jews. The 1920s Ku Klux Klan identifies Catholics as one of the country's most serious problems, and French-Canadians, with their Catholic faith, foreign language, and parochial schools were a major concern. With a motto of "One flag, One school, One language," the Klan made no apology in their attempt to enforce their view of "Americanism" on others.[8]

The Master Pedlar
Painting by Robert Perrizo

Assimilation, an attempt to fit in, was somewhat inevitable in the face of such social intimidation. Employers tended to hire individuals with more American names and, as a result, many French in Minnesota changed their French surnames to Anglo names, e.g., LeBlanc to White and Roy to King. Younger Americans soon realized that assimilation was the key to a better life and that English helped with earning power and a chance to fully participate in society. By the World War II generation,

[6] Blegen, Theodore C. *The Land Lies Open*, D.C. Heath and Company, Boston, 1938, p.122.; Lass, William E, *History of Minnesota*, W.W. Norton & Company, (2000).
[7] Blegen, Theodore C. *The Land Lies Open*, D.C. Heath and Company, Boston, 1938, p.149.
[8] Hatle, Elizabeth Dorsey, and Vaillancourt, "One Flag, One School, One Language, Minnesota's Klu Klux Klan in the 1920s," *Minnesota History*, 61/8, Winter 2009-10, p.365.

many parents insisted on their children speaking English in school and often chose public schools for their children.

A high rate of intermarriage with persons of other nationalities led to what historian Joseph Amato called "mongrel families,"[9] who had a rich heritage, but lost most of the focus on their countries of origin. American-born children tended to be more assimilated than their parents, while the third generation generally became mainstream Americans and lost their French heritage. Today, the French and French-Canadians are so assimilated that their heritage is difficult to trace. Many Minnesotans with English, German or Scandinavian names, who have grandmothers or great-grandmothers who were French or Acadian, do not consider themselves French or French-Canadian.

One reason that early French history in Minnesota is discounted may be the ties with Native Americans, whose story is also largely overlooked in the state's history. With a shortage of French women available for marriage, most of the French men in the fur trade married Indian women for companionship as well as economic and cultural benefits. In time, the small number of French in New France meant that most French-Canadians were related and, consequently, whether acknowledged or not, most Minnesotans with French-Canadian ancestry have some Indian blood, a fact not overlooked by the New Englanders and eastern American settlers whose experience with the Indians was negative.

Yet the French heritage in Minnesota is more conspicuous than in most states, starting with the state motto *L'Etoile du Nord (Star of the North)*. French place names show up all over the State, and Minnesota's history is full of stories and connections related to the French explorers and fur traders. But asking Minnesotans why towns have names such as Roseau or Mille Lacs is likely to draw a blank stare. Many French names in Minnesota now have an anglicized pronunciation. For example, prominent St. Paul settler Louis Robert, for whom Robert Street is named, would have pronounced his last name, "Row-bear." One reason French place names in Minnesota fail to generate curiosity is that the average Minnesotan's knowledge is fairly limited when it comes to our history before statehood. Students, in most Minnesota schools, will find little in their history books beyond a paragraph or two about the French and Indian relationship.

French Americans tend to identify more strongly with their North American ties, such as Quebecois, French-Canadian, Acadian, Cajun, or Louisiana Creole rather than their French background.

During the period known by some as the Quebec Diaspora of the 1840s–1930s, some one million French-Canadians moved to the United States, principally to New England, Minnesota, Wisconsin and Michigan.[10] Others moved to different regions of Canada, especially to Ontario and Manitoba. Historically, the French in Canada had among the highest birth rates in world history, which encouraged this emigration to areas where more opportunities existed. Farm families generally divided the farm among family members, but when a

---

[9] Amato, Joseph, *Jacob's Well: A Case for Rethinking Family History*, Minnesota Historical Society Press, St. Paul, 2008, p.3.
[10] Belanger, Damien-Claude, *French-Canadian Emigration to the United States, 1840-1930*, Department d'histoire, Universite de Montreal, and Department of History, Marianopolis College, last revised August 23, 2000.

farm family had fifteen children, some members had to look elsewhere for employment. During the 19th century, Quebec agriculture was strained not only by the fast growing population and available farm land, but also by crop failures and a suffering economy. A flood of Canadians entered Minnesota after 1850. This emigration slowed down during the Civil War, when a significant number of French-Canadians fought for the North, but was followed by the largest phase of French-Canadian migration in the years following the war. The French in Canada tended to settle along the rivers, and persons engaged in the fur trade and lumbering knew the river valleys, where they tended to settle. Thus, the principal concentration of Canadian settlers in Minnesota centered along the rivers and lakes – Hennepin and Ramsey counties, Duluth, Polk and Red Lake counties. Many of the men worked in the lumbering industry and, to a lesser degree, in the burgeoning mining industry of the Lake Superior region.

The Homestead Act of 1862 provided an opportunity for acquiring land in Minnesota and the Old Crossing Treaty of 1863 opened the Red River Valley for settlers, enabling the settlement of French-Canadians in northwestern Minnesota. The railroad opening between Chicago and St. Paul in 1867 changed the migration pattern of Canadians from wagons to train cars. Recruiters, such as Pierre Bottineau, were busy enticing persons from Quebec to settle in Minnesota. These immigrants tended to settle next to kinsmen, thus populating French-speaking communities like Little Canada, Mendota, Faribault, Centerville, and St. Michael, along with Gentilly and Terrebonne in northern Minnesota, where one can find cemeteries with headstones totally in French.

A melting pot mentality in the 20th century challenged people to adhere to one cultural norm and tended to create intolerance toward cultural differences. This often led to loss of some cultural heritage, such as the French-Canadians love for pea soup and *tourtiere* (pork meat pies) as well as the loss of their language.

In recent years, these long-suppressed languages and cultures are making somewhat of a resurgence in Minnesota. In part, this is due to new immigrants coming from the many countries throughout the world where French is spoken. Nearly all of the newer arrivals came seeking to escape excessive poverty or war. For example, Vietnam, Laos and Cambodia, the French Indochina Union, broke free from French colonial rule after the French were defeated in 1954. The fall of Saigon led to a large contingent of Vietnamese in Minnesota in recent years. Haiti, where French-based Creole and French are the official languages, also provided a number of new Minnesotans.

Groups, such as Minnesota's Vietnamese and Haitian citizens, as well as people from a number of African countries such as Congo, Rwanda, and Senegal strive to keep their cultures alive with festivals and educational efforts to bring an understanding of their culture.

This resurgence of French-speaking people is also evident in a renewed interest in learning the French language, reflected in such efforts as the *Alliance Francaise*, a French cultural center in the Twin Cities, and by a number of French Immersion Schools. French is the fourth most spoken language in the U.S., behind English, Spanish, and Chinese. In the U.S., half of the foreign films watched and 30 percent of foreign books are in French. France is the most visited country in the world. U.S. trade with Francophone countries, including many from which emigrants recently left for Minnesota, accounts for 33.5 percent of Minnesota's exports.[11]

Our region's French connection gives Minnesota something in common with those on the southern end of the Mississippi. Until the Conquest of 1760, and the end of the French and Indian War three years later, the French controlled the Mississippi from Louisiana to Minnesota as part of a French strategy to encircle the British colonies from New Orleans to Quebec. Had this French claim continued, the history of Minnesota would have been quite different. The map above shows the French territory prior to the French and Indian War and the Louisiana Purchase of 1803.

So, our North Star State may be known foremost for the accomplishments of its Scandinavian and German folks but, by golly, those who came here speaking French deserve a chapter in our history lessons too!

---

[11] American Association of French Teachers Advocacy, *Minnesota Francophone Connection*, August 2006.

Chapter Two
Early French Explorers, Pioneers and Fur Traders in Minnesota
By Mark Labine

Minnesota is situated in an area that used to be part of New France. Until the Conquest of 1760,[12] and the end of the French and Indian war three years later at the Treaty of Paris, the French controlled the Mississippi waterway between Louisiana and Minnesota. French was spoken at both ends of this mighty river.

French explorers from Quebec first set foot in Minnesota in the 1600s. They discovered a bountiful land with rich soil and an ideal habitat for animals that produced high quality furs which would in turn, be ideal for the fur trading industry. They encountered many Native American tribes, including Dakota (also known as Sioux), Ojibwe (also known as Chippewa), Arapaho, Cheyenne, Fox, Sauk, Iowa, Omaha, Otoe, Ottawa, Ponca, Winnebago, and Huron (aka the Wyandot). Before them, Paleo-Indians are believed to have inhabited Minnesota as early as 7,000 to 9,000 years ago.

"Return to Home Base"
Painting by Robert Perrizo

---

[12] This is term used by French-Canadians for the English takeover of Quebec and French Canada at the end of the French and Indian War.

Étienne Brûlé is credited with being the first European and first Frenchman to reach Lake Superior in 1622–23. We know Medard Chouart des Groseilliers and Pierre Esprit Radisson were in Minnesota in 1659. They established a French presence in Minnesota, and for the next two hundred years, French would be the dominant European language spoken in the state that has the motto "L'Etoile du Nord."

This chapter discusses some early explorers, pioneers and fur traders who helped pave the way for the development, settlement and organization of the future State of Minnesota.

Claude-Jean Allouez

Claude-Jean Allouez (1622-1689) was born in Saint-Didier-en-Velay in the département of Haute-Loire in south-central France. In 1639, he graduated from the College of Le Puy, and became a Jesuit novice in Toulouse, France. In 1655, he was ordained a priest of the Roman Catholic Church. Allouez arrived in Quebec in 1658 and immediately began a study of the Wyandot and Anishinaabe languages to prepare himself for work as a missionary among the American Indian tribes along the St. Lawrence River for three years.

Father Allouez in Canoe
Public Domain

In 1665, he established a Jesuit mission in La Pointe, Wisconsin, and ventured westward to explore the northern and western shores of Lake Superior. By 1671, he produced the most accurate and earliest maps of Lake Superior, which indicated the existence of land on the western edge of Lake Superior (modern day Minnesota). See a copy of this map below under "Dablon."

Jean-Pierre Aulneau

Father Jean-Pierre Aulneau de la Touche, S.J. (1705–1736) was a Jesuit missionary priest, who was briefly active in New France, and killed before he could take part in his first major assignment, which was to be an expedition to the Mandan. Born at Moutiers-sur-le-Lay in Vendee, France, he entered the Jesuit Novitiate in 1720 and spent a number of years as an instructor in La Rochelle and Poitiers, France. He came to New France in 1734 and died near Fort St. Charles, on Lake of the Woods in an area now in Ontario, Canada and Minnesota, United States. He was killed by Dakota warriors while traveling with Jean Baptiste de La Vérendrye, and is often referred to by the Catholic Church as "Minnesota's Forgotten Martyr."[13] The Church considered Aulneau a martyr because he died in an attempt to convert the Native Americans to Christianity. St. Mary's Catholic Church in Warroad, Minnesota, is also called the Father Aulneau Memorial Church in his honor.[14]

---

[13] Campeau, Lucien, *Jean-Pierre Aulneau*, Dictionary of Canadian Biography, 2000.
[14] Id.

Picture showing Jean Baptiste de La Verendrye and Father Aulneau leaving Fort St. Charles[15]
Minnesota Historical Society Collections

Historical Marker located at Baudette Wayside/Peace Park telling the story of the death of Father Aulneau and 19 voyageurs, including Jean-Baptiste La Verendrye, the son of Pierre Gaultier de Varennes de la Verendrye.

---

[15] Picture of Aulneau aken from "The Campion", a publication of the college in Regina, Saskatchewan, by the same name.

Alexis Bailly

Alexis Bailly
Minnesota Historical
Society Collections

Alexis Bailly (1798–1861) was the son of Joseph Bailly and Angelique McGulpin, born at Grand Haven (near Lake Huron). His grandfather (Michel Bailly de Messein) was in the 1735 punitive campaign against the Fox and in 1754, at the defeat of George Washington, then an officer in the Virginia militia, at Fort Necessity. Alexis served in the War of 1812 under the British flag and in 1812 was at Mackinac. Late 1821, he was at Ft. Snelling as a part of a cattle drive from the south up to the Red River Settlement. He and three others drove the cattle to the Selkirk Colony on the Red River of the North. By 1823, he was trading at Mendota (mouth of the Minnesota River) and in October of 1824, he was appointed Register of Probate for Crawford County by Michigan Territorial Governor Lewis Cass.

From 1825 to 1831 he was in partnership with Joseph Rolette and employed Alexander and Jean Baptist Faribault as his clerks, with posts at Traverse des Sioux and the mouth of the St Peter River (later called the Minnesota River). In 1834 Henry Sibley replaced Alexis as the American Fur Company agent in Mendota. From 1835-42 Alexis resided at Prairie du Chien. He moved to Wabasha in 1842, where he lived the remainder of his life. He was first married to Lucy Anne Faribault in 1826, who died in 1855. His second marriage was to Julia Marie Cory in 1857. In September of 1837, Alexis was part of a delegation of traders that accompanied twenty Native American leaders to Washington D.C. It has been said that he gave his hospitality at Wabasha to both Jefferson C. Davis and U.S. Grant while they served in the U.S. Army early in their military careers.[16] Today, the Alexis Bailly Vineyard near Hastings honors the memory of this man.

Judge Edmund W. Bazille

Judge Edmund W. Bazille (1855–1922) was born in St. Paul, the son of Charles A. Bazille (1812–1878) and Anna Jane Perret (Perry) (1832–1891).[17] Anna Perret was the daughter of Abraham Perret and Marie Anne Bourquin, who were Selkirk colonists and among the first settlers in St. Paul. Edmund was educated in St. Paul and at the St.

Judge Edmund Bazille
Minnesota Historical
Society Collections

Paul business college. He chose to study law and studied law in the office of the late Judge Cornish. He was admitted to the bar in 1880 and served as clerk of the district court from 1883 to 1887. Bazille was elected abstract clerk in 1894 and 1898, was elected as the probate Judge in St. Paul. He was a member of the American Bar Association, the Minnesota State Bar Association, the Ramsey Bar Association, a director in the Commercial Club,

---

16 Belliveau, Walter, *The Life of Alexis Bailly, Minnesota Pioneer*, Dictionary of Canadian Biography, 1928.
17 Castle, Henry A. History of St. Paul and Vicinity, Volume I, The Lewis Publishing Company, Chicago and New York, 1912

President of the Auto Club of St. Paul, and was a member of the St. Paul Rod and Gun Club. He married Clara Gravel in 1882. In 1907 Judge Bazille was one of the keynote speakers at the dedication of the building of the fourth cathedral of St. Paul.

His father Charles Bazille was a contractor who came to St. Paul in 1843 with Captain Louis Robert. He was born in Nicollet, Quebec. He erected the first frame building in St.

Charles Bazille
Minnesota Historical
Society Collections

Paul and built the first flour mill. He built his home on the bluff where the capital now stands. Hiram Stevens in his book states as follows: "The square or block now owned by the state, and on which the present state capital stands, was a gift from Charles Bazille to the United States for capitol purposes."[18] This gift is also noted in T.M. Newson's book titled *Minnesota and Biographical Sketches of Old Settlers, from the Earliest Settlement of the City, up to and including the year 1857*.[19] He had purchased part of the claim that now includes the State Capitol. He, together with Vital Guerin, according to Newsom, jointly gave the land to the United States, which subsequently became the property of the State. Charles Bazille was noted for his generosity and donated many lots and blocks for public purposes. He married the daughter of Abraham and Maria Perret (Perry) and was the brother in law to Vital Guerin.

Charles de la Boische, Marquis de Beauharnois

Charles de la Boische, Marquis de Beauharnois (1671–1749) was a French Naval officer who served as governor of New France from 1726 to 1746. The governor worked extensively with frontier traders, explorers, and missionaries. His term saw a great expansion in the number of western forts constructed with the leadership of people like La Vérendrye, and the linkage of Canadian and Louisiana colonies. Exploration was pushed west to the Rocky Mountains by La Vérendrye and his sons. Despite a generally peaceful and prosperous administration, he was blamed for the fall of Fortress Louisbourg in 1745, and was recalled in 1746, returning to France the following year. Many places carry his name including the town of Beauharnois, Quebec and Fort Beauharnois, Minnesota.[20]

Charles de la Boische
(Public Domain)

[18] Stevens, Hiram Fairchild, History of the Bench and Bar of Minnesota, Volume 2, Minneapolis and St. Paul Legal Publishing and Engraving Company, J. Clyde Lindsey, Manager, 1904, p. 110.
[19] Newson, T.M. St. Paul, *Minnesota and Biographical Sketches of Old Settlers, from the Earliest Settlement of the City, up to and including the year 1857*, published by the author in St. Paul, Minnesota in 1886, p.44.
[20] Birk, D.A. and J. Poseley, *The French at Lake Pepin: An Archaeological Survey for Fort Beauharnois, Goodhue County, Minnesota*, ,St. Paul: Minnesota Historical Society, 1978.

Colonel Clement H. Beaulieu

Colonel Clement H. Beaulieu (1811–1893) was born at Lac du Flambeau, in the then territory of Michigan, which included Wisconsin, Minnesota and a large portion of territory west of the Mississippi. His father, Bazil Hudon de Beaulieu (1783–1838) was actively engaged in the fur trade. Mr. Beaulieu was of mixed French and Algonquian blood. His mother was

Clement Beaulieu
(Public Domain)

Margaret Racine (Queen of the Skies). He married Elizabeth Farling, a daughter of one of the early Scotch missionaries.

He was listed as Justice of the peace in La Pointe County in 1848. It is believed he moved to Crow Wing at the time the Government was building Fort Gaines around 1849. In order to be independent of military regulations, Beaulieu decided to build off the reservation and settle opposite the north mouth of Crow Wing River. The geographical location of Crow Wing was on the Red River ox cart trail and wagon trail and was in the heart of Ojibwe country. He moved in with a large force of loggers, sawyers, and carpenters and erected a group of post buildings.

Eventually, Clement Beaulieu formed a partnership with John Fairbanks and the firm of Beaulieu and Fairbanks became the principal supplier of all Ojibwe or Chippewa Indian Posts in the area. One half of the Clement Beaulieu home was eventually moved to the old Jean Branchaud farm in Morrison County. It was known as the house at the south entrance of Camp Ripley on Highway 371. His son's house (Captain Charles Beaulieu) is currently located at Crow Wing State Park. A picture of this house is located elsewhere in this book.

Joseph Belanger

Joseph Belanger (1813–1900?) was the first white resident of Anoka County. He was born in St. Michel d'Yamaska, Quebec and came to Minnesota in 1836 with a party of ninety-three men to work for the American Fur Company. He built the first house in Anoka in

Joseph Belanger 1900
(Public Domain)

1844. He journeyed to Minnesota along the shores of Lake Ontario to the Niagara River, where they portaged around Niagara Falls. They then entered Lake Erie and followed the Detroit River to Lake St. Clair, then through the St. Clair River and Lake Huron to Mackinac Strait. They traveled down Lake Michigan, through Green Bay and up the Fox River to Fort Winnebago, then portaged to the Wisconsin River. They then took the Wisconsin River to the Mississippi and then up to St. Paul. Joseph Belanger worked for a time for the American Fur Company, engaged in rafting lumber from Stillwater to St. Louis, and was a riverboat captain for some twelve years. He was a continuous resident of Anoka from 1856 until the time of his death.[21]

Reverend Georges-Antoine Belcourt

Georges-Antoine Belcourt (1803–1874) was a French-Canadian Jesuit missionary and priest. Born in Baie-du-Febvre, Quebec, Belcourt was ordained in 1827. He established missions in areas of Quebec and Manitoba. He became an articulate spokesman for the free traders and the Métis in the Red River Colony, which included part of the Minnesota Territory. The Hudson Bay Company wanted all trade in furs and hides and other trade to go through them and were trying to stop the Métis from sending their goods south to St. Paul on the Red River Oxcart trail.[22]

Georges Antoine Belcourt
(Public Domain)

At the urging of the company's governor, Belcourt was recalled to Montreal. He was next assigned to Pembina, North Dakota. He established two missions in the 1840s to convert the local Ojibwe (also called Chippewa) and Métis to Catholicism. In 1859 he left Pembina for Quebec, but was quickly redeployed to North Rustico, Prince Edward Island. He established the Farmers' Bank of Rustico (the first community-based bank in Canada). Belcourt retired from his post in 1869 to live out his life in New Brunswick, but was recalled in 1871, this time to the Magdalen Islands. In May 1874, Belcourt was forced to retire due to ill health. He died in Shediac, New Brunswick on May 31, 1874. He was designated a National Historic Person by the government of Canada in 1959.

Henry Belland

Henry Belland (1816–1885) was a French-Canadian born in Canada who came to Minnesota in 1836. He lived near Fountain Cave in 1840 on a claim he bought from Pig's Eye Parrant. He was married at Lac Qui Parle in 1839. He was employed by the American Fur Company for sixteen years and worked for Henry Sibley. He acted as a guide and interpreter for the U.S. Government for almost 25 years, and was with George Armstrong Custer on his first campaign in 1874 out west. He was also a fur trader for Major Forbes at Redwood Falls, and was on his way to that place when the 1862 Sioux uprising began. Frank Blackwell Mayer (1827–1899) drew a sketch of Henry Belland in 1851

Henry Belland
By Frank Blackwell Mayer
(Public Domain)

---

[21] Goodrich, Albert M., *History of Anoka County and the Towns of Champlin and Dayton in Hennepin County, Minnesota,* (Minneapolis, 1905).
[22] Gilman, Rhoda R. and Gilman, Carolyn, and Stultz, Deborah, *Red River Trails, Oxcart Routes between St. Paul and the Selkirk Settlement 1820-1870,* Minnesota Historical Society Press (1979) p.14.

as shown above. He built a log house on the West side of St. Paul, overlooking the river and downtown St. Paul, where he owned 160 acres of land.[23]

George Bonga

George Bonga (August 20, 1802–1880) was a French speaking fur trader of African-American and Ojibwe descent. He was the second son of Pierre Bonga and an Ojibwe mother. Pierre Bonga worked as a fur trader with the Anishinaabe near Duluth, Minnesota. George had a brother named Stephen who was also a notable fur trader and translater in the region.

George Bonga (Public Domain)

George received his education in Montreal, Canada. He was fluent in French as well as Ojibwe and English. He later became a fur trader and interpreter. He was noted in Minnesota for being, as his brother Stephen claimed, "One of the first two black children born in the state." Bonga and his Anishinaabe wife named Ashwinn, opened a lodge on Leech Lake after the fur trade declined. George Bonga died in 1880.

Pierre Bottineau

Pierre Bottineau (1817–1895) was a Minnesota Frontiersman. Pierre was born in a hunting camp on the buffalo trail near Grande Fourche (present-day Grand Forks). His father Charles Bottineau was a French Protestant, who descended from French Huguenots who settled in Boston, and his mother, Marguerite Macheyquayzaince Ahdicksongab "Clear Sky Woman," was half Dakota and half Ojibwe from the Lake of the Woods band. She was a sister of Pembina Ojibwe Chief Misko-Makwa or "Red Bear."

Pierre had two wives. He first married Philomene Lormond and later Martha Gervais. He became a noted scout and voyageur and became known as the "Kit Carson of the Northwest." He played an important role in the history and development of Minnesota and North Dakota. He was an accomplished surveyor and was involved in founding a number of cities in Minnesota and North Dakota. Those settlements would become cities such as St. Paul, St. Anthony (today Minneapolis), Osseo, and Maple Grove (northwest of the Twin Cities) as well as Breckenridge, Red Lake Falls, and Wahpeton, North Dakota.

Pierre Bottineau.

Pierre Bottineau (Public Domain)

---

[23] Newson, T.M. St. Paul, *Minnesota and Biographical Sketches of Old Settlers, from the Earliest Settlement of the City, up to and including the year 1857*, published by the author in St. Paul, Minnesota in 1886, p. 53.

Pierre was one of the first land owners in St. Paul, and was one of the builders of the St. Paul Chapel. He also owned a large tract of land in the city of St. Anthony where the Metis oxcart drivers would camp as they passed through en route to St. Paul. Bottineau also took part in the founding of Orono Village, Sherburne County, Elk River, and the city of St. Anthony (later absorbed by Minneapolis). He was a renowned diplomat and translator, earning him the nickname "The Walking Peace Pipe." He played a part in forging many treaties with Native American tribes. According to his obituary he spoke French, English, Dakota, Ojibwe, Cree, Mandan, and Winnebago.

The U.S. government used Pierre, and others like him, to settle the land and help establish American sovereignty in the upper Mississippi country. His many invaluable services earned him celebrity status in his time. Upon Pierre's retirement, the United States Congress granted him a pension of $50 a month. He died in Red Lake Falls, Minnesota at the age of 78.[24] Bottineau County, North Dakota, and its county seat Bottineau, are named in his honor as well as the Pierre Bottineau branch library and Bottineau Park in Minneapolis and Bottineau Boulevard in Hennepin County, Minnesota.

René Boucher

René Boucher, Sieur de la Perriére (1668–1742) built Fort Beauharnois near present-day Frontenac, Minnesota in 1727. He led an expedition from Montreal in June 1727 with the purpose of establishing a post on Lake Pepin. His party arrived in at the lake in September 1727 and built a post on the west side of the lake at a place called the Point au Sable. Boucher built a stockade of pickets twelve feet high, forming a square of 100 feet, with two bastions, and he called the post Fort Beauharnois, in compliment to the governor of Canada. Michel Guignas and Nicolas de Gonnor, Jesuits missionaries, built, at Fort Beauharnois, a mission house, and this is said to be the first Christian church in what is now called Minnesota.[25]

Étienne Brûlé with Hurons (Public Domain)

René Bourassa dit La Ronde

René Bourassa (Bourasseau, Bouracas) dit La Ronde (1688–1778) was an early fur trader in the area we now know as Minnesota. He entered the fur trade in 1726, following the footsteps of his father. He was married to Catherine Leriger de La Plante. Bourassa first came to Upper Canada (*pays d'en haut*) in partnership with Nicolas Sarrazin and Francois Lefebvre Duplessis Faber. He was connected with business associates of Pierre Gaultier de Varennes and de La Verendrye. In 1735, he hired engagés to go to La Verendrye's posts at Fort Saint-Charles (on Lake of the Woods) and Fort Marepas (a few

---

[24] *Biographical Sketch of Pierre Bottineau, Compendium of History and Biography of Central and Northern Minnesota*, G. A. Ogle & Company: 1904, p.144
[25] Curtiss-Wedge, Franklyn, History of Goodhue County, Minnesota, published in Chicago, H.C. Cooper, Jr. & Co. 1909, p.51.

miles above the mouth of the Red River. Bourassa and Laurent-Eustache Gamelin, dit Chateauvieux constructed a post at near the mouth of the Vermilion River in present day Minnesota.

Étienne Brûlé

Étienne Brûlé (1592a–1633) was the first European explorer to journey beyond the St. Lawrence River in what is today Canada. Brûlé became an interpreter and guide for Samuel de Champlain, who later sent him on a number of exploratory missions. Among his many travels were explorations of Georgian Bay and Lake Huron, as well as the Humber River watershed in today's Toronto. In 1633, Brûlé was killed by the Bear clan of the Huron people. Brûlé is credited with being the first European to reach Lake Superior in 1622-23. [26]

Susan Frenier Brown

Susan Frenier Brown
(Public Domain)

Susan Frenier Brown, 1819–1904) was the wife of Joseph R. Brown. Her father, Narcisse Frenier, was a French and Indian trader and her mother, Winona Crawford, was the granddaughter of Walking Buffalo, a Dakota chieftan. She had eleven children with Joseph R. Brown, a French speaking trader who served as secretary of the Territorial Council, chief clerk of the House of Representatives, and a member of both the House and the Senate. He was appointed by Henry Sibley to serve as U.S. Indian Agent in 1857 for the Dakota and many believe that his later removal from this position was a major factor in the increased tension that led to the Dakota War of 1862. The granite ruins of Susan Frenier's home after her husband died in 1870 can be seen at the Joseph R. Brown Memorial and State Wayside Rest, on Renville County Highway 15, south of Sacred Heart, Minnesota.

In Minnesota, Brown County, Browns Valley, and Brown's Creek near Stillwater area all named after Joseph R. Brown.

Jean Baptiste Cadotte Jr.

Jean Baptiste Cadotte Jr. was the son of Jean Baptiste Cadotte Sr. and a Native American mother who was a member of the Owaazsii clan of the Anishinaabeg. She was a Roman Catholic convert whose French name was likely Marianne or Anastasia. Jean Baptiste Jr. had a brother Michel, who

Joseph R. Brown (Public Domain)

[26] Painting of Étienne Brûlé with Hurons in collection of Librairie du Centre (CFORP) located in Québec et autres provinces.

established fur trade outposts at the head of the Chippewa River and at Lac Courte Oreilles in Wisconsin. Michel is credited with establishing a trading empire throughout what became northern Wisconsin. Jean Baptiste Jr. was an interpreter for the French at Sault Ste. Marie, and established a trade post in present-day Red Lake Falls, Minnesota. Cadott, Wisconsin is named after his brother Michel. Alexander Henry "The Elder" (1739–1824) met him and spent the winter of 1762–63 with him and his wife Catherine Marcot Cadotte, who was of Ottawa-French parentage. In 1767 Cadotte, Jr. and Henry re-founded the post at Michipicoten. Alexander Henry was one of the leading pioneers of the British-American fur trade following the British conquest of New France.

Pierre Choteau Jr.

Pierre Chouteau, Jr. (1789–1865) also referred to as Pierre Cadet Chouteau, was an American merchant and a member of the wealthy Chouteau fur-trading family of St. Louis, Missouri.[27] Chouteau was born in St. Louis, where his father, Jean Pierre Chouteau, was one of the first settlers and part of the ethnic French elite. His mother was Pelagie Kiersereau (1767–1793). One of his brothers was Auguste Pierre Chouteau. A half-brother (by his father's second wife Brigitte Saucier) was François Chouteau, a trader who became one of the first European-American settlers of today's Kansas City, Missouri. Pierre, the Capital of South Dakota, is named after Fort Pierre which is named after Auguste Pierre Chouteau.[28]

Pierre Choteau, Jr.
Minnesota Historical Society

In 1844, Pierre Choteau Jr. and Company of St. Louis, through its Minnesota agent Henry H. Sibley, sent Norman W. Kittson to open a fur trading post at the U.S.—Canada border station of Pembina. Kittson organized brigades of two-wheeled oxcarts, which traveled between Pembina and St. Paul. These trails eventually became known as the Pembina or Red River Trails.[29]

Pierre Choteau Jr. held a substantial interest in a variety of Minnesota ventures, including the Central House and Ramsey House buildings in St. Paul, properties in Mendota, St. Anthony, Lac qui Parle, and Hastings. He held an interest in the Minnesota Packet Company, which controlled the steamboats linking St. Paul to St. Louis. Pierre Choteau contributed money towards the completion of St. Paul's new Catholic cathedral in 1857.[30]

---

[27] A portion of the Pierre Chouteau and Family Papers are available for research use at the Minnesota Historical Society.

[28] Boutros, David *Confluence of People and Place: The Choteau Posts on the Missouri and Kansas Rivers. See also* Hafen, LeRoy R, "Auguste Pierre Chouteau," *in French Fur Traders and Voyageurs in the American West*, ed. (Spokane, Wash; Aruthur H. Clark, 1995).

[29] Rife, Clarence W., *Norman W. Kittson: A Fur Trader at Pembina* in Minnesota History 6:246-48 (September 1925).

[30] Gitlin, Jay, *The Bourgeois Frontier: French Towns, French Traders, and American Expansion*, Yale University Press (2010).

Médard Chouart, Sieur des Groseilliers

Médard Chouart des Groseilliers (1618–1696) was an explorer and fur trader from French Canada. Médard was born at Charly-sur-Marne in France and called himself Sieur des Groseilliers, after a farm his parents managed in Bassevelle.

Medard Chouart des Groseilliers
Painting by Robert Perrizo

Groseilliers arrived in Quebec about 1641 and became a donné or lay helper at the Jesuit missions in the Huron country. Here, he learned the skills of a coureur des bois. In 1647 he married Helène, the daughter of Abraham Martin whose land later became the "Plains of Abraham," made famous as the site of the critically important 1759 Battle of Quebec between French and Indian forces. The British victory led to that nation's control of Canada. In 1653, he married his second wife, the widowed step-sister of Pierre-Esprit Radisson, Marguerite Hayet.

Grosseilliers is well known because he and his brother in law, Pierre-Esprit Radisson, with the assistance and financial backing of English and New England investors, helped form the Hudson's Bay Company in 1670. They did so in an attempt to try skirt around French licensing laws and taxes after running into difficulties. The company was incorporated by English royal charter in 1670 as *The Governor and Company of Adventurers of England trading into Hudson's Bay* and functioned as the de facto government in parts of North America before European states, and later, the United States laid claim to some of those territories. It was at one time the largest landowner in the world, with the area of the Hudson Bay watershed, known as Rupert's Land, having 15% of North American acreage. Grosseillier retired in Trois-Rivières, Quebec, and died in 1696.

Father Joseph Cretin

Joseph Crétin (1799–1857) was the first Roman Catholic Bishop of Saint Paul, Minnesota. Cretin Avenue in St. Paul, Cretin-Derham Hall High School, and Cretin Hall at the University of St. Thomas are named in his honor. He was born in Montluel, in the département of Ain, France, December 19, 1799; he died in St. Paul, Minnesota. He studied at the Petits séminaires of Meximieux (Ain), the Saint-Genis-l'Argentière (Rhône), at Alix (Rhône), and he studied theology in the seminary of Saint-Sulpice, Paris. He was ordained a priest on December 20, 1823, and soon afterward was appointed vicar in the parish at Ferney, France, eventually becoming its parish priest.

Bishop Mathias Loras, first bishop of Dubuque, Iowa, arrived in France in 1838 in search of priests for his vast diocese in the new world. Crétin volunteered, and on August 16, 1838, he embarked at Le Havre and landed in New York two months later. He spent the winter of 1838-39 in St. Louis, Missouri. He then traveled to Dubuque, where, he was appointed vicar-general of the new diocese. For over eleven years, he divided his time chiefly between Dubuque, Prairie du Chien, Wisconsin, and the Winnebago Indians in the neighborhood of Fort Atkinson, in Winneshiek County, Iowa. In 1851, Crétin was appointed the first Roman Catholic Bishop of the new diocese of St. Paul.

Bishop Joseph Cretin (Public Domain)

Crétin arrived in St. Paul on July 2, 1851. That same evening, he made his first appearance in the log chapel of St. Paul, his first cathedral, and gave his first episcopal blessing to his flock. Within less than five months, a large brick building was constructed, which served as a school, a residence, and a second cathedral. Another structure, begun in 1855, was finished after his death, and served as the third cathedral of St. Paul, until the present Cathedral (the fourth) was completed in 1915. He also oversaw the building of a hospital in 1853, and a cemetery in 1856. For the instruction of children, he introduced, in 1851, Sisters of St. Joseph of Carondolet, and in 1855, the Brothers of the Holy Family.[31]

Claude Dablon

Claude Dablon, (1618–1697) was a Jesuit missionary who was born in Dieppe, France. In 1668, he traveled on Lake Superior with Claude-Jean Allouez and Jacques Marquette. They navigated the lake with the help of two Indian guides. Their experience helped them create the picture of Lake Superior shown below in 1672. Their descriptions of Lake Superior was published in a book called "Jesuit Relations." These books were sold to help fund their missions to North America. The text that accompanied the map below explained how Lake Superior, with its clear waters and abundant fish, attracted people from twelve to fifteen Native American nations, who met by its shores, to fish and trade.[32]

---

[31] The Catholic Encyclopedia: An International Work of Reference on the Constitution, Doctrine, Discipline, and History of the Catholic Church, 1911.
[32] Wingerd, Mary Lethert, *North Country, the Making of Minnesota*, Illustrations complied and annotated by Kirsten Delegard, University of Minnesota Press, Minneapolis, (2010).

As you can see on the map made in 1672,[33] the lake is called "Lac Tracy ov Svperievr." The name "Tracy" was in honor of the Marquis Alexandre de Prouville de Tracy (1596a–1670), who was the Lieutenant General of the Carignan-Salieres Regiment that was sent to Quebec to fight the easterly tribes of the Iroquois Confederacy, resulting in a military victory.[34] He also labeled it "Svperievr" or 'Superior," and this is the name that stuck.

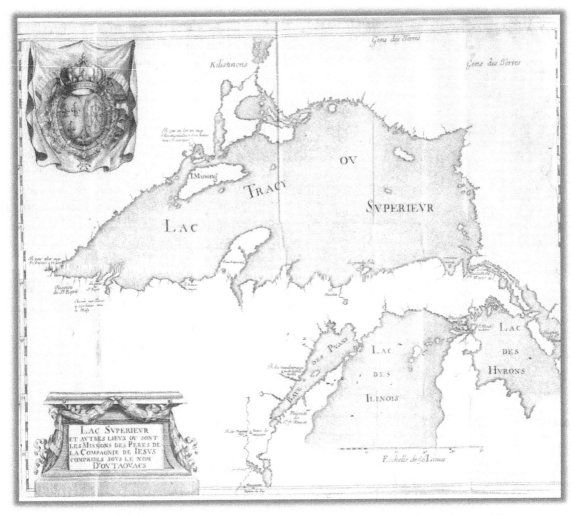

1672 Map of Lake Superior based on descriptions of Claude Dablon and Claude-Jean Allouez (Public Domain)

[33] The 1672 map of the Great Lakes was created by Claude Dablon and Claude Allouez based on their navigation of Lake Superior with the help of two Indian Guides (Paris: Sebastien Mabre-Cramoisy, 1673). James Ford Bell Library, University of Minnesota. Map found in book by Wingerd, Mary Lethert, *North Country, the Making of Minnesota*, Illustrations complied and annotated by Kirsten Delegard, University of Minnesota Press, Minneapolis, (2010).
[34] Wingerd, Mary Lethert, *North Country, the Making of Minnesota*, Illustrations complied and annotated by Kirsten Delegard, University of Minnesota Press, Minneapolis, (2010) (notes to plate 3).

Guillaume Delisle

Guillaume de Lisle (Public Domain)

Guillaume Delisle, also spelled Guillaume de l'Isle (1675–1726), was a French cartographer known for his popular and accurate maps of Europe, the newly explored Americas and Africa. Delisle's 1703 "Carte du Canada ou de la Nouvelle France" is praised as the first map to correctly depict the latitude and longitude of Canada. Delisle's 1718 Carte de la Louisiane et du Cours du Mississippi is an example of French cartography at its height, produced at a time when the rest of Europe looked to France for the most accurate maps. It had a wide circulation in Europe and remained in print for years, either copied exactly or used as a base map. It became a source map[35] for all succeeding maps of the Mississippi River as a result of its accurate representation of the lower Mississippi and the surrounding areas.[36]

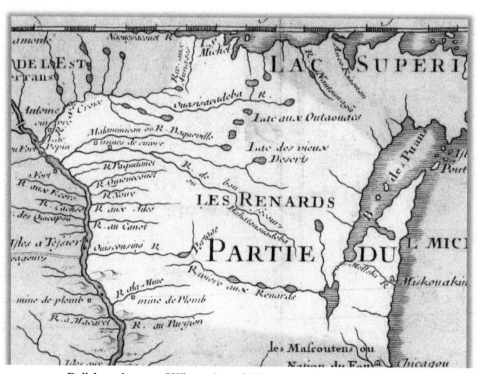

Delisle early map of Wisconsin and Minnesota (Public Domain)

---

[35] Guillaume Delisle- Library of Congress Public Domain Site: http://hdl.loc.gov/loc.gmd/g3700.ct000666
[36] Petto, Christine Marie, *When France was King of Cartography: The Patronage and Production of Maps in Early Modern France*, Lanham: Lexington Books, (2007).

Gabriel Dumont

Gabriel Dumont (1837–1906) was a Métis hunter, merchant, ferryman, and political and military leader. He was born in the Red River Settlement and lived for a time in the Pembina/St. Vincent area near present-day northwestern Minnesota. He was a buffalo hunter and was involved in the large buffalo hunts in the Red River Settlement. Gabriel Dumont is remembered principally for his role as Louis Riel's military commander during the North-West Rebellion of 1885. In 1886, Dumont accepted an offer from Buffalo Bill Cody and toured the eastern United States as a trick-shot artist with Buffalo Bill's Wild West Show.[37]

Gabriel Dumont
(Public Domain)

Dr. Clarence de Montreville

Clarence de Montreville, Sr. (1824-) was born in New York, to parents who were natives of France and Holland. He was a dentist and his wife Mary (1839-) was born in Missouri. Clarence de Montreville was the author of "A Practical Guide to Sound Teeth," or, "Family Manual of the Teeth," self-published in 1852. DeMontreville Lake in Washington County is named after him. Dr. Montre-

Gene DeMontreville
(Public Domain)

ville's son Gene, played major league baseball at the turn of the last century, and his 36 game hitting streak during 1896 and 1897 still ranks as the tenth longest in major league baseball history.

Phamphlet of Desnoyer Park
Published by Minnesota Historical Society

Stephen Desnoyer

Desnoyer Park and Desnoyer Avenue in St. Paul are named after Stephen Desnoyer (1805–1877) who owned a halfway house for stagecoach travelers between St. Paul and Minneapolis, located at approximately Fairview Avenue and interstate 94. He was a French-Canadian born in St. Jean d'Iberville, Quebec. He was a

[37] Macleod, Roderick C. *Gabriel Dumont*, Dictionary of Canadian Biography, Volume XIII (1910-1910), Univerity of Toronto/Universite Laval (2015).

farmer in New York state, a clothier in St. Louis, and a lumber merchant in Dubuque, Iowa before coming to Minnesota, where he purchased 320 acres between what is today Cleveland Avenue and the Mississippi River. Desnoyer Park is located at Pelham Boulevand and Doane Avenue, and the Desnoyer Park neighborhood is on the western end of the city bounded by Marshall and Cretin Avenue, the Mississippi River, and interstate 94.

Hypolite Dupuis

Hypolite Dupuis (1804–1879) was a fur trader with the American Fur Company. He was born near Montreal, Quebec and moved to Minnesota in 1831. He worked at Joseph Renville's Lac qui Parle trading post. Around 1840 he moved to St. Peters (present-day Mendota) and built a house on the property of Henry Sibley. He worked as a clerk for Sibley

and managed the company store. He married Angelique Renville, daughter of Jospeh Renville, and they had eight children. Dupuis was active in the local community, serving as a county treasurer in 1854, a justice of the peace in 1855, and as the Mendota Postmaster from 1854 to 1863.

Alexander Faribault

Alexander Faribault (1806–1882) was a second generation fur trader who came to the Cannon River Valley in 1826. He traded furs out of many posts along the rivers in present-day Rice County, one of which became the city of Faribault. His father was the fur trapper Jean-Baptiste Faribault.

Hypolite Dupuis
Minnesota Historical Society Collections

His son-in-law, William Henry Forbes (who spoke French fluently), also served in the Minnesota Territorial Legislature. Faribault died in Faribault, Minnesota. His house, the Alexander Faribault House, remains standing and is listed on the National Register of Historic Places. It was built in 1853. Alexander served as a government interpreter at the negotiations with the Dakota at Traverse des Sioux and Mendota in 1851, served as a representative of the Minnesota territorial legislature, served on the local school board, and was the first postmaster of Faribault.

Alexander Faribault
Minnesota Historical Society Collections

Jean Baptiste Faribault

Faribault House in Mendota
Minnesota Historical Society Collections

Jean-Baptiste Faribault (1775–1860) was a fur trader and early settler in Minnesota. His father, Barthélemy Faribault, a lawyer from Paris, France, settled in Canada towards the middle of the 18th century, and served as military secretary to the French army in Canada. After the conquest of 1760, he retired to private life in Berthier, Quebec, and held the office of notary public.

Faribault was born in Berthier and received a good education. He found a position with a fur trade company in Quebec, and in May 1798, he went with others to the island of Michilimackinac or Mackinac, one of the depots of the company he worked for. For over ten years, he traded with several Native American tribes on behalf of the Northwest Fur Company.

While living in Little Rapids, (located on the Minnesota River just upstream from present-day Carver, Minnesota), he married, in 1805, Elizabeth Pelagie Ainse, a half-Dakota daughter of Joseph-Louis Ainse, a British superintendent at Mackinac. In 1809, Jean and Elizabeth settled in the small village of Prairie du Chien, Wisconsin, where he commenced trading, on his own account, with the Indians of the Winnebago, Fox, and Sioux tribes. In addition to that, he conducted an exchange of lead with Julien Dubuque, at the point now occupied by the city of that name.

During the War of 1812, Faribault refused to enlist in the English army, and suffered imprisonment and the loss of all his goods in consequence. After the conclusion of the war, in 1815, he became a citizen of the United States, and recommenced his trade at Prairie du Chien. In 1819, he removed to Pike Island in the Mississippi River, and in 1826 to St. Peter Agency (Mendota, Minnesota), opposite the military post of Fort Snelling. There he remained until the last years of his life, which were spent with his children in the town of Faribault, Minnesota. The town of Faribault is named for his eldest son Alexander Faribault; while Faribault County is named after Jean-Baptiste. He died in Faribault, Minnesota, on August 20, 1860.[38]

Jean Baptiste Faribault
Minnesota Historical Society Collections

---

[38] Trap, Paul, *Biography of Jean Baptiste Faribault*, Dictionary of Canadian Biography, University of Toronto/Universite Laval (1974–2015).

Charles Eugene Flandrau

Charles Eugene Flandrau
Minnesota Historical Society Collections

Charles Eugene Flandrau (1828–1903) was an American Lawyer and colonel in the Union Army during the Civil War. Flandrau's father was Thomas Hunt Flandrau of New Rochelle, New York, a law partner of Aaron Burr. His mother was Elizabeth Maria Macomb, daughter of Alexander Macomb, the wealthy New York merchant, and half-sister of General Alexander Macomb, hero of the war of 1812 and afterward head of the United States Army. The Flandraus were descendants of Frenchman Jacques Flandreau, a Huguenot who came to New Rochelle in the 1690s. In 1853 he relocated to Traverse des Sioux, Minnesota to practice law. During the 1850s, he served on the Minnesota Territorial Council, in the Minnesota Constitutional Convention, and on the Minnesota territorial and state supreme courts. He was also appointed U.S. Agent for the Sioux in 1856. In August 1862, Flandrau and other Traverse des Sioux residents learned of a violent Dakota Uprising not far from their homes. Flandrau joined a surge of volunteers rushing to the defense of New Ulm. Citizens elected him their leader and he performed well in combat. It is in honor of his success there that both Flandrau State Park and the community of Flandreau, South Dakota, are so named. Governor Ramsey put him in charge of the defense of the southwestern frontier of the state, and he served in this capacity as colonel for two years, simultaneous to his position on the Minnesota Supreme Court. In 1867 he was the Democratic candidate for governor but was defeated by William Rainey Marshall. [39]

William Henry Forbes

William Henry Forbes
Minnesota Historical
Society Collections

William Henry Forbes (1815-1875) was a French Speaking American fur trader and Minnesota territorial legislator. Born in Montreal, Quebec, Canada, Forbes settled in Wisconsin Territory in 1837 and then moved to what is now Saint Paul, Minnesota in 1847 where he was the postmaster. Forbes worked for the American Fur Company, St. Paul Outfit. Forbes then served on the Minnesota Territorial Council from 1849 to 1853. During the Dakota War of 1862, Forbes served in the United States Army as a quartermaster and commissary. He was county auditor for Ramsey County, Minnesota. In 1871, he became the Indian agent for the Devil's Lake Agency, now the Spirit Lake Tribe. He died in Devil's Lake Agency in 1875, and was buried in St. Paul, Minnesota. His father-in-law was Alexander Faribault, who also served in the Minnesota Territorial Legislature. [40]

[39] Picture taken from Hennessy, W.B., *Past and Present St. Paul, Minnesota, being a relation of the progressive history of the capital city of Minnesota from the earliest historical times down to the present day*, published by Chicago, The S.J. Clarke Publishing Company (1906).
[40] *William Henry Forbes-obituary,*' The New York Times, July 27, 1875.

Alexis Jean Fournier

Alexis Jean Fournier (1865-1948) was an American artist.[41] He is well known in Minnesota for his naturalistic paintings of Minneapolis and St. Paul landmarks. He was raised in Wisconsin by French-Canadian parents and moved to Minneapolis in 1879 at the age of fourteen. Fournier studied at the Minneapolis School of Art, and later in Paris, France at the Académie Julian. In France, Fournier was influenced by the Barbizon school, a group of nineteenth century French painters who were drawn to natural landscapes and romanticism. At his death in Indiana, Fournier was revered as "the last of the Barbizon painters." A painting of the St. Paul Chapel by Fournier is located elsewhere in this book under Saint Paul Chapel.

Alexis Fournier
Minnesota Historical Society Collections

Sister St. John Fournier

Sister St. John Fournier was born in 1814 in France and entered the novitiate of the Sisters of St. Joseph in Lyons, France. She is credited with being the founder of the St. Paul Mission in 1851. She came to Carondelet, Missouri in 1837 and in November 1851, she came to St. Paul at the request of Bishop Joseph Cretin. She, along with Sisters Scholastica Vasques, Philomene Vilaine and Francis Joseph Ivory established in school at the little chapel in St.

Sister St. John Fournier
(Public Domain)

Paul, and then a hospital. They school and hospital became known as St. Joseph's Academy and St. Joseph's Hospital and became important institutions in the history and development of St. Paul.

Gabriel Franchére

Gabriel Franchère (1786–1863) was a French Canadian author and explorer of the Pacific Northwest. Franchère was a native of Montreal. He joined the American Fur Company when he was 24 years old. He was part of the founding of Astoria in 1811 at the mouth of the Columbia River. In 1834, he became John Jacob Astor's agent in Sault Ste. Marie, Michigan. Eventually he started his own Fur Trading

[41] Coen, Rena Neumann. Alexis Jean Fournier, the Last American Barbizon. St. Paul: Minnesota Historical Society Press, 1985

company. Franchere's life had many connections to Minnesota, including traveling and trading in the Rainy Lake and Lake of Woods area. He died at the St. Paul, Minnesota home of his stepson in 1863. He wrote Narrative titled *A Voyage to the Northwest Coast of America*, which was published in 1851.[42] This work was edited and translated into English, and published as part of the General Series of the Champlain Society in 1969.[43]

Gabriel Franchére (Public Domain)

Jean Baptiste Louis Franquelin

Jean-Baptiste-Louis Franquelin (1651–1712) was born in Saint-Michel de Villebernin, France. He was a cartographer, a royal hydrographer, and a teacher of navigation. He was also the first official cartographer in Canada.[44]

Between 1674 and 1708, Franquelin drew around fifty detailed illustrated manuscript maps of New France which included the Minnesota we know today. Franquelin came to Canada as a trader in 1671. Canadian Governor Frontenac recognized his talents and recruited him to draw maps of Canada. He recorded the explorations of Louis Jolliet and Cavelier de La Salle between 1674 and 1684. The French King appointed him royal hydrographer in 1688. He traveled to France in 1692 to complete a series of maps on the New England coast. He had thirteen children, but unfortunately, his wife and ten of his children drowned in a shipwreck in 1693. He held his Canadian appointment from 1686 to 1697 and again from 1701 to 1703. However, from 1694 to 1707 he worked for Louis XIVth military engineer Vauban, and never returned to Canada.[45]

[42] Franchere, Gabriel, *A Voyage to the Northwest Coast of America*, edited by Milo Milton Quaife, R.R. Donnelley & Sons Company, Chicago, 1954.

43 Friesen, Gerald, Gabriel Franchere, The Dictionary of Canadian Biography, University of Toronto/Universite Laval. (1974–2015).

44 Map of Franquelin taken from article by Burke-Gaffney, M. W. *Franquelin, Jean-Baptiste-Louis*. Dictionary of Canadian Biography, vol. 2, University of Toronto/Université Laval, 2003.

45 Burke-Gaffney, M. W. Dictionary of Canadian Biography, vol. 2, University of Toronto/Université Laval, 2003.

Map of Jean Baptiste Louis Franquelin (1688) (Public Domain)

John Charles Frémont

John Charles Frémont
Image from 1856 book on Fremont's expeditions (Public Domain)

John C. Frémont (1813—1890) was an American Explorer, politician and soldier. His father was a French Canadian named Louis René born in Québec City, Canada, on December 8, 1768. His French-Canadian ancestry goes back to Pierre Boucher, the Governor of Trois-Rivieres and the Sieur de Boucherville, who was married to Jeanne Crevier. Louis-René escaped imprisonment by the British during the Napoleonic Wars while traveling to Saint Domingue, and then settled in Norfork, Virginia calling himself Charles Frémon. Louis- René then had an affair with a married woman named Anne Beverly Whiting, and Fremont was born out of wedlock. [46]

Frémont was a strong abolitionist and became the first candidate of the anti-slavery Republican Party of the office of President of the United States in 1856. During the

---

[46] Rolle, Andrew F. *John Charles Fremont: Character as Destiny.* University of Oklahoma Press (1991).

Mexican-American War, Frémont, a Major in the U.S. Army, took control of California from the Mexican Government. He served as a U.S. Senator from California, a Major General during the American Civil War, and was the first Territorial Governor of Arizona. He is probably most famous for his five western expeditions to the American West to plot out and map this new territory.

When Joel R. Poinsett became Secretary of War, he arranged for Frémont to assist notable French explorer and scientist Joseph Nicollet in exploring the lands between the Mississippi and Missouri rivers, including present day Minnesota.[13] Frémont become a first rate topographer, trained in astronomy, and geology, describing fauna, flora, soil, and water resources.[14] Gaining valuable western frontier experience Frémont came in contact with notable men including Henry Sibley, Joseph Renville, J.B. Faribault, Étienne Provost, and the Dakota nation. In 1838, they traveled to present day Minnesota and Saint Anthony Falls. Here they explored land already named by the French, including the major prairie called "Traverse des Sioux" and the landmark called "Coteau des Prairies."

His son, John C. Fremont, was a career officer for the U.S. and attained the rank of rear admiral. Fremont, Minnesota, Fremont Avenue in St. Paul, Fremont Township and Fremont Street in Minneapolis, Minnesota are all named after him.

Louis de Baude de Frontenac

Louis de Buade, Comte de Frontenac et de Palluau (1622–1698)[47] was a French soldier, courtier, and Governor General of New France from 1672 to 1682 and from 1689 to his death in 1698. He established a number of forts on the Great Lakes and engaged in a series of battles against the English and the Iroquois.

In his first term, he supported the expansion of the fur trade, establishing Fort Frontenac (in what is now Kingston, Ontario) and came into conflict with the other members of the Sovereign Council over its expansion and over the corvées (mandatory free labor) required to build the new forts. In particular, despite the opposition of Bishop François de Laval, he supported selling brandy to the aboriginal tribes, which Laval considered a mortal sin. The conflict with the Sovereign Council led to his recall in 1682.

His second term was characterised by the defense of Quebec from a British invasion during King William's War, (1689—97), a successful guerrilla campaign against the Iroquois and English settlements which resulted in the elimination of the Iroquois threat against New France, and a large expansion of the fur trade using Canadian coureurs des bois. He died before his second recall to France. Frontenac and Frontenac State Park in Minnesota are named after him.

---

[47] Picture Courtesy of Biblioteque et Archive Nationales du Quebec. 52327/1956129

Louis de Baude, Comte de Frontenac
Meeting with leaders of the Five Nations of the Iroquois in 1673 (Public Domain)

Father Lucian Galtier

Lucien Galtier (1811a–1866) was the first Roman Catholic priest who served in Minnesota. He was born in southern France in the town of Saint-Affrique, department of Aveyron. The year of his birth is somewhat uncertain. Some sources state he was born in 1811, but his tomb at Prairie du Chien, Wisconsin, states he was born December 17, 1812. In the 1830s, people were settling across the Minnesota River (at the time called Saint Pierre by the French and St. Peter by the British and Americans) from Fort Snelling in the area of Mendota, Minnesota. Mathias Loras, bishop of the Roman Catholic Diocese of Dubuque, Iowa learned of these settlers and journeyed up the Mississippi River to visit the area. He wrote to his sister that "the Catholics of St. Peters amounted to one hundred and eighty five." The bishop saw a need to send a missionary to the area the next year. Galtier spoke little English when he arrived in 1840.

Galtier eventually learned that a number of settlers, who had left the Red River Colony, had settled on the east bank of the Mississippi River. He decided that the area with the settlers, in what is now downtown Saint Paul, Minnesota, needed a church. The location was near a steamboat landing, which had the potential for development. Two French settlers offered a location for a church, and other settlers provided materials and labor to build a log chapel. Father Galtier wrote, "I had previously to this time fixed my residence at Saint Peter's and as the name of Paul is generally connected with that of Peter. I called it Saint Paul."

Father Galtier
Minnesota Historical Society Collections

Jean Baptiste Faribault gave Galtier a small log house in Mendota. Galtier used one corner of it as a bedroom and used the rest for a chapel. In 1842, following the collapse of the house, the settlers at Mendota built a more permanent chapel. The church, now known as Saint Peter's Church, is the oldest Catholic Church in Minnesota. Galtier also conducted

Saint Peter's Church in Mendota

missionary trips to Chippewa Falls, Wisconsin, Hudson, Wisconsin, St. Croix Falls, Wisconsin, the new church in St. Paul, and traveled as far south as Lake Pepin.

In 1844, Galtier became ill as a result of "bilious fever" and the hard work necessary to minister in a frontier area. He was treated in the military hospital at Fort Snelling, staying there two months. In May 1844, Bishop Loras transferred him to Keokuk, Iowa, where he remained only for a few months, long enough to build the first Catholic church in that location. Galtier returned to Dubuque and subsequently traveled back to France without his bishop's permission, intending to quit the Dubuque Diocese for good, due to his disagreements with Mathias Loras. Following a two year absence from America, Galtier joined the Diocese of Milwaukee in 1847 and served at Saint Gabriel's Parish in Prairie du Chien, Wisconsin, where he remained until his death in 1866. The white marble tomb of the priest can be seen in front of Saint Gabriel's church. Galtier Plaza in downtown Saint Paul was named after him, as is the Galtier Society, a faith formation and service organization within the Roman Catholic Archdiocese of Saint Paul and Minneapolis.[48]

Paul Goodin

Paul Goodin (shown to the right) was born in York County, New Brunswick in 1813. He was married to Obeline Michaud in Van Buren, Maine. He arrived in Minnesota around 1850 and claimed the first homestead in what became Dayton. He established a trading post along the river. Goodin Island near present downtown Dayton is named after him. The following is taken from the Dayton Facebook page about Goodin: "Being French, the word spread quickly among the French pioneer community that Paul had found a good area to settle, and Dayton (although it wasn't called Dayton back then) became a magnet for French settlers."

Paul Goodin
(Public Domain)

Pierre Gaultier de La Vérendrye

Pierre Gaultier de La Vérendrye de Boumois (1714 −1755) was the second son of Pierre Gaultier de Varennes, sieur de La Vérendrye. An explorer and fur trader who served many years under the command of his father, he was born on Île aux Vaches, (Isle of Cows) near Sorel, Quebec.

The young Pierre spent two years in the colonial regular troops as a cadet, performing garrison duty in Montreal. In 1731, when his father planned an expedition to expand the fur trade westward and at the same time search for a water route to the Western Sea, he accompanied his father and brothers Jean Baptiste, François, and Louis-Joseph as a member of the expedition. He spent the winter at Fort Kaministiquia while his older brother Jean Baptiste and his cousin, the second in command, Christopher Dufrost de La Jemeraye, carried on to Rainy Lake and established Fort St. Pierre. In 1732 he accompanied his father to Lake of the Woods, where they built Fort St. Charles on Magnusen's Island. This post was abandoned by 1763. Today, a reconstruction of the old fort occupies the exact site on Magnusen's Island.

In the spring of 1734, after his father had left for Montreal, Pierre briefly was left in command of Fort St. Charles until relieved by La Jemeraye. In February 1737, Pierre accompanied his father to Fort Maurepas, and in June the two men left the west for Montreal and Quebec.

---

[48] Catholic Historical Society of St. Paul, "*Monsignor Augustine Ravoux, The Pioneer Missionary of the Northwest,*" in *Acta et Dicta*, Vol. 1, No. I, (July 1907) p.66. Also see Hennessy, W.B., *Past and Present St. Paul, Minnesota, being a relation of the progressive history of the capital city of Minnesota from the earliest historical times down to the present day,* published by Chicago, The S.J. Clarke Publishing Company (1906), page 37.

Pierre Gaultier de La Verendrye
Painting by Arthur Hilde (1870-1952) (Public Domain)

Pierre Gaultier de La Vérendrye was active as a fur-trader and explorer in the west, even after his father was relieved of his command in 1744. In 1749, he returned east and re-entered the army. He was active at Fort Beauséjour where he served until it was captured by the British in 1755. He died shortly after in Montreal, Quebec. It is believed he was assassinated.

Benjamin Gervais

Benjamin Gervais (1792-1876) was a French-Canadian pioneer and entrepreneur who is considered the founder of Little Canada. A former voyageur born in Riviére du Loup, Quebec, Gervais came to the Little Canada area in 1844 on the recommendation of his Dakota Indian friends and built the Gervais Grist Mill. Aided by his wife Genevieve and eight children, Gervais carved out a large farm along a creek and adjoining lake now named for him. After their first harvest, the Gervais family used the mill to make cornmeal and flour for the lumber camps of the St. Croix Valley. Today, a historical marker marks the site of his Grist Mill. It is described later in this book under French Heritage Sites.

Benjamin Gervais
Minnesota Historical Society Collections

Antoine Blanc Gingras

Antoine Blanc Gingras (1821-1877) was a Métis who was a pioneer and entrepreneur during the early days of Minnesota. He was an independent fur trader and concentrated on the buffalo trade, established the Gingras Trading Post, and also co-founded the town of St. Joseph near Pembina. Antoine was a leading merchant of St. Joseph in the Dakota Territory. He established his trading fort there in 1843 and it functioned up until 1873. He also served as a member of the Minnesota Territorial Legislature from 1851-1858. Gingras died on 26 September 1877 at St. Joseph, Dakota Territory.[49]

[49] Antoine Blanc Gingras, Metis Fur Trader and member of the Minnesota Territorial Legislature, 1852-1853, Visual Resources Database, Minnesota Historical Society, 2010

Antoine Gingras 1855
Minnesota Historical Society Collections

He became involved in the trade on the Red River Oxcart routes and created a business trading dried meat from Buffalo called pemmican. He would ship the pemmican to St. Paul in exchange for money or goods which he brought back to the Red River Settlement. This site has now become a historic site of the State of North Dakota.

Gingras became wealthy as a result of the oxcart trade and in 1861, his net worth was estimated to be $60,000, a large fortune for that time. Because of his prestige and business connections, Gingras was elected to represent the Nation Métis in the Minnesota Territorial Legislature in the years 1852 and 1853. Antoine Blanc Gingras was a fellow soldier with Métis Louis Riel in the struggles for the creation of Manitoba. When Louis Riel started the 1869 Red River Rebellion, Gingras participated in the events.

Gingras Pemmican Factory in Wahalla
Minnesota Historical Society Collections

Joseph Godfrey

Joseph Godfrey was born in the 1830s in Mendota near Fort Snelling, the son of a French-Canadian father, also named Joseph Godefroi, and a slave known by the name of Courtney (or Polly depending on the source.)[50] Joseph Godfrey's father's last name was also spelled Godfrey, Godfroi, and Godfroy. He was probably a descendant of Jean Baptiste Godfroy, (Godefroy) who arrived in New France with his brother Thomas about 1626 under the government of Champlain. In 1750, his descendant Jean Baptiste Godfroy de Linctot (also called Chevalier) came to Detroit with his wife, Jeanne Veron de Grandmenil. At the time of Joseph's birth, his mother Courtney was owned by Alexis Bailly. His father worked as a trader for Bailly. Godfroy lived in the Bailly household with his mother for many years. At some point Godfrey was taken to St. Paul, Minnesota, by a man named Bronson. During this

Joseph Godfrey (Public Domain)

[50] Bachman, Walt, *Northern Slave Black Dakota, The Life and Times of Joseph Godfrey,* Pond Dakota Press 2013.

time Godfrey served as an aide for Henry Hastings Sibley, prominent trader and later first governor of Minnesota, who also played a key role in the U.S.-Dakota War.

Godfrey eventually escaped from his owners to seek refuge among the Dakota as a fugitive slave. In 1857 he moved to the Lower Sioux Agency, where he married the daughter of Wahpaduta (Red Leaf). In August 1862, he felt compelled to join in their war against American forces. Along with a large group of Dakota fighters he surrendered after the Battle of Wood Lake in 1862. He was tried by the army and faced execution. In order to avoid execution, he testified against Dakota warriors. Thirty-eight Dakota men, including his father-in-law, were hanged the same year, eleven of who Godfrey testified against. His death sentence was commuted and he was later pardoned. After a prison term, he spent the rest of his life on the Santee reservation in Nebraska where he died in 1909.

Father Joseph Goiffon
(Public Domain)

Father Joseph Goiffon

Father Joseph Goiffon (1824-1910) was a Missionary priest. He spent much of his time among the Indians and Métis of the future North Dakota. In March 1859, after his arrival from France in the fall of 1858, he became the Roman Catholic pastor of the Missions at Pembina and St. Joseph. In November of 1860 Father Goiffon was caught in a blizzard near Neche, Dakota Territory, and was nearly frozen to death before being rescued and brought first to Pembina and then to St. Boniface where he recovered. In 1861, he was appointed missionary to Centerville, Dakota Territory. He returned to St. Paul in June of 1861.[51]

Daniel Greysolon, Sieur du Lhut (Duluth)

Daniel Greysolon, Sieur du Lhut (1639a-1710) was a French soldier and explorer who visited the area where the city of Duluth, Minnesota is now located and the headwaters of the Mississippi River. His name was anglicized as "DuLuth," and he is the namesake of Duluth, Minnesota as well as Duluth, Georgia. Daniel Greysolon signed himself "Dulhut" on surviving manuscripts. He was born in Saint-Germain-Laval, near Saint-Étienne, France, and first traveled to New France in 1674.

In September 1678, with seven other Frenchmen, he left Montreal for Lake Superior, spending the winter near Sault Sainte Marie and reaching the western end of the lake in the fall of the following year, where he concluded peace talks between the Saulteur and Sioux nations. In June of 1680, Duluth heard of the capture of a reverend by the name of Louis Hennepin. Hennepin was taken prisoner by the Nadouesioux, with whom Duluth was familiar. After receiving word of his capture, Duluth set out at once to find Hennepin

---

[51] Thein, Duane, *Father Joesph Goiffon: A Tale of a French Missionary*, White Bear Stereoptics Company, 2005.

Daniel Greysolon Sieur du Lhut at the Head of the Lakes-1679. By Francois Lee Jacques, 1922 (Public Domain)

and secured his release. Lured by native stories of the Western or Vermilion Sea (likely the Great Salt Lake in Utah), Duluth reached the Mississippi River via the Saint Croix River in 1680.

Vital Guerin

Vital (aka Vetal) Guerin (1812–1870) was one of the first settlers in St. Paul. His father was Louis Guerin (1782–1865), a voyageur. Vital was born in St. Remi, Canada and in 1832 he entered the employ of the American Fur Company and worked for Gabriel Franchere.[52]

Vital Guerin held a land claim between present-day Saint Peter and Cedar, Bench and Sixth Streets. Many of his neighbors sold out and moved further away but Guerin held on to his claim, refusing many offers and called a fool for doing so. In 1843, he was offered $1,000 for his land. Only a few years later,

Sketch of Vital Guerin's home in 1852 (Public Domain)

he sold his land for the amazing sum of $100,000.00. He built a fine house in 1849 at the corner of Wabasha and Seventh Street, where he lived until he died. He was known to be generous and gave away much of his wealth.[53]

Vital Guerin
Minnesota Historical Society Collections

Louis Hennepin

Father Louis Hennepin (1640–1705) baptized Antoine, was a French speaking Catholic priest and missionary of the Franciscan Recollet order and an explorer of the interior of

---

[52] Williams, J. Fletcher, "Memoir of William W. Warren," in William W. Warren, *History of the Ojibway People*, Minnesota Historical Society, (1885) p.97.
[53] Fletcher, J. Williams "Memoir of William W. Warren," in William W. Warren, *History of the Ojibway People*, Minnesota Historical Society, (1885) p.106

North America. He was born in present-day Belgium (then called Flanders) which was captured by the King of France in 1659. He joined the Recollect Friars at a monastery in Béthune, France, and was ordained a priest in 1666. In May, 1675, the Recollets sent four missionaries to New France, including Hennepin, who were accompanied by Rene Robert Cavelier, Sieur de la Salle.

Hennepin spent his first three years as a missionary in the area of the eastern St. Lawrence River, ministering to voyageurs, colonists, and American Indian communities. In 1678, Hennepin went with René-Robert Cavelier, Sieur de la Salle, on his exploration of the Mississippi. In 1680, while on La Salle's expedition, Hennepin and two other members of the party, Michel Accault and Antoine Auguelle (Picard du Gay), were sent to explore the section of the Mississippi north of the Illinois River. They encountered a Dakota war party who took the three men to a village near Lake Mille Lacs.

Father Louis Hennepin
(Public Domain)

In the summer of that year, Hennepin and Auguelle were allowed by the Dakota to canoe down the Mississippi to the mouth of the Wisconsin River. The fact that they were allowed this freedom raises questions about the nature of their relationship with the Dakota. There they planned to collect supplies left for them by the La Salle expedition. During this trip Hennepin and Auguelle first encountered the waterfall on the Mississippi that Hennepin named the Chutes de Saint-Antoine or the Falls of Saint Anthony after his patron saint, Anthony of Padua. The cover of this book shows the falls as they might have looked to Hennepin and his companions. His naming of the falls has stuck and has become an integral and important part of the culture of the twin cities area.

Hennepin, Accault, and Auguelle stayed with the Dakota until late summer of 1680, when Daniel Greysolon, Sieur du Lhut, is said to have rescued them. Since Hennepin and his associates seemed to have so much freedom of movement, it is questionable whether or not they were really being "rescued." Hennepin then returned to France, and wrote a book titled, *A Description of Louisiana, Newly Discovered to the South-West of New France,* which was published in Paris in 1683. It detailed his travels and experiences living with the Dakota, and his discovery of

St. Anthony Falls. His book was full of vivid descriptions and exagerations, but the public loved it, and it made him famous and also introduced the area in Minnesota to Europe.

Painting of Father Louis Hennepin at St. Anthony Falls by Douglas Volk, c. 1905 (Public Domain)

Hennepin would write two more books, published in 1697 and 1698, and continued to exaggerate his stay in the new world. He claimed he had traveled from Illinois down the Mississippi to the Gulf of Mexico and back, before being captured by the Dakota. The details of this improbable canoe trip, covering some three thousand miles in only a month, damaged his reputation but nonetheless, his books continued to be read by many in Europe. Little is known about the end of Hennepin's life. Around 1700 he traveled to Rome to seek funding from Franciscan authorities. Some say that Hennepin died in Rome around 1701, while other sources suggest he returned to Utrecht and died in 1705. Hennepin's memory lives on in the many parks, landmarks, schools, and streets, including one in his home city in Belgium, named in his honor. Minnesota's most populous county carries his name.

The picture above of Father Hennepin at St. Anthony Falls currently currently is displayed at the State Capitol of Minnesota in St. Paul. During renovations in 2016 and 2017, this painting was criticized for inaccurate depictions of Native American Dress and culture. The painting shows Father Hennepin standing among five members of the Dakota tribe and a fellow explorer on the east bank of the Mississippi River at St. Anthony Falls. It is assumed the fellow explorer is Michael Accault.

The painting previously hung in the Governor's Reception Room in the Minnesota State Capitol. After the renovations, the painting now hangs in the new exhibit space located on the third floor in rooms 317 and 317B.

Louis Joliet

Louis Joliet (Jolliet) (1645–1700) was born in French Canada, the third son of a Quebec wagonmaker and wheelwright. His father died when Louis was six years old, and at seventeen years of age, Louis Jolliet entered the Roman Catholic Society of Jesus. In 1673, Louis Joliet and Father Jacques Marquette (French Jesuit missionary) were the first to reach and map the northern portion of the Mississippi River which included present-day Minnesota. They traveled approximately halfway down the Mississippi to about Arkansas, but turned back to avoid capture by the Spanish who had a presence in the southern part of this territory.

Map Illustrating Father Hennepin's book titled "Description de la Louisiane" which was one of his popular books about his travels in New France, including present-day Minnesota.
Minnesota Historical Society Collections

Statue of Louis Joliet that stood in the St. Louis Plaza in Chicago's Columbian Exposition of 1893.

Norman Kittson

Norman Kittson (1814–1888) was a French speaking Canadian born in Sorel, Quebec. Norman's grandfather, John George Kittson (d.1779), was a junior officer in the British Army (his officer's sword still exists) who was said to have seen considerable action during the American Revolution. Kittson received a grammar school education at Sorel, Quebec, and was perfectly bilingual. In 1830, he accepted an apprenticeship with the American Fur Company at Michilimackinac, where Alexander Henry and many others from Sorel had been active. Kittson served at various posts in what became Minnesota Territory in the United States. Kittson collected furs and established strong connections to the local French-Canadians. Through his first wife, he became particularly attached to the Métis people, employing them as tripmen and trading extensively with them. All of this enabled him to play a significant role in bringing about free trade to the settlement in 1849. He was a long-time operator of Red River cart brigades on the Red River Trails, which served his trading businesses.[54]

Norman Kittson
Minn Historical Society

Edmund LaCroix

In 1861, Alexander Faribault sent to Montreal for Nicholas LaCroix to build him a mill. Nicholas came with his brother Edmund and his son Joseph. The LaCroix brothers were educated men, skilled millers and engineers, graduates of E'cole des Arts. Edmund LaCroix was a French inventor who, along with his brother Nicholas, brought the Middlings Purifier to Faribault, Minnesota in the early 1860's. The middlings purifier was first invented by Joseph Perrigault, but the machine was greatly improved upon by Edmund LaCroix. A middlings purifier is a device used in the production of flour to remove the husks from the kernels of wheat. It was developed to complement the emerging roller mill

---

[54] Rife, Clarence W., *Norman W. Kittson: A Fur Trader at Pembina* in Minnesota History 6:246-48 (September 1925).

technique of the late 19th century, which used corrugated metal rollers instead of abrasive grindstones to grind wheat into flour. The middlings purifier was used in this process to separate the bran from the usable part of the flour. The machine developed by LaCroix passed the partially ground middlings over a screen, and a stream of air blew away the particles of bran.[55]

This process was valuable because winter wheat, sown in the fall and harvested early the next summer, did not grow well in Minnesota. However, spring wheat, which was sown in the spring and harvested in late summer, grew well in this Minnesota climate. The problem was that conventional techniques of grinding grain between millstones did not work well with spring wheat and produced a darker flour than consumers wanted. The middlings purifier, however, was able to produce a nice white flour from spring wheat. After the invention of the middlings purifier, the Minnesota spring wheat business exploded, and in a short period of time, Minnesota became one of the leading flour producers in the world and Minneapolis developed a reputation as a "Mill City."

John La Farge

John La Farge, (1835-1910) was an American painter, muralist, and stained-glass designer. Both his parents were French and he was raised bilingually. He graduated from St. Mary's College in Maryland. La Farge studied law, but in 1856 he went to Europe to study art. He

John La Farge in 1902
Public Domain

studied briefly in Paris with Thomas Couture. He returned to the United States and went to Newport, Rhode Island, where he studied with the artist William Morris Hunt. La Farge produced landscapes and figure compositions in the 1860s and was among the earliest American painters to adopt the stylistic elements derived from progressive French landscape painting of the mid-19th century.

He took up mural painting in 1876 with a commission to decorate the interior of Trinity Church in Boston. He is most well known for his mural titled the Ascension (1887), in the Church of the Ascension in New York City. His writings include *Considerations on Painting* (1895), *An Artist's Letters from Japan* (1897), and *The Higher Life in Art* (1908).

At age 68, La Farge was the oldest artist to receive a commission to complete a work of art in the Minnesota State Capitol. He painted four murals in the Minnesota Supreme Court Chamber titled: "Moral and Divine Law;" "Recording of the Prcedents," "The Adjustment of Conflicting Interests," and "The Relation of the Individual to the State."

---

[55] Danborn, David B., *"Flour Power" The Significance of Flour Milling at the Falls*; Minnesota History 58(5) 271-285.

Joseph LaFramboise

Joseph LaFramboise (1805-1856) was a fur trader, interpreter and licensed United States buyer with Henry Sibley and the American Fur Company. He was an interpreter for the Indian treaty negotiations at Fort Snelling and in Washington D.C. He owned the Little Rock Trading Post on the Minnesota River. He also served as a guide for Jean N. Nicollet while he drew his maps of Minnesota.

Madeline LaFramboise (Public Domain)

Home of Madeline LaFramboise
In Mackinac Island, Michigan (Public Domain)

LaFramboise interpreted at two treaties signed between the Dakota and the U.S. Government. He married Jane Dixon at Traverse des Sioux in 1845. Their marriage was one of the first marriages in Nicollet County.[56]

Joseph was the son of Madeline LaFramboise (1780–1846), born Marguerite-Magdelaine Marcotte, who was one of the most successful fur traders in the Northwest Territory of the United States, in the area of present-day western Michigan. Of mixed Odawa and French-Canadian descent, Madeline was fluent in the Odawa, French, English, and Ojibwe languages, and partnered with her husband. After he was murdered, she managed the fur trade successfully for more than a decade. She retired from the trade, building a fine home on Mackinac Island.

---

[56] The monthly South Dakotan, *Joseph LaFramboise, First Settler*, in Watertown South Dakota Library Collection, March 1901, No. 11, Third Year, pp. 353-358.

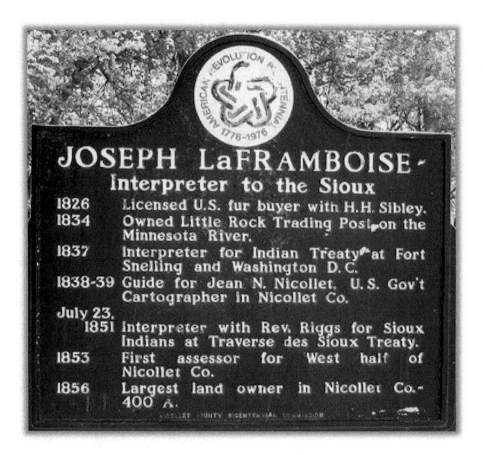

Here is another interesting note about Joseph Laframboise. His sister Josephine "Josette" Laframboise married Captain Benjamin Kendrick Pierce, who was the brother of Franklin Pierce, the 14th President of the United States.

Joseph La France

Joseph La France (1707–1745) traveled in Northern Minnesota from 1740 to 1742 and wrote written descriptions of the area.[57] La France was born at Michilimackinac, the son of a French fur-trader and an Ojibwa woman, in the area where Fort Michilimackinac was founded when he was a child. He became a trader early in his life working with his father and had varied and extensive training.

In 1739, having been refused a license to trade because he had been selling brandy to the Indians, he decided to align himself with the English traders at Hudson Bay. He began his trek toward there following the route of Pierre Gaultier de Varennes et de La Vérendrye through Rainy Lake, Lake of the Woods and the Winnipeg River to Lake Winnipeg. He must have made contact with some of the La Vérendrye forts although no written record confirms this assumption.

---

[57] Holcombe, I. and Bingham, William H, *Compendium of History and Biography of Polk County, Minnesota*, 30-33 (Minneapolis, 1916).

La France wintered in 1740–41 with natives of the Lake Winnipeg region. He spent the 1741–42 winter farther west and north in the region of Lake Manitoba and Lake Winnipegosis and the lower Saskatchewan River. He reached York Factory on Hudson Bay via the Hayes River in June 1742. Since Hudson's Bay Company posts were forbidden to harbour French traders and since La France refused to return to Michilimackinac, he was sent to England. He was apparently maintained there at the expense of the admiralty "on Prospect of his being of Service on the Discovery of the North-West Passage." In London about 1742 he met Arthur Dobbs, a leading critic of the HBC; the only known source of biographical information on La France is Dobbs' book, *An account of the countries adjoining to Hudson's Bay ...*, a compilation of narratives relating to the exploration of Hudson Bay and trade in the company's territories.[58]

Jacques Legardeur de Saint Pierre

Jacques Legardeur de Saint Pierre (1701–1755) was a grandson of Jean-Baptiste Legardeur de Repentigny, who had been elected the first mayor of Quebec City on October 17, 1663 and founded Repentigny, Quebec in 1670. His father Jean-Paul was an adventurer and had established a post at Chequamegon in what is now Wisconsin in 1718. It is believed that Jacques spent a number of years there with his father, where he gained knowledge of the Indian languages and of the business conducted at the trading posts. In 1724 he began military service as a second ensign with the colonial regular troops. Because of his skills as an interpreter, his early active duty involved building loyalty and support among the Ojibwa, Cree, and Sioux to assist the French in future campaigns against other Indian tribes. From 1734 to 1737, he was commandant at Fort Beauharnois in present-day Minnesota (on Lake Pepin). Fearing for himself and his garrison, he burned and abandoned the fort in May 1737.[59] He was killed during the French and Indian War at the Battle of Lake George in 1755.

Picture of reconstructed Fort Necessity, where in battle on July 3, 1754 British and colonial forces under Colonel George Washington surrendered to French forces under command of Louis Coulon de Villiers. Jacques Legarder de Saint Pierre and Michel Bailly, father of Alexis Bailly, were at this battle

[58] Dobbs, Arthur, *An account of the countries adjoining to Hudson's Bay in the north-west part of America* (London, 1744; repr. New York, 1967). Parl, G.B., *Report from the committee on Hudson's Bay.*
[59] Chaput, Donald, *Jacques Legardeur de Saint Pierre,* Dictionary of Canadian Biograph Online," Universy of Toronto/Universite Laval (2015).

Baron La Hontan's book

The present-day Minnesota River was formerly called the Riviére de Saint Pierre. Some believe this river may have been named after Jacques Legardeur de Saint Pierre.[60] On a side note, Saint-Pierre was in the party sent from Fort Duquesne that defeated Washington at Fort Necessity.[61] Also in that party was Alexis Bailly's father, Michel.

Louis-Armand de La Hontan

Louis-Armand de Lom d'Arce de La Hontan, Baron de La Hontan (1666–1716) was a French soldier and explorer who served in the French military in Canada and traveled extensively in the future Wisconsin and Minnesota regions and upper Mississippi Valley. Upon his return to Europe, he wrote an enormously popular travelogue. The "Travels" of Baron de La Hontan appeared in 1703, both in London and in Hague. His book was available for sale in Europe at the same time as Father Hennepin's book.

---

[60] Neill, Edward Duffield, Secretary of the Minnesota Historical Society, *The History of Minnesota from the earliest French Explorations to the Present Time*, Philadelphia: J. B. Lippincott & co. 1858.

[61] Stotz, Charles Morse (2005). *Outposts of The War For Empire: The French And English In Western Pennsylvania: Their Armies, Their Forts, Their People 1749-1764*. Pittsburgh: University of Pittsburgh Press. ISBN 0-8229-4262-3.

Auguste Louis Larpenteur

Auguste Louis Larpenteur (1823–1919) was born in Baltimore, Maryland on May 16th, the son of Louis Augustine and Melinda (Simmons) Larpenteur. His grandfather, Louis Benoist Larpenteur, owned a home on the banks of the Seine, forty-five miles from Paris, and was a personal friend and supporter of Napoleon Bonaparte. His grandfather immigrated to the United States after the fall of Napoleon in 1816. He came to St. Paul in 1843 and worked at the store of fur traders William E. Hartshorn and Henry Jackson as clerk and interpreter. From the 1850s through 1887 he was engaged, with partners or alone, in the fur trade, merchandise, wholesale grocery, commission, and real estate businesses. At various times throughout the 1860s and 1870s he had business associations with Henry C. Burbank, James C. Burbank, Amherst H. Wilder, and Channing Seabury. In 1888, after traveling to France and California, he retired in St. Paul. From the 1840s until his death in 1919, Larpenteur was active in many

Auguste Louis Larpenteur
Minn Historical Society Collections

civic and political affairs of the city, county, territory, and state. Larpenteur married Mary Josephine Presley in St. Paul in 1845; they had ten children.[62] Larpenteur Street in St. Paul is named in his honor.

Bishop Mathias Loras

Bishop Mathias Loras
(Public Domain)

Pierre-Jean-Mathias Loras (1792–1858) was born in Lyon, France on August 30th. He was a descendent of a French noble family. During the Reign of Terror in France, Loras's father and seventeen members of his family were put to death by guillotine. He was ordained a priest in 1815 in France and traveled to Mobile, Alabama in 1829. He was named the first Bishop of Dubuque, Iowa in 1837 and his diocese included the territory of Minnesota. When he arrived in Dubuque to assume his responsibilities as Bishop, he brought with him Joseph Cretin, Augsutin Ravoux, and Lucien Galtier. All three of these priests would play an important role in the early development of the Catholic Church in Minnesota. Bishop Loras made a missionary trip to the St. Pierre or also known as the St. Peters settlement (present-day Mendota, Minnesota) in June 1839.[63]

---

[62] Auguste L. Larpenteur and family papers. Minnesota Historical Society.
[63] The original records of Bishop Loras now form part of the Baptismal Register of the St. Raphael Cathedral in Dubuque, Iowa. In 1914 copeis were made for the St. Paul Catholic Historical Society and copies now exist in the Minnesota Historical Society.

René-Robert Cavelier, Sieur de La Salle

René-Robert Cavelier, Sieur de La Salle, or Robert de La Salle (1643–1687) was a French explorer. He explored the Great Lakes region of the United States and Canada, the Mississippi River, and the Gulf of Mexico. La Salle claimed the entire Mississippi River basin for France, a huge area that included modern day Minnesota.

René-Robert Cavelier was born on November 21, 1643, in Rouen, France, in the parish Saint-Herbland. As a youth, he enjoyed science and nature. As a man, he studied with the Jesuit religious order and became a member after taking initial vows in 1660. At La Salle's request on March 27, 1667, after he was in Canada, he was released from the Society of Jesus after citing "moral weaknesses." Although he left the order, never took final vows in it, and later became hostile to it, historians sometimes described him incorrectly as a priest or a leader.

La Salle's major legacy was establishing the network of forts from Fort Frontenac to outposts along the Great Lakes and the Ohio, Illinois, and Mississippi rivers that came to define French territorial, diplomatic and commercial policy for almost a century between his first expedition and the 1763 cession of New France to Great Britain. In addition to the forts, which also served as authorized agencies for the extensive fur trade, La Salle's encounters with the Illinois and other tribes cemented the French policy of alliance with Indians in the common causes of containing both Iroquois influence and Anglo-American settlement. He also gave the name Louisiana to the interior North American territory he claimed for France, which lives on in the name of a U.S. state. His efforts to encompass modern-day Ontario and the eight American states that border the Great Lakes became a foundational effort in defining the Great Lakes region.[64]

René-Robert Cavelier de La Salle
19th Century Engraving (Public Domain)

Pierre Charles Le Sueur

Pierre-Charles Le Sueur (1657–1704) a French fur trader and explorer in North America, was recognized as the first known European to explore what became known as the Minnesota River valley.

Le Sueur came to Canada with the Jesuits in their mission at Sault Sainte Marie, but very soon he turned himself to fur trade and became a coureur des bois. He was fluent in several native languages, which was crucial to his success in trade. Around 1683, he received some

---

[64] Parkman, Francis, *La Salle and the Discovery of the Great West*, France and England in North America, vol. 3 (Boston: Little, Brown, 1869), 7.

samples of bluish clay from the middle reaches of a tributary of the Mississippi and brought it back to France for analysis. A chemist, Alexandre L'Huillier, deemed it to be copper ore. Le Sueur returned to New France to mine this ore, but was waylayed by, among other things, a prison term for overreaching his trade privileges. He was present at the formal assertion of French sovereignty of Canada, declared in 1689 by Nicholas Perrot at Green Bay. Eventually, however, he was given a royal commission to open a copper mine (although some suggested he was more interested in mining furs).

In 1699, he was with the group that ascended the Mississippi River from Biloxi to the "country of the Nadouessioux," stopping to winter at Isle Pelée or Fort Perrot above Lake Pepin. He continued upstream as far as Saint Anthony Falls. After trading with the local Dakota bands (the Mdewakantons, Wahpetons and Wahpekutes) in the area, in the summer and fall of 1700, he and a group of twenty men went further up the river known to the native population as "minisota," or "cloud reflected water." This river was known to later voyageurs as the St. Pierre, but it is unclear if Le Sueur knew it by that name at the time. The group continued to the Blue Earth River, where they built Fort L'Huillier, named for the chemist who declared area soils held copper ore. They wintered at Fort L'Huillier, trading furs and other merchandise with the local Indian bands. They found the prairies full of bison, and learned to subsist largely on a meat diet. In May 1701, Le Sueur left a garrison of men at the fort under the command of d'Eraque and accompanied a large quantity of the blue earth (Dakota language: "mah kato") back to Fort Mobile for further analysis, which revealed that it was not copper and hence worthless. Later that year, Fort L'Huillier was attacked by Sac and Fox Indians. three men were killed in the attack on the fort, which was then abandoned.

Le Sueur sailed to France to secure a commission to serve as a local magistrate in what is now Alabama, but died of yellow fever shortly after his return in 1704. He never saw the future Minnesota country again, though a city and county in the state were named in his honor. Blue Earth County and its seat, Mankato, were named for the Dakota "blue earth" that Le Sueur had mined nearby. The supposed site of Fort L'Huillier is marked with a signpost along U.S. Route 169 south of Mankato.[65]

Jacques Marquette

Father Jacques Marquette S.J. (1637–1675) sometimes known as Père Marquette or James (Jim) Marquette, was a French Jesuit missionary who founded Michigan's first European settlement, Sault Ste. Marie, and later founded St. Ignace, Michigan. In 1673, Father Marquette and Louis Jolliet were the first Europeans to explore and map the northern portion of the Mississippi River, including areas of what would become Minnesota.[66]

[65] Dansereau, Antoinio, *LeSueur, Pierre*, Biography at the Dictionary of Canadian Biography, Univeristy of Toronto/Universite Laval.
[66] Catholic Encyclopedia, *Jacques Marquette*. New York: Robert Appleton Company. 1913.

Marquette meeting Indians at Mississippi
Oil Painting (1869) by Wilhelm Lamprecht (1838-1906)
at Marquette University (Public Domain)

Jacques Marquette was born in Laon, France, on June 1, 1637 and joined the Society of Jesus at age seventeen. After he worked and taught in France for several years, the Jesuits assigned him to New France in 1666 as a missionary to the indigenous peoples of the Americas. He helped found missions at Sault Ste. Marie in present-day Michigan in 1668, St. Ignace in 1671, and at La Pointe, on Lake Superior near the present-day city of Ashland, Wisconsin.

Emmanuel Masqueray

Emmanuel Masqueray
(Public Domain)

Emmanuel Masqueray (1861–1917) was born in Dieppe, France, on September 10th to Charles-Emmanuel and Henriette-Marie-Louise Masqueray, née de Lamare. He was educated in Rouen and Paris. Having decided to become an architect, he studied at the École des Beaux Arts, Paris, as a pupil of Charles Laisné and Léon Ginain, and was awarded the Deschaumes Prize by the Institute of France. He also received the Chandesaigues Prize. While in Paris, he served on the Commission des Monuments Historiques.

Masqueray arrived in St. Paul in 1905 and remained there until his death. He designed several parochial schools for the Catholic Archdiocese of St. Paul, and about two dozen parish churches for Catholic and Protestant congregations in the upper Midwest, including:

- Cathedral of Saint Paul in Saint Paul
- Basilica of Saint Mary, Minneapolis (1908)

- St. Paul's Episcopal Church on the Hill, St. Paul (1912)
- Bethlehem Lutheran Church, 655 Forest Street, St. Paul
- University Hall at the University of St. Thomas, St. Paul
- Incarnation Catholic Church in Minneapolis
- Chapel of St. Thomas Aquinas, 121 Cleveland Ave., St. Paul (1918)
- The Church of the Holy Redeemer, Marshall, Minnesota (1915)
- St. Louis, King of France Church in St. Paul
- Church of St. Peter, St. Peter, Minnesota (1911).
- Church of St. Edward, Minneota, Minnesota
- Church of St. Francis, Benson, Minnesota
- Sacred Heart Church, Murdock, Minnesota

Charles Mousseau

Charles Mousseau dit Desilets was born in Montreal around 1806. He found employment for the Hudson Bay Company, and in 1827, came to Fort Snelling with thirty other voyageurs. Charles helped construct buildings for the Fort and became a skilled carpenter. Charles lived for seven years near the Fort in a house Henry Sibley provided for him. He knew the Dakota language and helped serve as an interpreter for Sibley. While at the Fort, he met Franny Mary Anna Perret (Perry). Her parents (Abraham Perret and Franny Mary Anna Bourquin) were some of the first settlers from the Red River Selkirk colony who had established a farm about a mile north of the Fort at Camp Coldwater on the West side of the Mississippi.

Charles and Franny Perret married in 1836, and established a home at Mendota. In 1839, they established a claim on what is present day Dayton's Bluff. While Charles Mousseau resided in the Dayton Bluff area he offered Father Galtier an acre of his land on the bluff to build the chapel. In 1848, the Mousseaus sold their claim at Dayton's Bluff to Eben Weld and with the approval of the Fort Snelling Commander homesteaded 137 acres on the

John Stevens House built by Mousseau.
Photo by Mark Labine

southeast shore of Lake Calhoun. They built a house there to secure their claim. Today a portion of this land is part of the Lakewood Cemetery. At the time, this was still part of the Fort Snelling reservation so they could not legally own the land. Missionaries Samuel and Gideon Pond also had built their cabin on a part of this property in 1839.

On June 11, 1849, the first census taken in St. Anthony listed Charles Mousseau as a head of a household there. In 1849, Colonel John H. Stevens secured a permit from the government to use 160 acres of the Fort Snelling reservation on the west side of the Mississippi near St. Anthony Falls. Stevens was given permission to build here in exchange for providing ferry services across the river. He hired Charles Mousseau to build his house, which was completed in the winter of 1849-1850. Today this house is a museum and is located in Minnehaha Park in South Minneapolis.

In 1849, Ard Godfrey also hired Charles Mousseau to build his house which today is the oldest remaining frame residence in Minneapolis. The Ard Godfrey house is located at 28 University Ave SE, in Minneapolis, and is open as a museum.

Ard Godfrey House built by Mousseau.
Photo by Mark Labine

Charles Mousseau and Franny Perret (Perry) raised twelve children. Mousseau's first son, David, married Harriet Cloutier, the first white child born in St. Anthony. Other Mousseau children were David (1837), Anthony (1841), Sophie (1842), Mary Anna (1843), Ellen 1851), Bernard (1864), Paul (1856), Sophia ((1858), Henry, Mitchell, and Mary Fanny (1865). Henry was the first "cab man" to drive a horse drawn streetcar in Minneapolis in 1875. Mitchell was a streetcar operator who rose to assistant superintendant of the Twin Cities Rapid Transit. Charles Mousseau died February 22, 1882 and his wife Franny died April 10, 1878. Both are buried in the St. Anthony of Padua cemetery in Minneapolis.[67]

Mousseau Cabin in Minnetonka

The grandson of Charles and Franny whose name was Charles A. Mousseau (wife Mattie) build a log cabin in 1908 in Minnetonka that was purchased by the Hennepin History Museum around 2008. The Hennepin History Museaum intended to refurbish the cabin and reassemble the cabin on land near the museum.[68] Unfortunately, this never happened.

Jean Nicollet

Jean Nicollet (aka Nicolet) de Belleborne (1598a −1642) was a French coureur des bois noted for exploring Green Bay of Lake Michigan, in what is now the U.S. state of Wisconsin. Nicollet was born in Cherbourg-Octeville, France, the son of Thomas Nicollet, who was "messenger

[67] Information on Charles Mousseau and Stevens and Godfrey houses obtained from article published in Hennepin County History Magazine, Ray, Georgia, *Two Yankees on the Minnesota Frontier, The Shared Destiny of Ard Godfrey and John Harrington Stevens*, Henepin History Magazine, Fall 1986, p.3.

[68] Houlihan, Jesse, *Minnetonka Cabin on the Move*, Lakeshore Weekly News, October 20, 2008.

ordinary of the King between Paris and Cherbourg," and Marguerite de la Mer. He was a known friend of Samuel de Champlain and Etienne Brule. He was drawn to Canada to participate in Samuel Champlain's plan to train young French men as explorers and traders by having them live among Native Americans."[69]

1910 painting of Jean Nicolet's 1634 arrival in Wisconsin. Note he is wearing a Chinese robe. He thought he had found China! (Public Domain)

Nicollet is noted for being the first European to cross Lake Michigan. In 1634, he became the first European to explore what would become Wisconsin. Jean Nicollet landed at Red Banks, near modern-day Green Bay, Wisconsin, in search of a passage to the Orient. He and other French explorers had learned from their Native contacts that the people who lived along these shores were called Ho-Chunk, which the French translated as "People of the Sea." In their language, it meant "harvest (cutting) the rice," as they used wild rice as a staple of their diet.

Nicollet became the French ambassador to the Ho-Chunk people. He wore brightly colored robes and carried two pistols, to convey his authority. The Ho-Chunk people appreciated his ritual display. With some Ho-Chunk guides, Nicollet ascended the Fox River, portaged to the Wisconsin, and travelled down it until it began to widen. So sure was he that he was near the ocean, that he stopped and went back to Quebec to report his discovery of a passage to the "South Sea," unaware that he had just missed finding the upper Mississippi River. Jean Nicollet drowned after his boat capsized during a storm while traveling along the St. Lawrence River in Quebec.

Joseph Nicollet
MN Historical Society Collections

Joseph Nicollet

Joseph Nicolas Nicollet (1786–1843) also known as Jean-Nicolas Nicollet, was a French geographer, astronomer, and mathematician known for mapping the upper Mississippi River basin during the 1830s. Nicollet led three expeditions

---

[69] Hamelin, Jean, *Nicollet, Jean*, Dictionary of Canadian Biography, 2015, Univerity of Toronto/Universite Laval.

in the region between the Mississippi and Missouri Rivers, primarily in Minnesota, South Dakota, and North Dakota.

Before emigrating to the United States, Nicollet was a professor of mathematics at Collège Louis-le-Grand, and a professor and astronomer at the Paris Observatory with Pierre-Simon Laplace. Political and academic changes in France led Nicollet to travel to the United States to complete work that would bolster his reputation among academics in Europe.

Nicollet's maps were among the most accurate of the time, correcting errors made by Zebulon Pike. They provided the basis for all subsequent maps of the American interior. They were also among the first to depict elevation and the only maps to use regional Native American place names. Nicollet's Map of the Hydrographical Basin of the Upper Mississippi was published in 1843, following his death. Nicollet Tower, located in Sisseton, South Dakota is a monument to Nicollet and his accomplishments and was constructed in 1991.

Nicollet Avenue in Minneapolis is named for the mapmaker Joseph Nicollet, not the explorer Jean Nicollet.[70] Nicollet's home was located on Nicollet Island where the current Nicollet Island Inn is located.

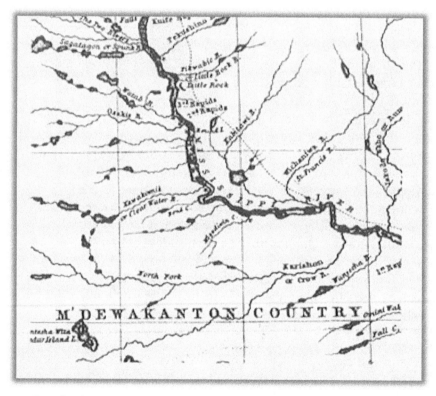

Joesph Nicollet Map of Upper Mississippi River (Public Domain)

---

[70] Nicollet, Joseph, *Joseph N. Nicollet on the plains and prairies: the expeditions of 1838-39* (reprinted. 1976). St. Paul: Minnesota Historical Society. p. 141

Jacques de Noyon

Jacques de Noyon (1668–1745) was a French-Canadian explorer and coureur des bois. He is the first known European to visit the Boundary Waters region west of Lake Superior. Jacques de Noyon was born on February 12, in Trois-Rivières, New France. His family moved to Boucherville not long after.

In 1688, de Noyon and three others traveled from the Montreal area to Fort Caministi-goyan on Lake Superior, located at present-day Thunder Bay, Ontario. From there they traveled inland up the Kaministiquia River. His group followed the canoe route of the in-digenous people over the Laurentian Divide past the present-day site of Atikokan, Ontario, through what is now Quetico Provincial Park and Voyageurs National Park, Minnesota. He built a fort, established ties to the local Assiniboine people, and spent the winter on the shore of Rainy Lake. There is some question as to whether de Noyon, in fact, made it as far as Lake of the Woods.

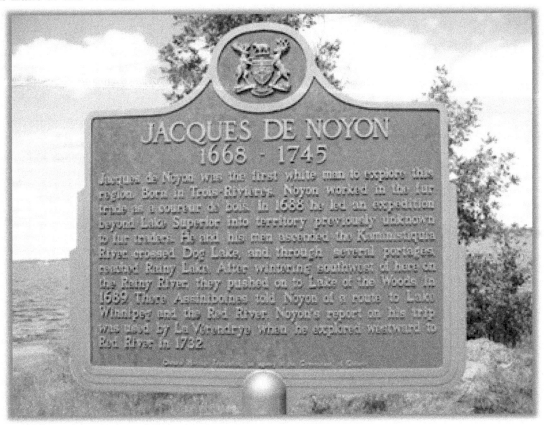

Jacques de Noyon Plaque on Rainy Lake

Jacques de Noyon continued to travel throughout New France and New England as a trader and coureur des bois. He married Abigail Stebbins in Deerfield, Massachusetts in 1704. He was still there when the French and Indians made the 1704 Raid on Deerfield. He was captured and brought back to Canada with his wife. Ruined, he became a soldier in Fort Pontchartrain du Détroit (Detroit). He died on the 12th of May 1745 in Boucherville.[71]

Pig's Eye Parrant

Pierre "Pig's Eye" Parrant (1777–1844) is believed to be the first person of European descent to live within the borders of what would eventually become the city of Saint Paul, Minnesota. The area where he lived became known as Pig's Eye for a time. The name of "Pig's Eye" came about by accident when a customer at Parrant's tavern mailed a letter with the return address of "Pig's Eye." Since everyone in the area knew Parrant, the response to the letter was delivered to Parrant's establishment. The area later became known as St. Paul's Landing, and a few years after, in 1846, a post office was established in what later became St. Paul.[72] St. Paul was incorporated as the city of St. Paul in 1854.

Pig's Eye Parrant, by Robert Perrizo

There are conflicting sources as to Pierre Parrant's exact history before settling in the Minnesota Territory. However, most sources agree that he was of French-Canadian origin and born near Sault Ste. Marie, Michigan, in or around 1777. Prior to settling in St. Paul, Pierre was a fur trapper working for the McKenzie and Chouteau Company. He was known as "Pig's Eye" Parrant, because he was blind in one eye, and apparently one of his eyes was ugly in appearance. He became known as a liquor dealer after settling in Minnesota, and would sell alcohol to the soldiers in the fort as well as to the local settlers and Indians. He located his business in a cave just to the west of downtown St. Paul, known as Fountain Cave. This was a nice cool place to store his goods before selling them. In 1844, Pierre Parrant lost his claim at Fountain Cave and was forced to vacate the land where he had become so successful. It is believed he died shortly after 1844.[73]

André Joseph Pénicaut

André Pénicaut (Pénigault, Pérricault), (1680–1750) carpenter and chronicler, was born in La Rochelle, France. He claimed to have accompanied Pierre Le Moyne d'Iberville on his first voyage to Louisiana in 1698, but that claim is very questionable, as the events he later relayed occurred on the second voyage. On September 24, 1699, Pénicaut signed a deed of indenture as a ship's carpenter. He went on Iberville's second voyage to Louisiana aboard Le Marin and established himself in Mobile. He later said that in 1701, he accompanied

[71] Russ, C.J., *Jacques de Noyon*, Dictionary of Canadian Biography, Univerity of Toronto/Universite Laval. (1974-2015).
[72] Brick, Greg, *What Happened to Fountain Cave—The Real Birthplace of St. Paul?*, Ramsey County History 29 (1995): 4-15
[73] Fletcher, J. Williams "Memoir of William W. Warren," in William W. Warren, *History of the Ojibway People*, Minnesota Historical Society, (1885).

Pierre Charles Le Sueur on an expedition to the upper Mississippi copper mines in what is now Minnesota. What historians know of his life derives almost entirely from his journals, titled "Annals of Louisiana from 1698 to 1722." The work is an important source of information on Native American life, geography and ecology, and historical events during the colonial period in the Gulf Coast region.

Pierre Pépin dit Laforce

According to L'Association des Familles de Pepin, Pierre Pepin, Sr., dit LaForce (1652–1722), along with his brother Etienne Pepin, took part in the Duluth expedition in 1678 which reached the upper Mississippi. Many believe that Lake Pepin was named in honor of these two Pepin brothers. Pierre Pepin's nickname, "LaForce," is said to come from his co-discovery of the Mississippi River. However, it is not certain if the lake is in fact named after Pierre or if it is named after his father, Guillaume Pépin dit Tranchemontagne, who was a Judge and Syndic of Trois Rivieres, Quebec and was known to have been granted large land concessions by King Louis XIII of France.

Pierre married Louise Lemire in Quebec in 1681, and had fourteen children. He lived on a large estate on the St. Lawrence River, near Nicolet, and lived to be 70 years old. A historical monument erected in Trois-Rivières, Quebec honors French explorers of the New World, including Jean Nicolet, René-Robert Cavelier, Sieur de La Salle and Pierre Pépin dit Laforce.

1840 Jacob C. Ward engraving depicting Lake Pepin
Minnesota Historical Society Collections

Jean Baptiste Perreault

Jean Baptiste Perreault (1761–1844) was a fur trader in Minnesota who wrote the book titled *"Narrative of the Travels and Adventures of a Merchant Voyageur in the Savage Territories of Northern America, Leaving Montreal the 28th Day of May, 1783 to 1820."* He worked at the following trading posts in Minnesota: Fond du Lac, Cass Lake, and Pine River. His book is available on the French-American Heritage Foundation website.

Jean Baptiste Perreault was born at Trois Rivieres, Quebec in 1761. He was educated in Quebec and entered the fur trade in 1783. His first engagement in the industry was for one year only, but he thrived, and twenty-two years would pass before he would return to visit his ailing father. His father was a Magistrate at Riviére Loup in Quebec. During his time in the fur trade he took an Indian wife and had many children. He worked for the Northwest Company from 1793 until 1805. After that, he worked for several different employers and ended up retiring and passing away in Sault Ste. Marie in 1844.

Nicholas Perrot

Nicholas Perrot (1641a–1717) lived in France between 1641 and 1644, perhaps at Darcey, in Burgundy, where his father was a lieutenant of justice.

Perrot came to New France around 1660 with the Jesuits, and traveled with them to the western Great Lakes, reaching present-day Wisconsin in 1665. He earned the friendship of the natives by swapping guns for furs, allowing the natives to defend themselves on an equal footing against their enemies, and was nicknamed the "trafficker of iron," or "iron legs."

Statute of Nicholas Perrot in Green Bay, Wisconsin

In 1667, he formed a fur trading company with three others from Montreal and on August 12, 1667, he returned to the Green Bay region. Then, in 1670, he was enlisted as a translator for Simon-François Daumont de Saint-Lusson, a military officer and deputy of Jean Talon, who had been sent "to lay claim to the land of the Ottawa, Amikwa, Illinois, and of other nations discovered or to be discovered in North America contiguous and adjacent to Lake Superior (French: Lac Supérieur), the great inland sea, including all its length and breadth, and including the resources therein, for Louis XIV" at what was called "The Pageant of the Sault."

In 1684, he participated in the peacekeeping mission of the Governor Lefebvre de La Barre and succeeded in bringing the warriors of several nations for the signing of a peace treaty. In the spring of 1685, he was appointed Commandant-in-Chief of Bais Des Puants (present-day Green Bay, Wisconsin) and the neighboring regions when war broke out between the Fox tribe and the Dakota and Ojibwe tribes. He worked endlessly to bring about peace, and was successful, at least for a time. After this, Perrot traveled to the northern waters of the Mississippi River, in the territory of the Dakota, where he built Fort Saint Antoine on Lake Pepin.

The first official document pertaining to Minnesota is Nicholas Perrot'a claim of that land for the King of France as follows:

> *"Nicholas Perrot, commanding for the King, at the post of the Nadouessioux, commissioned by the Marquis Denonville, Governor and Lieutenant-Governor of all New France, to manage the interests of commerce among all the Indian tribes, and people of the Bay des Puants, Nadouessioux, Mascoutins, and other western nations of the Upper Mississippi, and to take possession in the King's name of all the places where he has heretofore been, and whither he will go."*[74]

---

[74] Neill, Edward Duffield, Secretary of the Minnesota Historical Society, T*he History of Minnesota from the earliest French Explorations to the Present Time,* Philadelphia: J. B. Lippincott & co. 1858.

In the spring of 1687, he was in the region of Detroit taking part in an expedition. A fire broke out at the Jesuit mission at Bais De Puants, and 40,000 livres worth of his furs were destroyed. Perrot was financially ruined. He continued to serve as an interpreter and negotiator for the Governor of New France and the Natives, and was instrumental in resupplying the western Indians loyal to the French which may have saved New France from the Five Nations who were at war with the French. In subsequent years he was involved in the discovery of lead mines brought to his attention by Miami chiefs.

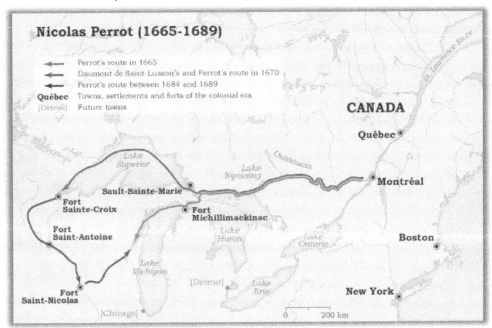

Nicholas Perrot Route map. Canadian Museum of History,
Virtual Museum of New France, IMG2013-0040-Dm

Plaque commemorating Nicolas Perrot, at Clergue
Park, Sault Ste. Marie, Ontario

In his later years, Perrot settled on his land grant at Bécancour, Quebec where he became a captain of the local militia and continued to serve as an interpreter and provide assistance to the governments in their relations with the native tribes. His final years were marked by financial difficulties and harassment from creditors due to the loss of his furs in 1687 and the government's refusal to compensate him for expense owed him and a pension promised him. He wrote his memoirs, which became valuable to later historians and helped secure his place in history.[75] Nicholas Perrot

---

[75] Perrot, Nicolas, *Mémoire sur les mœurs, coustumes et relligion des sauvages de l'Amérique septentrionale*, éd. Jules Tailhan (Leipzig et Paris, 1864; Canadiana avant 1867, Toronto, 1968).

died on the 13th of August 1717 at about the age of 74 and was buried the next day in the church at Bécancour. Nine of his eleven children along with his wife, Madeleine Raclot, outlived him. Madeleine died in 1724. A Wisconsin state park called Perrot State Park is named after him, near the confluence of the Trempeleau and Mississippi Rivers.

Charles Louis Perry (Perret)

Charles Perret (1816–1904) later anglicized to Perry, was a French speaking Swiss immigrant who originally settled in the Selkirk Colony. Charles was born in 1816 to Abraham Perret, a clock maker, and his wife Mary Anne in Berne, Switzerland. They emigrated to the Selkirk Colony in 1820. After only six years, they gave up their hopes of establishing themselves in the Red River Settlement. In 1826, after a devastating flood, they traveled by oxcart to the Fort Snelling military reservation.

Charles Perry (Perret) and Angeline Morrisette (Public Domain)

The Perret's were allowed to live at the Fort Snelling reservation for the next eleven years. In 1837, Abraham Perret, by then known as Perry, moved near Fountain Cave near downtown St. Paul. His son, Charles Perry, set out on his own and first married a Native American named Emilie Bruce who died at a young age after bearing three children. He then married Angeline (Orelia, Amelia, Aurelia) Morrisette, daughter of Jean Baptiste Morissette and Francoise LeTendre. They settled for a time near Lake Como, and then moved next to Lake Johanna in present-day Arden Hills. Perry Park in Arden Hills is named after him.

Louis Provencalle

Louis Provencalle (1780a–1850) was a French fur trader and explorer. He traded at Traverse des Sioux on the Minnesota River in the early 1800s. He is named in written accounts of travelers and missionaries and is often referred to as "Mr. Leblanc." His name appears, along with those of Jean Baptiste Faribault and Colin Campbell on a list dated June 21, 1814, of Canadian voyageurs who volunteered at Mackinac to fight under the leadership of Captain Thomas G. Anderson against the Americans at Prairie du Chien. It

Inside Provencalle's Trading House at Traverse des Sioux 1851 by Francis Blackwell Mayer (1827-1899) (Public Domain)

is believed he was born around 1780,[76] and died, according to Henry Sibley in his papers, at Mendota in 1850. His name appears in letters and papers written at the time by Henry Sibley, Alexis Bailly, Joseph Rolette, Major Lawrence Taliaferro, Father Gabriel Richard, George Boyd, Ramsey Crooks (general manager of the American Fur Company) and Jean Baptiste Faribault. His cabin remained standing at Traverse des Sioux in 1851 when the artist Frank B. Mayer[77] visited that place and made a sketch of it.

Louis Provencalle's Trading House at Traverse des Sioux
By Francis Blackwell Mayer (1827-1899) (Public Domain)

Pierre-Esprit Radisson

Pierre-Esprit Radisson (1636–1710)[78] was a French fur trader and explorer. He is often linked to his brother-in-law Médard Chouart des Groseilliers. They are considered the key players in the formation of the Hudson's Bay Company.

Pierre-Espirit Radisson
Image from 1785 Paris Print

Born in France in 1636, he came to New France as a child. At the age of fifteen he was captured by Mohawk Indians while out duck hunting. Spirited off to the Mohawk homeland, he was adopted by a family of a warrior who had nineteen French scalps on his belt. Radisson bided his time for two years, living as a Mohawk slave, before escaping to Albany and thence returning to Quebec or New France, as it was then known.

In Quebec, he came into partnership with the man who married his half-sister, a trader two decades his senior, named Médard Chouart, Sieur Des Groseilliers. They headed north in the spring of 1659 into the Canadian wilderness, in search of beaver fur, becoming some of the first European explorers in this vast area of the North American continent. Radisson and Groseilliers were successful in their venture into the wilderness but their furs were confiscated

---

[76] Babcock Willoughby M. *Louis Provencalle, Fur Trader*, published by the Minnesota Historical Society in St. Paul.
[77] Francis Blackwell Mayer (1827-1899) was a 19th century painter from Mayland who took a trip to the western frontier in the mid-nineteenth century and executed a series of drawings of Native Americans, including a painting of the Traverse des Sious Treaty. Mayer's paintings currently in Newberry Library, Chicago.
[78] Picture in this book available from Library and Archives Canada under the reproduction reference number C-015497.

because they had not secured a proper fur trade license from the French crown. Frustrated and angry, they went to the English, and after several efforts, helped form the Hudson Bay Company, which would become a highly successful business in future years. Radisson and Groseilliers worked on behalf of the Hudson Bay Company for a time, until they began to feel unappreciated. After a disagreement with others in the Company, they switched sides back to New France, only to later go back again to the Hudson Bay Company. He died in 1710.

Augustin Ravoux

Father Ravoux
Minnesota Historical Society
Collections

Monsignor Augustin Ravoux (1815-1906) was a French Jesuit priest and missionary who arrived in Minnesota in September 1841. He worked as a missionary priest in a number of locations. When Bishop Cretin died in 1857, Ravoux was named as the sole administrator of the St. Paul Diocese of the Minnesota Territory by Bishop Kenrick of the Archdiocese of St. Louis. He served in that capacity until Bishop Grace was installed as the second Bishop in 1859. Monsignor Ravoux was involved in many of the early events of Minnesota, including the early settlement of St. Paul, the establishment of a church in Chaska, and the baptizing of thirty-three of the thirty-eight Dakota hung in Mankato in 1865 as a result of the U.S. Dakota War of 1862.

Joseph Renville

Joseph Renville (1779–1846) was an interpreter, translator, and an important figure in dealings between white men and Dakota (Sioux) Indians in Minnesota. He contributed to the translation of Christian religious texts into the Dakota language.[79] The town of Renville, Minnesota, is named in honor of Joseph Renville, as are Renville County, Minnesota and Renville County, North Dakota.[80] Joseph Renville's father, also named Joseph Renville, was a French-Canadian fur trader, and his mother, Miniyuhe, was a Dakota, possibly a daughter of Mdewakanton-Dakota chief Big Thunder Big Thunder. Renville's bicultural formative years may have included some education in Canada.

Joseph Renville
Public Domain

[79] Drawing of Columbia Fur Company Post at Lake Traverse in 1823 by Samuel Seymour engraved by J. Hill, in Keating, William H. *Narrative of an Expedition to the Source of St. Peter's River…under the Command of Stephen H. Long* (Philadelphia, 1824). Public Domain
[80] Ackermann, Gertrude, *Joseph Renville of Lac qui Parle*, Minnesota History 12 (September 1931) 231-246.

In 1822, he with other experienced trappers and traders organized the Columbia Fur Company of which he was the leader, but some time after, the American Fur Company bought them out. They retained the services of Renville, and Renville settled permanently

at Lac qui Parle in 1826 where he erected a trading house to conduct business with the Indians. The Lac qui Parle mission was established in 1835 largely through Mr. Renville's influence.

Columbia Fur Company Post at Lake Traverse in 1823
(Public Domain)

Captain Louis Robert

Robert Street in downtown St. Paul is named after Captain Louis Robert, (1811–1874) an early resident of Saint Paul.[81]

Louis Robert was a fur trader, an early St. Paul land owner, and a steamboat owner and pilot. He came to St. Paul from the Creole community of Carondelet in St. Louis, Missouri. Carondelet is a neighborhood in the extreme southeastern portion of St. Louis that was annexed into the city in 1870.

Captain Louis Robert
Minnesota Historical Society
Collections

Louis Robert arrived in St. Paul in the winter of 1843. Before that he had been a trapper in the Rocky Mountains and a trader on several rivers. Robert bought Pigs Eye Parrant's claim near the lower landing, and extensive tracts of property in St. Paul. His house was on the bluff where Kellogg and Robert Street now meet, and his trading post made of tamarack poles was located at the site which is now the east side of Jackson Street under the bluff. This was a good steamboat landing site, and became the "Lower Landing." Robert bought a steamboat named "The Greek Slave" in 1853, followed by "The Time and Tide," "The Globe" and the "Jeannette Roberts," which was named after his daughter. Even though he gave up steamboating by 1859, he was always known as Captain Roberts. Robert remained active in trading posts along the Minnesota River. During the Dakota uprising of 1862, Louis Robert escaped death near Fort Ridgely by crawling into a swamp and lying with only his nose above water while Dakota braves searched for him. In 1869, Louis Robert donated bells to the frame church of the French speakers of the city called St. Louis, King of France. The bells remain at the "new" church, built in 1909, at the corner of Tenth and Cedar Street.

[81] Empson, Donald L. (2006). *The Street Where You Live: A Guide to the Place Names of Saint Paul.* University of Minnesota Press. p 232; Neill, Rev. Edward D., edited by Charles S. Bryant, *History of the Minnesota Valley: Including the Explorers and Pioneers of Minnesota,* by North Star Publishing Company, Minneapolis, 1882.

On them, an inscription reads "Presente a la Congregation Francaise de l'Eglise St. Louis par Capt. Louis Robert, Juillet, 1869." [82] Louis died in 1874 and is buried at the Calvary Cemetery in St. Paul.

Louis Robert house in St. Paul
Minnesota Historical Society Collections

Joseph Rolette

Joseph Rolette (1820–1871) was a well-known American fur trader and politician during Minnesota's territorial era and the Civil War. His father was Jean Joseph Rolette, often referred to as Joe Rolette the elder, a French-Canadian and a trader himself. Joseph Rolette's mother was Jane Fisher, who married Joe the elder in 1818 when she was either 13 or 14 years old. Jane's relatives brought young Joseph to New York. Joseph's parents never divorced as they were Catholics, but the couple became separated in 1836. As part of the settlement, the elder Rolette built what is today known as the Brisbois House, for his estranged wife on Water Street, St. Feriole Island, Prairie du Chien, Wisconsin.

Joe Jr. headed back west in 1840, and by the time he was twenty one he was working for his father's partners in the Red River valley area of Minnesota. Some of the best-known names in Minnesota history (Henry Hastings Sibley and Ramsey Crooks) were active and running a fur trading company in the area. While in their service, Joseph Rolette rebuilt a trading post at Pembina. He was responsible for the building and the defense of the post as well as managing the business being conducted there. The area where the Pembina Trail crossed the Red Lake River is now the county seat for Red Lake County.

In 1842 young Rolette helped develop a supply route along the Red River Oxcart Trails between Pembina and Mendota, Minnesota. As a result, a substantial portion of the trade enjoyed by the Hudson's Bay Company in Canada was diverted to the United States. In 1845, he married Angelique Jerome. Together they had eleven children.

[82] Mississippi River Field Guide, site submitted by Steve Lee and story on Louis Robert submitted by Patricia Condon.

In 1851, he was elected to the Minnesota Territorial Legislature and served four terms. It was from his time in the legislature that the best-known story about him originates. A bill naming St. Peter the capital of Minnesota was about to be enacted, and since he was chairman of the enrollment committee, bills of this nature had to pass through him. Rolette took physical possession of the document and disappeared for the rest of the session, not returning until it was too late to pass any more bills. St. Peter did not become the capital and it ended up in St. Paul where it remains today. According to the story, he spent the week away from the legislature drinking and playing poker in a hotel room with some friends. From 1857-1858, he served in the first Minnesota State Constitutional Convention and the Minnesota State Senate.

Joe Rolette
Minnesota Historical Society
Collections

Augustin Rocque

Augustin Rocque (1787–1856) and his father Joseph Rocque, were fur traders and Indian interpreters in the service of the British. Augustin was born at Prairie du Chien. At the conclusion of the War of 1812, called the Blackhawk War in the Wabasha area, Augustin Rocque, accompanied by a government appointee named Long, traveled up the Mississippi River and established his home in the western part of Wabasha on the Mississippi River, just north of Wabasha's St. Elizabeth Hospital. Wabasha County was named in honor of a Dakota Chief Wa-pa-shaw, whose tribe was on the Mississippi River in that area. Augustin Roque was Wa-pa-shaw's nephew because his father, Joseph Rocque, was married to Chief Wa-pa-Shaw's sister, Wapashaw.

In 1830, a treaty was made with the Dakota, Sacs, Foxes, Iowas, Omahas, Otoes and Missouri Indians at Prairie du Chien. The Mdewakanton Dakota and their many Metis relatives from the fur trade days had a special article put in the treaty to benefit the mixed bloods. The United States agreed to allow mixed bloods of the Dakota Nation a tract of country beginning at a place called the Barn, below and near the village of Red Wing Chief and running back fifteen miles, then in a parallel line with Lake Pepin and Mississippi River, thence fifteen miles to the Grand Encampment opposite the Beef River. The United States agreed to let the Metis occupy this county, holding title in the same manner that the other Indian titles were held. Certificates were issued to many Métis. There ensued much litigation over them in subsequent years. In time, these land titles, labeled "half-breed certificates" became very valuable to its holders.

In September 1837, Augustin Rocque accompanied the Dakota leaders to Washington, D.C. to cede their lands east of the Mississippi. In July, the Ojibwe ceded their claims east of the river by signing the Dodge Treaty. Augustin accompanied the Chiefs along with Alexis Bailly, Joseph LaFramboise, Francois LaBathe, Henry H. Sibley, Alexander Rocque, and Alexander and Oliver Faribault.

**Seigneuret Gravestone
in Henderson cemetery
Photo by Mark Labine**

Dr. H. J. Seigneuret

H.J. Seigneuret, M.D. was born at Fontainebleau, France on March 7, 1819. He received his medical degree at the Academy of Paris and University of France in 1841. He later went back to school and graduated from the school of law in Paris in March 1846. He was a leader in the French insurrection of June 1848, and as a result, had to flee France. He first went to Jersey Island, one of the Channel Islands, and then migrated to Henderson in Sibley County, Minnesota in 1854.

In 1862, when the Sioux Indian outbreak took place, Dr. Seigneuret was appointed the brigade surgeon of the expedition with General H.H. Sibley. He later was the surgeon for the Battalion of Minnesota volunteer cavalry during the civil war and served at a number of frontier posts.

Henry Hastings Sibley

Henry Hastings Sibley (1811–1891) was the first governor of the State of Minnesota and a U.S. Representative of the Minnesota Territory and the Wisconsin Territory. Henry Sibley spoke fluent French[83] and worked as a supply-purchasing agent of the American Fur Company at Mackinac. He became a partner and was relocated to their headquarters in the settlement of St. Pierre or St. Peter which is now called Mendota.

**Henry Sibley
Minnesota Historical
Society Collections**

Over the winter of 1839-40, he entered a de facto marriage with Red Blanket Woman, granddaughter of a Mdewakanton Dakota chief; a daughter, Helen Hastings Sibley, also known as Wahkiyee (Bird), was born in August 1841. In 1862 Sibley was appointed colonel of the state militia. He was sent to the upper Minnesota River to protect exposed settlements as the U.S.—Dakota War raged. Sibley was promoted to brigadier general after the Battle of Wood Lake.[84]

[83] Gitlin, Jay, *The Bourgeois Frontier: French Towns, French Traders, and American Expansion,* Yale University Press. p. 177.
[84] West, Nathaniel, *The ancestry, life, and times of Hon. Henry Hastings Sibley,* Pioneer Press Publishing Company, Saint Paul, (1880).

Gilles Robert de Vaugondy

Gilles Robert de Vaugondy (1688–1766) also known as Le Sieur or Monsieur Robert, and his son, Didier Robert de Vaugondy (1723a–1786), were leading cartographers in France during the 18th century. Gilles and Didier Robert De Vaugondy produced their maps and terrestrial globes working together as father and son. Globes of a variety of sizes were made by gluing copperplate-printed gores on a plaster-finished papier-mache core, a complicated and expensive manufacturing process, employing several specialists. In some cases it is uncertain whether Gilles or Didier made a given map. Gilles often signed maps as "M.Robert," while Didier commonly signed his maps as "Robert de Vaugondy," or added "fils" or "filio" after his name.

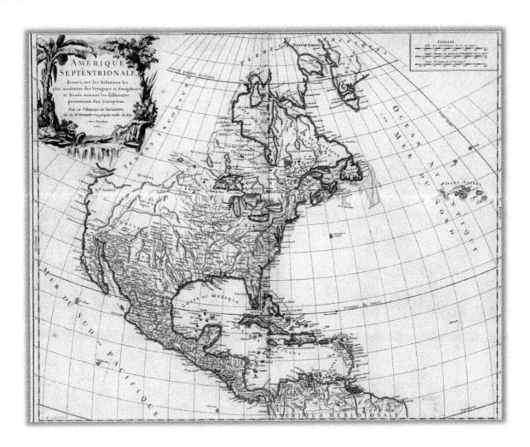

De Vaugondy map of North America- 1750 (Public Domain)

The Robert de Vaugondys were descended from the Nicolas Sanson family through Sanson's grandson, Pierre Moulard-Sanson. From him, they inherited much of Sanson's cartographic material, which they combined with maps and plates acquired after Hubert Jaillot's death in 1712 to form the basis the Atlas Universel. Sources from the Dépôt de la Marine, the official French repository for maritime-related information, were used for their maps of Canada and South America. He created early maps of Minnesota.

Jim Thompson

Jim Thompson was a French speaking mulatto who was the slave of an officer from Kentucky. The Reverend Alfred Brunson, who had established a Methodist mission at the Dakota village of Kaposia, purchased Jim's freedom for the price of twelve hundred dollars. Thompson then married a daughter of Cloud Man, the Dakota leader of the Lake Calhoun ban. Cloud Man had other daughters who were married to other leaders in the area. Captain Seth Eastman and Major Lawrence Taliaferro both had children with their Dakota wives. Jim Thompson lived with the French speaking settlers of early St. Paul. His name was asociated with men who were selling liquor to the Indians and troops, such as Menk, Pierre "Pig's Eye" Parrant, Joseph R. Brown, and Donald McDonald. He lived with the French-Canadian community and was treated as an equal. He went to the rescue of a ten year old girl who had been taken and savagly attacked, and testified at the trial which was conducted by Henry Sibley, the Justice of the Peace. It was unheard of at that time to allow a black man to testify against a white man. He also had an incident with Edward Phelen after Phelen stole his pig. The story goes that after Phelen disputed that the pig belonged to Thompson, he proposed they fight, and "If you lick me, the pig is yours, and if I lick you, the pig is mine." Thompson won. He later ran the first ferry across the Mississippi near downtown and helped construct the Methodist Church on Market Street in 1849.[85]

Joseph and Amable Turpin

Joseph Turpin (1775–1865) is said to be the first man to build a house east of the Mississippi in the St. Paul area.[86] Mr. Turpin was born in Montreal, Quebec and emigrated to Prairie du Chien with his brother Amable. He lived in the Selkirk Colony for a time but returned to St. Paul in 1831, staying at the Fort Snelling Military reservation for a time before building a house on the east side of the Mississippi. He later sold this house to Joseph Rondeau (Rondo) and moved to Mendota. Amable Turpin (1766-1866) was also born in Montreal and lived to be almost 100 years old. He was a fur trader who traveled to Mackinac, to Green Bay, Prairie du Chien and finally to St. Paul.[87] He worked for the American Fur Company. He was said to possess extraordinary power and endurance. Amable Turpin's daughter married Captain Louis Robert.[88]

William Whipple Warren
Minnesota Historical Society Collections

William Whipple Warren

William Whipple Warren (1825–1853) was a French speaking historian, interpreter, and legislator in the Minnesota Territory. His father was Richard Warren and his mother Mary Cadotte. Mary

[85] Information on Jim Thompson found in Green, William D. *A Peculiar Imbalance: The Fall and Rise of Racial Equality in Early Minnesota*, Minnesota Historical Society Press.

[86] Fletcher, J. Williams, *The History of the City of Saint Paul and the County of Ramsey, Minnesota*, (Minnesota Historical Society Press, St. Paul, 1983) p.61

[87] The Picture of Settler's Cabins shown above is by Albert Bierstadt (1830-1902). Pictures available for purchase at webstie www.albertbierstadt.org.

[88] Fletcher, J. Williams, *The History of the City of Saint Paul and the County of Ramsey, Minnesota*, (Minnesota Historical Society Press, St. Paul, 1983) p.86

Cadotte was the Metis daughter of French-Canadian Michel Cadotte and Ikwesewe, an Ojibwe. His grandfather, Michel Cadotte, was a French fur trader, for whom Cadott, Wisconsin is named. He was educated at Protestant mission schools in Lapointe, Wisconsin and Mackinac Island, and later attended Clarkson Academy and the Oneida Institute in New York. Warren wote "A Brief History of the Ojibwas," which the Minnesota Democrat newspaper published in several installments in 1851. He used the perspective of his American education to present the stories of the Ojibwe people. He recounted their wars, political leaders, and history, and always credited his sources. In 1851, Warren was elected a legislator from the Minnesota Territory, serving in the Minnesota Territorial House of Representatives. Warren married Mathilda Aitken, who also shared a multi-racial ancestry like his.[89]

Settler's Cabins by Albert Bierstadt (1830-1902) (Public Domain)

---

[89] Fletcher, J. Williams *"Memoir of William W. Warren,"* in William W. Warren, *History of the Ojibway People,* Minnesota Historical Society, 1885.

Chapter Three
French Mining in Minnesota
By Greg Brick, Ph.D.

All three European nations that extensively colonized North America—Britain, France, and Spain—were interested in potential mineral deposits in their new lands. In the sixteenth century, even before the founding of New France, the Saguenay River valley of Quebec had attracted Jacque Cartier's attention, because the legendary kingdom, perhaps an echo of Norse traditions, was said to be replete with gold, silver and copper. La Rocque de Roberval, sent to Canada to establish what proved to be abortive settlements, also sought precious metals. Samuel de Champlain, the father of New France, spent much time looking for copper, lead, and iron mines in Acadia and elsewhere. Jean Talon, the first royally-appointed Intendant of New France (served 1665–1668), so energetic in diversifying and expanding French activities in Canada generally, made efforts to locate new mines, as did a successor, Gilles Hocquart (served 1731–1748). The French hoped that the Mississippi valley would prove comparable to Spanish Mexico, with its rich mines, a sentiment that played into the disastrous financial speculations associated with John Law's "Mississippi Bubble" in the 1720s.[90]

Mineral identification was imperfect. The Jesuit historian Francois-Xavier de Charlevoix, who is usually noted for the careful account given in his *Histoire et description generale de la Nouvelle France* (1744) occasionally made mistakes, as when he described as diamonds what were later determined to be merely quartz. The Quebec plateau, known as Cap aux Diamants, was a shining example. This gave rise to the expression "as false as Canadian diamonds" which in turn became ironic with the discovery of valuable Canadian diamond mines at Ekati in our own times.[91]

Lead Mines

The French seemed to have had the best luck establishing lead mines, some of which are still in operation today. Lead was found in the form of galena (lead sulfide) which could be smelted to remove the sulfur, after which it was turned into lead bullets and shot that was available for use on the Minnesota frontier.[92]

French prospectors delineated the great lead deposits of what are now Missouri, Wisconsin, Illinois, and Iowa. Hennepin's map of 1687 shows a lead mine near Galena, Illinois. Nicolas Perrot discovered the lead mines near Dubuque, Iowa, about 1690. In the wake of Law's speculative "Mississippi Bubble," Philippe Francois Renault arrived in the Midwest with miners, working the La Motte lead mine in Missouri from 1720 to 1744, even extracting some silver from the lead ores. Julien Dubuque shipped lead down the Mississippi River from his "Mines of Spain" (now in Iowa) to St. Louis from 1788 to 1810. Dubuque had

[90] For background information, see Winsor, J., *Cartier to Frontenac: Geographical Discovery in the Interior of North America in its Historical Relations 1534-1700* (Boston and New York: Houghton, Mifflin and Company, 1894). Also Trudel, M., *Introduction to New France* (Toronto and Montreal: Holt, Rinehart and Winston of Canada, Limited, 1968).

[91] Eyles, N. and Miall, A., *Canada Rocks: The Geologic Journey* (Markham, Ontario: Fitzhenry and Whiteside, 2007), pp. 407, 409.

[92] The best source on this topic is Jillson, W.R., Early mineral explorations in the Mississippi Valley (1540-1840), *Transactions of the Illinois State Historical Society* (1924): 41-57.

obtained the concession from the Spanish authorities, who had secretly accepted France's succession of land west of the Mississippi River in 1762.[93]

Copper Mines

In prehistoric North America, there was a widespread trade in the native (elemental) copper of the Great Lakes region, usually associated with the Old Copper Culture. Copper was used for making ornaments, tools, and weapons. "A large mass of copper" had been reported four leagues above the mouth of the St. Croix River in 1700 and marginal copper mines existed along that river into the nineteenth century.[94] But a single nugget did not necessarily mean that a mother lode was nearby, something not well understood until the advent of glacial theory about 1840 (thus post-dating the period of French occupation) when it was realized that glaciers had transported minerals from distant places. Float copper, or glacially transported nuggets, are found scattered widely across North America.

The biggest player in copper was the French explorer and fur trader Pierre-Charles Le Sueur (1657–1704), born in Artois, France, who came to Quebec as a donne of the Jesuits. He soon adopted the adventurous life of a fur trader, associating himself with the aggressively expansionist and controversial policies of the Governor-General of New France, Buade de Frontenac (served 1672–82 and 1689–98). When Nicolas Perrot established Fort St. Antoine on the Wisconsin shores of Lake Pepin in 1689, proclaiming the Upper Mississippi valley in the name of the French king, Le Sueur was there, signing his name to the document.[95]

The state geologist Newton Horace Winchell gave the best summary of Le Sueur's copper mining ventures in Minnesota. This involved the establishment of "Fort L'Huillier" or "Fort Vert" (sometimes rendered Fort Green) at the site of a supposed copper mine on the Blue Earth River, near Mankato, Minnesota, in 1700. The fort's namesake, Alexandre L'Huillier, was a French farmer-general (tax official) who supported Le Sueur's "compagnie des Sioux," which had royal permission to exploit mines in the Sioux country:

> In April, 1700, with a single shallop and about twenty-five persons, he started from the settlements on the lower Mississippi for the mouth of the Minnesota river, where he arrived on the 19th of September; and on the last day of the same month, being stopped by ice forty-four leagues above its union with the Mississippi, he determined to build his fort. His narrator, Penicaut, who was also his carpenter, states that this place was a league up the Green river (now the Blue Earth) on a point of land a quarter of a league distant from the woods. This river was so called "because it is of that color by reason of a green earth, which, loosening itself from the copper mines, becomes dissolved in it and makes it green." ... The blue, or green, earth, which was mistaken for an ore of copper by Le Sueur, was obtained in a mine three-quarters of a league distant from the fort. The fort was named L'Huillier, from one of the chief collectors of the king, who had assayed the ore in Paris in 1696. Having spent the winter at his fort, in the spring of 1701 he descended the Mississippi with a large quantity of the ore, 4,000 pounds of which were sent to France. He intended to return, but in 1703

---

[93] Trewartha, G.T., A second epoch of destructive occupance in the Driftless Hill Land, *Annals of the Association of American Geographers* 30 (1940): 109-142.

[94] Winchell, N.H., Historical Sketch of Explorations and Surveys in Minnesota, IN *The Final Report, Geology of Minnesota*, (Minneapolis: Johnson, Smith & Harrison, 1884), Vol 1, pp. 17, 97-98.

[95] *Dictionary of Canadian Biography*, University of Toronto/Universite Laval, 1974. (Hereafter, DCB.)

the garrison left by him arrived at Mobile, in charge of Derague, having been compelled to abandon the post on account of ill treatment by the Indians, and lack of supplies. This river is further described as being near a range of hills (Keating says mountains) ten leagues long that seemed to be composed of the same substance. Charlevoix says: "After removing a burnt, black crust, as hard as a rock, the copper could be scraped with a knife." Penicaut says: "This mine is situated at the beginning of a very long mountain which is upon the bank of the river, so that boats can go right to the mouth of the mine itself. At this place is the green earth, which is a foot and a half in thickness, and above it is a layer of earth as firm and hard as stone, and black and burnt like coal by the exhalation from the mine. The copper is scratched out with a knife. There are no trees upon this mountain. If this mine is good, it will make a great trade, because the mountain contains more than ten leagues running of the same ground. It appears, according to our observations, that in the very finest weather there is continually a fog upon this mountain."[96]

Le Sueur's men loaded the boat with beaver pelts worth far more than the ore itself. Bochart de Champigny, Intendant of New France, cynically wrote of Le Sueur, "I think the only mines that he seeks in those regions are mines of beaver-skins."[97] Indeed, Le Sueur's activities appear to be in violation of Louis XIV's 1696 order of cessation against the fur trade in New France.[98] French markets had been glutted with beaver pelts, severely depressing prices, so they petitioned the king for relief. French officialdom was suspicious of so-called explorers for this very reason and Le Sueur was already among those noted for his defiance of government orders, having worked as a *coureur de bois* (illegal trader) earlier in life. Explorers such as La Verendrye and his sons, searching for the so-called Western Sea on the Canadian plains in the 1730s and 1740s, also indulged heavily in fur trading.[99]

There is no record of continued mining at Fort L'Huillier (Figure 1). Upon returning to France afterwards, Le Sueur solicited a judgeship in Mobile (in what is now Alabama). He was appointed and secured permission for his family to settle in Louisiana with him. On the return trip he was stricken with yellow fever at Havana, Cuba, where he perished in 1704.[100]

In 1835, the English geologist G.W. Featherstonhaugh, upon observing nothing more than blue siltstone in the vicinity of Fort L'Huillier, commented, "I found myself obliged to come to the conclusion that these discoveries were fables invented to give [Le Sueur] influence at the court of France." Used as body paint, "the Indian blue earth or clay" was reexamined several years later, in 1838, by the French émigré scientist Joseph Nicollet, who was informed by Chief Sleepy Eye that "great numbers" of Indians were sent to collect "the famed blue or green earth, used by the Sioux as their principal pigment."[101] Winchell summed up the results of his own inquiry into Le Sueur's copper mine as follows:

It is more probable that Le Sueur was honest in his conviction, but was mistaken in the value of the green earth which he mined. Charlevoix, La Harpe and Penicaut agree in the statement of the main

---

[96] Winchell, pp. 16-17.
[97] DCB
[98] Wedel, M.M., Le Sueur and the Dakota Sioux, IN E. Johnson (editor), *Aspects of Upper Great Lakes Anthropology: Papers in Honor of Lloyd A. Wilford*. Minnesota Prehistoric Archaeology Series (St. Paul: Minnesota Historical Society, 1974), pp. 157-171.
[99] Morton, A.S., La Verendrye: commandant, fur-trader, and explorer, *Canadian Historical Review* 9 (1928): 284-298.
[100] DCB
[101] Winchell, pp. 60, 71-72.

facts, and if Le Sueur took a quantity to France for assay, it is not likely that he wilfully falsified the facts as to its origin and nature. There can be no question of the existence of both green and blue earth in that vicinity. The shales of the Cretaceous are common in that part of the state.[102]

Figure 1. Historical marker at the conjectured location of Fort
L'Huillier, near the "Mount Kato" ski resort, south of Mankato, MN.
Note the variant spelling "Fort Le Hillier" on the plaque.

That was the end of French copper mining in Minnesota, but not New France. Louis Denys de la Ronde learned of several copper-bearing islands in Lake Superior in the 1730s, collecting samples and sending them to France to be assayed at the royal mint, where they were declared "more than 90 per cent pure copper." Third parties called in for a second opinion, however, declared that the cost of obtaining the copper would outweigh the expense involved. This did not stop La Ronde from continuing to promote the venture, leading others to suspect his motives.[103]

---

[102] Winchell, pp. 16-18.
[103] DCB

Saltpeter Caves

The extended French presence in the Upper Mississippi valley required gunpowder and the usual assumption (valid in most cases) is that it was imported. One of the most important constituents of gunpowder is saltpeter (potassium nitrate), a mineral sometimes obtained from caves. Le Sueur, while ascending the Mississippi, reported saltpeter caves in his Journal, which previous researchers have reasonably interpreted as being located along the west side of Lake Pepin, in Minnesota.[104] Under the dates September 10 to September 14, 1700, we read that:

> *In these regions, a league and a half to the northwest, there is a lake named "Pein" which is six leagues long and more than a league wide. It is bordered on the west by a chain of mountains; on the other side, to the east, there is a prairie, and to the northwest of the lake a second prairie two leagues long and wide. Near by there is a chain of mountains which must be two hundred feet high and more than a half league in length. Many caves are found there in which bears hibernate in winter. Most of these caverns are more than forty feet deep and between three and four feet high. A few have very narrow entrances, and all of them contain saltpeter. It is dangerous to enter them in summer because they are filled with rattlesnakes, whose bite is very dangerous. M. Le Sueur saw some of these snakes that were six feet long, although usually they are only about four feet.*[105]

Le Sueur's comments about the caves being inhabited by bears in winter and rattlesnakes in summer suggests that they were visited (by someone) throughout the year, and presumably there would have been a reason for this. Apparently Le Sueur himself had no need of saltpeter on this particular trip, because his Journal records that he gave away gunpowder to various individuals.

Although Le Sueur described the Lake Pepin caves as containing "saltpeter" he was more likely referring to calcium nitrate, not potassium nitrate. The prevailing humidity in Minnesota caves is too high for him to have encountered anything other than deliquescent salts (dissolved in the sediment) rather than the crystallized saltpeter seen in desert regions.[106] Apart from whitish snow-like efflorescences, not even experienced saltpeter prospectors could identify nitrate-rich sediments by sight and the usual confirmation was a bitter taste and other subtle clues until modern chemical tests for nitrates were developed. However, it has been documented with more certainty that the French were harvesting saltpeter from caves in Missouri by 1720.[107]

The location of Le Sueur's saltpeter caves, in Goodhue County, MN, as inferred from his Journal, was examined in 2004 (Figure 2). Sediment samples collected there and from other rock crevices in the Lake Pepin bluffs revealed a high nitrate content (up to 3.5%) in the

---

[104] Shaw, T.R., *History of Cave Science: The Exploration and Study of Limestone Caves, to 1900*, second edition (New South Wales, Australia Sydney Speleological Society, 1992), p. 52.

[105] Conrad, G.R. (editor), *The Historical Journal of the Establishment of the French in Louisiana. by Jean-Baptiste Benard de La Harpe. Translation by J. Cain and V. Koenig* (Lafayette: University of Southwestern Louisiana, 1971), pp. 32-33.

[106] Hill, C.A. and Forti, P., *Cave Minerals of the World*, second edition (Huntsville, AL: National Speleological Society, 1997), p. 157.

[107] Breckenridge, W.C., Early gunpowder making in Missouri, *Missouri Historical Review* 20 (1925): 85-95.

laboratory.[108] This compares favorably with the nitrate content of sediments from known American saltpeter caves in Kentucky, which "range between 0.01% and 4%."[109]

No mining tools or indications of saltpeter mining were observed in any of the Minnesota caves, though nearby archeological sites had the potential to contain mining artifacts. In 1727, under the directive of the Governor-General of New France, the first French trading fort on the west side of Lake Pepin, Fort Beauharnois, was established. Traditionally, the fort was assumed to have been located at Sand Point near the town of Frontenac, MN, but during a systematic archeological excavation in 1976, no French cultural remains were found.[110] This unfortunately precluded the possible identification of potential saltpeter-related implements in artifact inventories.[111]

Figure 2. Interior view of low, narrow crevice in the Lake Pepin bluffs showing the sort of saltpeter cave that Le Sueur described in 1700. The crevice contains nitrate-rich sediments. Photo by author, 2004.

Even though actual saltpeter or tools were not identified in the Lake Pepin caves during this recent study, the presence of abundant nitrate (likely of organic origin) in cave sediments at the approximate location described by Le Sueur corroborates that there was a kernel of truth to what was reported in his Journal.

---

[108] Brick, G., Le Sueur's Saltpeter Caves at Lake Pepin, Minnesota, and Wilderness Gunpowder Manufacture, *Minnesota Archaeologist* 71 (2012): 7-20.
[109] Hill, C.A., Origin of cave saltpeter, *National Speleological Society Bulletin* 43 (1981): 110-126.
[110] Birk, D.A. and Poseley, J., *The French at Lake Pepin: An Archaeological Survey for Fort Beauharnois, Goodhue County, Minnesota* (St. Paul: Minnesota Historical Society, 1978).
[111] Faust, B., Saltpetre Mining Tools Used in Caves, *National Speleological Society Bulletin* 17 (1955): 8-18. Apart from the largest operations, which employed diagnostic leaching hoppers and log pipelines, many of the tools used to harvest, transport, and process the cave sediments have uses not unique to saltpeter mining. Examples are picks, shovels, and boiling kettles.

French Mining on Later Maps

Guillaume Delisle, together with his father, Claude, cartographers to Louis XIV, and successors to the Dutch cartographic tradition, prepared one of the first maps showing the entire Mississippi River, in 1702.[112] This five-part map, largely based on notes made during Le Sueur's trip up the river to construct Fort L'Huillier, shows the locations of some genuine mineral resources identifiable today, such as the lead mines of Dubuque, Iowa, and Galena, Illinois. A "mine de terre verte" (green earth) is shown at "le Fort Vert" (Figure 3).

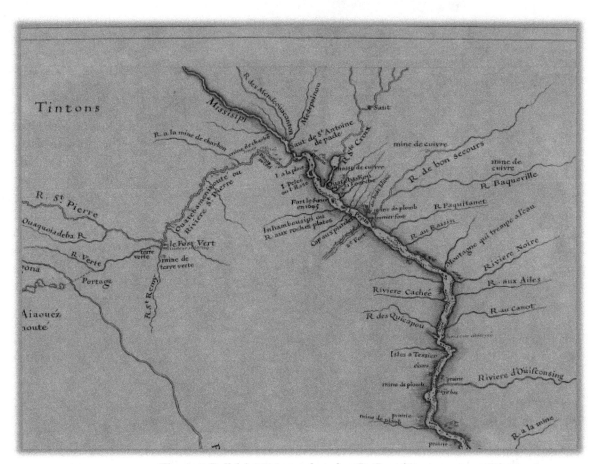

**Figure 3. Delisle's 1702 map, based on Le Sueur's notes,
showing copper and lead mines in the Upper Midwest.**

The French geologist Jean-Etienne Guettard prepared one of the earliest geologic maps of North America, his 1752 *Map of Louisiana and Canada*. While Guettard never visited New France, he consulted Charlevoix's *Histoire* and had correspondents send him samples.[113]

[112] Wood, W.R. and Birk, D.A., Pierre-Charles Le Sueur's 1702 Map of the Mississippi River, *Minnesota Archaeologist* 60 (2001): 31-35. A large scale complete version of the Delisle map was published by W. Raymond Wood, An Atlas of Early Maps of the American Midwest: Part II, *Illinois State Museum Scientific Papers* XXIX (2001), Plate 4.

[113] Cailleux, A., The Geological Map of North America (1752) of J.-E. Guettard, IN C.J. Schneer (editor), *Two Hundred Years of Geology in America* (Hanover, NH: The University Press of New England, 1979), pp. 43-52. See also Lamontagne, R., La participation canadienne a l'oeuvre mineralogique de Guettard, *Revue d'histoire des sciences et de leurs applications* 18 (1965): 385-388. Winchell, N.H., *The Aborigines of Minnesota* (St. Paul: Minnesota Historical Society, 1911), p. 49, describes a 1768 map of North America as "probably the earliest

One of them was the scientifically oriented Governor-General of New France, the Marquis de la Galissoniere (served 1747–1749), who impressed even the Swedish traveler Pehr Kalm, a pupil of the great botanist Linnaeus, with his attainments. The mineral deposits and mines marked on the Delisle map are not shown on the Guettard map, which includes 37 kinds of minerals, rocks, and fossils. Nor are they shown on the geological map of a French traveler, the Comte de Volney's informative 1803 classic, *Tableau du climat et sol des Etats-Unis d'Amerique.*[114]

Nor did Deslisle's supposed mines survive the Louisiana Purchase of 1804, which ended French mining interests in North America. What is perhaps the last and best French cartographic work, coming right at the end of the fur-trade era, Joseph Nicollet's famous 1843 "mother map" of Minnesota, though concerned to document such occurrences, does not depict mines in Delisle's locations.[115] Nicollet's interest in mines is attested by a paper that he prepared on the "mines of the west" for the Association of Geologists and Naturalists.[116]

Already by 1815, however, geologic maps had taken a different stylistic turn, the rock layers being represented by broad color washes in the manner of William Smith (1769–1839), widely regarded as the father of English geology. William Maclure (1763–1840), the father of American geology, mapped the geology of the eastern United States in the new style. David Dale Owen (1807–1860) subsequently extended these methods to the Upper Midwest, including Minnesota, when the U.S. General Land Office employed him to survey public lands, reserving the mineral deposits for the Federal government. No longer would isolated, poorly identified, mineral deposits be represented by X's in the wilderness, in the manner of a pirate's treasure map.[117]

geological map of the state ever made," showing copper and lead deposits, as well as "pit coal" along the Minnesota River. However, the identity and whereabouts of this map are unknown.

[114] Wells, J.W., Notes on the earliest geological maps of the United States, 1756-1832, *Journal of the Washington Academy of Sciences* 49(1959): 198-204.

[115] Nicollet, J.N., *Hydrographical Basin of the Upper Mississippi River* (Washington, 1843). French contributions to American geology during the period 1750-1850 are described by Taylor, K.L., American geological investigations and the French, 1750-1850, *Earth Sciences History* 9 (1990): 118-125.

[116] Bray, M.C., Joseph Nicolas Nicollet, Geologist, *Proceedings of the American Philosophical Society* 114 (1970): 37-59.

[117] Merrill, G.P., *The First One Hundred Years of American Geology* (New York and London: Hafner Publishing Company, 1969), pp. 31-37, 271-275.

Chapter Four
The Voyageurs
By Mark Labine

Frances Anne Hopkins[118]

You cannot write a book on French heritage in Minnesota without talking about the voyageurs. Most historical references to voyageurs describe them as French-Canadian and paid employees of fur trading companies who engaged in the transportation of furs and trade supplies between the fur trading posts of Canada and the upper Midwest and Montreal. The term itself, "voyageur" means "traveler" in French. The voyageurs have almost become legendary, not only in French Canada, but in Minnesota as well. They are celebrated in folklore and music and re-enactment groups such as "La Compagnie de la Hivernants des Riviére St. Pierre,"[119] which is a Voyageur and Fur Trade era re-enactment group.[120]

La Compagnie de la Hivernants des Riviére St. Pierre. Photo from their website.

Henry Hastings Sibley, the first Governor of Minnesota, made the following statements about voyageurs:

It affords me pleasure to bear witness to the fidelity and honesty of the Canadian French voyageurs.

[118] Frances Anne Hopkins, Library and Archives of Canada. Public domain.
[119] "La Compagnie de la Hivernants des Riviére St. Pierre," is a Voyageur and Fur Trade Era Re-enactment Group in Minnesota. This historical re-enactment club meets generally on the first Wednesday of each month at the DePuis house in Mendota at the Henry Sibley Historic Site at 7 p.m. Visitors are welcome, although you should check first to make sure that meeting will take place.

In after years, when at the head of a district, as a partner of the great American F[...]
New York, comprising the vast region north of Lake Pepin to the British boundary, [...]
streams tributary to the, Missouri River, I had within my jurisdiction hundreds of t[...]
and voyageurs, almost all of whom were Canadian French, and I found abundant occ[...]
their honesty and fidelity. In fact, the whole theory of the fur trade was based upon good
employers, and employed. Goods, amounting to hundreds of thousands of dollars, nay millions, were
annually entrusted to men, and taken to posts in the Indian Country, more or less remote, with no
guarantee of any return except the honor of the individual, and it is creditable to human nature, that
these important trusts were seldom, if ever, abused.[121]

The fur trade was big business in New France and was very lucrative. In early years, the fur trade business was wide open and many early settlers risked the perils of traveling through Indian country to seek out Native trappers to trade with. These *coureurs des bois* were not looked upon favourably by Montreal authorities or royal officials. By 1681, the French authorities realized the traders had to be controlled so that the industry might remain profitable, but also so that they could tax profits to raise needed capital to run their government. There were simply too many coureurs des bois and the fur supply was flooding the market. The authorities limited the numbers of coureurs des bois by establishing a system requiring permits (*congés*). This legitimization created a "second-generation" coureur des bois known as the voyageur. This name change resulted from a need for the legitimate fur traders to distance themselves from the unlicensed ones. Voyageurs therefore, held a permit or were allied with a Montreal merchant who had one. In time, they were associated with being the men who paddled the canoes on the supply lines of the fur trading company who employed them.

Shooting the Rapids, by Robert Perrizo

[121] Sibley, Henry Hastings, *The Unfinished Autobiography of Henry Hastings Sibley,"* page 336, Found in the Henry Hastings Sibley Papers of the Minnesota Historical Society's Manuscript Collection.

Voyageurs were the crews hired to man the canoes that carried trade goods and supplies to "rendezvous posts" in exchange for furs. To keep (and pass) their time while paddling, the voyageurs would sing. Nearly 13,000 French-Canadian songs are believed to have existed during the height of the fur trade.

A couple of well known rendezvous posts were Grand Portage in Minnesota and Michili-mackinac[122] in Michigan. Over time, voyageurs came to be known as those men who performed the hard labor required to trade furs. The voyageurs were highly valued employees of trading companies, such as the North West Company (NWC) and the Hudson's Bay Company (HBC). Many young French-Canadians took jobs as voyageurs to find adventure and to earn a valuable wage.

Fort Michilimackinac

The reality of the voyageur life was grueling. For example, they had to be able to carry two 90 pound bundles of fur over portages. More suffered from strangulated hernias than from any other injury. Voyageurs were expected to work fourteen hour days and paddle at a rate of 55 strokes per minute. Few could swim. Many drowned in rapids or in storms while crossing lakes.[123] Portages and routes were often marked by lob trees, or trees that had their branches cut off just below its top. Voyageurs who only paddled between Montreal and Grand Portage were known as "*mangeurs de lard*" (pork eaters) because of their diet, which consisted mostly of salt pork. This was considered to be a derogatory term and the implication was that only the strongest and the most hardy would spend the winter in the wilderness. Those who wintered and ate "off the land" (mainly fish, pemmican and rubaboo) were called "*hommes du nord*" (northern men) or "*hivernants*" (winterers).

Fort Mackinac, by Seth Eastman, 1872 (Public Domain)

---

[122] Map of Fort Michilimackinac on this page taken from State Park brochure.
[123] Charles Guidry dit Labine's brother Marin (Mauthurin) died in the rapids at Lachine, Quebec.

When a voyageur left Montreal, it was said he was leaving for the *pays d'en haut*, or the high country. Over time Quebec was to become known as Lower Canada while Ontario and the western lands Upper Canada.[124] This had something to do with the elevation, since the water from Lake Superior and Minnesota drained towards the lower elevations of the east. Voyageurs were *"engagés"* which came to mean experienced voyageurs. This term came from the contract or engagement that voyageurs would sign, as shown below. They were known to carry packs or *piece* that generally weighed 90 pounds.

Grand Portage Rendezvous Point
Minnesota Historical Society Collections

Other terms associated with the voyageurs:

Voyageur Term	English Translation
A la facon du Nord	The way of life of French voyageurs in the interior and in their relations with the Indians
Allumez	Smoke breaks
Bourgeois	Clerks
Campément	Camp
Ceinture fléchée	Sash
Chansons	Songs. Voyageurs were known for singing while they canoed.

---

[124] Prior to conquest of 1760 Quebec was called "New France." After the Conquest it was called "Lower Canada" and "Eastern Canada," and then finally "Quebec."

Cordelle	Towing a canoe
Décharges	Areas where water was shallow but canoes could be towed through
En derouine	Meaning fur traders visited the Indians instead of having Indians take their furs to the trading post.
En roulant	Singing a refrain in a song
Galanterie	Reputation of Voyageurs to grace a lady
Galette	Form of bread used by voyageurs
La ronde	Dance around campfire at night
La Vielle	Soft gentle breeze
Lard	Grease, pork or bacon
Lève, lève no gens	Get up!
Mangeurs de lard	Pork eaters, reserved for rookies or those who did not spend the winters in the interior wilderness.
Pemmican	Dried meat
Portage	Dry land between waterways
Pour l'amour de dieu	For the love of God
Pose	Rest stops in portages
Rendezvous	Meeting place
Rubbaboo	Pemmican made into a kind of soup by boiling in water.
Sac-à-feu	Beaded bag
Saccajé chien	Cussing or swearing
Saults	Rapids
Trois Pipes	About 12 miles. The distance it took to smoke three pipes.
Traverses	Crossing a large stretch of water

Below is a copy of a voyageur contract signed by Charles Guidry dit Labine on April 20, 1779, on St. Paul Street in old Montreal, right behind the Notre Dame Cathedral. This contract provided that Charles Guidry would travel by canoe to Michilimackinac and Lake Superior to secure furs for the Northwest Company. The literal translation of the "engagement" was as follows:

*"Before the Notary of the town and District of Montreal, in the province of lower Canada, there resident, the undersigned, Charles Guidry, of the parish of St. Jacques, who of his own free will has engaged and engages himself by these present to Messrs. McTavish and Frobisher, to this agreeing and accepting, at their first command to leave this town in the position of **voyageur mileau** in one of their canoes to make the voyage, as much going up to Michilimackinac as for coming down, to go and come and to take good and due care during the voyage, and in the said place of the Merchandise, Edibles, Furs, Utensils and of all the things necessary for the trip; to serve, obey and execute faithfully all that the said McTavish and Frobisher or any of their agents may command that is lawful and honest; to make their profit, avoid damage to them, warn them of it if it comes to his knowledge, and generally all*

*that a good "engage" must and is obliged -to perform; without being able to make any private agreement, neither to absent himself from or to quit the said service, under the penalties imposed by the law, and to lose his wages. This Engagement thus made, for and providing the sum of **two hundred and forty livre or old shillings** of this province, which they promise themselves to give and pay to the said "engage" one month after his return to this town, and on his departure a simple ordinary kit. Charles Guidry recognizes that he has received in advance on account of the said wages four piastres[125]."*

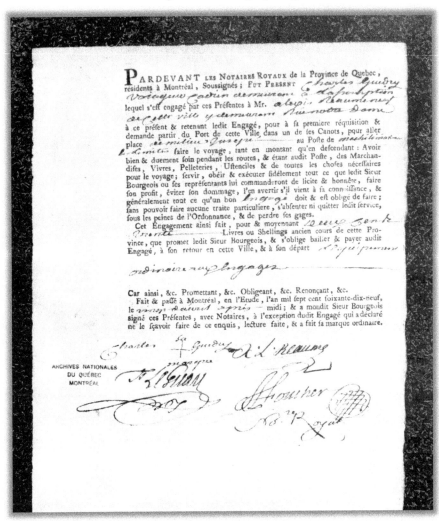

Copy of 1779 Charles Guidry Voyageur Contract [126]

There are several interesting things to note about the Voyageur contract signed by Charles Guidry dit Labine in 1779.

---

[125] Piastres was a word used for "dollar" so 4 piastres would equal four dollars.

[126] Library and Archives of Canada. The University of Ottawa is set up a database that consolidates the information found in more than 35,000 notarized contracts signed by the voyageurs between 1755 and 1870 in the Montréal-Trois-Rivières corridor. Copies of these contracts are also available in the Quebec Archives.

- **First,** he was only 19 years old.

- **Second**, the contract is filed under the name "Guidry" and not "Labine." The family of Charles Guidry continued to use the name Guidry or Guildry in their formal legal documents until at least 1879. Some church records used the name Guildry. Charles Guidry's grandson, Modeste Labine, signed a mortgage in 1870 using the signature "Modeste Guildry." Sometime after that the name Guidry disappears and is replaced by the name Labine. This was common in French-Canadian families, in that descendants would use "dit" names[127] of their ancestors and the former surname would be dropped from their name.

- **Third**, Charles could not sign his name and simply wrote an "X." This common in that time period.

- **Fourth**, Charles was signed up to be a voyageur mileau or a middle canoeman and paid 240 livres. The more experienced voyageurs were in the front and back of the canoe. More experienced voyageurs would earn 400 livres or even more. According to one source, a cargo canoe cost 500 livres in 1755 and the total cost to move two tons of merchandise from Montreal to the upper country cost $2,300 livres.[128]

- **Fifth**, Charles received 240 livres or old shillings (shilling ancient) for his work. Livres were used by the French Republic until 1794. In 1795, the Franc was introduced and livres were no longer the official currency. Webster's New World Dictionary says that the livre at the time it was discontinued in 1795, was worth about the same as an English pound. There is a website called www.measuringworth.com which provides a table that compares the worth of money between different time periods. According to this website's calculator, 240 livres or old shillings in 1779 would be worth $15,078.00 pounds in 2007 using the average earnings index.[129] Other calculators show the earnings to be even higher. Trying to equate the actual value of money in 1779 compared to today is very difficult, but I believe it is a fair statement to say that the amount of money earned by Charles Guidry dit Labine as a voyageur was considered a good wage and it must have been a sought after job by young French-Canadian men in the province at the time.

- **Sixth-** The voyageur contracts are said to number around 35,000. The University of Ottawa is setting up a database that will consolidate the information found in more than 35,000 notarized contracts signed by the voyageurs between 1755 and

---

[127] "dit" means "otherwise called" and is used to show nick names or names used by French-Canadians that are different than their surname.

[128] Skinner, Claiborne, *The Upper Country, French Enterprise in the Colonial Great Lakes*, The John Hopkins University Press, 2008, p.139.

[129] From the Roman denarius came the French denier. Twelve deniers equaled one sou, or sol (same thing), equivalent to a French penny. Twenty sous equaled one livre. The livre tournois, minted in the Touraine region of France, was comparable to an English pound. Three livres tournois equaled one écu, and three deniers equaled one liard. Source: Fisher, David Hackett, *Champlain's Dream*, Vintage Canada, (2009), also Goodwin, Sandra, "Podcast MSS-036-Money in New France," *Maple Stars and Stripes*, http://maplestarsandstripes.com.

1870 in the Montréal-Trois-Rivières corridor. Copies of these contracts are also available in the Quebec Archives.

Charles signed a contract to canoe from Montreal to Fort Michilimackinac and back. These canoes would depart in April or May from above Lachine Rapids in Montreal and paddle up the St. Lawrence River to the Ottawa River, up the Ottawa River to the Mattawa River, through Lake Nippissing, down the French River to Lake Huron, around Lake Huron to Sault Ste. Marie and then either through Lake Superior to Fort William in Thunder Bay or down to Fort Michilimackinac. At Fort William in mid July there would be a rendezvous where the furs from the interior would be exchanged for the goods being brought from Montreal. The "mangeurs de lard" or summer voyageurs would then head back to Montreal with the furs and the "hivernants" would take the goods and head back into the interior.

Northwest Company Coat of Arms

We don't know how long Charles was a voyageur, although we know he eventually settled down on his father's farm in St. Jacques, Quebec. He married Marie Doucet in 1783 at the age of 22, and started a family shortly thereafter, so it would be a good guess that he was a voyageur for only a few years.

The voyageur legacy lives strong in Minnesota, where many locations and historical sites celebrate their history. A fur trading post museum exists in Pine City, Minnesota celebrating the lives of the voyageurs. At Fort William, Ontario, which is just north of the Minnesota border, one of the largest living history attractions in North America exists: devoted to the recreation of the North West Company and the Canadian fur trade. Fort William Historical Park is recognized as one of the "Top Ten Attractions" in Canada and one of the world's most impressive historic sites.

Located on Lake Superior, Fort William became the key midway transhipment point for voyageurs ("winterers") paddling from the west carrying precious furs and voyageurs ("pork eaters") coming from the east bearing valuable trade goods and supplies. This allowed for an exchange of trade goods--all within a single season.

Every year, in July, an annual meeting known as The Great Rendezvous was held at Fort William. It became the centre of frenzied activity as hundreds of natives, voyageurs, clerks, partners and agents arrived. These rendezvous meetings conducted much business but also allowed time for fun, with numerous campfires and many stories told.

Voyageurs at Dawn, by Frances Anne Hopkins[130]

Today, the Great Rendezvous is held each year in July, when hundreds of period re-enactors from across Canada and the United States gather at Fort William Historical Park to re-live the lively fur trade spirit, much like their predecessors of centuries past. [131]

[130] "Frances Anne Hopkins, Voyageurs at Dawn" 1871. Library and Archives of Canada.
[131] Note: References for information of Voyageurs include Blegen, Therodore C. *Five Fur Traders of the Northwest*, and edited by Charles M. Gates, (Minnesota Historical Society, St. Paul, 1965), and Nute, Grace Lee, *The Voyageur* (Minnesota Historical Society, St. Paul, 1955).

Chapter Five
Early French-Canadian Fur Trade in Minnesota
By Jerry Foley

As soon as Europeans settled in North America, the fur trade quickly became the primary economic force. Fishermen coming to the banks of North America had already conducted trade with the Indians, especially for beaver pelts as these pelts were already in demand in Europe, especially for making beaver felt hats.[132] Beaver pelts were becoming scarce in Europe, so reports of quality furs in North America spurred immigration and, before long, fights broke out among the Indian tribes over trading and competition between the French and English to claim the western region for their fur trade. The Indians were happy to exchange pelts for European goods such as cloth, knives, kettles and guns.

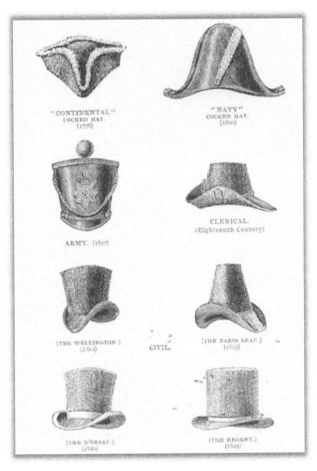

Hats made from Beaver Fur (Public Domain)

Europeans also were searching for a water passage westward to the Orient, and this brought the first explorers to Minnesota. But it was the fur trade which pushed expansion westward as furs became less available in the eastern regions and ultimately led traders westward. French traders began arriving in Minnesota about 1650 to establish trading posts among the Indians. When New France ceded the territory east of the Mississippi to Britain in 1763, British and Scotch merchants took over much of the fur business, but the clerks and canoemen continued to be mostly French-Canadian and the language of the fur trade was French.

The Indians, who had hunted fur bearing animals for clothing and meat, now had a valuable commodity for trade. Intermarriage of the Indians with fur traders, who lived among them and learned their language and customs, was integral to the fur trade and the exchange of furs for European goods, which made the Indians' life easier, was viewed as an exchange between family members.

---

[132] Martin, Horace T., *Modifications of the Beaver Hat, Castorologia, or the History and Traditions of the Canadien Beaver* (Montreal: W. Drysdale, 1892), p.125, Minnesota Historical Society.

The French Fur Trade Era- 1600s to 1763

This period marked the beginning of French exploration and influence in Minnesota. After the Treaty of Utrecht ended the St. Anne's War in 1713, French traders, forts, and trading posts began to appear this far west.[133] Before Europeans reached the Upper Mississippi Valley, Indian middlemen brought furs to Montreal to trade for European goods. Early in the settlement of New France, Samuel de Champlain sided with the Huron Indians against the Iroquois, which led to ongoing skirmishes with the Iroquois for many years and made it hazardous for other Indian tribes to bring their furs to Montreal so the French fur traders headed out to the Indian haunts, creating a group of independent traders called *coureurs de bois*.

The fur trade in New France was tightly controlled and never opened to everyone who wished to become a trader. A royal license was required, obtained through the governor and very limited in number. Licensed traders could sell their furs, after paying a heavy tax, only to a single buyer at prices fixed by the government. Many young men, especially the less privileged, viewed life among the Indians as an exciting escape from an oppressive semi-feudal French society.

The first Frenchmen entering Minnesota territory were explorers, who also saw their chance to profit by the fur trade as *coureurs de bois*, including Radisson and Groseilliers, Sieur Duluth, La Salle, Louis Joliet, Pierre La Verendrye, and Charles Le Sueur. Medard Chouart, Sieur des Grosseilliers, and his bother-in-law, Pierre Espirit Radisson, provide a good example. On their first trip west in 1654, these two explorers had permission from the governor and the fur trading monopoly, *Compagnie des Habitants*, to trade in the west. After travelling around Lake Superior, they returned accompanied by fifty Ottawa canoes filled with furs. When they applied for a license to return west again in 1659, their application was denied, so they slipped out of Quebec to join Indians heading west. On this trip they entered Minnesota on the Pigeon River and obtained a large collection of furs from the Cree Indians. Returning to New France, they were considered illegal, received a short jail sentence, and had most of their furs confiscated. When their proposal for a new trade route through Hudson Bay was rejected in New France and again in France, they went to New England where their proposal led to a trip to England and acceptance by King Charles II and his cousin, Prince Rupert. When a British ship with Groseilliers aboard returned from Hudson Bay in 1668 with a cargo of beaver skins, English investors sought a royal charter, which led to the establishment of Hudson's Bay Company in 1670 and a monopoly to trade in all the rivers emptying into Hudson Bay.[134]

In 1663, the fur trade in New France was placed in the hands of a new monopoly, the *Compagnie de l'Occident*.[135] With a growing number of *coureurs de bois* heading west in search of any beaver pelts the Indians could supply, even poor quality furs, an oversupply of furs led to lower prices and the *Compagnie des l'Occident* went bankrupt in 1674. In an effort to keep the young men at home, French officials set up a system of licensing, allowing only

[133] Lass, William E, *History of Minnesota*, W.W. Norton & Company, (2000) p.62
[134] Lavender, David, *Winner Take All, The Trans-Canada Canoe Trail*, McGraw-Hill Book Company, New York, (1977) pp.91-107.
[135] Lavender, David, *Winner Take All, The Trans-Canada Canoe Trail*, McGraw-Hill Book Company, New York, (1977) pp.118,107.

25 permits (conges) annually for persons going into the interior and a stiff penalty for illegal trade. Voyageurs needed a contract for employment. The system failed and, by 1700, there were perhaps 400 contracted voyageurs and likely more than 3,000 *coureurs de bois*.

In the late 1660s, a temporary peace between the Iroquois and the French allowed a great westward push of French fur traders into the Great Lakes area. Nicolas Perrot first travelled to Wisconsin in 1667, and in 1670 brought a large cache of furs to Montreal. Perrot would soon become known for his trading post, Fort St Antoine, on the east bank of Lake Pepin in 1686 and Fort Perrot at Read's Landing about 1687. The French built Fort Beauharnois on the west side of Lake Pepin in 1727 near Frontenac. It was rebuilt and named Fort Jonquiere in 1750. Pierre Charles Le Sueur built Fort Le Sueur in 1694, on what is likely now Prairie Island. He built another trading post near St. Anthony Falls in 1695, and in 1700 built Fort l'Huillier for trading in the Mankato area.

Jacques de Noyon reached Rainy Lake in 1688 and wintered there. When Pierre Gaultier de La Verendrye came through Grand Portage in 1731 on his way to Lake of the Woods, fur posts began to appear on Minnesota's northern border. La Verendrye built Fort St. Pierre in 1732 at the outlet of Rainy Lake and Fort St. Charles on Lake of the Woods the same year. Another La Verendrye fort was built on the Roseau River. Rene Bourassa, who had traveled west with La Verendrye, built a fort in 1736 at the mouth of the Vermilion River near Crane Lake.

Forts, like the one at Grand Portage, were built as permanent structures with the idea

"Portage Push," by Robert Perrizo

that the Indians would bring furs annually for trade. However, most trading posts were small buildings where traders reached out to the Indians. Such wintering posts were occupied from about September through May and often abandoned after several years. Clerks managed the post while their Voyageurs spent the winter making trips to Indian villages to buy furs. Operating largely on credit kept both the traders and Indians dependent on each other.

The Treaty of Paris ending the French and Indian War in 1763 gave England claim to the vast interior of North America.[136] As the British began taking over French posts throughout the region, resentment grew among the Indians. The Ojibwa and other Indian groups had allied with the French traders, with whom they lived, traded and intermarried. The

[136] Lass, William E, *History of Minnesota*, W.W. Norton & Company, (2000) pp.77-79.

British approach was to treat the Indians as a conquered people. The Indians were aware that in the east the Natives had been pushed off their lands by English colonists and feared the same would happen in the west. Urged on by an Ottawa chief, Pontiac, a loose federation of Indian nations launched a series of attacks that threated British hold on the area.[137]

The British Trade Era

Following the collapse of New France, a rush of British traders headed to the upper country, leading to a British attempt to control the fur trade as the French had done earlier. The British attempt to impose imperial control did not work as hundreds of *coureurs des bois* headed for the Great Lakes area. British traders soon found they could not trade with the Indians without help from the French-Canadians, who continued to be the majority of traders heading west. British fur traders hired seasonal voyageurs and picked up where the French had left off.

For more than a century, the Hudson's Bay Company had the Indians come to them with their furs. Now, they somewhat reluctantly began to send out small expeditions to the Indian tribes. Where they had previously used flat-bottomed "York boats," they began to use canoes to expand their business. In 1789, a group of competing fur traders in Montreal organized the North West Company to expand the fur trade further north and west.[138] While Hudson's Bay Company employees worked on a salary, North West Company employees worked for a commission and were highly motivated. As "Nor'westers" followed old trade routes and re-occupied abandoned French forts, the Northwest Company grew more rapidly than Hudson's Bay Company. Each wintering partner was in charge of a large area known as a district. For example, John Sayer managed the Fond du Lac and Folle Avoine areas south of Lake Superior and the northern reaches of the St. Croix River. From his post at Snake River, where his chief assistant was Seraphin Lamare, his journal in 1804 mentions supervising two other traders, Joseph "La Prairie" Duchene and Joseph Reaume. He also mentions Joseph Girard and Louis Bellair as Voyageurs and Francois Bouche' as interpreter.[139]

The prominence of Frenchmen in the fur trade was apparent when Alexander MacKenzie of the North West Company became the first European to cross the upper continent to the Pacific. His crew consisted of six Voyageurs named Beauchamp, Beaulieux, Bisson, Courtois, Ducette, and Landry, along with two Indian hunters and interpreters.[140]

After the American Revolution, the United States claimed the region west of the Mississippi, but Great Britain refused to give up their military posts, accusing the United States of not living up to its promise to compensate Loyalists for their loss. When the two countries signed Jay's Treaty in 1794, the British agreed to give up their posts. However, the treaty stipulated that British and French-Canadian traders be allowed to continue trading

---

[137] Lavender, David, *Winner Take All, The Trans-Canada Canoe Trail*, pp.200-201.
[138] For a description of the Northwest Company and the Hudson's Bay Company, see: Peterson, Chris, *Birchbark Brigade; A Fur Trade History*, Calkins Creek, Honesdale, Pennsylvania, (2009).
[139] Minnesota Historical Society Handout, *People of the Fur Trade: on the backs of men, in the hands of women*, Northwest Company Fur Post.
[140] Peterson, Chris, *Birchbark Brigade; A Fur Trade History*, Calkins Creek, Honesdale, Pennsylvania, (2009) p.76.

in the Midwest, which allowed British companies in Canada to control the fur trade in that area until 1816, with almost no Americans trading in the region during this time.[141]

In 1797, a breakaway group of traders from the North West Company formed the New North West Company, better known as the XY Company after the marks used to identify their goods. The XY Company headquartered at Grand Portage, by then a flourishing post which each summer hosted a Grand Rendezvous of Indians, Voyageurs, and fur traders, bringing together about 1000 people for trade and socializing. In 1804, the XY Company reconciled with the North West Company and they again focused their opposition against the Hudson's Bay Company.

When the United States declared war on Britain with the intention of conquering Canada in 1812, control of the western fur trade was one of the primary reasons. The War of 1812 disrupted the fur trade and folks in the Minnesota region fought on the British side. After the treaty was signed ending the war, the United States retained the western region and Congress passed an act excluding foreigners from the fur trade in American territory. John Jacob Astor's American Fur Company purchased posts of the North West Company south of the border, but by this time the English had moved the center of their fur trade north to Fort William.[142]

A frontier skirmish after the war, named the Pemmican War, broke out between the North West Company fur traders and settlers brought to the Red River by a Scotch investor in Hudson's Bay Company, Lord Selkirk. The Nor'westers viewed the Selkirk colony as an effort by Hudson's Bay Company to establish a base for further penetration into the interior. Selkirk sent followers to capture the western headquarters of the North West Company and to raid northern Minnesota trading posts. The bitterness gradually died down when the North West Company went into debt and in 1821 the North West Company and Hudson's Bay Company merged.[143]

John Baptiste Cadotte and Jean Baptiste Perrault were French fur traders active in the Minnesota area during the English regime. Cadotte, who had first ventured west in 1742, and his new partner, Alexander Henry, were granted exclusive rights by colonial authorities in 1765 to trade on Lake Superior. Married to a Nipissing wife, Cadotte's name appears frequently at places such as Grand Portage, Pembina, and the Red Lake River. Also married to an Indian wife, Jean Baptiste Perrault first worked for the North West Company and then became an independent trader. He built trading posts at Fond du Lac in 1783, Prairie Portage in 1785, and Red Cedar Lake (Cass Lake) in 1794, also wintering at the Crow Wing River and Sauk Rapids.[144]

---

[141] Information obtained from article titled *The Fur Trade-Indian Country, Wisconsin.*
[142] Lass, William E, *History of Minnesota*, second edition, W.W.Norton & Company, (2000), pp.70,83. For a more complete history of the War of 1812, see Borneman, Walter R., *1812, The War that Forged a Nation*, Harper Collins Publishers, New York (2004).
[143] Ferguson, Will, *Canadian History For Dummies*, 2nd Edition, John Wiley and Sons, Mississauga, Ontario, (2005). Pp. 181-182, 184.
[144] Information on Jean Baptiste Perreault can be obtained in his book titled *Narrative of the Travels and Adventures of a Merchant Voyageur in the Savage Territories of Northern America," Leaving Montreal the 28th Day of May, 1783 to 1820.* Written in 1830, (Found in Schoolcraft Manuscripts in the Smithsonian Institute in Washington, D.C.)

The British phase in Minnesota fur trade ended with the Treaty of Ghent ending the War of 1812. Fur traders in the area needed to apply for U.S. citizenship to continue in the fur trade and most did so.[145]

Fur Trade in the American Era

John Jacob Astor of the American Fur Company was very competitive and determined to hold a monopoly on the fur trade in the United States. Once foreigners were excluded from the fur trade in Minnesota, a large portion of the Canadians joined Astor's company and became U. S. citizens.

American Fur Company Trading Post in 1926. Published in 1940 by Artvue Post Card Company.
Minnesota Historical Society Collections

Ramsey Crooks, a Scotchman who came to Canada as a teenager, joined Astor's subsidiary, the Pacific Fur Company, rapidly climbed to the exclusive management of the American Fur Company, and by 1823 was manager of the northern and western departments, including the Minnesota area. Crooks quickly turned his attention to a competitor active in Minnesota, the Columbia Fur Company, an energetic company composed mostly of former employees of the North West Company who had migrated to St. Louis after the North West Company merger with Hudson's Bay Company.

The Columbia Fur Company opened four posts in the Minnesota Valley: at the north side of the Minnesota River near Fort Snelling, at Little Rapids (Carver), at Traverse des Sioux and at Lac Qui Parle. The post at Lake Traverse served as the anchor point for the new company. Determined to beat the Columbia Fur Company but unable to drive them out of

[145] Lass, William E, *History of Minnesota*, 2nd edition, W.W. Norton & Company, (2000)pp.,80,83.

business, Crooks' offer to buy the company in 1826 was rejected. The real leader of the Columbia Fur Company was Kenneth McKenzie, another Scotchman whom Crooks hoped would join him with American Fur Company. McKenzie refused to join the American Fur Company unless some of his men would also be employed and, when this happened, the American Fur Company had a virtual monopoly in Minnesota.

When Fort Snelling was built in 1819, the fur trade in Minnesota was quite vigorous. New Hope (later Mendota) quickly became a fur trade hub. Major Lawrence Taliaferro, Indian agent at the Fort, listed seventeen posts on the Upper Mississippi in 1826, most of them American Fur Company trading posts under the control of Joe Rolette, who had his headquarters at Prairie du Chien. The American Fur Company supplied trade goods to Rolette, who in turn, supplied goods to local fur traders on credit, which they often traded to the Indians on credit for a 100 percent and sometimes a 300 or 400 percent profit, assuring the traders a good profit.

The situation along the northern border of Minnesota was a bit more complicated. Parts of northern Minnesota were thought to be part of Rupert's Land, a large territory owned by Hudson's Bay Company. Until 1818, the entire Red River Valley was considered to be British and was occupied by Metis of the Red River Colony established to supply the British fur trade. In 1818, the border between the United States and British North America was established at the 49th parallel, but the point where the Red River crossed the border was not marked until 1823, when the fur post at Pembina was found just inside the U.S. border. In 1833, the American Fur Company agreed to withdraw from competition with Hudson's Bay Company along Minnesota's northern border and for a decade after this, there were few American traders along the boundary waters.[146] The exception was the Red River Colony, which neglected the agreement with Hudson's Bay Company and brought furs to St. Paul.

The American Fur Company reorganized in 1834, with Ramsay Crooks replacing John Jacob Astor, and Henry Sibley came as a partner with responsibility for trade from Prairie du Chien to the Little Falls of the Mississippi, north and west to Pembina in the Red River Valley, and the valley of the Minnesota River westward to the streams which flowed into the Missouri River. Two of Sibley' friends, Joe Rolette and Hercules Dousman, traders at Prairie du Chien, became partners with Sibley as the "Western Outfit" of the American Fur Company. The "Northern Outfit" included Crow Wing, Sandy Lake, Sauk Rapids, and Watab.

The year 1837 was a turning point for the fur trade in Minnesota. Prior to this, the Indians owned the land. When the Dakota and Ojibwa signed a treaty with the U. S. Government for all the land east of the Mississippi, people started moving into the pine forests of the St. Croix Valley right away, while others staked out farms on land that was not yet surveyed. As more treaties took land from the Indians, the areas for harvesting furs diminished and before long the Indians were pushed further westward onto reservations. The success of

---

[146] Nute, Grace Lee *Rainy River Country* in Minnesota History, Minnesota History Press (1959) p.33

the treaty negotiations between the U. S. and the Indian tribes, was in large part, facilitated by fur trade families such as the Faribaults and Renvilles.

By 1837, the fur bearing animals had been greatly reduced while in Europe silk hats had replaced the beaver felt hats that had been in vogue for 300 years. Prices of furs dropped sharply, putting the American Fur Company into financial difficulties. Sibley began sending furs south by river boats and purchasing goods from P. Chouteau and Company of St. Louis. By 1841, this St. Louis Company also began purchasing furs in Minnesota, challenging the monopoly of the American Fur Company, which went bankrupt in 1842.[147]

When the American Fur Company failed, Sibley and Rolette transferred to Pierre Chouteau, Jr. and Company. Seeking to expand their business and challenge the agreement with Hudson's Bay Company, Sibley sent Norman Kittson to Pembina in 1843 to encourage the Red River Colony to trade with St. Paul. To skirt around the agreement between Hudson's Bay Company and the American Fur Company, Sibley considered Kittson an independent trader, although many of the furs coming south were caught by Indians north of the border.

When Sibley became involved in a public career in 1848, he had his brother Fred and Dr. C.W. Borup manage his fur interests until he left the fur trade in 1853. Some of the French-Canadian traders working for the American Fur Company in Minnesota included:

> John Baptiste Faribault at Little Rapids and other upper Mississippi posts
> Alexis Bailly at Mendota and Wabasha
> Joseph Renville at Lac Qui Parle
> Louis Provencalle at Traverse des Sioux
> Joseph Laframboise at Little Rock and Coteau de Prairie
> Alexander Faribault at Cannon Falls
> Clement Beaulieu at Crow Wing
> Francois Labathe at Winona
> Joe Rolette at Prairie du Chien and the upper Mississippi Valley
> Eustache Roussain at Fond du Lac, Swan River and Rainy River
> Louis Robert at St. Paul.

---

[147] Milwaukee Public Museum, *The Fur Trade-Indian Country, Wisconsin.*

Women in the Fur Trade[148]

Samuel Champlain, the early leader of French settlement in North America, witnessed firsthand the appalling inhumanity perpetrated against American Indians in Spanish South America. In settling Quebec, Champlain dreamed of a different attitude toward Indians, seeing them as equals and expecting that his French settlers and Indians might intermarry. Champlain told the Indians that "Our young men will marry your daughters, and henceforth we shall be one people."[149] By 1615, the term "Metis" referred to children of mixed racial unions and soon became a term of pride.

The Trapper's Bride, by Alfred Jacob Miller (1810-1874) Walters Art Museum. Depicts a Trapper paying $600 in trade goods for an Indian woman to be his wife. (Public Domain)

Intermarriage established bonds of kinship and supported trading alliances. Traders quickly grasped the economic and social significance of intermarriage. Young Indian women had nearly as much freedom in choosing their marital partner as did men and welcomed the traders into their families. Most of the French-Canadians in the fur trade were laborers, such as voyageurs and Coureurs des Bois, who intended to remain on the frontier and embraced Indian culture with enthusiasm. A few married Indian wives in Catholic weddings but most by Indian custom – *"a la facon du pays"* (after the custom of the country), and lived among their wives' kinsmen. While the bourgeois and their clerks, many of them Scotch or English, intended eventually to return to Montreal or Europe, the canoe men and laborers in the fur trade were committed to the frontier for life.

In Minnesota, most of the intermarriages were between French-Canadian men and Ojibwe women, who had invaluable skills for subsistence and trade. As Maggie Siggins notes in her book *Riel*:

"These marriages were encouraged by Natives and Europeans alike for they established an economic symbiosis which fueled the fur trade. The Indian women ground corn to make sagamite, chopped firewood, collected berries, snared hares and partridges and caught fish, which frequently saved the white traders from starvation and scurvy. She also provided her man with a never-ending supply of moccasins from deer or moose skins, and she netted the intricate webbing which gave the essential snowshoe its support. She collective wattappe (roots from the spruce tree) and with the resulting twine repaired his canoe, she dressed the beaver

[148] For a more complete treatise on the role of Indian women in the fur trade, see Van Kirk, Sylvia's *"Many Tender Ties," Women in Fur-Trade Society in Western Canada*, 1670 -1870, Watson and Dwyer Publishing Ltd, 1980.
[149] Fischer, David Hackett, *Champlain's Dream*, Toronto, Vintage Canada Edition, 2009, p. 457.

and otter furs and prepared the staple food of the Northwest – the famous pemmican, a mixture of buffalo meat, fat and berries. She also acted as a guide, a language teacher, and perhaps most important, an advisor on the traditions and customs of various Indian tribes with which her husband must deal."[150]

By the time the French-Canadians began to penetrate Minnesota at the end of the 17th Century, traders more often married mixed blood women and produced a close-knit society of Metis families where family life was highly valued. With the decline of the fur trade and the rush of new settlers to Minnesota, Indian women had a lesser role to play and were supplanted by European wives. Mary Lethert Wingerd notes in her book, *North Country*, that the wives of soldiers and settlers held the ideal that women's role was domestic and confined to the household and family, and "the interracial partnership between traders and their wives – who paddled canoes, hauled packs, bartered goods, and involved themselves in every aspect of their husband's enterprises – seemed to transgress all the middle-class white culture deemed womanly and proper."[151]

Fur Trade Forts and Posts in Minnesota[152]

Basswood Lake - Several French trading posts and Hudson Bay Company
Belle Prairie – Henry Rice
Big Stone Lake – Fort Greene in 1826, American Fur Company; Hazen Mooers; Martin McLeod
Bowstring Lake – Perrault mentions Patchatchanban post about 1785
Brown's Post – At headwaters of Minnesota River, AFC Joseph Brown
Cannon River – 1786 Fort La Pointe with Charles Patterson; AFC Alexander Faribault
Cass Lake – 1794 NWC John Baptiste Perrault; another NWC post further east; AFC about 1820
Cedar Lake – NWC in 1806
Cottonwood River – AFC 1826, Joseph Laframboise by 1839
Crane Lake – NWC
Crow Wing River – James McGill 1771; J.B. Perrault 1790; AFC 1826; 1837 Clement Beaulieu; Henry Rice.
Elk River – David Faribault in 1846
Faribault – Alexander Faribault
Fisher's Landing
Fond du Lac – 1793 Fort St Louis by Perrault of NWC; 1816 AFC
Fort Charlotte – NWC; XY Company
Frontenac – 1727
Fort Beauharnois; 1750
Fort Marin; AFC
Grand Forks – Junction of Red Lake and Red Rivers AFC
Grand Marais – 1823 AFC
Grand Portage – 1785 NWC; 1793 David and Peter Grant; XY Company; AFC

[150] Siggins, Maggie, *Riel, A Life of Revolution*: Toronto, HarperCollinsPublisherLtd, 1994, page 7.
[151] Wingerd, Mary Lethert, *North Country, The Making of Minnesota*: Minneapolis, University of Minnesota Press, 2010, page 146.
[152] This listing of fur trade posts is taken in large part from: Nute, Grace Lee's *Posts in the Minnesota Fur-Trade area, 1660-1855*, Minnesota History, Vol. 11, No. 4 (December 1930), pp 353-385

Great Oasis – AFC Joseph Laframboise
Gregory – 1850 William Aitken
Grey Cloud Island – AFC Joseph R. Brown, Hazen Mooers, Andrew Robinson
Grand Rapids – Early French post; 1804 NWC post on Pokegama Lake; AFC
Gull Lake – AFC Ambrose Davenport
Hastings – AFC Joseph R. Brown
La Crescent – 1755 Fort Le Sueur
Lac Qui Parle – 1816-17 James Lockwood; 1837 Columbia Fur Company Fort Adam; 1835 AFC Joseph Renville; Martin McLeod
Lake Bemidji – 1785 trading post; another by 1832
Lake of the Woods – 1732 Fort St. Charles by La Verendrye
Lake Traverse – 1800 Robert Dickson post; 1823 Fort Washington by Columbia Fur Company; AFC
Lake Winnibigoshish – AFC
Leaf Lake – Fort Bolivar by Columbia Fur Company
Leaf River – 1792 Joseph Reaume; AFC
Leech Lake – NWC 2; AFC 2; William Johnson
Little Falls – 1750s French Fort Duquesne
Little Rapids – 1826 Fort Lewis, John Baptiste Faribault
Little Rock – AFC Joseph Laframboise, Hazen Mooers
Lower Sioux Agency – At least four fur traders had posts here.
Lynd – Lynd's post
Mankato – 1700 Fort L'Huillier by Pierre Charles LeSueur
Mendota – 1820 J. B. Faribault at Pike's Island; AFC Alexis Bailly and Henry Sibley; Columbia Fur Company
Mille Lacs – French posts on south shore; AFC
Minneapolis – Benjamin Baker's Post at Coldwater, Columbia Fur Company; AFC Land's End post one mile north of Ft. Snelling on Minnesota River
Moose Lake – HBC
Morristown – Alexander Faribault of AFC
Ortonville – AFC Hazen Mooers
Ottertail Lake – Several trading posts including AFC
Pembina – (Minnesota side) 1790s Peter Grant of NWC; HBC; XY Company; AFC
Pine City - NWC
Pine River – NWC by 1784
Platte Lake – AFC
Prairie du Chien – 1686 Fort St. Nicolas by Nichols Perrot; many other posts including AFC.
Prairie Island – 1694 Fort Le Sueur by Le Sueur
Prairie Portage – 1785 post built by J. B. Perrault
Rainy Lake – 1732 Fort St. Pierre by La Verendrye; NWC, XY Company; HBC; AFC
Rainy River – NWC
Red Lake – Early British fort; NWC; AFC; Joseph Reaume wintered at Red Lake in 1784-85, J.B Cadotte in 1794-95.
Red Lake Falls – NWC with J. B. Cadotte in charge by 1798

Rice Lake – William Morrison of NWC

Roseau – 1730's post by La Verendrye; NWC; HBC; AFC

Rum River – British posts by 1805; AFC

Rust's Post – Henry Rust's post

Sandy Lake – NWC post from 1794; AFC

Sauk Rapids – J. B. Perrault there in 1789, Francois Giasson

Sauk River – AFC David Gilman

St. Cloud – Robert Dickson post 1805

St. Croix Falls – Columbia Fur Company; AFC

St. Peter – Patterson's Rapids post

Shakopee – AFC David Faribault

Snake River – AFC

Snake River (North) – 1803 NWC post built by John Cameron (MN side east of Grafton, ND)

Standing Cedar

Sturgeon Lake – Early French post

Sunrise River - Maurice Samuel's post on west bank of St. Croix River near Sunrise River

Swan River – William Aitken post

Thief River Falls – Vincent Roy's post by 1794

Traverse des Sioux – Columbia Fur Company Fort Union; AFC; Martin McLeod post erected 1840

Vermilion Lake – NWC; AFC Eustache Roussain

Vermilion River – Rene Bourassa of La Verendrye party build fort here in 1736

Wabasha – Augustin Rocque; Alexis Bailly of AFC; Joseph La Bathe

Warroad – AFC

Watab – AFC

Waterville – AFC Alexander Faribault

Whitefish Lake – NWC (two forts); AFC

White Oak Point – Three independent traders had posts here.

Winona – AFC Francois La Bathe

Yellow Lake – AFC

Yellow Medicine

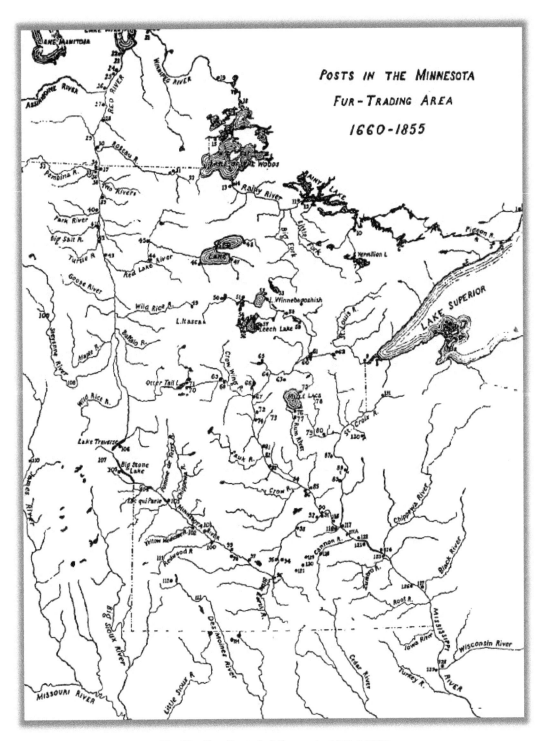

Fur Trading Posts in Minnesota 1660-1855[153]

[153] Picture taken from article written by Grace Lee Nute titled *"Posts in the Minnesota Fur-Trading Area, 1660-1855"* published by Minnesota Historical Society and reprinted with their permission.

Chapter Six
Unseen: Métis and Mixed Bloods in Minnesota
By Jane Skinner Peck

Formation of Red River Metis and Mixed Blood Communities Minnesota; Natives and Newcomers.

Almost from the start, mixed blood families were among the Huron and Jesuit settlement, along the St. Lawrence River in early 17th century Quebec.[154] Recent genealogical research indicates many of the original voyageurs were actually already mixed blood before arriving in Minnesota or the "Northwest." With their native boating, tribal language, and extensive guiding skills, entering the fur trade was natural for the males of mixed blood families. The first large-sized birch bark canoes in the fur trade were built by the Huron tribe. The fur traders followed pre-established native trade practices and routes. Only the goods were different, bringing new European and Asian technologies to native peoples.

Ojibwe Village, Courtesy of Hennepin County Library

The area of present-day Minnesota was reached by fur traders from various directions. French fur posts from 1700 have been discovered along the Mississippi River, especially at Frontenac, MN. This trade was licensed and promoted by French King Louis XIV, done by coureurs de bois that mostly came down the Fox and Wisconsin Rivers from Lake Michigan to the Prairie du Chien area of the Mississippi and then north. The 17th century was a time of French settlement to the east of the future Minnesota, in Michigan and Wisconsin. The British Hudson Bay Company (1670) was operating up in the current area of Manitoba, entering through the Hudson Bay from the north. They continued down the Red River to Pembina where they met traders moving west from Lake Superior along the Pigeon River route, in the area now called the Boundary Waters. This was the route of La Verendrye in the mid 18th century. Thus one can imagine there was much more trade in Minnesota in the first half of the 18th century than we know about. Mixed blood families were part of the fur trade community wherever it went, settling all across the center of the continent and along its waterways. They were closely connected to the tribal communities in those areas, where their relatives lived.

Metis with Two Spouses Painting by Peter Rindisbacher (1806-1834) Alberta Public Archives

---

[154] Morin, Gail. *First Metis Families of Quebec,* 5 volumes. Clearfield Company, Baltimore, Maryland. 2012-2015

As the fur traders moved west looking for plentiful beaver both the Metis and the Ojibwe (from Quebec) followed. The arrival of the Ojibwe in future Minnesota in the mid-1700s gradually pushed the Dakota to its southern and western regions and began years of tribal violence. The Montreal-based North West Company formed in late 18th century and pushed west through Lake Superior and the Pigeon River route. Many Metis in the fur trade were actually moving with their native relatives. The fur trade center in what has become Minnesota was Pembina where both the Hudson Bay Company and North West Company had posts. Pembina was a center for mixed blood communities because of the fur trade. There were minor posts across the state and mixed blood families in those locales. The Red River Community or Assiniboia, now the Winnipeg area of Manitoba at the junction of the Red and Assiniboine rivers, was another trading center and quickly became a populous Metis community, long before the Selkirk Colony came to that area. Families were a mix of Cree, Ojibwe, French, Assiniboine, and Scottish.

Business vs. Settlement

Business, not settlement, was the basis of the relationship between the fur traders and the tribes. This is a crucial point to remember. The "Northwest Territory'"or "Le Pays du Nord," which included today's Minnesota and points west and north, was officially Indian territory before the mid to late 19th century. There were some land arrangements made for fur posts before then. In the case of Hudson Bay Company a large area called Rupert's

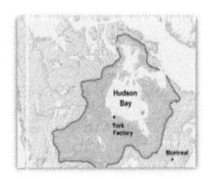

Rupert's Land, small finger follows Red River south into MN

Land was negotiated with the English crown. The area was the watershed of the York and the Red rivers up to Hudson Bay, included the Pembina area and the current Winnipeg area. Apart from Rupert's Land, there was no legal settlement for immigrants in the Northwest Territory before treaties, unless they were married to tribal members. Mixed blood fur trade families were encouraged to live in Rupert's Land. In the years before the treaties, the tribes so outnumbered the traders that it would have been nearly suicidal for traders and voyageurs to be involved in rape or theft. It would have ruined their trading connections, their business, and endangered their lives. This population difference promoted a far more civil and equal relationship between the tribes and the traders. Most racial abuse came later, when the treaties to buy Indian land began and the white population grew dramatically.

Intermarriage

In an era when arranged marriages were the norm in Europe and in tribal cultures of North America, marrying for prestige and business was commonplace in the fur trade as well. Tribal leaders*[155] often wanted a blood connection to a fur trade company to ensure a de-

---

[155] *Tribal leader is the correct term, not chief, as that was a corruption of the French word for leader, 'chef'. There was seldom only one person in charge in a band or tribal group. This caused many problems in negotiations and later in treaties, as there was not one unique person elected to negotiate. Consequently, one tribal leader might agree to something that another of his band would later annul.

pendable flow of goods, and suggested alliances with their daughters. Fur traders, especially the bourgeois or group leaders, always wanted a blood connection to the tribe to ensure continuing business with their company. There was bargaining and a sizable exchange of goods given to the tribal family before a trader-Indian marriage, followed by a feast and dance. This was called a "bush marriage," or "a la facon du pays," which meant it lacked the authority of the Catholic Church. Some were lasting marriages and some ended in a few years, with the trader later marrying a white woman in Quebec (or St. Paul) to improve his social image.

Most often traders and voyageurs who intermarried were French, though in later 18th century there were many Scotsmen who followed suit. There was more informal social interaction between the tribes and French voyageurs, rather than with English or Americans. The sense of humor was more similar, and after the 1763 transfer of Canada to Britain, most of the French-Canadian men and Scotsmen were working class, with no attachment to preserving hierarchy. This allowed more romances and friendships to form between the French and Indians.[156] To this day reservations in the Upper Midwest and Canada have a majority of French last names.

Value of the Metis to the Fur Trade

As the mixed blood families had blood bonds with one or more tribes, they generally spoke many languages and had a more intimate knowledge of the land as well as an available client base. They maintained their skills at hunting and canoeing as well, making them important employees of the fur companies. They often travelled back and forth across sections of the continent. Some of them accompanied Lewis and Clark on their journey, listed as French surnamed interpreters and boatmen, and referred to as hunters and dancers, all classic jobs of Metis men.[157] From the early 17th century throughout the fur trade era, Metis were essential to its success. The Hudson Bay Company recognized this from the start by encouraging them to live in Rupert's Land, where they were not pressured by either tribal or colonial powers. This was a unique opportunity that allowed the Metis culture to develop and flourish in a way that was not possible elsewhere.

Decline of the Fur Companies

It took time after the Louisiana Purchase and Lewis and Clark's voyage for the American Fur Trade Company to expand north and west into presemt-dau Minnesota. By 1820 they were entering the area and creating pressure on the fiercely competitive Hudson Bay and Northwest Companies who knew their time in U.S. territory was limited. During the years preceding this, the competition between the two caused them to offer ever more alcohol to native tribes to win their trade loyalty. Native peoples have an increased vulnerability to alcohol addiction, according to recent genetic and endocrine research. This caused degradation of cultures and values among all the people involved and precipitated increasing violence on all sides. The two companies finally merged under the Hudson Bay Company,

---

[156] Peterson, Jacqueline and Brown, Jennifer. *The New Peoples*, Edmund, R. David, "Unacquainted with the laws of the Civilized World...", Minnesota Historical Society Press, St. Paul, Minnesota. 2001.
[157] DeVoto, Bernard. *The Journals of Lewis and Clark*, Appendix II. Note names of interpreters and boatmen. Mariner Books, NYC, NY. 1997.

whose area was northern U.S. border lands and north through Canada. The American Fur Trade Company moved into the southern area of present-day Minnesota, increasing their use of alcohol in trade. Furs were declining and population growing and they found they soon needed to move further west. Metis families living in Rupert's Land along the Red River suffered under the monopoly of Hudson Bay, and by 1840s began the ox cart trips to the growing St. Paul area to sell buffalo furs and dried buffalo meat to the American Fur Company. By then the fur –bearing animals were becoming rare, but buffalo were still plentiful.

What is Metis Culture?

This author has great respect for the bravery required to live between two such different cultures as the European and the First Nations. Many languages were required to negotiate that middle ground between French, English, Ojibwe, Dakota, Cree peoples. It was most difficult to negotiate a place for a mixed blood life in more populated areas where they were often forced to choose one or the other. In Rupert's Land, the French-Indians were undisturbed and able to form a unique merged culture, including a new language, Michif. They also had blended dance and music, blended spiritual beliefs and stories, and blended visual arts and handcrafts. This is the only place in the United States or Canada where this happened, though it was more common in Mexican mestizo culture.

Ox Carts going through Main Street in St. Anthony.
Printed with permission by Hennepin County Library

The Metis or Michif language is considered an actual language and not just a dialect of French. Most nouns are French and most verbs are Cree, with some Ojibwe words. Each culture offered the type of words it had in most abundance. Trade objects had no Cree names, so French names became nouns and Cree/Ojibwe verbs, far more varied and explicit, were adopted.[158] There were also localized dialects of Michif, that had more or less French or Cree. Fewer Metis speak Michif with each added year, though Canadian reserve schools are actively teaching Michif.

Dance, Music, Life Style

Metis lifestyle in Rupert's Land was an interesting blend of log cabins and gardens part of the year, and buffalo hunting with tipis during other parts of the year. They adopted both Catholic and native spirit beliefs, which they selected at will. There were very few priests available in the Northwest until the late 18th century. Clothing was a blend of deerskin

---

[158] Fleury, Norman. *Michif Dictionary 2013*. Gabriel Dupont Institute, Saskatoon, Saskatchewan. 2013.

and fur trade cloth and decorated with beads, ribbons, and silver from the trade. The 'ceinture fleché' or arrow sash was a useful fur trade article that was recreated for regular Metis use. The native women maintained many of their skills of processing wild foods, making moccasins and snowshoes, while their French husbands would hunt bison for the fur trade and also serve as fur trade voyageurs or "engages." Metis families went together on the buffalo hunts, with women and children in charge of cutting and drying bison meat.

Metis Dance
Drawing by Corporal Louis Voelkerer ca. 1870 (Public Domain)

Metis families were famous for enjoying life to the fullest: dancing all night and fiddling or singing at any occasion. The Scottish traders brought some of their dance and music to the blend as well. The fiddle was the prized instrument, though often people sang and played spoons for dancing because there was no fiddler available. A blended dance style called the Red River Jig developed and was popular for parties and competitions. The jigging became part of the quadrilles, or square dances as well. Dances were held in the small cabins, after moving the handmade furniture out of the house. Many 21st century Metis families in Canada and northern United States still play the fiddle and jig today at dances and at contests. One such contest is held every February in Winnipeg at the Festival de Voyageur.

Metis or Mixed blood?

The name 'Metis' is a fairly modern term. It means 'mixed or mixed blood' in French, but was originally used to refer to a woman, "metisse." In the fur trade era, they called themselves "bois brulé" or burnt wood, referring to their skin color. There has been so much intermarriage since those days that the current United States requirement to qualify for reservation status is generally only 25% full blood. It was Louis Riel who first used the term "La Nation Metisse," referring to the Red River mixed bloods as a political group. The Ojibwe term, "Michif," referred to mixed blood and was in use in the fur trade. The English used the term "half-breed." For a long time the word "Canadian," referred to a French –Indian person. Metis has come to identify those mixed blood of white/Cree and some Ojibwe descent with ancestors who lived in Rupert's Land (Red River area). Mixed French/Caucasian and Indian families from other regions and tribes are referred to as "mixed bloods." Today Metis and mixed blood families are more comfortable claiming their mixed heritage than in the past, especially in Canada. However, individuals within the same family may self-identify with different specific heritages or with their own blended background.

Louis Riel and Metis Political Identity

Metis men could be well educated. Even illiterate Metis usually spoke five languages due to trading and alliances with many groups. Wealthy fur traders sent their sons for education in Montreal in either the French or the British communities. They returned as lawyers, priests, teachers. When Rupert's Land was dissolved by the British government in Canada, the Metis leaders and lawyers quickly wrote a provisional constitution for the new Manitoba province where they lived. Though they later lost most of their land in that province, that original Metis constitution still stands today.[159]

Provisional Metis Government of Manitoba, Louis Riel center (Public Domain)

Born in the Red River settlement to French and Metis parents, Louis became one of the heroes of the Metis people. He was the president of the temporary Metis government of Manitoba and he was a respected leader. Sent by Bishop Taché and his parents to Montreal to become a priest, Louis spent time as a law student. On his return to the Red River, Rupert's Land was to become a part of British Canada, which was a threat to the Metis population and their sovereignty. Riel led the Metis in forming a provisional army and a provisional government, which was overturned by Ottawa. Many of the Metis fighters fled to Saskatchewan and Montana where the fight continued under Riel's General Gabriel Dumont. It was there that Riel was hunted down and finally hung. After over a century of viewing them as criminals, modern Canadians respect the courage of these Metis leaders.[160]

Homeland

The Metis never again had their homeland on the Red River, though many lived there under British rule, some denying their Indian blood. Many fled to the far Northwest in Canada, as well as the Turtle Mountains near Pembina in North Dakota and Fort Peck in Montana. The Turtle Mountain Ojibwe Reservation is west of Pembina. The Metis had many relatives on that reservation that welcomed them in and generously shared their meager government rations with them. Many residents of Turtle Mountain continue to be

---

[159] A popularly elected convention in 1869 supported a provisional Metis government dominated by Louis Riel. Lists of Metis rights were drafted by the provisional government; the final version became the basis of federal legislation called the Manitoba Act, which was approved as part of the Constitution of Canada in 1870 and exists to this day. A plaque at the statue of Louis Riel which stands adjacent to the magnificent Manitoba Legislative Buildings in Winnipeg reads: *In 1992, the Parliament of Canada and the Legislative Assembly of Manitoba formally recognized Riel's contribution to the development of the Canadian Confederation and his role, and that of the Métis, as founders of Manitoba.*

[160] Neering, Rosemary. *Louis Riel*, Fitzhenry and Whiteside, Ontario, Canada. 1999.

proud of their Metis/Michif heritage. The Turtle Mt. cemetery at St. Anne's Catholic Church is full of French names and a New Orleans-style 18th century cemetery.

Canada formed Metis Reserves (reservations) in many locations of the Northwest, where there is an active Metis Federation. These reservations have maintained the Metis culture, language, and identity in Canada. In the United States there is no legal identification for

Brien family of Turtle Mountain at end of Metis jigging and fiddling show. Photo by Jane Peck

mixed bloods, and no attached land rights, other than for those who meet the 25% full blood tribal identification. This fact has had a destructive effect on Metis culture in the U.S.. Some native peoples find it a threat to their reservation status to admit Metis heritage. Strangely, Metis reserves in Canada require the same 25% blood level that U.S. "full blood" reservations require. Canadian full blood requirements are much higher than in the U.S.

There were many Metis families who joined the dominant white culture in Minnesota and Montana and adapted culturally as best they could. Mixed blood families would sometimes join the tribe of their relatives, sometimes stay in the dominant culture, and sometimes shift back and forth. Many people today are just learning through genealogical research that they have Metis or mixed blood heritage. Admitting First Nations heritage has only recently become acceptable.

Some Metis and Mixed Blood Families who Formed Minnesota

Pierre and Charles Bottineau, were both Metis of the Red River Settlement (now Winnipeg or Les Fourches) who married Indian

George Bonga

women. They were leaders and guides for Selkirk Colony retreats to St. Paul, as well as many Metis from Les Fourches settlement. Bottineau brothers were founders of Minneapolis (St. Anthony Falls and Northeast), St. Paul (Mears Park area), Osseo, and finally Red Lake Falls and region.

George Bonga and sister Marguerite were African/Ojibwe but spoke French. George married an Ojibwe woman and settled in Leech

Pierre Bottineau

Lake area. Marguerite who married Swedish trader Jacob Fahlstrom, from Fond du Lac area (Duluth) settling first in St. Paul, and later Afton. Negotiators, traders.

Jean-Baptiste Faribault family, of Mendota and Faribault. Jean-Baptiste, a French Quebecois lawyer but fur trader in Minnesota, who married French Dakota woman Pelagi, also a trader. They had a large mixed blood family who lived in the Twin Cities, Mendota, and Faribault. Son Alexander started town of Faribault. Faribault County named after the family.

Joseph Renville family of southwest Minnesota. French- Canadian trader who married Dakota woman and together raised a large mixed blood family. Descendants in Twin Cities area as well as western Minnesota. Renville County named after the family.

Martin McLeod was a Scotsman from the Red River area who married a Dakota woman after moving further south. Together they raised a mixed blood family. McLeod County is named after them.

John Beargrease- Mixed blood dogsled mail carrier, Grand Marais to Duluth and south to the Mississippi River. A popular, present-day dogsled race is named after him.

Governor Henry Sibley. Before his marriage to Sarah Jane Steele, he had a child with a Dakota woman, Red Blanket Woman, who bore his daughter Helen. His mixed blood daughter was supported by him, but brought up in a different household.

Gabe Brien, Metes fiddler with the author as historic Metis woman

Chapter Seven
Early French-Canadian Settlements in Minnesota

In the 1830s silk was introduced to England, lowering the demand for beaver fur. Combined with over-trapping, this lowered demand greatly changed the fur trade and the relationships between traders and Native Americans. Many of the French-Canadians who had made their living in the fur trade industry now had to look for other ways to earn a living. Since they were in what was to become Minnesota, and had established family ties and connections with local Native Americans in this state, it only makes sense that they would now look to establish themselves here.

Painting by Seth Eastman of early settler's house and barn (Public Domain)

1899 Map showing Half Breed Tract off Lake Pepin (Public Domain)

This chapter will discuss the settlement of French-Canadians in Minnesota, which occurred in three distinct tiers or time frames.

The first tier of French-Canadian settlement occurred in the 1820s and 1830s. By the 1830s, although what was to become Minnesota remained officially closed to settlement, isolated agricultural outposts were being formed in the State at fur trading posts, at Fort Snelling by remnants of the Selkirk Colony, and in what U.S. treaty makers labeled the Half-Breed Tract around Lake Pepin.[161]

---

[161] Wingerd, Mary Lethert, *North Country, the Making of Minnesota*, Illustrations complied and annotated by Kirsten Delegard, University of Minnesota Press, Minneapolis, 2010, p.125.

Fur traders and their families who had established ties in the territory by working at fur trade posts and who had children with native American women began to plant crops, raise livestock, and build homes. Most of the early French-Canadian settlers had some kind of connection with the fur trade and had blood relations with the local tribes. In Mendota, a frontier community called St. Pierre was forming to serve the needs of the soldiers and squatters on the military reservation.

Other settlers in this first tier were members of the Selkirk Red River Colony. The Red River Colony (or Selkirk Settlement) was a colonization project set up by Thomas Douglas, 5th Earl of Selkirk in 1811, on land granted to him by the Hudson's Bay Company. Selkirk died in 1820. The colony was made up of Scottish, French speaking Swiss and some French-Canadians. This settlement was more or less a failure, and many of these early settlers ended up taking the Ox Cart trails south to Fort Snelling and beyond to escape the harsh conditions of the Red River Colony.

Selkirk Red River Colony 1880 Map
(Public Domain)

Red River Ox Carts
19th Century drawing (Public Domain)

Between 1821 and 1835, it is estimated that 489 refugees from Selkirk's Colony arrived at Fort Snelling, and they continued to come in following years.[162] For a number of reasons, the Selkirk colonists decided their prospects would be better in the Fort Snelling area and beyond, rather than remain up in the Red River. The War of 1812 had changed the international border line so that Lord Selkirk no longer owned the land in the United States he had formerly purchased from the Hudson's Bay Company. There was an ongoing rivalry causing problems between the fur trading companies, namely the Hudson's Bay Company, the Northwest Company, and the American Fur Trade Company. Grasshoppers, the annual flooding of the Red River, and the harsh winters, were all factors in the decision by these Selkirk settlers to journey to the Fort Snelling Reservation.[163]

---

[162] Wingerd, Mary Lethert, *North Country, the Making of Minnesota*, Illustrations complied and annotated by Kirsten Delegard, University of Minnesota Press, Minneapolis, 2010, p.124
[163] Ramsey, Walter Reeve, *The Selkirk Colony of the Red River of the North…and its profound influence on early development of the Twin Cities; a factual research*, originally published before 1923, reprinted Nabu Press (2011).

The Selkirk colonists traveled by ox cart down to Fort Snelling. In the early years, they followed the Red River down to present-day Breckenridge, then along the Bois des Sioux River to Lake Traverse and Lac qui Parle, then followed the Minnesota River to Fort Snelling. It was essential to always have a water source during their journey, and this route followed waterways all the way to Fort Snelling.

Some of these Selkirk colonists continued south where lands were open for settlement since the future Minnesota region was not officially open to settlement until 1837. One such group established themselves in Galena, Illinois. Some stayed on the Fort Snelling Military Reservation and established farms and

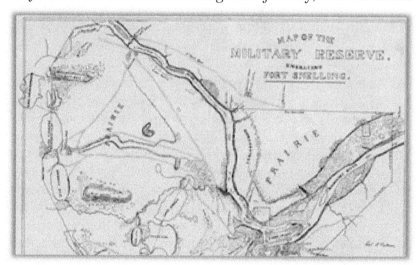

19ᵗʰ Century drawing of Fort Snelling Military Reservation
(Public Domain)

raised livestock in the reservation, even though they had no valid claim to this land. This was a concern of the fort Commander and these settlers would eventually be evicted in May 1840.

The second tier of French-Canadian settlement began in Minnesota after separate U.S. treaties with the Ojibwe and Dakota opened up land between the St. Croix and Mississippi Rivers. There were two treaties in 1837, one with the Ojibwe and one with the Dakota. At that time, the land ceded was in the Wisconsin Territory and Minnesota did not yet exist. Below is a map showing lands ceded by the Anishinaabeg[164] tribes to the U.S. Government in the 1800s.

The family of Joseph Labissoniere (b.1786) and Francois Desjarlais (b.1796) were part of this second tier of French-Canadian settlers. Joseph had been a clerk for the North West Company in Grand Forks *(Les Grandes Fourches)*, Wahalla, and Pembina in the future Dakota Territory. Pierre Bottineau's father was also a clerk at fur trading posts in the Red River Valley area and he was part of this second tier. Joseph was living at St. Boniface in Canada before he decided to move to Fort Snelling. His wife, Francois Desjarlais, was the daughter of fur trader Antoine Desjarlais and Pert Won, an Ojibwa woman from the Little Snake Tribe of Manitoba.

---

[164] **Anishinaabe** (or **Anishinaabeg**, which is the plural form of the word) is the autonym often used by the Odawa, Ojibwa, and Algonquin First Nations in Ontario. They all speak closely related Anishinaabemowin-Anishinaabe languages, of the Algonquian language family. The Ojibwas in Minnesota were Anishinaabe. The Dakota tribes are not considered Anishinaabe.

19th Century Treaty Map (Public Domain)

In 1837, Joseph Labissoniere and his family joined sixty Selkirk colonists and traveled by ox cart down to Fort Snelling, and spent the winter of 1837–38 on the reservation. On July 15, 1838, it was announced at the fort that the U.S. Senate had ratified the 1837 treaties with the Ojibwe and the Dakota, which opened up for settlement the land between the Mississippi and the St. Croix River. Ojibwe leaders signed an agreement with U.S. commissioner Henry Dodge at St. Peters in July 1837. Two months later, twenty Dakota chiefs and elders journeyd toe Washington accompanied by Major Taliaferro, agent at Fort Snelling, and representatives from the American Fur Company including Major Taliaferro, their agent, and repre sentatives from the American Fur Company, including Henry Sibley, Alexis Bailly, Joseph LaFramboise, Augustine Rocque, Labathe, the Faribaults, and other fur traders.

In the fall of 1838, Joseph Labissoniere and a number of French-Canadians moved to an area known as the Grand Marais,[165] which is the lowlands located just to the southeast of where the current city of St. Paul is located. It was here where Joseph Labissoniere established a claim, near where the present Fish Hatcheries are located in the lowlands to the north of Pig's Eye Lake.

Fort Snelling in 1850
By Sergeant Edward Kirkbride
Minnesota Historical Society Collections

In May 1840, the Selkirk colonists living on the Fort Snelling Military Reservation were evicted and most of them set out new claims in the area east of the Mississippi and in the lowlands area. By 1842, there were at least nineteen French-Canadian families in this area. In

---

[165] This name was given to this area due to its low position by General Pike in his expedition of 1805.

addition to Joseph Labissoniere, other French-Canadians included Francis Gammel, Benjamin Gervais, Henry Belland, Pierre Parrant, Michael LeClaire, Francois (Amable) Morin, Charles Mosseau, Denis Cherrier, Charles Sévère and Pierre Bottineau, Vetal Guerin, and Antoine LeClaire.[166] These are among the first French-Canadian settlers in what would become Minnesota and this French-Canadian community went on to build a small chapel known as the chapel of Saint Paul which is where the name Saint Paul came from. More on the story of the first Saint Paul Chapel is described elsewhere in this book.

Early Minnesota enjoyed a very strong French influence. In the book "History of the City of Saint Paul," by J. Fletcher Williams, first published in 1876, it is noted that "a knowledge of the French language was indispensable to a trader." Williams states in his book that St. Paul's early stores often bore the sign, "*Ici on parle Francais* (French spoken here)." French was spoken nearly everywhere during the early Territorial days in Minnesota.

1888 Painting by James Desvarreaux Larpenteur (1847-1937) titled "St. Paul from Pig's Eye." The Fish Hatcheries are currently located in the middle left of the picture.
Minnesota Historical Society Collections

Historical records also show that the preferred language of business in Minnesota during its territorial and early statehood period was often French. As Judge Charles Flandau commented, "nearly all the people were French, and that language was quite as usually spoken as English. The town of Mendota was almost exclusively French and half-breed Sioux, the latter speaking French if they deviated from their native tongue."[167]

Henry Sibley, the first governor of Minnesota, was fluent in French, and included in his papers is a pamphlet he wrote in French in 1877, to promote the sale of railroad bonds. The title of his pamphlet was "Les Bons de Chemin de Fer de l'Etat."[168] William Forbes and Norman Kittson, business associates of Sibley, both spoke French fluently, having grown up in Montreal and Sorel, Quebec, respectively.[169]

The third tier came after the United States government passed the Homestead Act in 1862 and continued making treaties with the Native American tribes for their lands, and land opportunities opened up for settlers. It is estimated that over one million French-Canadians

[166] Fletcher, J. Williams, *The History of the City of Saint Paul and the County of Ramsey, Minnesota*, Minnesota Historical Society Press, St. Paul, (1983) pp.87-88.
[167] Flandrau, Charles, *The History of Minnesota and Tales of the Frontier*, CreateSpace Independent Publishing Platform, (2015).
[168] Sibley Papers located at the Minnesota Historical Society.
[169] Flandrau, Charles, *The History of Minnesota and Tales of the Frontier*, CreateSpace Independent Publishing Platform, (2015).

emigrated to the United States between the 1840s and 1930s. Many of these came to Minnesota, after some going first to New England, and then to the Midwest. This group was not related to the fur trade and were generally farmers by occupation. They ventured to Minnesota because of the perceived economic opportunity provided by the large amount of land available at cheap prices.

This third tier of French-Canadian immigrants began to migrate to the United States and Minnesota in the 1840s. The French-Canadian population in New England almost doubled during that decade.[170] French-Canadians also arrived in substantial numbers to Midwestern states such as Michigan, which by 1850, boasted a French population of about twenty thousand. More than two thirds of these were recent arrivals from Canada, with the remainder being the "first wave" Francophones who had settled in towns such as Detroit and Monroe many years prior.[171]

There were several reasons for the migration of French-Canadians to Minnesota in the 1840s and 1850s. Large families and limited amounts of farmland forced sons and daughters to look elsewhere for a livelihood. The production of wheat and timber declined in Quebec and the Ottawa Valley during the 1840s. There was political instability in Canada at that time, with the failed rebellions of 1837-1838 and the Act of Union of 1840 in Canada. The Act of Union proposed to establish a new English regime, which threatened the language and religion of the French-Canadians.

After the American Civil War, a large number of French-Canadians moved to the United States. It is estimated that during the years 1871 to 1901, more than two million people emigrated from Canada to the United States. During this period (1873 to 1896), Canada was suffering through a long, sustained and difficult economic depression. The economy in the United States was more mature and diversified and was in need of workers. A large amount traveled to Minnesota and other Midwestern states.[172] Minnesota shows the second highest concentration of Francophones in the United States in the 1900 census records.

The early Francophones in Minnesota came from a variety of places. The majority had connections to Canada, but some like Auguste Larpenteur, Eugene Villaume, Joseph Cretin, Lucien Galtier, and others, came directly from France. Many like Louis Robert came from the St. Louis area, some from Illinois where earlier French settlements had been established before the Revolutionary War, and others from New England. Many were from mixed ethnic and cultural backgrounds, such as Pierre Bottineau and Joseph Labissoniere, who had Ojibwe mothers, and the sons of Jean Baptiste Faribault who were part Mdewakanton Dakota.

In 1891, the Twin Cities area of Minnesota contained approximately eighteen thousand French-Canadians. Outside of the Minneapolis-Saint Paul metropolitan area, the largest

[170] Gitlin, Jay, *The Bourgeois Frontier: French Towns, French Traders, and American Expansion,* Yale University Press (2010).
[171] Lamarre, Jean, *French-Canadians of Michigan* Wayne State Community Press (2003); See also McQuillan, D. Aidan, "*French-Canadian Communities in the Upper Midwest during the Nineteenth Century,*" Cahiers de géographie du Québec, vol. 23, n° 58, 1979, p. 53-72. " and also Dulong, John P., *French-Canadians in Michigan,* Michigan State University Press, (2001).
[172] Roby, Ives, *The Franco-Americans of New England: Dreams And Realities* Mcgill Queens Univ Pr (May 16, 2005) P. 11-12.

settlements were in Polk County in the Red River Valley.[173] French-Canadians founded more than three dozen French language newspapers in the Midwest in the nineteenth century, mostly in Michigan, Illinois[174] and Minnesota. Most were short lived, but *Le Canadian* in St. Paul survived more than two decades.[175]

Below is a list of French or French-Canadian settlements in Minnesota in alphabetical order. Most of these settlements established Catholic churches where French was spoken for a time. Many French churches took the names of patron saints, such as St. Louis, St. Anne, St. Jean Baptiste and St. Clotilde. The establishment of a church name may be a key to the ethnic identity of the parish. This also means that the French-Canadian population was large enough to support a church. French-Canadians settled in other places, in smaller numbers, where they did not have enough to establish a French speaking church. These populations are harder to find. As a result, some of these smaller settlements may not be listed here. And now the list:

Afton
French-Canadians settled here in 1837. Village was not platted until 1855.

Albertville
French-Canadians settled near the junction of the Crow and Mississippi rivers, where the counties of Hennepin, Wright, Sherburne and Anoka join. French-Canadian group settled in the Albertville area where the Church of St. Albert was established in 1902.

The first church was built under the leadership of Fr. Joseph Jagerman in 1906, in what was then called Saint Michael Station. He was also the first resident pastor. The village began to be called "Albertville" in 1909 after the St. Albert parish. Eventually a rectory and a convent were built on either side of the church. A parish school opened in September of 1915 and continued to function here until 1968. The School Sisters of Notre Dame de Namur (their origins were in France) staffed the school. In 1981, the school building was torn down to make room for the Parish Center.

Church of St. Albert

Anoka
Early residents of Anoka remember a log house which stood on the east side of the Rum River near its mouth. This was the first house built in Anoka County. It was built in the fall of 1844 by a French trader named Joseph Belanger, assisted by George Cournoyer, Pierre Crevier, Joseph Brunet and Maxime Maxwell.[176] Joseph Belanger was born in St. Michel d'Yamaska, Quebec in 1813.

---

[173] Clayton Andrew R.L. and Sisson, Richard and Zacher, Chris, *The American Midwest: An Interpretive Encyclopedia* p.199
[174] "Illinois" is the modern spelling for the early French Catholic missionaries and explorers' name for the Illinois Native Americans.
[175] Clayton Andrew R.L. and Sisson, Richard and Zacher, Chris, *The American Midwest: An Interpretive Encyclopedia*, Indiana University Press, 2007, p.199
[176] Goodrich, Albert M., *History of Anoka County and the Towns of Champlin and Dayton in Hennepin County, Minnesota*, (Minneapolis, 1905), p.23

He came to Minnesota in 1836 to join a group of men who were going to work for the American Fur Company. In 1846, two brothers, Peter and Francis Patoille, started a trading post at Anoka.[177] A French-Canadian named Antoine Guion was one of the first landowners in Anoka. In 1856, a group of French-Canadians founded a church in Anoka near where the Red River Trail ferry crossed the Mississippi River.[178]

Argyle

The first settler of Argyle was Basil Gervais and his son Pierre, French-Canadians who came from the Province of Quebec in 1877. Pierre Gervais filed his homestead claim on May 25, 1878. Other French-Canadian families soon arrived, many from the area just out-

St. Rose de Lima in Argyle

side the city of Montreal. The first settlement was called "Louisa" and was located near the Middle River. The railroad station was later established about a mile south of the river and was called Argyle, which is the name adopted for the town. In 1880, French-Canadian settlers signed a petition to use the local school for religious services. The names help identify who the original settlers of Argyle were. French-Canadian names on this petition were as follows: Joseph LaFond Jr., Gaspard Ethier, Dosethe Tessier, Eugene Labine, H. Morin, Alex Chouinard, Pierre Gervais, Michael Troumble, Levia Sourdine, George Prenevous, Xavier Legault, Ernest Messier, Alfred Lafond, William Martell, George Morin, Albert Proulx, Challe Choinard, Samuel Cormier, and Medard Landreville, among others. The names illustrate the strong French-Canadian presence in the early days. The St. Rose de Lima Church was established in Argyle by French-Canadians in 1881 and Father Fortier came from St. Boniface, Canada to minister to this first congregation.

A history book of the St. Rose of Lima Parish lists most of the early French-Canadian settlers and families who lived in Argyle during the early years. This book is available to purchase from the St. Rose parish in Argyle.

[177] Williams, J. Fletcher, *History of the Upper Mississippi Valley*, Minnesota Historical Society Press, St. Paul, (1881), p.224.
[178] Holmquist, June Drenning, *They Chose Minnesota, a Survey of The State's Ethnic Groups*, Minnesota Historical Society Press (1981); Goodrich, Albert M., *History of Anoka County and the Towns of Champlin and Dayton in Hennepin County, Minnesota*, (Minneapolis, 1905).

Badger

French-Canadians in this area were traders and trappers, and later worked for the lumber industry. The French-Canadians and others in town organized a St. Mary's Catholic Church in 1898 which was served by French speaking priests from Red Lake Falls, but the mixed congregation used English during the services.[179]

St. Mary's Catholic Church in Badger

Belle Prairie

French-Canadians from Crow Wing spread down the east bank of the Mississippi to Little Falls and Belle Prairie in Morrison County. Anton Bisson settled in area in 1853, and was the first French-Canadian to settle in the town.[180] Belle Prairie had between thirty to forty families by the end of the 1850's and started a church called Holy Family.

**Holy Family Church
Belle Prairie**

**Belle Prairie Convent called
Academy of St. Anthony, 1889**

By 1881, French-Canadians constituted a majority of the propulation of Belle Prairie.[181] In 1872, Belle Prairie founded a Convent and Academy of St. Anthony which was operated by the Missionary Franciscan Sisters of the Immaculate Conception, who taught all classes in French.

---

[179] Rubenstein, Sarah, "The French-Canadians and French," found in Holmquist, June Drenning, *They Chose Minnesota" a Survey of The State's Ethnic Groups*, Minnesota Historical Society Press (1981), p.52; *"History of the Red River Valley : past and present, including an account of the counties, cities, towns, and villages of the Valley from the time of their first settlement and formation.* Written by various writers, published by C.F. Cooper & Company, Chicago, (1909).
[180] Williams, J. Fletcher, *History of the Upper Mississippi Valley*, Minnesota Historical Society Press, St. Paul, (1881), p.591
[181] Rubinstein, p.41.

Our Lady of the Angels Academy

The Missionary Franciscan Sisters of the Immaculate Conception are the only religious congregation ever founded within the boundaries of the St. Cloud Diocese. Their convent burned down on April 26, 1889, and the sisters left Belle Prairie. Some of the sisters returned to the east coast. Others, including Sister Mary Francis Beauchamp, moved to Little Falls and established the Franciscan Sisters of the Immaculate Conception. Eventually, the Missionary Franciscans returned to Belle Prairie and Mother Mary Columba (daughter of Mr. and Mrs. Elzear Doucet, later spelled Doucette) opened Our Lady of the Angels Academy on November 11, 1911.

Breckenridge

Most of the town now platted as Breckenridge, Minnesota was once owned by three French Dakota women, namely Angelique Martin, Mary R. Marlow and Angeline Lagree with a small portion owned by Thomas Provencelle.[182] Pierre Bottineau helped map out the Breckenridge area for the railroad and received lots in exchange for his services.[183] Despite this, there was not a large population of French-Canadians settling in Breckenridge.

Brooks

Brooks was established in 1904 as a station on the Soo Line Railroad. Many of its early settlers were French-Canadians. By 1926, Brooks had two general stores, a grocery store, a bank, hardware store, butcher shop, blacksmith shop, a livery barn, two saloons, a

Original St. Joseph's Catholic Church in Brooks

community hall and a hotel to accommodate travelers. Brooks was primarily a service town for the surrounding agricultural townships, and a creamery was established as the local dairying business developed on neighboring farms. St. Joseph's Catholic Church in Brooks was established there. Parishes in Red Lake County in the 1930's reported 578 French-Canadian members in Brooks.[184]

The Brooks Cheese Factory was built by the Aurelius J. Parenteau family in 1926 and operated until 1980, producing cheddar cheese and noted for its cheese curds.

[182] Lakem, Neoma, *History of Wilkin County, Minnesota*, published on Wilken County Website at co.wilkin.mn.us.
[183] Snodgrass, Mary Ellen, *Settlers of the American West, The Lives of 231 Notable Pioneers*, published 2015, pp.19-20.
[184] Holmquist, June Drenning, *They Chose Minnesota, a Survey of The State's Ethnic Groups*, Minnesota Historical Society Press (1981).

Brown's Valley

The church of St. Anthony of Padua church in Brown's Valley was established by French-Canadians. The Reverend C. Thiebaut was the first Pastor.

Buffalo

In 1851, Canadian fur trader Edmund Brisset (Brissette) created a path from present-day Minneapolis to Buffalo Lake by cutting through the dense forests once occupying the area. In paving the way for others, Brisset and crew made it possible for ambitious settlers to create Winnebago City, the tiny village now known as Buffalo.[185] In 1850, Edmund Brisset had established a fur trading post on the west end of Lake Pulaski for the purpose of obtaining pelts from the Winnebago Indians. This post was abandoned in 1855. Edmund Brisset was a French-Canadian who came to Fort Snelling in 1832 and engaged in carpentry and interior woodwork. He once told a story to J. Fletcher Williams, who wrote a book on the history of St. Paul, that he wrote a letter while at Pig's Eye Parrant's tavern and decided to use the word "Pig's Eye" for the return address. The return letter was delivered to Parrant's tavern, and this is where the term Pig's Eye began to be used for the St. Paul area.[186] He also became a fur trader and ran a post near Lake Harriet in Minneapolis. In 1851, Brisset and his associates cut a road through the timber from Lake Harriet and Lake Calhoun to the present site of Buffalo, and from there a trail to the west end of Lake Pulaski. After leaving Lake Calhoun, the road passed along the west shores of Medicine Lake, Independence Lake, and Lake Sarah, crossing Crow River at Rockford, then passing north of present-day Rockford and Buffalo Road, and crossing the creek between the marsh and the lake. It was a crooked narrow path, but the traders used it extensively and the early settlers found this road to be very useful.[187]

Centerville

The Church of St. Genevieve of Paris Catholic Church was established in Centerville in 1853.[188] The village of Centerville was organized in 1857 and incorporated on September 27, 1910. The village was laid out and platted by Charles Peltier, F.X. Lavallee and F. Lamott in the spring of 1854. French-Canadian names found there included LaMotte, Peltier, Cardinal, Dupre and LaValle. The name Centerville refers to it being between the Mississippi and St. Croix rivers and it was equal distance from Stillwater, St. Paul and Anoka. The settlers of this village were mostly French-Canadians, and it came to be known as a French Settlement. The first sawmill in the county was built here by Charles Peltier.

---

[185] Taken from article Hertwig, Michele, *History of Buffalo*, posted on City of Buffalo website.
[186] Story taken from Scholberg, Henry, *The French Pioneers of Minnesota, Les Pionniers Francais du Minnesota*, Northstar Publications, 1995, p.33
[187] Curtiss-Wedge, Franklyn, *History of Wright County, Minnesota* (Volumne I, Chicago, H.C. Cooper Jr. & Co. 1915
[188] Broden, Holly, *French Immigrants and the Catholic Church in Centerville*, published in History Center News, a Newsletter of the Anoka County Historical Society. Vol 39, No.3 May-June 2009.

1870 picture of Church at Centerville

Church of St. Genevieve, Centerville, Minnesota

Chaska

In 1842, Jean Baptiste Faribault invited Father Ravoux to establish a mission among the Dakota Indians in what would become the town of Chaska. Father Ravoux built a small chapel there, but dismantled it three years later when the Indians threatened to burn it down. The chapel was sold to the Catholics of Wabasha and floated down the river where it was rebuilt.

Cloquet Voyageur located beneath Highway Eighty-Eight bridge in Cloquet.

Cloquet

In Cloquet, the first Catholic Church was organized in 1881, under the name "The Church of the Holy Names of Jesus and Mary." The first pastor was Father A. LeMay, who served until October 1, 1883. The first trustees of the new parish were Andrew Gowan and Dennis Harrigan. The latter was the grandfather of Harry Lillis Crosby, Jr., better known in later years as Bing Crosby, and internationally known singer and movie star.[189] The church was known as the "French Church" because Father Giraux and predecessors in Cloquet had given their sermons in French; however, some fifteen ethnic groups worshiped in the parish.

Corcoran

In 1860, a number of French-Canadians settled in the area now known as Corcoran. On December 3, 1881, the parish of St. Jeanne de Chantel was established. It was located just a few miles west of the present St. Thomas site. The official incorporation papers used the American name St. Jane. However, most of the parishioners used the French version, St. Jeanne de Chantel. The church closed in 1953 after sustaining damage from a tornado. At that time its congregation merged with St. Thomas the Apostle Church in Corcoran.

St. Jeanne de Chantal
Corcoran

---

[189] Taken from article titled "*History of Our Parish*" in website for Queen of Peace Church in Cloquet.

Crookston

The area in which Crookston is located was traversed by trappers and traders including Ojibwa and Lakota Indians, Metis, and other mixed-race people as well as white men between 1790 and 1870. A branch of the Red River Trails passed nearby; it was used by fur traders between the 1840s and 1870s. Many French-Canadians were members of St. Anne's in Crookston and French-language newspapers in 1895 reported that Crookston's French-Canadian population numbered 950.[190] St. Joseph's Academy was established in 1903 by the French speaking St. Joseph of Medaile sisters.

St. Annes Church in Crookston

Crow Wing

The Church of St. John the Baptist in Crow Wing was established in 1863. The settlement of Crow Wing, which began in 1839, only existed for about forty years.[191] From 1839 to 1844, it was primarily a trading post where William Aitkin traded merchandise to the Indians in exchange for furs. He also employed quite a number of French-Canadian and mixed bloods (French-Canadian and Indian) who acted as voyageurs by canoeing up surrounding lakes, rivers, and streams to trade on his behalf with the natives.

In 1845, the East Woods Trail was opened from Pembina, in the Red River Valley, to St. Paul. Crow Wing then became a favorite stopping place for the long caravans of ox cart teams that led south each summer hauling buffalo hides, furs, and pemmican and afterwards returned north laden with food staples, manufactured goods, liquor, guns, and ammunition.

With the signing of the Fond du Lac and Leech Lake treaties in 1847, Ojibwa lands north of the Crow Wing, Long Prairie, and Leaf Rivers were opened for lumbering. The advent of lumbering brought in more French-Canadians from Quebec, New Brunswick, Maine, Vermont, Wisconsin, and Michigan. By 1860, Crow Wing had a population of over two hundred and was ranked as the largest inhabited place north of St. Paul. This expansion ended in 1861 when the Civil War began. The U.S. Dakota War of 1862, and the Ojibwe troubles of the same year, frightened people so that even after the Civil War ended in 1865, few were interested in settling here.

---

[190] Holmquist, June Drenning, *They Chose Minnesota, a Survey of The State's Ethnic Groups* , Minnesota Historical Society Press (1981) p.43.
[191] The above picture of Crow Wing Village painted by Charles Hallock from article *"The Red River Trail"* in Harper's New Monthly Magazine 19:47 (June 1859).

In 1868, the Ojibwa Indians from Crow Wing, Gull River, Gull Lake and North Long Lake were removed to the White Earth Reservation. The Northern Pacific then bypassed Crow Wing and decided to run its line where a new town called Brainerd was built in 1870-71. Brainerd became the county seat in 1872 and many of the businesses in Crow Wing moved there. Residents began moving elsewhere during 1873–74. Some went to Brainerd, many of the French-Canadians to Little Falls, while most of the mixed bloods joined their relatives at White Earth. By 1879–80, old Crow Wing was almost a deserted ghost town. Below is a list of French-Canadian occupants of Crow Wing in 1860.[192]

A View of Crow Wing, when First Settled, in 1859.

Crow Wing Village found in page 250 of Col Hankins Dakota Land Or the Beauty of St. Paul, published in 1868

Clement Beaulieu, Henry Beaulieu, Jacques Currier, Cyrillo Dunard, Mary Colombe, Joseph Dagol, Narcisse Gravelle, Cyrillo Beaudette, John Fumadi, A. L. Crapotte, Joseph Teasroux, Francois Thibaud, Joseph Laporte, Charles La Rue, Michael Contois, Jonah Contois, Louis Mayrand, Eli Berthniaud, Moses Dupuis, Jules LeDuc, Andrew Dufort, Laurent Darupt, Joseph Tescely, Peter Roy, Lxdia Choumard, Gideon Le Sage, Peter Lecotte, and Antoine Bourgeious.

Dayton

The city of Dayton occupies the northern part of Hennepin County. Its eastern and northern boundaries follow the Mississippi River while on its western and northwestern boundary is the Crow River. The topography of the town is generally rolling, and it was originally covered with a growth of hardwood, and an unlimited supply of limestone. The soil is known for its fertility, and there are many streams and lakes in the area.

The earliest settler of Dayton was Paul Godine, a Frenchman who settled there in 1852. One article written by Rev. David

St. John the Baptiste Church in Dayton (1885)

Brooks states that Mr. Godine was from France. The Dayton Historical Society Internet Facebook page states that Paul Goodin was born in France in 1810.

---

[192] Information on early French-Canadian settlement obtained from article written by Leslie, Earl C. titled *"Our French-Canadians"*.

Other French-Canadians, including Marcellus Bonlee, Benjamin Leveillier, and others, made claims along the rivers, and on the lakes in the area. Nearly all of the pioneers of Dayton were French-Canadians, although it is possible there were some who came directly from France.

**St. John the Baptist in Dayton
Built in 1904**

The Church of St. John the Baptist in Dayton was established in 1857.[193] A church building was erected the same year; its location being on the claim of Paul Godine. The first priest of the parish was Father Jennis. The present church building was built in 1904.

Below is the McNeil building in downtown Dayton. The second floor was dance hall. In the book titled "Letters to George" collected and submitted by Ellen Nelles Leger, Minneapolis, Minnesota, 2005, page 52, there is a statement in one of the letters in the book written on January 25, 1934 that states: "I went to the old French town (Dayton) again last night for a dance," referring to the McNeil building.[194]

McNeil Building in Dayton. Dance Hall on Second Floor

[193] Brooks, Rev. David, *History of Dayton.*
[194] Leger, Ellen Nelles, *Letters to George*, self published in Minneapolis, Minnesota, 2005.

Delano

Prior to 1874, the Catholics in the Hamel area, chiefly Irish, German and French-Canadian, had been served by a visiting priest from Osseo or had attended Mass in other communities. In 1874, they began planning for their own church, and in 1879, their church (St. Peter Church) was completed and they were assigned their first permanent pastor, Father Z.L. Chandonnet.

Delavan

Delavan is a small town settled by a group of French-Canadians. The Perrizo family lived there (formerly Pariseau) and notables from this area include Mitchel Perrizo (1917–2011) who was an attorney, a member of the Minnesota House of Representatives, a captain

Delano St. Peter Church in 1874

in the U.S. Navy who served during

St. Dorothy's Church in 2007

World War Two, and a naval officer during the Vietnam War. He was campaign manager for Senator Hubert Humphrey when Humphrey ran for a second term.

Dorothy

Dorothy was a small town in Section 5, Louisville Township, Red Lake County, Minnesota. It is no longer an ongoing community. It was named after St. Dorothy's Catholic Church, which was built in 1919 for the French-Canadian families in the area.[195]

The roots of St. Dorothy's Parish go back to the Huot area, where Father Pierre Champagne offered mass at the home of Louis Huot as early as 1880. At that time, there were about 25 Canadian families located in the area. A church, St. Aloysius, was built at Huot in 1883. In 1919, a new church was built in the village of Dorothy (five miles north) and the St. Aloysius Church was closed.

Duluth

The French left their mark on Duluth as early as 1679, when namesake Daniel Greysolon Sieur DuLuht portaged across Minnesota Point at Onigamiinsing ("Little Portage"), the spot where Duluthians later dug a ship canal. Soon after came the voyageurs. When the fur trade died, French-Canadians worked in mines and lumber camps.

---

[195] Upham, Warren, *Minnesota Place Names, A Geographical Encyclopedia*, Minnesota Historical Society Press; 3rd Revised & Enlarged edition (May 15, 2001) Third Edition p.478

Prior to the 1880s, Duluth's Catholic French-Canadian population attended Mass at Sacred Heart. By 1884, the French-Canadians made up the largest Catholic population in Duluth and organized their own French national parish, St. Jean-Baptiste. A year later, they built a modest wooden structure in the heart of The Glenn beneath Point of Rocks at Eleventh Avenue West and Superior Street. The French-Canadian population, employed for the most part as laborers and building tradesmen, continued to grow. In 1888, two hundred French-Canadians called Duluth home; by 1902, that number had grown to five hundred. In 1904, the parish decided it was time for a bigger church.

The French moved deeper into Duluth's west end in 1905, building a new church and school called St. Jean-Baptiste at Third Street and Twenty-Fifth Avenue West. The two-story red brick church employed an unusual design, with its school on first floor and church on second. The front gable's tall triple-arched windows stood over a stone arched entrance; the gables were adorned with decorative brick work.

St. Jean-Baptiste Church in Duluth in 1904

St. Jean-Baptiste absorbed St. Clement's congregation in 1975 when the German church was sold and joined with Saint Peter and Paul's, originally built to serve Duluth's Polish Catholics. The congregation celebrated Mass at both churches until 1996, when St. Jean-Baptiste was razed and replaced by the Holy Family Catholic Church, where both former parishioners of and artifacts from all three churches found a new home.[196]

---

[196] Dierkins, Tony and Norton, Maryanne, *Lost Duluth, Landmarks, Industries, Buildings, Homes and the Neighborhoods in Which they Stood.*, Zenith City Press, Duluth, Minnesota, 2012.

East Grand Forks

The Catholic Church reported that there were seventy French-Canadian families at the Church of the Sacred Heart Catholic Church in East Grand Forks in 1915.[197]

Elk River

In 1848, Pierre Bottineau built a trading post on an elevation between what was called Upper Town and Elk River. In 1850, Pierre Bottineau built the Elk River House, a small tavern.[198]

Faribault

Alexander Faribault, the Métis son of fur trader Jean Baptiste Faribault, founded a French-Canadian colony in 1844, in what is

Church of Sacred Heart and Rectory East Grand Forks

now the city of Faribault in Rice County. He brought Edmund and Nicholas La Croix from Montreal to Minnesota to oversee his flour mill, and they developed a middlings purifier that made it possible to produce white flour from the spring wheat grown in the region.

Church of the Sacred Heart, Faribault

The first mass offered in the Faribault area is recorded in 1848 in the home of Alexander Faribault, which at the time, was a log cabin.[199] The Reverend Augustine Ravoux, a French mission priest, officiated at that first Mass. The first parish in Faribault was established by Bishop Joseph Cretin in 1856 and was called Immaculate Conception. By the 1860s, European immigrants had moved into the area in large numbers, many of them German. In 1870, the German Catholic immigrants in the area received permission to start their own church which they called St. Lawrence. In 1877, French-Canadian families in Faribault petitioned the Bishop to start their own French speaking parish which was called Sacred Heart Church. Eventually, all three of the Catholic parishes in Faribault merged into one church now called Divine Mercy Catholic Church.

[197] Holmquist, June Drenning, *They Chose Minnesota" a Survey of The State's Ethnic Groups*, Minnesota Historical Society Press (1981).
[198] Williams, J. Fletcher, *History of the Upper Mississippi Valley*, Minnesota Historical Society Press, St. Paul, (1881)m p.296.
[199] O'Leary, Johanna, *A Historical Sketch of the Parish of the Immaculate Conception, Faribault, Minnesota*, Faribault Journal Press (1938).

French Lake- Annandale

A few French-Canadian's settled in the French Lake and Marysville Township in Wright County around 1860. Pierre Bottineau made an attempt to start a French colony in Wright County in 1879, when he tried to persuade 200 to 300 families from Ontario to settle near Maple Lake. The village, township, and lake known as French Lake was named by the early French-Canadian settlers who arrived here in the late 1850s and early 1860s.[200]

The church of St. Ignatius was incorporated in 1873 and was built at the present site of the French Lake cemetery, located about four miles southwest of Annandale. The first pastor of the church was Father Joseph Darche, succeeded by Father T. G. Plante.

French-Canadians attended Catholic services at East Maple Lake, Marysville, French Lake and Buffalo. A French priest remained at St. Timothy's in Maple Lake until 1905. Some French-Canadian names at French Lake were Bistodeau, Cayouette, Chartier, Chevalier, Dagenais, DeChaney, Fashant, Gerard, Guttry, Lambert, Logeais, Potrin, Provo, Purcell, Rehaume, Rochette, Rousseau, Rungette, and Verhey.

St. Ignatius Catholic Church in French Lake

Fort Ripley

St. Mathias, one of the older parishes in the Duluth Diocese, is located to the east of Fort Ripley at 4529 County Road 121. Monsignor J.F. Buh began to visit the area in 1887. Mass was first celebrated in the homes.

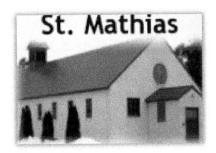

Originally, St. Mathias was a French settlement, and although the parish was a mission of St. Francis Church in Brainerd, it was looked after by Father Arthur Lamothe from Belle Prairie in the St. Cloud Diocese. Fr. Lamothe was pastor from 1890 until 1905. A frame church was constructed under his direction on land donated by the Gideon Matte family which also included the cemetery.

[200] Holmquist, June Drenning, *They Chose Minnesota" a Survey of The State's Ethnic Groups*, Minnesota Historical Society Press (1981)

Gentilly

Gentilly was first settled by French-Canadian settlers in 1878. Historians believe that Joseph Beaudette and others, who came from the parish of Gentilly on the right bank of the St. Lawrence River in Quebec, gave this name to the village seven miles east from Crookston. The French-Canadian settlers established St. Peter's Church of Gentilly in 1878. The first pastor of Red Lake Falls, a missionary priest, Pierre B. Champagne, celebrated the first mass in Gentilly. From 1878 to 1880, he occasionally offered Mass in the village schoolhouse.

St. Peters Church in Gentilly

Father Alexander Bouchard, the first resident priest, erected a small chapel and a modest rectory. At that time 118 families comprising 769 persons made up the parish. Except for two Irish families, all were French-Canadian.[201]

Ghent

The village of Ghent, located in Lyon County, is named after the city in Belgium and was named in 1881, after a large number of Belgian colonists settled there. The town had previously been named Grandview. The original Ghent is in the Flemish region of Belgium, but it certainly has many ties to the French language. Today roughly 40% of Belgium is French speaking. The Belgian colonists were soon joined by a large group of French-Canadian settlers who came from Kankakee County Illinois, lead by Joseph Letourneau and George Regnier. They chose Ghent because the local residents had established a church named St. Eloi that employed a French speaking priest named Father Julius De Vos.[202] The French-Canadian settlers were prosperous and paid cash for land in the area. Some of the French-Canadian family names found at Ghent in the early years were Letourneau, Bergeron, Regnier, and LeBeau.

St. Eloi Church and Rectory in Ghent

[201] Minnesota History (Winter 1975) p. 270.
[202] Holmquist, June Drenning, *They Chose Minnesota, a Survey of The State's Ethnic Groups*, Minnesota Historical Society Press (1981), p. 44.

Grand Marais

The term "Grand Marais" in French means "Great Marsh." It is used in a number of locations throughout Minnesota, and is the name of a town on the North Shore. The village of Grand Marais, on the North Shore of Lake Superior was named by the French voyageurs who traded furs along these shores. The Ojibwe had a settlement at what is now Grand Marais, and they made good use of the harbor by fishing from canoes in the Great Lake. The harbor at Grand Marais also proved useful during the 17th through 19th centuries for the French Voyageurs in their fur trading. In 1855, Father Dominic du Ranquet founded the mission at Grand Marais.[203]

In 1839, the area around the present-day Pig's Eye Lake near downtown St. Paul was also known as the Grand Marais. Some sources refer to it as the "Point LeClaire" Settlement, because Michel LeClaire was the first to settle there. Zebulon Pike, who visited the area in 1805, referred to this area as the Grand Marais.[204] After the Dodge Treaty of 1837, this land was open for settlement and a number of French-Canadians settled there with their families. During the summer of 1839, the following French-Canadians were living there with their families: Amable Turpin, Michel LeClaire, and his Dakota wife, Antoine LeClaire, Francis Gammel, Mr. Lasart, Joseph Labissoniere, Henry Belland, Mr. Chevalier, Amable Morin and Charles Mosseau. Historical accounts state they were employed as voyageurs of the American Fur Company a portion of the year, and when not needed by the company, cultivated their small farms.[205]

Grand Portage

The village of Grand Portage was an early location for French voyageurs. In June 1731 Pierre Gaultier de Varennes, Sieur de la Verendrye, with three of his four sons, brought

their flotilla of canoes to Grand Portage. He built a trading post there and between 1731 until about 1805, it was a link in the route between Montreal and the trading posts at Rainy Lake and Lake of the Woods. In 1805 the Northwest Company abandoned this post and moved their operation up the coast to Fort William in Ontario. In 1835 the American Fur Company opened a Fishery there. In 1851, Father Dominic du Ranquet build a chapel there which serves as the sacristy of the present church.[206] The church was originally built of logs, but was covered with siding in 1940.

Holy Rosary Church in Grand Portage

[203] Ahern, Reverend Patrick H. *Catholic Heritage in Minnesota, North Dakota and South Dakota*, published by the Most Reverend Archbishop and Bishops of the Province of Saint Paul 1964, p.69.

[204] Fletcher, J. Williams, *The History of the City of Saint Paul and the County of Ramsey, Minnesota*, Minnesota Historical Society Press, St. Paul, (1983).

[205] ID, p.86.

[206] Ahern, Reverend Patrick H. *Catholic Heritage in Minnesota, North Dakota and South Dakota*, published by the Most Reverend Archbishop and Bishops of the Province of Saint Paul 1964, p.69.

Green Valley

The Church of St. Clotilde in Green Valley was incorporated November 14, 1912, as a new parish of the Diocese of Saint Paul. Archbishop John Ireland appropriately chose the name

after a sixth century French queen named St. Clotilde, because the saint was responsible for much of the growth of Catholicism in France, and the original twenty nine members of the new parish were predominately French.[207] Green Valley is an unincorporated community in Fairview Township, Lyon County, Minnesota. The community is sandwiched between the cities of Marshall and Cottonwood, near the junction of State Highway 23 and Lyon County Road 8.

St. Clotilde in Green Valley

Greenbush Township

Between 1860 and 1880, over 250 French-Canadians left Franklin County, New York and St. Regis, Quebec and settled in Greenbush Township, located near Princeton, Minnesota. They were referred to as the "French Settlement." They created a cemetery, and later a church called St. Frances de Chantal for worship. The Greenbush Catholic Cemetery still

St. Frances de Chantal Church

exists today but the church burned down in the 1950s. Some of the French-Canadian surnames who were part of this community are: Blair, Belair, Boisvert (Greenwood), Fredette, LaBissoniere, LaFantasie, Mailhot, Mallotte, Mallett, DesChamps, DuHaut, DeShaw, DesChamps, Shaw, Goulet, Grow, Gros, LeGros, LeGrow Garrow, Garreau, Jasmin, Jesmer, Mercier, Plamandon (Plumadore) Raiche, Robideau, Robidou Robideaux, Robidoux, Rabideau, Rocheford, Rubido, and Verboncoeur. St. Frances de Chantal Catholic Church was built in Greenbush in 1875, and was the only local Catholic Church until 1896 with the opening of St. Ed's in Princeton.[208]

[207] Holmquist, June Drenning, *They Chose Minnesota, a Survey of The State's Ethnic Groups*, Minnesota Historical Society Press (1981); Rubenstein, Sarah, "The French-Canadians and French," found in Holmquist, June Drenning, *They Chose Minnesota" a Survey of The State's Ethnic Groups*, Minnesota Historical Society Press (1981).
[208] Information obtained on Greenbush provided by Teresa Mercier, Circulation Services Supervisor, Hennepin County Library.

Hamel

St. Anne Church was established in Hamel by French-Canadians in 1879. The first church was built by the parishioners on land donated by J. O. Hamel, for whose family the village was named. It was constructed before the parish even had a priest, because the Archbishop had no one to send to care for the congregation. Missionaries served temporarily.

The existence of the church, in fact, was unknown to the Archbishop. The building was almost completed by the time the parish petitioned him for a pastor. That was in 1875. Four years later, the Archbishop appointed Father L. Chandonnet pastor of the Hamel Church, and the building was moved westward to newly acquired property.

St. Anne Church in Hamel

As soon as Father Chandonnet arrived, the parish built a house for him. Hamel was originally settled by French Catholics. A mile south, the Germans settled in the little village of Holy Name, with the church at its center. Nearby, the Irish had settled in Corcoran and built a church. There was also a settlement and a Catholic Church (St Joseph's) at Medicine Lake. However, the French in Hamel wanted a parish where sermons would be in French, so they decided to build a church of their own. Hamel had to wait four years for a pastor, but when one was finally appointed, they were so overjoyed that they made their church a show place with hand-made lumber, sacristy furniture and an altar lovingly carved by hand.

The little church of St. Anne survived until 1933 when it was razed to build the present brick building. Through time, Hamel changed from a French speaking village to an American small town.[209]

Henderson

French and French-Canadians were early settlers of Henderson, Minnesota in Sibley County. A section of Henderson, Minnesota, was known as "Frenchtown." In 1852, when Joseph Renshaw Brown arrived to purchase land in the area, he found three Frenchmen already there, namely Hyacinth (aka Jesse) Camirand, Numidique (aka Medic) Labissonnière, and Esdras Beliveau. They were all French-Canadians.[210] Jessenland Township just outside Henderson is said, by one story, to be named after Hyacinth "Jesse" Camirand.

---

[209] Taken *from an article entitled 75th Anniversary to be Celebrated by Saint Anne's at Hamel in Fall, Transcibed from "The Minnetonka Herald" newspaper dated August 12, 1954, Wayzata, Minnesota.*
[210] Sibley County Historical Society *Henderson Then and Now, in the Minnesota River Valley 1852-1994, 3rd edition,* published by the Sibley County Historical Society, 2005

Medic Labissonière's claim was filed February 16, 1856, for 160 acres in the NW ¼ of Section 2, but he and his wife Mary, née Jutras, later returned to Québec and are recorded in Arthabaska, Quebec in 1863. Numerous Beliveau families still live in the area. The Camirand name seems to have been Anglicized into Cameron; as is shown by the man named "Camerand (Cameron), Emanuel (Manuel)" in the index. Frenchtown was later platted as Camirand's Addition, but became known as Cameron's Addition.

In 1854, Dr. Hyppolite Joseph Seigneuret arrived in Henderson. He was born 1819 in France. He "had degrees in both Medicine and Law from Paris universities... and had edited a French political newspaper."[211] He was on the losing side of the French Revolution of 1848 and fled with his family to the Isle of Jersey in the English Channel. (Victor Hugo also lived in exile on Jersey after 1852.)

The Hyacinth Bisson family also came to Henderson from France by way of the Isle of Jersey. This family apparently had mechanical and engineering skills. Hyacinth Bisson owned the first flour mill in the area. His sons owned the steamer *Otter* on the Minnesota River. Bisson relatives from Geneva opened a jewelry store in 1876. There are numerous Bisson descendants in the area today.

Although there was a 'Frenchtown' and many prominent citizens were of French and French-Canadian background, today there is little French presence in Henderson. The community festival has long been Sauerkraut Days. French family names associated with Henderson are, Beaudette, Beliveau, Bigaouette, Bisson, Boudin, Buley, Cameron/Camirand, Carpenter, Chevalier, Denoir, Desilets, Durocher, Ethier, French, Gadbois (Gadbaw), Geronime, Gondreau, Goulet, Guibert, Hoyez, Jarvis, Lefto, LeMere, LeMire, Lovett, Maisonneuve, Manuel (Hebert dit Manuel), Moisan, Morell, Morissette, Norman, Peltier, Piquette (Pecket), Prudhomme, Pruden, St. Denis, Terrio (Terriot), Tousignant, Schouviller and Seigneuret. There was never a separate French-Catholic church in this community.

Hugo

In 1850, French immigrants and French-Canadians became the first permanent settlers of Hugo when the Lake Superior and Mississippi Railroad established a station called Centerville Station. It bypassed the already established city of Centerville. Early entrepreneurs were French natives Louis and Françoise Kuchli. They came to the area in 1872 and built a store, hotel, and "sample room," the first businesses in the village. St. John the Baptiste Church in Hugo was established in 1902 by French-Canadians.[212]

Family names in the 1850 territorial census which later appeared in the parish registers of St. Geneevieve of Paris at Centerville and St. John the Baptiste in Hugo included: Arcand, Asseline, Bernier, Bellanger, Bourdon, Bonin, Campbell, Carpentier, Cournoyer, Crevier, DeMars, Derosier, Dubois, Dupre, Durand, Faucher, Gadbois, Gagnon, Garneau, Gauthier, Goulet, Godin, Granger, Gregorie, Guerin, Houle, Jerome, LaBelle, LeBlanc, Lambert, Lacroix, Labore, Levasseur, LaPointe, Laderoute, Lavallee, LeRoux, Maheu,

---

[211] Id, page 279.
[212] See article on history of Hugo in Washington County History Guide.

Martelle, Martin, Morrissette, Moran, Morin, Mercier, Nadeau, Parent, Peltier, Pelkey, Pelletier, Perreault, Plant, Roy (King), Rondeau, St. Marin, Martin, and Thibault.[213] The 258 people in the area decided to incorporate in 1906. However, the post office requested the village be incorporated under a different name to avoid confusion between Centerville in Anoka County and Centerville Station in Washington County. The name Hugo was said to have been proposed by Michael Houle after the name "Houle" was rejected by the village. The story is that the town name honors the French author Victor Hugo.

St. John the Baptist Church in Hugo in 1947

Huot

Huot is an unincorporated community in Louisville Township, Red Lake County, Minnesota. The location of Huot was originally dubbed the "Old Crossing." In the 1840s and 1850s, this was a ford or crossing of the Red Lake River used by Red River ox cart trains en route from Pembina and Fort Garry in the Red River Colony to St. Paul, Minnesota. After negotiating the difficult and sometimes dangerous crossing, these cart trains typically camped overnight nearby, and the location became known as a regular stopping place on the "Woods Trail.

Old Crossing Treaty Park near Huot

A substantial French-Canadian farming community developed nearby in what later became Red Lake County. One of these settlers, Louis Huot, arrived from Quebec in 1876. He established a ferry at the Old Crossing, just below the Black River, in 1877. The resulting village site and surrounding Louisville Township both were named after Louis Huot. As the neighborhood was homesteaded by other farmers, the village grew to include St. Aloysius Catholic Church, a school, general store, a creamery (which later became the town hall) and a post office, as well as several homes. A bridge was built across the river, replacing the ferry, around 1900.

[213] Info obtained from St. Genevieve Council of Catholic Women, *Heritage Recipes and Historical Notes from Centerville and Hugo, Minnesota, a Collection of Recipes and Remembrances*, published 2013 by Morris Press Cookbooks.

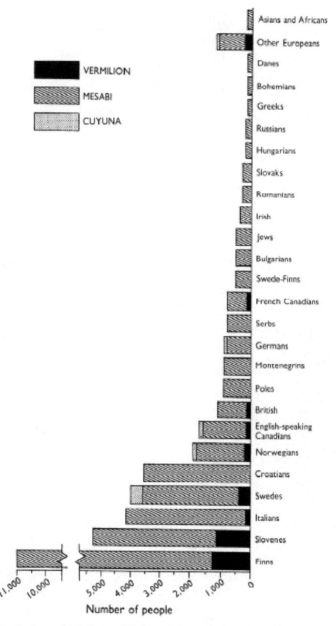

VERMILION

MESABI

CUYUNA

Asians and Africans
Other Europeans
Danes
Bohemians
Greeks
Russians
Hungarians
Slovaks
Romanians
Irish
Jews
Bulgarians
Swede-Finns
French Canadians
Serbs
Germans
Montenegrins
Poles
British
English-speaking Canadians
Norwegians
Croatians
Swedes
Italians
Slovenes
Finns

11,000 10,000 5,000 4,000 3,000 2,000 1,000 0

Number of people

*Foreign-born population on Minnesota's iron ranges, 1910. Source: Ethnicity
has been determined from listings of country of birth and mother tongue as
given in manuscript schedules for the 1910 federal census (see n. 46).*

**Graph showing ethic breakdown in Iron Range showing low percentage of French-Canadians
(Public Domain)**

International Falls

This area was well known to French speaking missionaries and voyageurs as early as the 17th century. International Falls was situated on "the "Voyageurs Highway" between Grand Portage and Winnipeg. Fur Trade centers were established here by French-Canadian voyageurs in the 1700's.

Iron Range

Many early French-Canadian settlers in Minnesota ended up in the Iron Range since jobs were available there. French-Canadians were present here early as French explorers and fur traders and remained after the fur trade era ended. After the Iron Range and North-eastern Minnesota were open to settlement, many different ethnic groups arrived, including: Slovenian, Croatian, Italian, Polish, Czech, Hungarian, German and Irish. There were parishes served by priests of Irish, Slovenian and sometimes French backgrounds. The chart below shows the breakdown of ethnic groups in 1910 with French-Canadians only a fraction of many other groups. The number of French-Canadians in Northeast Minnesota were small. A 1909 study of thirteen towns on the Mesabi Ranges showed only 875 French-Canadians out of a total population of 50,191.[214]

St. Genevieve Catholic Church

Lake Benton

There was an early French-Canadian settlement in Lake Benton, Minnesota. Second Generation French-Canadians from Marshall were prominent in the founding of St. Genevieve Catholic Church in 1897.[215]

St. Francis Xavier Church, Lambert 1899

Lambert

Alfonse F. Lambert and his wife, Cesarie, of Quebec, Canada, came to Lambert Township, Polk County, in 1881. Here they built their home in what was to become the Village of Lambert. Alfonse assisted in the organization of the new township that bears his name and was a leader in founding St. Francis Xavier Catholic Church. At one time, the village consisted of the church, a hotel, a blacksmith shop, a post office, four stores, and several homes. St. Francis Xavier Church was built in 1899, in Lambert Township

214 Rubenstein, Sarah, *The French-Canadians and French*, found in Holmquist, June Drenning, *They Chose Minnesota" a Survey of The State's Ethnic Groups* , Minnesota Historical Society Press (1981) p.45.
215 Rubenstein, Sarah, *The French-Canadians and French*, found in Holmquist, June Drenning, *They Chose Minnesota" a Survey of The State's Ethnic Groups* , Minnesota Historical Society Press (1981) p. 53.

under pastor Father J. Archambault. It was moved to Oklee in 1917. The Catholics around Lambert were formed into two distinct parishes in 1917. The territory in the east half became the Oklee parish.

Early picture of Lambert, Minnesota

Little Canada

Many of early French-Canadian settlers in Minnesota ended up migrating to the areas in present-day Little Canada, Dayton, and Osseo, Minnesota. The church of St. John the Evangelist was established by French-Canadians in 1852.

Benjamin Gervais was the first white man to claim land in Little Canada. After he left St. Paul in 1844 to build a cabin at Lake Gervais, a number of his fellow French-Canadians followed him to establish Little Canada in northern Ramsey County. In 1850, the French settlers erected a school with Eliza la Barre as its first teacher. Other French-Canadian names in early Little Canada were Auger, Auge, Barette, Beauchamp, Belland, Bernier, Bibeau, Bouvier, Cardinal, Charette, Clouette, Demers, Ducharme, Donais, Dupre, Flibotte, Forcier, Godbois, Gagne, Garceau, Gervai, Ciroux, Gobin, Guerin, Houle, Labore, Labonne, Lalancette, Lambert, Landroche, Langliere, Langevin, Langlois, Lapointe, Lemay, Hamelin, Loiselle, Millette, Mingo dit Dumaine, Melancon, Moosbrugger, Morisette, Nadeau, Parenteau, Pariseau, Patrin, Paul, Peltier, Pepin, Papin, Perron, Perry/Perret, Picard, Plouffe, Racine, Rioux, Rivard dit Dufresne, Rondeau, Ste-Marie, St. Martin, Sempere, Theroux, Tereau, Therrien, Thibault, Vadnais, Vandale, Vanney, and Vincent.
Al Dahlquist has written a book titled "Little Canada's First Generation French-Canadian Settlers and their Ancestors." This book lists the ancestors of all the above original settlers of Little Canada. This book is available on the French-American Heritage Foundation website.

St. John the Evangelist
Little Canada- 1851

Little Falls

The French were in Morrison County and the Little Falls area during the fur trading era. One of the first French-Canadian settlers of Little Falls was Martin Bisson, who was born in 1790 in Maskinonge, Quebec. He was employed by the Northwest Company and when the fur trade ended, he moved back to Quebec and purchased a farm. When Minnesota opened for settlement, however, he sold his farm and returned to Belle Prairie with his neighbors, John Branchaud and Theodore Bellefeuille.

Other early settlers from Quebec who came to Morrison County were Peter Picotte (from Louisville, Quebec) Charles Chartier, Michel Heroux, Michel Ledoux, Wilfrid and Ludger Dugas, Joseph Doucette, Charles Lamontagne, Felix Bastien, Narcisse Grael, Louis Hamlin, Joseph Fournier, David Morin, Cyriaque Dufort, Czias Roy, Alec Riendeau, William and Alfred Racicot, Elie Paquin, Eusebe Monchamp, Calixte Vallee, Frank Thiebault, Joseph Dugal, Joseph, Antoine, and Leo Boisjoli, Moses Lafond, and Periche Roy. Both Moses Lafond and Periche Roy were elected to the Minnesota Legislature. Representative Periche Roy is claimed to have helped Joseph Rolette hide the bill that proposed moving the State Capital to St. Peter.

St. Francis Xavier Church in Little Falls

The church of St. Francis Xavier in Little Falls was a French Catholic Church started for the French-Canadian immigrants who settled there.

Another early prominent French-Canadian who settled in Little Falls was William Butolier. He came to Little Falls in 1855 and anglicized his name to William Butler. He was

William Butler Building (Butolier) in Little Falls

listed as Butolier in the 1857 Minnesota Territorial Census but as Butler in the 1860 Census.[216] Another Little Falls resident who anglicized his name was Joseph Le Mieux listed as Joseph Better in the 1857 Census and later as Joseph Batters in the 1865 Census. William Butler (aka William Butolier) is known for his commercial interest and his Butler building in Little Falls.

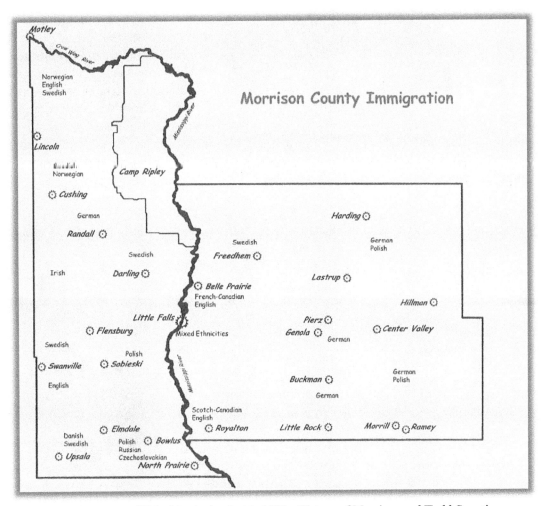

Above is a map published in the book titled "The History of Morrison and Todd Counties, Minnesota, Their People, Industries and Institutions" by Clara K. Fuller

[216] Minnesota Cenus Records MNTC57, MC60,MnSC65 and MC70. Also Richardson, "History" 18, interview by Linda and Peavy and Billy Batters Bennett, Little Falls, March 26, 1988). See also Rubenstein, Sarah, *The French-Canadians and French*, found in Holmquist, June Drenning, *They Chose Minnesota" a Survey of The State's Ethnic Groups* , Minnesota Historical Society Press (1981) pp. 36-54.

Louisville

French language newspapers in 1895 claimed that there were ninety French-Canadian families in Louisville, which is located in Red Lake County. Below is a picture of the Louisville Church which was also the Huot church.

Louisville Church

Marshall

Marshall, the county seat of Lyon County, received an infusion of French-Canadians after 1895, some from the town of Bourbonnais, Illinois. In the mid-1890s, an historian of Holy Redeemer Catholic Parish noted that of the one hundred families in the church, forty were French or Belgian, and it was thought at that time that Marshall would become a predominately French town. However, other ethic groups soon overwhelmed the French-Canadians. A French school was started and staffed by the French nuns of the Sisters of St. Joseph of Carondelet.[217] The Sisters operated the parish's educational system from 1900 to 1996, including a small elementary school until the early 1950s, when it was replaced by a modern elementary and high school.

Medicine Lake

A group of French-Canadian settlers organized the Church of St. Joseph in Medicine Lake in 1856. That is when this Catholic community celebrated its first Mass in a tiny log cabin just off the shores of Medicine Lake. St. Joseph's began as a mission parish for mostly French-Canadian settlers and was officially named St. Francis. Mass was celebrated only once a month. The log church was a mere 24 by 32 feet, but was large enough to house the congregation for almost twenty years.[218]

Medicine Lake's First Catholic Church
As shown on website of St. Joseph's parish

Church of Holy Redeemer in Marshall

[217] Rubertus, Donald, *History of the Holy Redeemer Catholic Church, 1869-1916, Marshall*, typescript, 1956, in Southwest Minnesota Historical Center, Marshall, copy in MEHP Papers.
[218] Rubenstein, Sarah, *The French-Canadians and French*, found in Holmquist, June Drenning, *They Chose Minnesota" a Survey of The State's Ethnic Groups*, Minnesota Historical Society Press (1981)

Medina

A group of French-Canadian settlers established farms in the northeast section of Medina prior to 1868. Older maps of Medina show a town call Lenz located at the junction of two Indian trails: the north/south trail from Shakopee to the junction of the Crow and Mississippi River (roughly County Road 101) and the east/west trail that later became Rockford Road. Rockford Road was the main street through town. Medina probably received its name from Leonard Lenzen, who built a mill on Elm Creek and set up the post office on 5 Jan 1861. The area had been settled by French-Canadians who had spread from the Osseo and Medicine Lake areas that had been settled a couple years prior. The town boasted several businesses: Authier's Shoes, Beaupre's Wagon Works and the Huot Grist Mill among them. St Anne's Catholic Church was founded on

St. Anne Catholic Church in Medina

land donated by J. O. Hamel in 1875. The local French-Canadian Catholic population did not feel comfortable in the German speaking churches at Holy Name or Loretto or at the Irish church in Corcoran. The first full time priest arrived in 1879. That same year, the church was improved and a rectory was built. The current church was built in 1933.[219]

Mendota

Mendota is a city in Dakota County, Minnesota. The name is derived from the Dakota language, meaning "mouth or junction of one river with another." The town was one of the first permanent settlements in the state of Minnesota, being founded around the same time

Father A. Ravoux
Minn Historical Society

as Fort Snelling. In its early days, the settlement was known as St Pierre or St. Peter and French was the primary language spoken. It houses a small museum which used to be the Hypolite Dupuis house, the Henry Hastings Sibley house, the Faribault house, and buildings associated with the American Fur Company, all dating from the 1830s. The church of St. Peter's in Mendota was established in 1842 by French-Canadians and Fa-

St. Peter's Church in Mendota
Built in 1853

ther Lucien Galtier. At first mass was performed in a small log chapel. After Father Galtier left, Father Ravoux took over as pastor and had a limestone church constructed in 1853 which still stands today.

219 Scherer, Bill, *History of Medina*, published in Western Hennepin County Pioneers Association, Volume 158/Spring 2013.

Mendota in 1848, by Seth Eastman (Public Domain)

Minneapolis

The Church of St. Clotilde was established as a French church in 1884 and was later re-named to the Church of St. Anne. The parish named in honor of St. Clotilde was the eighth oldest in Minneapolis. St. Clotilde was formed to meet the needs of French-Canadian immigrants. The first St. Clotilde Church was a frame building purchased from a Protestant congregation and was replaced by a brick church in 1886, at the corner of 11th Street and Lyndale Avenue North. Some of the French names associated with the church were Marsolais, Deschene, Faubert, Joncas, Gagnon, Jasmine, Chouninard, Dubay, Laramee, Labreche, Saucier, Valiere, Trepanier and LeGardeur.

St. Anne Church in 1886

St. Clotilde Church at 11th & Lyndale Ave North

In 1899, the church was destroyed by fire and the Parish of St. Clotide declared itself bankrupt. As a result, Archbishop John Ireland ordered the dissolution of the Parish of St. Clotide and in its place established the Parish of St. Anne. St. Anne became the parochial church of all French-Canadians who lived in the neighborhood then known as West Minneapolis. Today, we know it to be the North Side. The first pastor of St. Anne was Father LeGardeur who welcomed 373 French-Canadian families as members of the new parish.

St. Anne Church at Queen Ave and 26th Ave North

The Parish of St. Anne prospered for a time as a French speaking parish but eventually transitioned to English. In 1922, it moved to its present location at the corner of Queen Avenue and 26th Avenue North. Over time, it eventually lost its association with being a French-Canadian church.

Our Lady of Lourdes Church in St. Anthony Main sits perched on a hill high above the St. Anthony Falls. It was originally built as a Universalist church in 1857 when that side of the river was still the village of St. Anthony. In 1877, it was pur chased by the French-Canadian Catholics who converted it to a French Gothic Revival structure. Most of these French-Canadians were from the St. Anthony of Padua Parish who were overwhelmed by the Irish Catholics and wanted to have their own parish and services in their native language.

Also in Minneapolis is a French-Lebanese community including members of the Maronite Catholic churches in both St. Paul and Minneapolis. The Maronite community started as a monastic community in the Monastery of St Maron on the Orontes River in Syria, but considerably grew and sought refuge from persecution in the Mountains of Lebanon. Lebanon's French roots date back to the mandate which assigned Ottoman Syria, including modern day Lebanon, to France after the First World War in 1923. French remains the primary foreign language taught in public schools in Lebanon, and much of the French influence remains today. The first Lebanese who came to Minnesota did not speak

Our Lady of Lourdes Church
(Public Domain)

French, but after the 1920's, many of those who came to Minnesota did, and even today, many speak French.

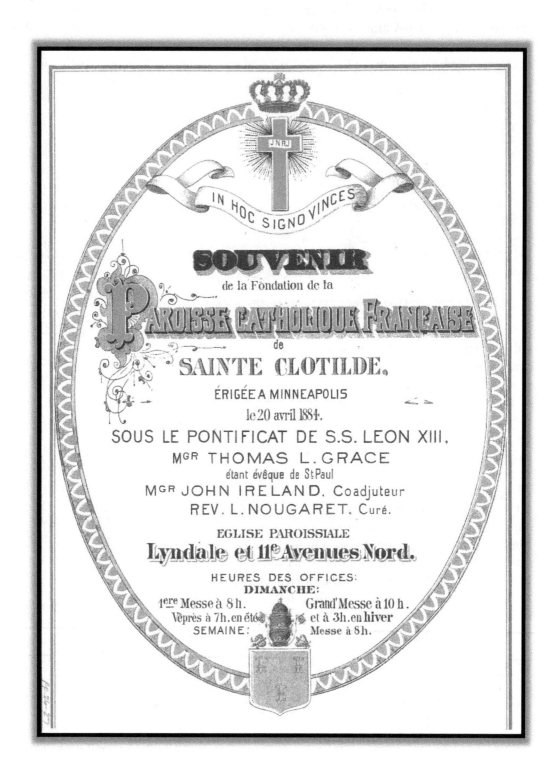

Minnesota River Valley

Along the Minnesota River Valley, French-Canadians settled at Henderson and Jessenland in Sibley County in the 1850s. By the following decade, they could be found in counties to the west of Glencoe, including Helen Township, Hutchinson and Rocky Run (just west of Winsted) in McLeod County and Roseville Township in Kandiyohi County. The French-Canadian population in these areas were sparce and many of their children eventually left for the Twin Cities.[220]

St. Francis Xavier Church in Oklee

Oklee

Oklee is a city in Red Lake County, Minnesota, on Minnesota State Highway 222. The Church of St. Francis Xavier was established by French-Canadians and moved from Lambert Township to Oklee in 1917. Father Pierre Champagne first ministered to this church.

Oakwood, North Dakota

Oakwood, North Dakota is near the Minnesota border and it's French-Canadian population mixed freely with people in Minnesota. Oakwood was first settled by Joseph Charpentier who immigrated from the French settlement in Corcoran, Minnesota. In 1878, and for years following, many French-Canadians settled in the Oakwood area. Some names found in this community are: Boivin, Bourcier, Boutin, Brunelle, Chaponneau, Collette, Desautels, Dechenes, Donelly, French, Girard, Goulet, Huard, LaBerge, LaBonte, LaChappele, LaRoche, Lessard, McLernan, Parent, Patenaude, Pellant, Poole, Suprenant, Bellegrade, Bolduc, Courure, Demers, Faille, Fortier, Lacoste, Lamarre, Garant, Sabourin, Savard, Sevigny, Soucy, Suprenant, Vary. The community built a church called The Church of the Sacred Heart (see right) and in 1906, St. Aloysius Academy was founded at

[220] Rubenstein, Sarah, *The French-Canadians and French,* found in Holmquist, June Drenning, *They Chose Minnesota" a Survey of The State's Ethnic Groups,* Minnesota Historical Society Press (1981).

Oakwood.[221] Sisters of St. Mary of the Presentation, whose mother house wsa located in Broons, Cotes du Nord, France, taught classes there.

St. Aloysis Academy in Oakwood, North Dakota

Osseo

Osseo was first marked for settlement in July 1852 by Pierre Bottineau and his traveling companions. The area would become known as the "Bottineau Prairie." In 1854, Warren Sampson, Isaac Labissonniere, Clark Ellsworth, Senaca Brown, D.B. Thayer, and James McRay settled on "Bottineau Prairie." The years 1855-1856 saw much growth, and in 1856, the settlement was renamed Osseo, and platted by Sampson and Issac Labissonniere. It is said that Osseo is a Native American name, "Waseia," meaning "there is light" although more commonly known as "Son of the Evening Star." The author Henry W. Longfellow mentions Osseo in one of his Native American legends contained in his poem "The Song of Hiawatha." It is also claimed that Longfellow visited Osseo while in St. Anthony. The Church of St. Vincent de Paul in Osseo was established in 1855 by French-Canadians. In 1864, a second church was built. This facility was built on Main Street Osseo on land donated by Peter Gervais. As the parish grew, the sanctuary was enlarged and a

Second St. Vincent de Paul Church, Osseo

---

[221] Information obtained from Centennial Book of Sacred Heart Church, published 1981.

sacristy was added in 1880. A new steeple was added in 1890 to house the existing bell that had been purchased in the year 1865.[222] The first doctor to make his home in Osseo was Dr. A. Guernon, a French-Canadian, who came to Osseo in 1866.

Red Lake Falls

Red Lake Falls is yet another French-Canadian settlement. It is located near the Red Lake and Clearwater Rivers. These rivers provided habitat for a wide range of wildlife and was a successful location for a fur trading post. In 1798, Jean Baptiste Cadotte Jr. established a trading post near the junction of the two rivers in the present-day site of Sportsmen's Park in Red Lake Falls.

As oxcarts began crossing the area while transporting goods between St. Paul and Selkirk or River Colony (Winnipeg), the "old crossing" of the Red River near Huot became a place of historical importance. At this site in 1863, a peace treaty was signed between the Red Lake and Pembina bands of the Chippewa Indians and the U.S. Government. This treaty ceded to the United States nearly eleven million acres of some of the most fertile land in the world.

Original St. Vincent de Paul Church

St. Joseph's Church in Red Lake

In 1876, the famous Métis guide, Pierre Bottineau, is credited by his efforts with bringing the first settlers to the area, one hundred nineteen families of French-Canadian descent, who founded the towns of Red Lake Falls and Gentilly. Settlers of European descent followed, attracted by the same waters that enticed the Indians and trappers before them. Newspapers of the time advertised the abundant supply of water power provided by the two rivers.[223] The French-Canadian settlers established St. Joseph's Catholic Church in Red Lake Falls.

Red Lake Indian Reservation

The Red Lake Indian Reservation is located in northern Minnesota counties of Beltrami and Clearwater, approximately thirty miles north of

---

[222] Excerpts from 100 Year History of the City of Osseo.
[223] Taken from Red Lake Falls Visitor Information Guide.

Bemidji. Fur trading brought the Ojibwe into contact with French-Canadians which resulted in inter-marriage between them. During the Seven Years War, otherwise known as the French and Indian War, the Ojibwe allied with the French against the English. After this war, the Ojibwe continued to mainain their fur trade as well as family associations with the French-Canadians. The Red Lake Nation has a website that provides more information about these connections. The Red Lake Band, through treaties and agreements in 1863 (amended in 1864), 1889, 1892, 1904, and 1905, gave up land but never ceded the main reservation surrounding the Lower Red Lake and a portion of Upper Red Lake. This unceded land is spoken of as the "diminished" reservation and "aboriginal" land. It is 407,730 acres. Today you find many members of the Red Lake Tribe who can trace their ancestry back to the French-Canadians. A look at the 1940 Red Lake Census reveals many French-Canadian names, including: Moreau, Durand, Beaulieu, Bellanger, Lussier, Gervais, Perrault, Hebert, Jourdain, Roy, Desjarlais, Petite, Bedeau, Nedeau, Defoe, Lajeunesse, Benoise, Nadeau, Garneau, Sylvestre, Michaud, Frenchman, French, and Martin.

Red River Valley

The first European explorer to reach the Red River Valley was the French voyageur, Pierre Gaultier de Varennes, Sieur de La Verendrye. He reached the Red River in 1732 and established a series of posts in the area, including Fort Rouge on the present site of Winnipeg. He called it the Red River because of the reddish-brown silt it carries. The French trade cut severely into Hudson's Bay Company profits at its post by the bay and forced the company to expand inland.

Minnesota Historical Society Collections

The first permanent settlement by Europeans in the Red River Basin was founded on the banks of the Red River near the mouth of the Assiniboine River (in present-day Manitoba). The Red River Settlement colony, who's official name was Assiniboia, was founded in 1811-12 by the Earl of Selkirk, who purchased a land grant from the Hudson's Bay Company of 116,000 square miles in the Red and Assiniboine River valleys.

The Red River Valley below the 49 degree of North Latitude became a part of the United States by treaty with Great Britain after the War of 1812. Pembina became an important hunting and trading center and a major link in the transportation network which developed between St. Paul and the "lower" Red River Basin. There were trails along both sides of the river to carry products to the Selkirk Settlement or to St. Paul.

The flat plains and uniquely designed ox carts made it much easier and cheaper to supply the Red River Valley settlements from Minnesota than from eastern Canada. In the early 1800s, supplies were shipped on trails from St. Paul, via St. Anthony to Fort Garry and other Red River Valley settlements. The earliest trail led south along the Red River from Pembina to Lake Traverse and followed the Minnesota River southeastward. By 1850, hundreds of carts were making the trip each year. The Red River ox carts were built entirely of wood. Though crudely made and inherently noisy because of the wheels' screeching on the wooden axles, the carts provided effective transportation. The boxlike body of the cart, resting on the wooden axle, rode high, making the fording of streams easier. A single ox could pull a cart with a load of eight or nine hundred pounds.

Minnesota became a state in 1858. Its western boundaries were cut back from the Missouri River to the Red River. The fur trade declined, but the Homestead Act of 1862 was passed by the U.S. Congress, giving title to 160 acres of unoccupied public land to each homesteader on payment of a nominal fee and required five years of residence. This legislation opened up the Valley to a flood of pioneers who transitioned to wheat farming.

In 1871, railroads reached the Red River from St. Paul and Duluth, Minnesota, providing a vital trade link between the Valley and St. Paul, and further opening the basin to settlement. The railroads influenced development of the Red River Valley by selling vast acres of railroad lands, and by promoting and advertising it's attributes.[224]

Saint Anthony (Saint Antoine)

The Church of St. Anthony of Padua, located at Main Street and 9th Ave NE, was founded by a group of French-Canadians in 1849 under leadership of pioneer priest Father Ravoux. In November 1853, Sisters Philomene Vilaine and Ursula Murpsh were sent to open a school in St. Anthony Falls, the only town in the Minnesota Territory besides St. Paul that had a resident priest, namely Father Ledon, a Frenchman. The congregation, at that time, consisted of primarily French-Canadians which included a large Métis population. [225] The sisters began a school in an old frame house that had been the property of fur traders.[226]

Some of the names associated with the early church were Cloutur, Poncin, Crepan, Huot, Crepeau, Martin, Lapointe, Blais, Rainville, Menard, and Boutin. Pierre Bottineau donated fourteen lots

St. Anthony of Padua Church in 1860's

[224] Cooper, C.F. & Company, History of the Red River Valley, Volume II, Chicago 1909.
[225] Picture of Oxcarts above from Minneapolis Historical Collections, Minneapolis Public Library.
[226] Savage, Sister Mary Lucida PhD, *The Congregation of Saint Joseph of Carondolet*, Second Edition, Published by B. Herder Book Co. 1927; p. 89.

for the building of the church. The French members were soon outnumbered by incoming Irish and left to join our Lady of Lourdes, which is located in present-day Minneapolis.

Oxcarts in St. Anthony heading east around 1855.
Minnesota Historical Society Collections

Saint Boniface

The Saint Boniface Church in Northeast Minneapolis in 2015 was home to a French speaking Haitian group. They said French Mass every Sunday at noon. In 2015, Father Jules Omalanga was the pastor in residence of this parish and Bishop Lee A. Piché was the Parochial Administrator. Chapter twelve of this book discusses this French speaking African community.

St. Boniface Catholic Church
Photo by Mark Petty

Saint Paul

The first settlers in St. Paul were French-Canadians. In 1841, they built a chapel near the intersection of Kellogg Boulevard and Minnesota Street. Father Lucian Galtier was the

missionary priest who helped direct the building of this chapel.[227] Eight French-Ca-nadians built this first chapel. These men were as follows: Issac Labissoniere, Joseph Labisoniere, Pierre Gervais and Pierre Ger-vais (most likely Benjamin Gervais and Pierre Gervais[228]) Pierre Bottineau, Charles Bottineau, Francois Morin, and Vetal (Vi-tal) Guerin.[229], The Saint Paul chapel was built in a week and completed in October 1841. It was named Saint Paul which com-plimented the name of the church built at Mendota called Saint Peter.

Saint Paul Chapel
Painting by Alexis Jean Fournier
Minnesota Historical Society Collections

---

[227] Catholic Historical Society of St. Paul, "Obituary of Issac Labissoniere," in *Acta et Dicta*, Vol. III, No. 1, (July 1911) p. 188.

[228] No records exist that support the contention that there were two Pierre Gervais's who lived in St. Paul at the time the log chapel was built. Historians who have studied this believe that the two Gervais who built the chapel were brothers, Pierre and Benjamin. This makes sense since they both donated land for the chapel. Pierre Gervais was the younger brother of Ben Gervais, who is credited with being the first white man to settle in Little Canada, Minnesota. See Scholberg, Henry, *The French Pioneers of Minnesota (Les Pionniers Francais du Minnesota)* Northstar Publications Minnesota, 1995, p. 65

[229] *Acta et Dicta*, Vol. 1, No. 1.

The presence of the Catholic Church in St. Paul attracted Catholic settlers, especially the Irish, whose numbers quickly overwhelmed the Francophone makeup of the early church. By 1868, the French-Canadians had abandoned the cathedral parish and established the Church of St. Louis, King of France. A parish school, the Ecole St. Louis, provided education in French from its founding in 1873 until the 1960s. In Minneapolis, a French parish, Notre Dame de Lourdes, was established in 1877 with a parochial school operating from 1888 to 1959.[230]

St. Paul Chapel built in 1841 by French-Canadians later became the St. Paul Cathedral when Father Cretin was named the first Bishop of Minnesota. There would be three other cathedrals built, with the last one sitting on the bluff overlooking St. Paul. Below is a picture of the third St. Paul Cathedral.

King Louis, King of France Church

The third St. Paul Cathedral build by Bishop Cretin around 1860.
The first mass in this Cathedral was celebrated June 13, 1858.[231]
Minnesota Historical Society Collections

[230] Gitlin, Jay, *The Bourgeois Frontier: French Towns, French Traders, and American Expansion*, Yale University Press (2010), notes to pages 177-179.
[231] Trimble, Steve, *Historic Photos of St. Paul*, Text and Captions by Steve Trimble, published in 2008 by Turner Publishing company.

Saint Vincent/Pembina

Saint Vincent is located just across the river from Pembina and shares its early French speaking history. This area was long inhabited by various indigenous peoples, including the Lakota (Sioux, as the French called them), the Chippewa (Ojibwe), and the Assiniboine.

The North West Company built a fur trade post at the Saint Vincent site on the east side of the Red River between 1784 and 1789. This post disappeared by 1801.[232] Later the Hud-

son's Bay Company built a small post in Saint Vincent on the east side of the Red River in 1801. French speaking fur traders and their mixed blood descendants known as Metis lived in this area which became known as the Red River Settlement. The Metis from the Red River Settlement became famous for their involvement in the Red River Ox Cart Trails and the large buffalo hunts.

Red River Settlement at Pembina
Published in *Harper's Monthly* in 1860 (Public Domain)

Red River Métis on Buffalo Hunt[233] **Created in 1860 and published in Harper's Monthly** (Public Domain)

---

[232] Halpenny, Francess G. and Hamelin, Jean *Dictionary of Canadian Biography, 1836-1850.* Springer Science & Business Media, (1 January 1988). p. 356
[233] From Whitney's Gallery St. Paul Collection.

Fort Daer of the Hudson Bay Company on the left and old Fort Pembina built by the Northwest Company on the right. The Pembina River is in the center. (Painted by Peter Rindisbacher in 1822). (Public Domain)

Somerset, Wisconsin

The Catholic Church in Somerset was first called St. Vincent de Paul of Somerset but was later changed to St. Anne.[234] A large French-Canadian population settled in Somerset, and although it is not in Minnesota, many descendants of these Somerset French-Canadians ended up in Minnesota.

Stillwater

St. Joseph Parish in Stillwater was established by French-Canadians in 1882. It closed in 1959 and merged with St. Michael Parish.

St. Annes in Somerset

---

[234] *Somerset, Wisconsin: 125 pioneer families and Canadian connection: 125th year,* from The State of Wisconsin Digital Collection (1984).

Terrebonne

French-Canadians from Montreal founded Terrebonne in the spring of 1879. They established the church called St. Anthony of Padua and built their first church building in 1882. In 1895, French language newspapers reported 633 French-Canadians in Terrebonne, located in Red Lake County. [235] The church of St. Anthony was closed in the year 2000. [236]

Tower

In 1884, a Roman Catholic mission church was established in Tower, Minnesota. It was made up of Irish, Germans, Italians and French-Canadians

St. Anthony Church and Parsonage in Terrebonne

St. Joseph's of Stillwater

for a total of 120 members. The French-Canadians were among the first to settle in the Iron Range, but their numbers were generally small when compared to the other ethnic groups.[237]

Two Harbors

At Two Harbors, some of the first settlers were French-Canadian. Early priests were French, but the settlement was predominately Scandinavian. At the corner of Highway 61 and Stanley Road in Two Harbors, "Pierre the Voyageur" stands overlooking the town. A picture of Pierre the Voyageur is shown to the left.

---

[235] Holmquist, June Drenning, *They Chose Minnesota" a Survey of The State's Ethnic Groups*, Minnesota Historical Society Press (1981) p.43.
[236] Picture of St. Anthony Church and Parsonage taken from Red Lake County History website at redlakecountyhistory.org.
[237] Congressional Series of United States Public Documents, Volumne 5677.

Wabasha

Pierre the Voyageur in Two Harbors

Wabasha is one of the oldest cities on the entire upper Mississippi River and has been occupied continuously since 1826.[238][239] U.S. Government records and "The 2nd Treaty of Prairie du Chien" (1830) establishes Wabasha to be the oldest city in Minnesota, established 1830. Wabasha was named in honor of an Indian Chief of the Dakota Nation, Chief Wa-pa-shaw. In 1850, the population of the whole county of Wabasha was 243. Nearly all of the old French traders who settled here had married Dakota wives. In 1837, the government set apart 450 square miles of territory for the benefit of these so called half-breeds. The land extended fifteen miles back and thirty miles on the river, from a point three miles below Wabasha to Mdewakanton village of Red Wing. In 1857, the French fur trader mixed-bloods and their families each received 480 acres of land scrip from the government in exchange for their reserve land. Some ten or twelve French fur traders settled at Wabasha, and received scrip for their wives and families.

The Catholics built a small log church as early as 1845; which was afterwards used as a printing office. The city was first platted in 1854, in the name of Oliver Craft and Joseph Buison.[240] St. Felix Catholic Church was built in Wabasha on land that Augustin Rocque donated in 1862. It was named after the pastor's patron saint.

St. Felix Catholic Church in Wabasha

[238] Upham, Warren, *Minnesota Geographic Names, Their Origin and Historic Significance*, Minnesota Historical Society, 1920

[240] Andreas, A.T., *An Illustrated Historical Atlas of the State of Minnesota*, published by A.T. Andreas, 1874.

Warroad

In Warroad, French services at the local Catholic Church were held in the early days.[241] Warroad is the site of St. Mary's Church, also called the Father Aulneau Memorial Church, which commemorates a French Catholic priest who accompanied French explorers and soldiers in their search for the Northwest Passage and was killed, along with several other people, presumably by Native Americans. The history of St. Mary's has been traced to 1732, when the first Mass in the St. Mary's Parish territory was offered on Magusson Island in Lake of the Woods by the French Priest, Father Charles Mesaiger. When Father Masaiger became ill, he was replaced by Father Jean-Pierre Aulneau in 1735. Father Aulneau and twenty members of his expedition were killed in June of 1736. The Aulneau Peninsula in Lake of the Woods is named after Father Aulneau.

Father Aulneau Memorial Church n Warroad

Waverly

Many early settlers of Waverly were French-Canadians who established farms there, but the population was never enough to establish their own French speaking church.

---

241 *"History of the Red River Valley : past and present, including an account of the counties, cities, towns, and villages of the Valley from the time of their first settlement and formation.* Written by various writers, published by C.F. Cooper & Company, Chicago, (1909) 2:265.

White Bear Lake

The Church of St. Mary of the Lake was established by French-Canadians in White Bear Lake in 1881. The French-Canadian Catholics who helped start the St. Mary's parish generally came from Little Canada. The services were held in French for the first five years.

St. Mary of the Lake

White Earth Reservation

Beaulieu Township within the Mahnomen County portion of the reservation was named after families of French-Canadian and Indian descent who owned farms there after the Civil War. French-Canadian family names can still be found in this area.[242] An example of some of the names found are Beaulieu, Bellecourt, Brunette, St. Clair, Dufault, LaDuke, and Trotochaud.

Wild Rice, North Dakota

St. Benedict Church, Wild Rice Settlement

The first French farming community in North Dakota was the settlement at Wild Rice in Cass County, located on land near the junction of the Red River and the Wild Rice River. This settlement was located just across the Red River from Minnesota.[243] The first settlers to this community arrived in 1869. Many of the French-Canadians who settled here were from Trois Rivieres in Quebec. The original settler was Ulphi Cossette. Other family names were Morin, Dorval, Hebert, Denis, DuBord, Richard, Trottier, Pronovost, Brunette, Fugere, Rheault, Tessier, Brunelle, Duval, Belemar, Lajoie, Monplasir, Bailly, Grandbois and Rivard. St. Benedict Church became the center of this Wild Rice community.

---

[242] Rubenstein, Sarah, "The French-Canadians and French," found in Holmquist, June Drenning, *They Chose Minnesota" a Survey of The State's Ethnic Groups*, Minnesota Historical Society Press (1981).
[243] Sherman, William C. and Thorson, Playford V. editors, *Plains Folk, North Dakota's Ethnic History*, part of North Dakota Centennial Heritage Series, published by The North Dakota Institute for Regional Studies at North Dakota State University, 1986

Chapter Eight
French Influence on Education in Minnesota
By Mark Labine

Arrival of first Ursuline Nuns in Quebec in 1639
(Public Domain)

The French were very involved and instrumental in setting up schools and providing education in Minnesota in the 1800s. The French speaking Sisters of St. Joseph of Carondolet started the first school in St. Paul on November 7, 1851. [244] They went on to provide instruction and administration to numerous schools in Minnesota through the years. This chapter lists some of the schools and French religious orders that made a contribution to education progression in Minnesota.

In addition to the orders listed below in this chapter, there were numerous other French religious orders in the United States and Canada that provided educational opportunities in other states, including the following:

Congregation de Notre-Dame de Montréal, Filles de Marie (France), Sœurs de Ste-Croix de Montréal, Sœurs de la Providence de Montréal, Sœurs de la Présentation de Marie de St-Hyacinthe, Sœurs de Ste-Anne de Lachine, Sœurs Grises de Montréal, Sœurs de la Merci, Sœurs Grises d'Ottawa, Sœurs de l'Assomption, Sœurs du Bon Pasteur de Québec, Sœurs Dominicaines, Sœurs Franciscaines Missionaires de Marie, Sœurs Grises de St-Hyacinthe, Sœurs de Jésus-Marie de Sillery, Ursulines des Trois Rivières, Congrègation Notre-Dame (Villa Maria), Sœurs de la Sainte Union des Sacrés-Cœurs, Sœurs du Saint-Esprit, Sœurs du Saint-Rosaire, Filles de la Sagesse, Petites Sœurs des Pauvres, Sœurs de St-Joseph (Le Puy), Sœurs du Sacré-Cœur, Sœurs de St-Joseph (Chambéry), Sœurs Servantes du Cœur Immaculé de Marie, les Fidèles Compagnes de Jésus, Sœurs du Bon Pasteur (Angers), Petites Sœurs Franciscaines de Marie (Malbaie), Dames de Sion, Frères de Ia Charitè de St-Vincent de Paul, twenty seven members; Frères Maristes d'Iberville; Frères de St-Gabriel; Frères des Ecoles Chrétiennes; Frères du Sacré-Cœur.

---

[244] The painting of the arrival of first Ursuline nuns is from the Hôtel-Dieu, Quebec. Painted by Masselotte, 1911.

Belle Prairie's Academy of St. Anthony

The Franciscan Sisters operated the Convent and Academy of St. Anthony in Belle Prairie, Minnesota and taught all classes in French for a number of years. The French language was used in some services in Belle Prairie's Holy Family Catholic Church until World War II.[245]

Brothers of the Holy Family

The Institute of the Brothers of the Holy Family was founded in the diocese of Belley in France by Brother Gabriel Taborin Ponce. It is a religious Institute of Brothers, dedicated to the service of Catholic parishes and villages, in tasks such as teacher acquisition, and catechist instruction. When Bishop Cretin became Bishop in St. Paul, he brought the Brothers of the Holy Family to Minnesota to aid in the education of his diocese.

Academy of St. Anthony

**Gabriel Taborin Ponce
Founder of Brothers of
Holy Family**

Crosier Fathers and Brothers

The Order was founded in 1210 by Blessed Theodore de Celles and companions in France. The name Crosier is derived from the French word croisés which means "signed with the cross." In medieval England, Crosiers were known as the Crutched (crossed) Friars. This designation refers to the cross and the spirituality of the Order. Theodore and four companions came from Liège in Belgium and formed a community near the city of Huy called Clairlieu.

The primary feast day of the Crosiers, the Exaltation of the Holy Cross, reflects a spirituality focused on the triumphant cross of Christ and our glorified Lord. A distinctive mark of the Crosiers is the red and white crusader's cross worn on the scapular of their religious habit.

The Crosier Community of Onamia, Minnesota is a center for Crosier religious life. This Crosier Community has been an important part of Crosier presence in the United States since the Order came over from Europe more than a century ago. Its members serve in a variety of ministries, working as parish priests, retreat leaders, and jail ministers, and the community is home to the Crosiers in formation.

---

[245] Holy Family Church Files located in St. Cloud Visitor Office, St. Cloud.

Cretin-Derham High School

Cretin-Derham Hall High School is a private, co-educational Catholic high school located in Saint Paul, Minnesota. Located in the Roman Catholic Archdiocese of Saint Paul and Minneapolis, it is co-sponsored by the Brothers of the Christian Schools and the Sisters of St. Joseph of Carondelet. Cretin High School was named after Joseph Crétin, the first Roman Catholic Bishop of Saint Paul. Derham is named for Hugh Derham, a Minnesotan farmer who donated money to start an all-female Catholic boarding school.

Cretin-Derham High School

Christian Brothers

The Midwest District is one of four districts in the Lasallian Region of North America, also known as the Région Lasallienne de l'Amérique du Nord (RELAN). RELAN is comprised of Lasallian ministries in the United States and Canada. The Midwest District encompasses eight states and includes three universities, fifteen high schools, five middle schools, four retreat centers, two publishing houses, and one Provincialate office. Within the District there are currently 118 Brothers and hundreds of their lay partners, all working together to further the mission of the De La Salle Christian Brothers.

DeLaSalle High School

DeLaSalle opened in 1900 and has been administered by the Christian Brothers throughout its history. The "Brothers of the Christian Schools" (also known as the "Christian Brothers," the "Lasallian Brothers," the "French Christian Brothers," or the "De La Salle Brothers," is a Roman Catholic religious teaching congregation, founded in France by Jean-Baptiste de La Salle (1651–1719), and now based in Rome, Italy. The Brothers use the post-nominal abbreviation of "F.S.C." to denote their membership of the order, and use the honorific title of "Brother", abbreviated "Br."

1913 drawing of St. John Baptiste de la Salle Founder of the "Christian Brothers." (Public Domain)

Elementary French Immersion Programs in Minnesota

There are a number of Elementary French Immersion programs in Minnesota. Three such programs are as follows:

- Normandale Elementary French Immersion School http://www.edina.k12.mn.us/normandale/

- Edina Public Schools French Immersion Program (since 1991): Elementary school is early total immersion. Middle continuation program include the following subjects taught in French: Math, French Language Arts, and Social Studies. The High School continuation program encompasses French literature, French culture and cinema.

- l"Étoile du nord, St. Paul Public Schools French Immersion program http://www.frenchimmersion.spps.org/

Grey Nuns

The Sisters of Charity of Montreal was a French-Canadian community of sisters known as the Grey Nuns. More information on them is found in the section "Sisters of Charity of Montreal."

Holy Cross Fathers

The Congregation of Holy Cross or "Congregation a Sancta Cruce" (C.S.C.) is a Catholic congregation of priests and brothers founded in 1837, by Blessed Father Basil Anthony-Marie Moreau, C.S.C., in Le Mans, France. Father Moreau also founded the Marianites of Holy Cross, now divided into three independent congregations of sisters. The Congregations of women who trace their origins to Father Moreau are the Marianites of Holy Cross (Le Mans, France), the Sisters of the Holy Cross, (Notre Dame, Indiana), and the Sisters of Holy Cross, (Montreal, Canada).

From the late 1920s through the mid-1930s, the Holy Cross Fathers, who ran the University of Notre Dame, also controlled the College of St. Thomas's administration. The St. Paul diocese called in those priests to help with the school's financial problems. At that time, the Holy Cross Fathers were known as a crisis intervention team of sorts for parochial schools.[246] Here are a list of some of the higher education institutions which the Holy Cross Fathers are associated with:

- University of Notre Dame, Notre Dame, Indiana (1842)
- St. Edward's University, Austin, Texas (1878)
- University of Portland, Portland, Oregon (1901)
- King's College, Wilkes-Barre, Pennsylvania (1946)
- Stonehill College, Easton, Massachusetts (1948)
- Notre Dame College, Dhaka, Bangladesh (1949)
- Holy Cross College, Notre Dame, Indiana (1966)
- Holy Cross College, Agartala, India (2009)
- Saint Mary's College, Notre Dame, Indiana (1844) (Sisters of the Holy Cross)

[246] O'Neill, Arthur Barry, "Congregation of the Holy Cross." in *The Catholic Encyclopedia*. Vol. 7. New York: Robert Appleton Company, 1910. 10 Sept. 2015.

- Our Lady of Holy Cross College, New Orleans, Louisiana (1916) (Marianites of Holy Cross)
- Notre Dame University Bangladesh, Dhaka, Bangladesh (2013)
- University of St. Thomas, St. Paul, Minnesota (Holy Cross Fathers controlled the College's administration from late 1920s to mid 1930s).

Jesuits

On August 15, 1534, Ignatius of Loyola (born Íñigo López de Loyola), a Spaniard of Basque origin, and six other students at the University of Paris, France, met in Montmartre outside Paris, in a crypt beneath the church of Saint Denis, now Saint Pierre de Montmartre. The term "Jesuit" (of 15th-century origin, meaning "one who used too frequently or appropriated the name of Jesus"), was first applied to the society in reproach (1544–52). Many young Frenchmen became Jesuits. Though it was never used by its founder, in time, members and friends of the Society adopted the name in its positive meaning. The Jesuits operate the Retreat House Demontreville located in Lake Elmo, Minnesota. Most of the Jesuit Missionaries who came to North America were French.

Mendota School (Public Domain)

Mendota School

Sister M. George and the Sisters of St. Joseph of Carondolet established a boarding and day school in the former home of Henry Sibley, the first Governor of Minnesota. The school served children in the surrounding area, including Dakota Indian children camped near Mendota.

Our Lady of Lourdes School

Our Lady of Lourdes (Notre Dame de Lourdes) school operated in St. Anthony from September 1888 until 1906. It was originally staffed by four Grey Nuns from Montreal, namely Sister Tassi, Superior, and Sisters Derome, Bissionette, and St. Thomas. In 1906, the Grey Nuns (Sisters of Charity of Montreal) were replaced by the Sisters of Saint Joseph of Carondolet. Many in the parish were sad to see the Grey Nuns leave because when they left the school all classes were taught in English except for the French Language class.

Our Lady of Lourdes School
at 5th Street and 6th Avenue N.E. (Public Domain)

Many blamed this on Bishop Ireland who was known to urge all Catholics to become American and speak English, and leave their old world languages behind.[247]

Our Lady of Angels Academy

The Missionary Franciscan Sisters of the Immaculate Conception operated a French speaking school for young girls in Belle Pairiere from 1873 until 1889, when the building was destroyed by fire. Sister Mary Francis Beauchamp remained in Little Falls. Eventually in 1911, the Franciscan teachers led by Mother Mary Columba (daughter of Mr. and Mrs. Elzear Doucet (Doucette) opened Our Lady of Angels Academy in Little Falls.[248]

Our Lady of Angels Academy in Little Falls (Public Domain)

Saint Joseph's Academy in Crookston

According to "Footprints of Yesterday, Crookston 1879-1979," the Sisters of St. Joseph had arrived from France in 1903, in order to escape anti-religion movements there, and had first traveled to Argyle, Minnesota. Under the supervision of Mother Marie Jeanne Humbert, the sisters arrived in Crookston in 1905, with the intention of opening a parochial school, where there already was a large French population. At first, they had but one student in a small home at 436 Ash Street, but within a few months, their school population had increased to seventeen. In 1903, the home owned by J.R. Clements was purchased to house teachers and students at the new school called the St. Joseph Academy. The old French Provincial home was used for classes until

St. Joseph's Academy in Crookston (Public Domain)

---

[247] Hazel, Reverend Robert, *Notre Dame de Minneapolis,* "*The French-Canadian Catholics,* (Second Printing 2003) p.20-21.
[248] Information obtained from Our Lady of the Angels History.

1912, when the first two stories of the brick academy were built on the property. Later a third story was added.

Saint Joseph's Academy in St. Paul

The first school in St. Paul opened on November 7, 1851 in the vestry of the log chapel built in 1851, in St. Paul. Four sisters from the Sisters of St. Joseph from Carondolet in St. Louis, arrived by steamer to teach the children of French-Canadian Catholics and other children. The four sisters who began this school were Mother St. John Fournier, Sister Philomene Vilaine, Sister Francis Joseph Ivory, and Sister Scholastica Vasques. Mother Fournier was trained in St. Etienne, France. From 1851 to 1859, the school was known as St. Mary's school. In 1859, the name was changed to St. Joseph's Academy. The Sisters of St. Joseph staffed this school until 1971.

St. Joseph's Academy in St. Paul in later years. (Public Domain)

Saint Mary's School of St. Anthony Falls

In 1853, the Sisters of St. Joseph of Carondolet established St. Mary's School in St. Anthony Falls.

Saint Mary's School of Bird Island Minnesota

The Saint Mary's School of Bird Island (shown to the left) was operated by the Sisters of St. Joseph of Carondolet from 1897 to 1986.

St. Mary's School, Bird Island

Saint Mary's School of White Bear Lake

The Sisters of St. Joseph of Carandolet operated a school in White Bear Lake called Saint Mary's. It was located right next to Saint Mary's Church as shown in the picture below.

Sisters of Charity of Montreal

The Sisters of Charity of Montreal was a French-Canadian community of sisters known as the Grey Nuns. In 1846, Sister Gosselin and Sister Quimet stopped at the Fort Snelling military reservation while en route to St Boniface from their motherhouse in Montreal.

They disembarked from the boat they had taken to Fort Snelling, and while waiting for transportation to St. Boniface on ox carts, they arranged to instruct the children of the local residents. In return for the lessons, they were provided with food and lodging until the Red River Oxcarts arrived. They did this again in 1850, teaching the children for six days, while waiting for transportation to St. Boniface.

St. Mary's School of White Bear Lake-1916
Courtesy of Robert Vadnais Family

These were the first recorded records of French Speaking nuns providing education to Minnesota children. Although the Grey Nuns instructed the children of early settlers, including those at Our Lady of Lourdes church in St. Anthony from 1888 to 1906,[249] they did not establish any permanent schools in Minnesota.[250]

Sisters of the Holy Names of Jesus and Mary

The Sisters of the Holy Names of Jesus and Mary (Soeurs des Saints Noms de Jésus et de Marie) is a teaching religious institute founded at Longueuil, Québec, Canada in 1843, by Blessed Mother Marie-Rose (Eulalie Durocher 1811- 1849) for the Christian education of young girls. Their motto is: "Jésus et Marie, Ma Force et Ma Gloire" ("Jesus and Mary, my strength and my glory").

Since 1843, the SNJM's mission to educate young girls has extended beyond Québec into other Canadian provinces, including Ontario and Manitoba. Their mission of education also continues internationally, in the United States, Lesotho, and South America. Within the United States, the Sisters have established ministries in California, Oregon, Florida, Minnesota, Mississippi, New York, the Mid-Atlantic States and Washington among other states. The Sisters of Jesus and Mary taught school at the St. Jean the Baptist School in Duluth and in 1920 there were 12 sisters on the staff at that school.[251]

---

[249] Hazel, Reverend Robert, *Notre Dame de Minneapolis,"The French-Canadian Catholics*, (Second Printing 2003).
[250] Raiche, Annabell CSJ, and Biermaier, Ann Marie OSB, *"They Came to Teach" the Story of Sisters who Taught in Parochial Schools and Their Contribution to Elementary Education in Minnesota.* North Star Press of St. Cloud, Inc. 1994.
[251] Article written by Don Martens on French school in Duluth, published in Chez Nous, Vol. 8, No. 6, Juin-Juilet Newsletter, 1987.

Sisters of Notre Dame de Namur

The Sisters of Notre Dame de Namur are a Roman Catholic religious institute of sisters, dedicated to providing education to the poor. The institute was founded in Amiens, France in 1803, by St. Julie Billiart and Marie-Louise-Françoise Blin de Bourdon, Countess of Gézaincourt, whose name as a Sister was Mother St. Joseph. It's organizational headquarters moved to French Namur in 1809, from which it spread to become a worldwide organization. The Sisters now have foundations in five continents and in twenty countries. They have offices in Minnesota and provide outreach and services for the poor. They staffed the school located at St. Albertville from 1915 to 1981.

The St. Jean Baptiste School was on first floor and church above it. The Sisters of Holy Names of Jesus and Mary taught here.

Sisters of St. Joseph of Carondelet

The Sisters of St. Joseph, also known as the Congregation of the Sisters of St. Joseph and abbreviated C.S.J., is a Roman Catholic religious congregation of women founded in Le Puy-en-Velay, France in 1650. In 1994, this Congregation had approximately 14,000 members worldwide: about 7,000 in the United States; 2,000 in France; and were active in fifty other countries.

The Congregation of the Sisters of St. Joseph began in 1650, with six women meeting in a small kitchen in Le Puy, France, motivated by a common desire to serve God and the poor in their community. These women, with the spiritual direction of a Jesuit priest, Jean-Pierre Medaille, formed the first community of the Sisters of St. Joseph. (Some early accounts attribute the founding of the order to Father Medaille's younger brother, Jean-Paul Medaille S.J.)

The sisters of St. Joseph of Carondolet came to Minnesota at the request of Bishop Cretin and arrived on the evening of November 2, 1851 from St. Louis. Within two weeks, they opened their school in the vestry of the log chapel built by the French-Canadian settlement in 1841. Fourteen pupils were enrolled on their first day of classes,[252] including the daughter of Major Fridley, Mary Bottineau, daughter of Pierre Bottineau, and the niece of Henry M. Rice.[253]

---

[252] Savage, Sister Mary Lucida, PhD, *The Congregation of Saint Joseph of Carondolet* Second Edition, Published by B. Herder Book Co. 1927.
[253] Henry Rice was first U.S. Senator from Minnesota, member of the board of regents of the University of Minnesota, and President of the Minnesota Historical Society.

The four sisters who began this school were Mother St. John Fournier, Sister Philomene Vilaine, Sister Francis Joseph Ivory, and Sister Scholastica Vasques. They arrived by steamer from St. Louis. Mother Fournier was trained in St. Etienne France. Eventually this group of nuns would teach in seventy eight schools in Minnesota, including the following:

St. Joseph's Academy opened in the vestry of the St. Paul Chapel in 1851 (Public Domain)

1. St. Anne's in Anoka from 1894 to 1945
2. St. Rose in Avoca from 1890 to 1902
3. St. Mary's in Bird Island from 1897 to 1986
4. Nativity of Mary in Bloomington from 1951 to 1973
5. St. Raphael's in Crystal from 1952 to 1987
6. Immaculate Heart of Mary in Currie from 1907 to 1919
7. St. John the Baptist in Excelsior from 1952 to 1977
8. St. Gabriel's in Fulda from 1901 to 1932
9. St. Eloi's in Ghent from 1902 to 1971
10. St. Mary's in Graceville from 1885 to 1969
11. Guardian Angel in Hastings from 1872 to 1971
12. St. Boniface in Hastings from 1872 to 1890
13. St. Teresa's Academy in Hastings from 1872 to 1876.
14. St. Joseph's in Hopkins from 1923 to 1969
15. St. Columbia's in Iona from 1901 to 1912
16. St. Canice in Kilkenny from 1910 to 1926
17. St. Anne's in LeSeur from 1902 to 1971
18. St. Mary's in LeCenter from 1914 to 1971
19. Indian Mission in Long Prairie from 1852 to 1855
20. St. Joseph's in Marshall from 1900 to 1950
21. Holy Redeemer in Marshall from 1950 to ?
22. St. Peter's in Mendota from 1867 to 1879
23. Ascension in Minneapolis from 1897 to ?
24. Basilica of St. Mary in Minneapolis from 1913 to 1971
25. Catholic Boy's Home in Minneapolis from 1878 to 1960
26. Christ the King in Minneapolis from 1939 to ?
27. Good Shepherd in Minneapolis from 1959 to 1982
28. New Holy Angels in Minneapolis from 1931 to 1947
29. Old Holy Angels in Minneapolis from 1877 to 1928
30. Holy Name in Minneapolis from 1923 to 1971

31. Immaculate Conception in Minneapolis from 1866 to 1913
32. Notre Dame in Minneapolis from 1906 to 1959
33. Notre Dame de Lourdes in Minneapolis from 1906 to 1959
34. St. Anthony's in Minneapolis from 1853 to 1970
35. St. Charles Borromeo in Minneapolis from 1939 to 1971
36. St. Helena's in Minneapolis from 1926 to 1971
37. St. Lawrence in Minneapolis from 1922 to 1970
38. St. Margaret's Academy in Minneapolis from 1907 to 1920
39. St. Stephen's in Minneapolis from 1915 to ?
40. St. Thomas the Apostle in Minneapolis from 1925 to 1971
41. St. Edwards in Minneota from 1938 to ?
42. St. Mary's in Morris from 1911 to 1943
43. St. Peter's in North St. Paul from 1917 to 1928
44. St. Aloysius in Olivia from 1914 to 1974
45. St. Peter's in Richfield from 1946 to 1987
46. Assumption in St. Paul from 1858 to 1885
47. Blessed Sacrament in St. Paul from 1918 to 1981
48. Cathedral in St. Paul from 1855 to 1914
49. New Cathedral in St. Paul from 1914 to 1970
50. Girl's Orphanage in St. Paul from 1869 to 1953
51. Holy Spirit in St. Paul from 1937 to ?
52. Nativity in St. Paul from 1923 to ?
53. Project Discovery in St. Paul from 1970 to 1977
54. St. Cecilia's in St. Paul from 1924 to 1968
55. St. Columbia's in St. Paul from 1922 to ?
56. St. Gregory in St. Paul from 1953 to 1971
57. St. James in St. Paul from 1913 to 1975
58. St. John's in St. Paul from 1892 to 1970
59. St. Joseph's in St. Paul from 1876 to 1914
60. St. Joseph's Academy in St. Paul from 1851 to 1926
61. St. Kevin's in St. Paul from 1952 to 1972
62. St. Leo's in St. Paul from 1947 to 1971
63. St. Louis in St. Paul from 1873 to 1962
64. St. Luke's in St. Paul from 1904 to ?
65. St. Mark's in St. Paul from 1913 to ?
66. St. Mary's in St. Paul from 1868 to 1970
67. St. Pascal Baylon in St. Paul from 1950 to ?
68. St. Patrick's in St. Paul from 1885 to 1992
69. St. Therese in St. Paul from 1949 to 1971
70. St. Vincent's in St. Paul from 1902 to 1970
71. Transfiguration in St. Paul from 1953 to 1971
72. St. Thomas Aquinas in St. Paul Park from 1949 to 1971
73. St. Peter's in St. Peter from 1914 to 1934
74. St. Michael's in Stillwater from 1873 to 1970
75. St. Mary's in Waverly from 1886 to 1971

76. St. Michael's in West St. Paul from 1885 to ?

77. St. Mary of the Lake of White Bear Lake from 1914 to 1977

78. St. Piux X of White Bear Lake from 1955 to 1971

St. Joseph's Hospital (Public Domain)

The early curriculum used was based on a book entitled "Method of Instruction" printed in Lyons, France in French for the Sisters of Saint Joseph. It is a book of three hundred pages, a model course of study, with minute instructions regarding the matter to be taught and the manner of presenting each subject.[254]

During the first one hundred years (1851-1950), the parochial school system became well established and highly respected in Minnesota. The schools run by the the "Sisters" were known for their quality education as well for their Christian values and beliefs. Catholic parishes were expected to build and support Catholic Schools and were expected

St. Joseph's Novitiate and Provencial House in St. Paul (Public Domain)

to send their children to these schools. Between 1950 and 1965, the number of parochial schools increased as did the enrollment. In 1965, however, this trend changed. After 1965, the number of students attending decreased, schools were closed, sisters began to move to new apostolates and lay teachers and others assumed major responsibility for Catholic education. Today, the transfer of leadership from the sisters to the laity is all but complete.[255]

St. Joseph's Hospital opened its doors in 1853 in Saint Paul, Minnesota and was Minnesota's first hospital. The Sisters of St. Joseph of Carondelet founded the facility in response to the outbreak of cholera in the community. They used the little log chapel as their first hospital to fight the cholera outbreak. A picture of this log cabin still exists in the lobby of the hospital.[256]

[254] Methode D'Enseignement pour les Classes de Soeurs de St. Joseph, Lyons, France, 1832.

[255] Raiche, Annabell CSJ, and Biermaier, Ann Marie OSB, *"They Came to Teach" the Story of Sisters who Taught in Parochial Schools and Their Contribution to Elementary Education in Minnesota.* North Star Press of St. Cloud, Inc. 1994.

[256] Savage, Sister Mary Lucida PhD, *The Congregation of Saint Joseph of Carondolet,* Second Edition, Published by B. Herder Book Co. 1927.

St. Catherine University was founded as the College of St. Catherine in 1905, by the Sisters of St. Joseph of Carondelet, under the leadership of Mother Seraphine Ireland. The University is named for St. Catherine of Alexandria, the fourth-century Egyptian lay philosopher who suffered martyrdom for her faith. The limestone chapel on campus named "Our Lady of Victory" is modeled after the cathedral of St. Trophime at Arles, France.

College of St. Catherine in St. Paul (Public Domain)

The St. Paul, Minnesota Province includes the Archdiocese of St. Paul and the dioceses of Winona and Fargo. The Sisters of St Joseph of Superior, Wisconsin joined the congregation in 1986, becoming part of the St. Paul Province. The St. Paul Province sponsors Cretin-Derham Hall High School, St. Paul, Minnesota and St. Catherine University. Derham Hall, an administrative building at St. Catherine's is listed on the National Register of Historic Places.

Sisters of St. Joseph of Medaille

The Congregation of Sisters of Saint Joseph was started in Le Puy, France by the Jesuit Jean Pierre Médaille and accepted by Bishop Monsignor de Maupas, on October 15, 1650. They have the same origins as the Sisters of St. Joseph of Carondolet but evolved into separate orders. The Sisters of St. Joseph of Medaille, also known as the Sisters St. Joseph of Bourg, were initially recruited in 1903, to teach in the predominantly French-Canadian parish of St. Rose of Lima in Argyle, Minnesota. They came from Bourg, France and found conditions in Argyle to be very difficult for the first few years. Living conditions gradually improved and before long were able to use their limited resources to open the Villa Rosa School in Argyle. Eventually this small group of nuns would teach in fifteen schools in Minnesota, including the following:[257]

1. Villa Rosa in Argyle (Later renamed St. Joseph's School and then St. Rose School) from 1903-1988
2. St. Joseph's Academy in Crookston from 1905-1969
3. St. Boniface in Stewart from 1927-1969
4. St. Canice in Kilkenny from 1929-1970
5. St. Peter's in Park Rapids from 1944-1972
6. St. Joan of Arc in Minneapolis from 1948-1974
7. St. Joseph's in West St. Paul from 1949-1971
8. St. Richard's in Richfield from 1953-1987
9. St. Joseph's Primary in Crookston from 1968-1975

---

[257] Raiche, Annabell CSJ, and Biermaier, Ann Marie OSB, *"They Came to Teach" the Story of Sisters who Taught in Parochial Schools and Their Contribution to Elementary Education in Minnesota.* North Star Press of St. Cloud, Inc. 1994.

10. Brady High School in West St. Paul from 1968 to 1991
11. Redwood Catholic in Redwood Falls from 1969-1971
12. Holy Redeemer in Marshall from 1971-1976
13. St. Peter's in Mendota from 1971-1972
14. Crookston Cathedral Elementary School from 1975-1984
15. St. Croix in Stillwater from 1978-1981
16. St. Luke's in St. Paul from 1983-1989

Villa Rosa Catholic School

This school was run by the St. Joseph Sisters from Bourg Ain, France in Argyle, Minnesota. Built in 1901, it operated until 1949, when a new school building was built on the same site.

Villa Rose, built in 1901 in Argyle (Public Domain)

Villa Maria Academy

This school was run by Roman Catholic Ursuline Nuns as a private religious oriented boarding school. The school was open from 1889 to 1969.

Villa Maria Academy south of Red Wing, Minnesota (Public Domain)

The Ursuline Sisters were the first Catholic nuns to land in the new world. In 1639, Mother Marie of the Incarnation (née Marie Guyart (1599–1672), two other Ursuline nuns, and a Jesuit priest left France for a mission in Canada.[258] When they arrived in the summer of 1639, they studied the language of the native peoples and then began to educate and teach the catechism to the native children. They also taught reading, writing as well as needlework, embroidery, drawing and other domestic arts. The Ursuline Convent established by Mother Marie has been in continuous use by the Ursuline Sisters since its construction. There is an Ursuline convent in Quebec City that is the oldest educational institution for women in North America. Their work helped to preserve a religious spirit among the French population and to Christianize native peoples and Métis.

---

[258] Chabot, Marie-Emmanuel, O.S.U., *Guyart, Marie, dite Marie de l'Incarnation*, Dictionary of Canadian Biography, University of Toronto/Universite Laval

Chapter Nine
French-Canadian Influence on Hockey in Minnesota

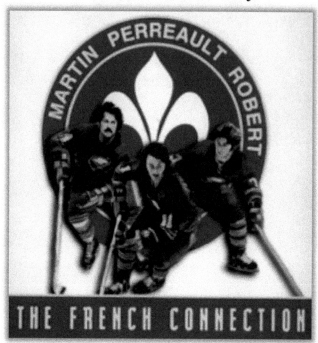

Miracles Still Happen on Ice
By Jerry Foley

Folks debate about where in Canada the first ice hockey game was played, but they agree that Montreal was at the center of ice hockey development. Teams played an ice hockey game using a circular piece of wood in Montreal in 1875 and, by the next year, students at McGill University had developed rules for the game. The first world championship of ice hockey, part of Montreal's annual winter carnival in 1883, was won by the McGill University team. The first known ice hockey game in the United States was between student teams from Yale and John Hopkins universities in 1893. By 1907, there were hockey leagues in Manitoba, Ontario and Quebec.

Ice hockey is Canada's national sport. "The game is invariably tied to our (Canada's) sense of what it means to be Canadian and is perhaps our most identifiable icon," says Heather Wentworth.[259] Hockey, Canada's most wide reaching sport, "is the game that makes us a nation" says Morley Callaghan[260] recognizing how hockey has helped heal the division between separate communities that was Canada in the late 19th Century. Ice hockey lives in the hearts and minds of Quebecers, in large part because of the once all-French-Canadian team, the Montreal Canadians. It would be rare to find even the smallest community in Quebec without a rink available for organized play.

---

[259] Wentworth, Heather, *Hockey Culture*, Canadian Living, February 15, 2011.
[260] Quoted by Paul W. Martin, "Hockey and Canadian Culture," online, 2010.

Perhaps a major reason that ice hockey became a favorite French-Canadian sport hinged on the size of players. French-Canadian voyageurs were usually short, strong, highly competitive men. Many of today's football and basketball players would tower over them, although professional hockey players today also tend to be larger.

Ice hockey began creeping into Minnesota and the northern United States in the 1890s through border towns like Roseau and Warroad and the Iron Range towns of Eveleth, Virginia and Hibbing. Eveleth had a team in 1903. Hockey in Warroad, today styled as "Hockeytown U.S.A.," started in 1904 when George Marvin got off a train from Manitoba to manage a grain elevator and a lumber and coal business. At first, Eveleth and Warroad teams played Canadian teams in the adult hockey leagues. Before long hockey teams appeared in Minnesota's northern communities, such as Roseau, Thief River Falls, Crookston, Hallock and Baudette. In 1909 Roseau and Warroad began a high school hockey rivalry that continues today.

Many Minnesota kids get interested in ice hockey by playing on frozen ponds, rivers, and lakes that dot the land of 10,000 lakes. Hockey is a pick-up sport for long winters, and even a few frozen ears and toes can't discourage hockey lovers, including the infatuated fans standing in the snow banks to watch the games. Most communities have strong youth hockey programs, where kids learn to skate almost as soon as they learn to walk. In the smaller northern Minnesota towns like Eveleth and Warroad, with only one ice rink, the kids learn to play alongside the adult stars. Townspeople and coaches already often know who will be a future star before a child reaches high school age. Parents love to watch their kids play hockey, even at the pee-wee level. Talented kids often dream of playing in the Quebec International PeeWee Hockey Tournament, which draws a number of U.S. teams for the tourney. Hockey creates a culture that brings the community together.

Minnesota's passion for hockey, reflected in Warroad, is indicative of hockey throughout Minnesota. Minnesotans are well aware of such hockey families as the Marvins and Christians in Warroad and the Broten brothers in Roseau, who have won six state high school championships and produced seven Olympic hockey players. Warroad has sent eight hockey players to the Olympics since 1956, four of them from the Christian family. The U.S. has never won an Olympic gold medal without at least one player from Warroad. Cal Marvin, Warroad coaching legend, called Henry Boucha "the most colorful hockey player to come out of Northern Minnesota," noting that even the folks in senior care homes came to watch Henry play.[261] When Warroad High School teams reach the state hockey tournament, the school closes for spring break. In towns like Warroad and Roseau, each now with an arena with more seats than the number of town residents, the ice rink is literally the community's focal point. The Lakers, Warroad's adult hockey team, despite the struggle of a small town to sustain them, was considered the best senior hockey team in North America, traveled worldwide for tournaments, won twenty Manitoba Hockey titles, and was the only team to win the prestigious Canadian Allan Cup three consecutive years. In general, hockey is deeply ingrained in the culture and tradition of folks who live in Minnesota.

---

[261] U. S. Hockey Hall of Fame

Canadians have helped make Minnesota a hockey state. For example, a group of kids in Thief River Falls, were awed by the local senior team with whom they shared the town rink. Paul Bedard, the "Thieves" young coach from Canada, offered to coach the boys, taught them hockey fundamentals, and made them into a real team. When this group of youngsters won the 1956 state hockey tournament, Paul Bedard was there to cheer them on. Louis Nanne, who came from Sault Ste. Marie, Ontario to the University of Minnesota to play hockey in 1959, remained in Minnesota, played pro hockey and later became general manager and coach of the Minnesota North Stars. Nanne has also served as the Minnesota State High School Hockey Tournament TV analyst for fifty years. His dedication reflects his love for high school hockey and Nanne says he "has never seen an event like the state tournament." [262]

By the 1920s, hockey was sponsored by about twenty-five high schools, but the popularity emerged after World War II when colleges were leading the way and youth hockey programs appeared. Women's hockey teams began to form at Midwest colleges in the 1970s. In 1994 Minnesota became the first state in the U.S. to sanction girl's ice hockey as a high school varsity sport. Although Minnesota's population is less than that of many states, Minnesota leads the nation in the number of hockey players, including girl hockey players. Today the state high school hockey tournament is Minnesota's biggest single athletic event. Now some names of women hockey players are also becoming familiar because of the Olympics, e.g. Gigi Marvin of Warroad, Cal Marvin's granddaughter. The University of Minnesota, where most Minnesota kids would like to play, has a proud tradition of using, almost exclusively, Minnesota players.

Mike Snee, Executive Director of College Hockey, Inc. says: "We take pride in the number of players that make it to the National Hockey League and the Division 1 colleges, but I think what we take most pride in is just the number of people that play." Warroad, Roseau, and Eveleth reflect the importance of hockey to local communities, where pride comes in representing the community. "Other states don't have a big state high school hockey tournament. The state tournaments for bantam and peewee aren't nearly as big a deal as they are in Minnesota. In Minnesota, you really see how big a deal it is that hockey is such a part of the community here."[263]

A significant number of Minnesota hockey players play in junior hockey leagues, both in the United States and Canada, often for the experience they hope will lead to NCAA hockey opportunities. For example, four nineteen year old English-speaking Minnesotans played for the St. Jerome Pantheres, a Quebec French- speaking team near Montreal, in 2014-15, residing with families in that community. Hockey is the focal point of St. Jerome, a community of 70,000. Noting that the Quebec Junior Hockey League is known to be speed and skill-oriented, compared to other Canadian and American junior leagues, Bill Hattem, owner of the Pantheres, says that playing hockey at St. Jerome, is a developmental and

---

[262] Nelson, Loren, *Voice of the Tourney*, Minnesota Hockey Hub News, March 8, 2011.
[263] Snee, Mike, *NCAA men's hockey: Minnesota the capital of hockey nation*, espn sports online, April 5, 2011.

cultural experience that will help propel the players on this team maturely into their future hockey and life opportunities[264]

Hockey players from Canada and the United States dominated the game until recently. A young group of U.S. hockey players, twelve of the twenty from Minnesota, defeated a highly-favored veteran team from the Soviet Union at Lake Placid in the 1980 Olympics' "Miracle on Ice," coached by Minnesotan Herb Brooks, who tried to summarize the culture of hockey in Minnesota by saying that "we think of ourselves as Southern Manitobans." The Miracle on Ice united Minnesotans almost like hockey has done in Canada and many Minnesotans can still name the players on the 1980 U.S. Olympic hockey team.

The National Hockey League was formed in 1917 with all Canadian players and first expanded to the United States at Boston in 1924. Minnesota kids today follow the Minnesota Wild hockey team, which uses the moniker "State of Hockey" to declare that Minnesota is the hockey capital of the U.S. Professional hockey has introduced French-Canadian players to Minnesota, such as Jason Pominville, Justin Fontaine, Alexandre Daigle, and Stephane Veilleux, and French names of Minnesota players are also appearing on the Wild roster, including Zach Parise of Minneapolis and Keith Dallard of Baudette. Darby Hendrickson, a favorite Minnesota hockey player who played with the Minnesota Wild, com-

Lou Nanne, Minnesota North Stars

mented that "the Canadian guys who come through here say it's like where they grew up. I think the weather and our culture are what we have going for us here. My kids are on the ice at three years old."

Jacques Lemaire, Former coach of Minnesota Wild

French-Canadian Jacques Gerard Lemaire (born September 7, 1945) is a former ice hockey forward for the Montreal Canadiens and a long-time coach, most notably with the New Jersey Devils and the Minnesota Wild. After retiring at the end of the 2010–11 NHL season, he accepted a position as special assignment coach for the Devils. He currently works as a special assignment coach for the Toronto Maple Leafs. Lately, Bruce Boudreau, a man with French-Canadian ancestry, was hired to coach the Wild.

The United States Hockey Hall of Fame is located in Eveleth, a town which has produced ten per cent of the inductees thus far. Although a fairly small mining town, Eveleth High School has won the Minnesota State High School Championship title seven times.

---

[264] Hamre, John, *The Minnesota to St. Jerome Connection*, Let's Play Hockey, October 16, 2014.

Of course, we cannot forget to mention college hockey in Minnesota, with Minnesota teams competing each year for the National Championship. Since the NCAA national tournament began fifteen years ago in 2001, the University of Minnesota women's team has won six National Championships in 2004, 2005, 2012, 2013, 2015, and 2016. In 2013 they had a perfect 41-0 season. The University of Minnesota-Duluth women's team has won five national championships, in 2001, 2002, 2003, 2008 and 2010. The University of Minnesota men's team has won the National Championship in 2003, 2002, 1979, 1976 and 1974. The University of Minnesota Duluth Men's team won the National Championship in 2011.

In 2007, Senator Gen Olson first introduced a bill in the Minnesota legislature to make hockey the state sport, saying that "ice hockey has a unique relationship with Minnesota." Minnesota's hockey craze was apparent when Olson's bill passed in 2009, stating that "Ice hockey is adopted as the official sport of the state of Minnesota."[265]

As writer and hockey fan Roy MacGregor explained in an article for Canadian Living, "the values respected in hockey—teamwork, resourcefulness, tenacity, humility and triumph— are the principles Canadians try to uphold on the world stage, and as individuals."[266]

Ditto for Minnesota nice folks, eh!

[265] HF2088 Laws of Minnesota, Chapter 78, 2009.
[266] Watterworth, Heather, *Hockey Culture*, Canadian Living, February 2, 2011.

Chapter Ten
Haitian Diaspora in Minnesota
By Jacqueline Regis

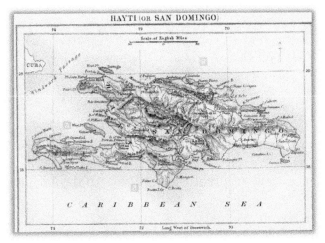

19ᵗʰ Century Map of Haiti & Santo Domingo
(Public Domain)

The French heritage contributes mightily to the richness and diversity in the Twin Cities. This heritage includes an emerging Haitian community with its deep French and Afro-Caribbean roots as one of the growing immigrant communities in this region. It is estimated that over one million Haitians live in the United States.[267] Displacement of any people from their homeland can be a lifelong trauma, particularly for the first generation. The hopeful side of such displacements, however, is the blending of rich and disparate human experiences.

It underscores the human bond we share regardless of race and culture. In this is the strength of the project that shaped the American experience. The Haitian culture is a *pot pourri*, a mixture of strong French and African traditions, handed down and blended in subtle and less subtle ways. That culture has been seasoned and transformed through slavery, revolt and the ultimate independence bought and paid for with blood.

Haiti often referred to as "*la perle des Antilles*"[268] (the Pearl of the Antilles), is that notorious western third of the island of Hispaniola in the Caribbean Sea initially known as Saint-Domingue. Christopher Columbus claimed the island populated by Taino natives and named it Hispaniola in 1492 as the first Spanish conquest in the New World. [269] In 1697 under the terms of the Treaty of Ryswick, France acquired Saint-Domingue, which later regained its Taino name Haiti, the mountainous island.[270] Under French colonial rule, which depended on slavery as free labor, Saint-Domingue's plantations yielded a prosperous coffee and sugar agricultural economy and provided great wealth to France and its colonial landowners. [271] Haiti was the rich jewel from which France governed its other dependencies including Louisiana and the expansive Mississippi River watershed.

At the end of the eighteenth century, the American and French Revolutions had extensive ripple effects on colonialism worldwide, and especially in Haiti. New thoughts on liberty and human rights were a catalyst for a massive slave uprising which began in 1791.[272] This

---

[267] Camarota, Steven, *Fact Sheet on Immigrants in the United States*, Center for Immigration Studies (January 2010).

[268] New World Encyclopedia Contributors, *Hispaniola*, February 24, 2014.

[269] Pamphile, Leon D., *Haitians and African Americans: A Heritage of Tragedy and Hope*, University Press of Florida, 1ˢᵗ Edition (December 30, 2001).

[270] *Ibid.*

[271] *Ibid.*

[272] Ibid.

revolt was, in fact, the basis for liberty throughout the rest of Latin America. It is from Haiti that Simon Bolivar,[273] liberator of South America, launched his independence struggle against Spanish hegemony over South America with Haitian men and arms. The celebrated Haitian freedom fighter Toussaint L'Ouverture, credited as the great leader of the rebellion in Saint Domingue which led to Haiti's independence in 1804, was born into slavery in Haiti in 1743 on the Breda Plantation.[274] It is reported that, although born into slavery in Haiti, Toussaint received a classic education from Jesuit missionaries and from his French godfather. Toussaint was an avid reader and absorbed himself in the writings of Greek philosophers. Like his fellow Haitians, black, mulatto or white, he read among others the writings of Julius Caesar and the French Enlightenment thinker, Guillaume Raynal, who condemned slavery. He also read the French *"Declaration des Droits de l'Homme"* (Declaration of Human Rights) which resonated with the African zeal for liberty. In 1776, Toussaint was granted freedom, and thereafter he steadily rose to leadership positions, including that of assistant overseer. When the slave uprising began in 1791, Toussaint quickly became involved as a general and eventually as the leader of the independence movement.[275]

The Haitian revolution led by Toussaint was ultimately successful in ending slavery and colonization in Haiti. The world has credited its success to Toussaint's unparalleled leadership. But Toussaint did not live to see the culmination of his efforts with Haiti's independence in 1804. In 1801, Napoleon Bonaparte sent 20,000 French troops to reclaim the island. While the French troops could not recapture the island from the former slaves, they succeeded in capturing Toussaint and taking him to prison in France where he died of pneumonia in 1803.[276] As Toussaint left Haiti he uttered the following prophetic words, immortal to Haitians: *"En me renversant on a abattu a Saint-Domingue le tronc de l'arbre de la liberté des noirs. Mais elle repoussera par ses racines, car elles sont puissantes et nombreuses."* The ideal Toussaint conveyed with those words can be translated as follows: *"by overthrowing me, they've only succeeded in bringing down the trunk of the tree of freedom for blacks. Freedom will nonetheless sprout again through its roots which are powerful and numerous."*[277] Toussaint's life

19th Century Engraving of Toussaint Louverture (Public Domain)

symbolizes Haitian culture, which includes French intellectual and cultural traditions, interfused with remnants of its African origin, toughened by the cruelties of slavery, exalted

[273] Leger, Jacques Nicolas, *Haiti, Her History and Her Detractors*, New York, Neale, (1907); Lynch, John "Simon Bolivar: a Life;" Yale University Press (July 5, 2007).
[274] Edwards, Owen, *A Larger Than Life Toussaint Louverture*, Smithsonian Magazine, www.Smithsonian.com, May 2011.
[275] Ibid.
[276] Ibid.
[277] Feard, Rev. Joh R.D.D. *Toussaint L'Overture of Hayti*, James Redpath, Publisher (1863).

by the success of a revolution that ended slavery and burdened by the unfulfilled promise of a dearly-bought freedom.

The illustrious history of this tiny French and Creole speaking nation has nonetheless been and continues to be embroiled in turbulence and instability, resulting in the migration of scores of Haitians to other nations in search of a better life. With the rise to power of Haitian dictator for life, Francois (Papa Doc) Duvalier, the phenomenon of massive emigration of Haitians accelerated steadily since the late 1950's and continues relentlessly to present-day.[278] In 1980, just as the Mariel Boatlift brought scores of Cuban exiles to the United States, a simultaneous migration of Haitians seeking refuge from brutal dictatorial repression and misery occurred, when some 60,000 desperate Haitians left Haiti on barely seaworthy boats.[279] Many Haitians ultimately found solace and established strong communities in most major cities throughout the world, including American cities notably, New York, Boston, Miami, Chicago, New Orleans, Washington D.C., and in many Canadian cities as well.

There are many Haitians in the diaspora who have distinguished themselves and further illustrate the richness found in the tiny island nation. The acclaimed scholar and a founder of modern social science W. E. B. Du Bois is of Haitian origin, as his father emigrated from the island.[280] Jean Baptiste Point du Sable from Saint-Domingue was declared the Founder of Chicago on October 26, 1968 by the State of Illinois and the City of Chicago.[281] The former Governor General of Canada and now Secretary-General of the *Organization Internationale de la Francophonie*, Michaelle Jean, came from Haiti to Canada in 1968 at the age of eleven.[282] The State of Florida has produced at least two Haitian-American state lawmakers.[283] Most recently in July 2015, Xavier University in New Orleans, Louisiana installed its newest University President, Dr. C. Reynold Verret, a first generation immigrant from Haiti with undergraduate and graduate degrees from Columbia University, the Massachusetts Institute of Technology (MIT) and post graduate studies at Yale University. The celebrated Haitian novelist, Edwidge Danticat, [284] author of *Breath, Eyes and Memory* and acclaimed by the McArthur Foundation, is a first generation Haitian immigrant who continues with a broader world audience, the celebration of the rich Haitian cultural heritage started by renowned Haitian writers such as Jean Price-Mars and Jacques Roumain.[285] The U.S. Ambassador to South Africa, the Honorable Patrick Gaspard, is also of Haitian descent.

Unlike most other major American cities on the east coast, settlement of Haitians in the Twin Cities is rather recent. The explanation for this may well be the stark contrast between the extreme climates of Haiti and Minnesota. Despite the brutal cold winters of

---

[278] Chiamaka Nwosu, Jeanne Batalova, *Haitian Immigrants in the United States*, Migration Information Source (May 29, 2014).

[279] Stepick, Alex and C.D. Stepick.) *Haitian Boat People: A Study in the Conflicting Forces Shaping U.S. Immigration Policy. Law and Contemporary Problems.* Duke University Law Journal 45/2 (spring 1982).

[280] Lewis, David Levering, *W.E.B. Du Bois Biography of a Race, 1868-1919*, Owl Books (1994).

[281] Andreas, Alfred Theodore, History of Chicago. *From the earliest period to the present time, volume 1.* Retrieved January 25, 2011.

[282] *Jean, Michaelle,* The UN Refugee Agency. Retrieved June 11, 2010.

[283] Jaggi, Maya, Island Memories (Profile: Edwidge Danticat" The Guardian. Retrieved 2013-05-12.

[284] http://www.britannica.com/biography/Edwidge-Danticat

[285] Mohl, Raymond, *Review of Pamphile, Leon D., Haitians and African Americans: A Heritage of Tragedy and Hope,* University Press of Florida, 1st Edition (December 30, 2001).

Minnesota, since the 1990s a vibrant Haitian community in the Twin Cities has emerged. In the early to mid-1980s only a handful (less than a dozen known to this writer) of Haitians mostly professionals and university students lived in the Twin Cities. In the early 1990s following a military *coup d'état* against then Haiti's president Jean-Bertrand Aristide, a new wave of Haitians ran away *en masse* from violence and repression and left Haiti through any available means seeking refuge in other parts of the world.[286]

The growing Haitian community in the Twin Cities appears to have closely followed the 1990's Haitian exodus. There is some indication in *The Advocates for Human Rights'* records that some Haitians immigrants began to settle in Minnesota during the 1990s. *The Advocates for Human Rights* is a non-profit organization headquartered in Minneapolis whose mission is "*to implement international human rights standards to promote civil society and reinforce the rule of law.*"[287] One core project of The Advocates for Human Rights is *pro bono* legal representation of qualified low-income immigrants seeking asylum. The Advocates for Human Rights has provided pro bono legal services to a few Haitians beginning in the 1990s.

Afoutayi Haitian Arts, Dance & Music Company

Today, the Twin Cities metro area includes a Haitian community which, conservatively, has at least 500 members and which has begun to make its presence visible. One visible sign of the presence of the Twin Cities Haitian community is the formation of the Minnesota Haitian Cultural Center under the leadership of first generation Haitian immigrant Anne Florence Celestin Adabra. Through its Facebook page the Minnesota Haitian Cultural Center provides a means of connection and communication for community members and friends regarding current events and activities. It is a shared space for expression, discovery and sharing of Haitian art, culture and history. The small Minnesota community in the metro area includes several graduate students at the University of Minnesota, one church congregation (offering regular worship services in French and Haitian Creole), one Haitian Dance Troupe, *Afoutayi Haitian Arts, Dance & Music Company*, at least two university faculty members, a handful of professionals including several businessmen, members of the clergy, a physician, lawyers and one member of the Minnesota judiciary.

---

[286] Mohl, Raymond, *Review of Pamphile, Leon D., Haitians and African Americans: A Heritage of Tragedy and Hope*, University Press of Florida, 1st Edition (December 30, 2001).
[287] www.advocatesforhumanrights.org (October 2015).

It is also reported that Minnesota has a connection with Toussaint L'Ouverture through Hayward Toussaint, a light-middleweight boxing figure in Minnesota also known as "*Honey Boy*" Conroy. Hayward Toussaint was reportedly the great-great-great-grandson of the brother of Toussaint L'Ouverture who escaped to New Orleans, Louisiana when Napoleon Bonaparte captured Toussaint in 1802.[288] Minnesota claims Alex (Al) Sands, also known as the "*Haitian Temptation*" a nationally recognized cruiserweight boxer from Duluth, Minnesota. Al Sands, despite his American name and American upbringing, is also Haitian by birth (born Gregory Sean Noel). Al was adopted when he was only eighteen months old by a single mother from Duluth, Minnesota from an orphanage in the outskirts

"Haitian Tempation" Al Sands

of Port-au-Prince, the capital of Haiti. At age eleven life's circumstances nonetheless resulted in Al being raised in foster care by Tim and Jennifer Myles in Floodwood, Minnesota. In the course of his childhood journey in foster care through his adolescence, Al credits the Myles' loving guidance and discipline and the support of his community in Duluth as enabling him to overcome many obstacles leading him to discovering his incredible talent in the sport of boxing at the age of 21. He now ranks 8th among cruiserweights in the nation and 55th worldwide. Al uses his public image to speak to youth in the community promoting a healthy and purposeful lifestyle. He has joined forces with organizations committed to advancing the development of infra-structure in his homeland of Haiti. Al lives the Haitian spirit so evident in many Haitians in the diaspora. His strength, courage and talent are inspiring and he lives in Duluth, Minnesota.

Minnesota's connection with Haiti and commitment to Haiti's full development and self-reliance go a lot farther than through people of Haitian origin living in the state. Minnesota is the home base of at least thirty non-profit organizations dedicated to the development and advancement of certain aspect of life in Haiti. For example, the Minnesota-based non-profit organization, *Haiti Outreach* headquartered in Hopkins, Minnesota and Pignon, Haiti, has exclusively focused its efforts over the last 18 years on developing the country of Haiti as opposed to just providing relief. Their primary activity has been creating the availability of community-managed, sustainable potable water systems to mostly rural communities in Haiti. Haiti Outreach's hope for the future is to be the catalyst for Haitians to develop sustainable infrastructure as found in developed countries and, in particular, the wide availability of potable water and sanitation to everyone on the island nation. *No Time for Poverty*, a non-profit organization headquartered in Eagan, Minnesota, operates *Klinik Timoun Nou Yo* (Our Children's Clinic) staffed 100% by Haitians in the village of Port-Salut in southern

---

[288] Hiebert, Gareth, Columns of Oliver Towne, *City on Seven Hills*, Pogo Press (1989) p.4.

Haiti. *Klinik Timoun Nou Yo* is a large pediatric medical center providing a number of services including primary and urgent care, dental treatment, well baby evaluation and vaccination, and food supplementation for severely and moderately malnourished children. A number of other Minnesota religious organizations and groups support hospitals, clinics and schools in various other parts of Haiti.

The Haitian complex cultural heritage is also visible in the Twin Cities and surrounding communities through the presence of Haitian art. The Milwaukee Art Museum in the neighboring state of Wisconsin boasts hosting *"the world's foremost collections of 20ᵗʰ-century Haitian art,"* featuring the work of world -renowned Haitian artists. The Museum's website describes its Flagg Haitian art collection as follows: *"The Flaggs began collecting Haitian art in 1973 and proceeded to amass one of the world's foremost collections of 20th-century Haitian art. Featuring some 90 paintings and sculptures, the Richard and Erna Flagg Collection includes works by artists such as Hector Hyppolite, Castera Bazile, Wilson Bigaud, Préfète Duffaut, Philomé Obin, Rigaud Benoit, and Georges Liautaud."*[289]

Recently, the *Afoutayi Haitian Arts, Dance & Music Company,* a renowned Haitian dance company (with existing branches in Haiti, California and now the Twin Cities) under the direction of Artistic Director, acclaimed dance master and first generation Haitian immigrant Djenane St. Juste has added a new dimension to Haitian cultural presence in Minnesota. The acclaimed Haitian dance company held in 2015 its annual Haitian Cultural Festival in Minnesota on September 26 and 27 at the Sundin Music Hall, Hamline University. [290]

Haitians are a people of deep faith. The most significant sign of the presence of a Haitian community in any major city around the world is a church congregation providing worship services exclusively in both French and Haitian Creole. At least one Haitian church has been present in the Twin Cities since prior to the 2010 earthquake, holding regular worship services exclusively in French or Creole. Following the 2010 earthquake, this congregation provided a place and forum for local Haitians to gather, pray, mourn and contribute to the world's response to rebuilding Haiti.

Haiti's cultural presence in the Twin Cities is also evident through the recreation of cultural culinary habits of the homeland. While this writer is not aware of a Haitian restaurant in the area at this time, Haitian delicacies are readily available through a Haitian-American catering service called *Caribbean Delights, Inc.,* operated in her spare time by Dr. Barbara Pierre-Louis, a first generation Haitian immigrant who is a professor at a local Twin Cities university. This catering service features culinary favorites such as fried plantains, chicken, sweet potato and rice and beans. The Twin Cities lie at the origin of the mighty Mississippi. Let's remember that red beans and rice, gumbo and other delicacies of the lower Mississippi came from that island and like many Haitians, became American.

---

[289] Milwaukee Art Museum, *The Richard and Erna Flagg Collection of Haitian Art,* (2015).
[290] Minnesota Monthly, *The Music and Dance of Haiti* (2015).

Chapter Eleven
French Africans in Minnesota

African French (French: Français Africain) is the generic name for the varieties of French spoken by an estimated 120 million (2010) people in Africa spread across 24 Francophone countries. This includes those who speak French as a first or second language in these 31 Francophone African countries (dark on the map), but it does not include French speakers living in non-francophone African countries. Africa, is thus, the continent with the most French speakers in the world. French arrived in Africa as a colonial language. These African French speakers are now an important part of the Francophonie.

In Africa, French is often spoken alongside indigenous languages, but in some areas, it has become a first language, such as in the region of Abidjan, Ivory Coast or Libreville, Gabon. In some countries, it is a first language among some classes of the population, such as in Tunisia, Morocco and Algeria, where French is a first language among the upper classes. Many people in the upper classes are simultaneous bilinguals in Arabic/French, but only a second language among the general population. In each of the Fancophone African countries French is spoken with local specificities in terms of pronunciation and vocabulary. To the left is a map of Africa showing countries where French is spoken.

As of 2015, there are twenty-nine independent nations where French is an official language. The following is a list of sovereign states and territories where French is an official or de facto language.

Sovereign States

	Country	Continent	Population (2010)
1.	Democratic Republic of the Congo	Africa	67,827,000
2.	France	Europe	65,350,000
3	Canada	North America	34,207,000
4.	Madagascar	Africa	21,146,551
5.	Cameroon	Africa	19,958,692
6.	Ivory Coast	Africa	21,571,060
7.	Burkina Faso	Africa	16,287,000
8.	Niger	Africa	15,891,000
9.	Senegal	Africa	12,861,259
10.	Mali	Africa	14,517,029
11.	Rwanda	Africa	10,277,282
12.	Belgium	Europe	10,827,951
13.	Guinea	Africa	10,324,437
14.	Chad	Africa	11,274,337
15.	Haiti	North America	10,188,000
16.	Burundi	Africa	8,519,005
17.	Benin	Africa	9,212,000
18.	Switzerland	Europe	7,782,520

19.	Togo	Africa	6,780,000
20.	Central African Republic	Africa	4,410,873
21.	Republic of the Congo	Africa	4,043,318
22.	Gabon	Africa	1,501,000
23.	Comoros	Africa	734,750
24.	Equatorial Guinea	Africa	700,401
25.	Djibouti	Africa	888,716
26.	Luxembourg	Europe	506,953
27.	Vanuatu	Oceania	239,651
28.	Seychelles	Africa	86,525
29.	Monaco	Europe	35,407

Territories

1.	French Polynesia	Oceania	267,000	Overseas Collectivity of France
2.	New Caledonia	Oceania	224,824	Overseas Collectivity of France
3.	Aosta Valley	Europe	128,000	Autonomous Region of Italy
4.	Jersey	Europe	91,533	British Crown dependency
5.	Guernsey	Europe	66,000	British Crown dependency
6.	Saint-Martin	North America	29,376	Overseas Collectivity of France
7.	Wallis and Futuna	Oceania	16,448	Overseas Collectivity of France
8.	Saint-Barthélemy	North America	7,492	Overseas Collectivity of France
9.	Saint-Pierre and Miquelon	North America	7,044	Overseas Collectivity of France
10.	French Southern and Antarctic Lands	Antarctica, Africa	140	TAAF districts

Sub-national regions located within countries where French is an official national language are not included in this list. The five overseas regions of France (*Départements d'Outre-Mer*, or DOM): Guadeloupe, French Guiana, Martinique, Mayotte, and Réunion, have the same status as metropolitan France and are not listed here. French has a certain legal status in the American state of Louisiana but it is not considered de jure official.

West Africa, also called Western Africa and the West of Africa, is the westernmost subregion of the African continent. West Africa has been defined in Africa as including the eighteen countries Benin, Burkina Faso, the island of Cape Verde, Gambia, Ghana, Guinea, Guinea-Bissau, Ivory Coast or Cote d'Ivoire, Liberia, Mali, Mauritania, Niger, Nigeria, the island of Saint Helena, Senegal, Sierra Leone, Sao Tome and Principe and Togo. The French established their presence in West Africa in 1659, by building a fort at St. Louis at the mouth of the Senegel River and capturing Goree Island from the Dutch.[291]

---

[291] Mitchell, Peter, *Peoples and Cultures of Africa, West Africa*, Chelsea House Publishers 2006, p.17.

In Minnesota, it is estimated there are around 5,000 people in the past five years (2015),who are recent immigrants from French West Africa and who still speak French. There is a large Francophone African Catholic Community of approximately 300 households who are members of the St. Boniface Catholic Church in Northeast Minneapolis. Father Jules Olamanga is their pastor. This congregation celebrates a French mass every Sunday at noon. They have an international choir called the Saint Mary African Choir and they sing songs in French. The following chapter talks about this French Speaking community.

Chapter Twelve
The Francophone African Catholic Community
By Rev. Jules O. Omalanga

In 2006, the Archdiocese of Saint Paul and Minneapolis assigned Fr. Jules Omalanga as hospital chaplain for the Catholic patients at the Hennepin County Medical Center in downtown Minneapolis. As a priest chaplain, his primary job was to minister to the Catholic patients and their families, to support them, and to respond to their spiritual needs and concerns. From that time on, he started to minister not only to the Catholic patients and their families, but also to a very diverse and multicultural black community. Later, he found himself ministering to many patients from different ethnic groups and religious backgrounds. Because of his French background (he is from the Democratic Republic of Congo, the largest Francophone country) most of his French speaking patients and their relatives connected with him easily. The French language was their common bond and heritage. It helps them to communicate fluently without any linguistic barriers.

The next year—2007—he received an additional assignment as Parochial Administrator (equivalent of Pastor) at the church of Saint Leonard's of Port Maurice in South Minneapolis. There, about twenty of his Francophone patients and acquaintances followed for different reasons, including pastoral and sacramental needs in French: confession, baptism, sacrament of the sick, marriage, spiritual support and guidance, healing prayers, counseling, blessing of their houses or cars, etc. Even few of them became members of St. Leonard's church. Among them were six Togolese couples and their kids, one French Caucasian couple and their two daughters, and a single mother from

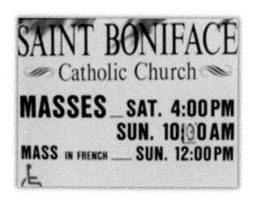

Photo by Mark Petty

the French Guyana and her son. This group were the pioneers of today's Francophone African Catholic Community in the Twin Cities. A French African choir was created, and they began to celebrate masses in French occasionally.

In the summer of 2008, Fr. Jules received a new assignment as full time pastor at the Church of St. Philip's in North Minneapolis. Once he was installed, the entire Francophone African group left St. Leonard's and joined St. Philip's. In both parishes, they were not easily welcomed. In fact, they were new immigrants in the United States. Most of them were young couples with young children. Their kids were making noise during the mass and their hosts were very challenged to accept them. This is one of the reasons some Caucasian parishioners were leaving the parish. Fr. Jules had to assure everyone that the Catholic Church was a home for everyone. No one was at the wrong place at a wrong time. All were welcome and had to embrace each another. "Differences are gifts from God Himself," he liked to repeat. However, not all parishioners welcomed these words. At Saint Philip's, the Francophone African community grew a little bigger with about fifty households. In four years, fifteen African couples were married in the church, many children were baptized and received their first communion, and a few African adults converted to Catholicism.

In the spring of 2012, St. Philip's Church merged with the Church of Ascension. Meanwhile, Fr. Jules was assigned as hospital chaplain at North Memorial without a parish to minister to the Francophone Africans. The African Community was dispersed and struggled to find a worship place - a parish. Many of them got discouraged and stayed home on Sundays. In effort to gather the community, a few events were organized during the summer: meetings with the Archdiocese leaders, a picnic in Brooklyn Park, and a French mass at the Church of St. Austin in North Minneapolis.

In October 2012, the Archdiocese of St. Paul and Minneapolis found a worship place for the Francophone African community at the Church of St. Boniface in Northeast Minneapolis, where it was established as a Francophone African chaplaincy. But, "New place, few challenges!" Beside his hospital ministry Fr. Jules and his African friends worked hard to bring back their dispersed folks into the church. The community struggled, but was strengthened with a regular celebration of Sunday mass in French, the celebrations of many weddings, baptisms, first communion, the creation of an International choir named "Sainte Marie," and the apostolate of the Legion of Mary. In Minnesota, the Francophone African Catholic Community is the only place that offers mass in French every Sunday.

Francophone African Catholic Community- St. Boniface
(Photo by Mark Petty in November 2015)

In three years (fall 2012 to fall 2015), the Francophone African Catholic community grew much bigger to two hundred fifty households. They are people from Togo, Cameroon, Democratic Republic of Congo, Ivory Coast, Benin, Guinea Conakry, Republic of Congo, and Senegal. There are also four Caucasian Americans who joined this community after the merging of St. Philip's with the Church of Ascension. This is a heartfelt welcoming community. Every Sunday, people are excited to attend the mass in French. The mass is always followed by a warm-felt hospitality. They sing in French and other African languages. The spirit of the Francophone African Catholic community reflects the ideal of the first Christian community: *"Day after day they met together…they broke bread together in different homes and shared their food happily and freely, while praising God. Everyone liked them, and each day the Lord added to their group others who were being saved"* (Acts 2:46-47).

Although formed by people from different parts of Africa, this community is like one unique family strengthened by Christian values and the philosophy of African solidarity. They share their joys and sorrows, their success and failures, their dreams and challenges. Therefore, the hospitality following the mass is, for them, a precious moment that energizes their daily life. During their hospitality they eat traditional African meals (Akoume, Ablo, Fufu, Pondu, Atseke, Mbongo-tshopi, Kwanga, Mfumbwa, etc). However, the most important thing, they actively listen to each other stories, struggles, concerns, and worries. The hospitality is then transformed into a place of encouragement and counseling, a source of healing and integral well-being. All of these makes Saint Boniface Church a unique place where African Catholics feel at home and respected, but not like second class citizens in the Catholic Church.

In caring for each other, these Africans definitely understand they are immigrants and cannot survive in a foreign land without God's help from their brothers and sisters. Since their well-being and success depend also on their children and grandchildren, they have the responsibility to educate them with the same Christian values and the spirit of African solidarity.

Today, there are many Francophone Africans in Minnesota. Because they are not all Christians or Catholics or legal immigrants, it is hard to establish the exact statistics. Below, are some statistics received by Father Omalanga from the leaders of African communities in Minnesota.

Togo- 5,000 persons
Cameroun- 4,000 persons
Democratic Republic of Congo- 2,000 persons
Ivory Cost- 1,000 persons
Guinea Conakry- 2,000 persons
Republic of Congo/ Brazzaville- 25 persons

Father Jules Omalanga, Founder and Priest-Chaplain of the Francophone African Catholic Community, with Service Attendants. (Photo by Mark Petty in November 2015)

Chapter Thirteen
French Vietnamese Influence in Minnesota

French Indochina, officially known as the Indochinese Union after 1887, and the Indochinese Federation after 1947, was a grouping of French colonial territories in Southeast Asia. A grouping of the three Vietnamese regions of Tonkin (north), Annam (centre), and Cochinchina (south), with Cambodia was formed in 1887. Laos was added in 1893 and Kouang-Tchéou-Wan (Guangzhouwan), in 1898. French was Indochina's official language from the beginning of French colonial rule in the mid-19th century until the dissolution of the South Vietnamese government in 1975.

After the fall of France during World War II, the colony was administered by the Vichy government and was under Japanese occupation until March 1945. Beginning in May 1941, the Viet Minh, a communist army led by Ho Chi Minh, began a revolt against the Japanese. In August 1945, after Japan's defeat, they declared Vietnamese independence, forming the Democratic State of Vietnam, and extended the war, known as the First Indochina War, against France. In Saigon, the anti-Communist State of Vietnam, led by former Emperor Bảo Đại, was granted independence in 1949. On November 9, 1953, the Kingdom of Laos and the Kingdom of Cambodia became independent. Following the Geneva Accord of 1954, the French evacuated Vietnam and French Indochina came to an end.[292]

Alexander de Rhodes, French missionary priest and creator of the Vietnamese alphabet (Public domain)

The Roman Catholic Church in the future Vietnam is evidence of the French influence in the country. Vietnam has the fifth largest Catholic population in Asia, after the Philippines, India, China and Indonesia. According to Catholic Hierarchy Catalog, there are 5,658,000 Catholics in Vietnam, representing 6.87% of the total population. There are twenty-six dioceses (including three archdioceses) with 2,228 parishes and 2,668 priests.[293]

The first Catholic missionaries visited Vietnam from Portugal at the beginning of the 16th century. However, it was not until the arrival of Jesuits from France in the first decades of the 17th century that Christianity became established within the local population. Between 1627-30, Alexander de Rhodes and Antoine Marquez, priests from the region of Provence in France, converted more than 6,000 people.

[292] Turner, Robert F. *Vietnamese Communism: Its Orgins and Development*, Hoover Institution Publications, 1975.
[293] Cheney, David M. *Statistics by Country by Catholic Population* (1996-2005)

In the 17th century, de Rhodes created an alphabet for the Vietnamese language, using the Latin script with added diacritic marks. This language, introduced by the French colonizers, continues to be used today, and is called Quc Ng (literally "national language").

Most Vietnamese in the United States arrived in a series of three waves. The first was in 1975, after the fall of Vietnam. The second was in 1977, as a result of new re-education policies in Vietnam. A third wave came in the early 1980s, when more than two million Vietnamese, known as the "boat people" fled Vietnam in small, overcrowded boats seeking asylum. Many of the Vietnamese who came to Minnesota were Catholic and sponsored by Catholic Charites and other Christian organizations. In a sense, therefore, the French Christian influence was indirectly responsible for their immigration to Minnesota. In Minnesota today, there are approximately 25,000 Vietnamese. About 85% of Minnesota's Vietnamese live in the Twin Cities metropolitan area. The remaining 15% live in places such as St. Cloud, Rochester, and Duluth.[294]

Much of the Vietnamese food that we enjoy today in Minnesota has been heavily affected by French colonialism in Indochina, with the French influence staying within the Vietnamese culinary culture. With these influences come new flavors, ingredients and combinations that give Vietnamese food a unique and wonderful taste, incorporating both the historical tastes of the Vietnamese people with the food introduced to them by the French.

The French brought many ingredients and flavors to Vietnam. The most popular and noticeable is probably the baguette, which the Vietnamese adapted and today create their own style of baguette using rice flour. Bánh mì, or Vietnamese baguettes, as they are known to those outside of the country, are bursting with Asian spices and flavors.

Many of the vegetables introduced to the country are common in Western cooking, and their names in Vietnamese reflect their origins. Potatoes, carrots, artichokes, onions and asparagus are just some of the more obvious vegetables that are included here, with the Vietnamese word for potato (khoai tây) literally meaning "Western yam."

Influences are not limited to simple ingredients, but stretch to methods of cooking also, with the use of butter and wine in the preparation of meals as a nod towards the French. The increase of beef into the cuisine is also apparent, as seen in dining experiences such as bò 7 món, which is a multi-course meal of beef created by the French to celebrate the rise in the availability of meat, which followed their arrival in the French colonial era. There are a number of Vietnamese restaurants in Minnesota where you can experience Vietnamese and Thai meals, with a French and American influence.

---

[294] From article written by Dung Pham, Vietnamese Social Services of Minnesota.

Chapter Fourteen
Acadian or Cajun Heritage in Minnesota
By Mark Labine

Map of Old Acadia (Public Domain)

Acadia was an early French settlement in the present-day Maritime Provinces in Canada. The map above shows the location of this settlement. Acadia, as a French settlement, existed from 1604 to 1710. In 1710, the land was ceded to Great Britain at the end of Queen Anne's War, but it still remained largely a French speaking colony. During the French and Indian War, the French in Acadia tried to remain neutral but were suspected of aiding France. In 1755, some six to seven thousand Acadians were forcibly deported from Acadia to the lower British American Colonies. Many died and their families and lives were cruelly disrupted and forced to endure tremendous hardships for many years. Eventually, many ended up in Louisiana and are known today as Cajuns. A number ended up back in the Maritimes and in Quebec.

An excellent article written about the Acadian Expulsion was written by Andrew O'Hehir for the Salon Media Group who describes the Acadians as a unique hybrid people. The Acadians offered a wiser, kinder vision of settling the continent. Instead, they became the victims of what has been called North America's first ethnic cleansing campaign. As Yale historian John Mack Faragher documents in his major new history of the Acadians and their downfall, "A Great and Noble Scheme," this semi-literate fishing and farming people forged a prosperous, autonomous and nearly idyllic society that was unique in the Western world. O'Hehir describes Faragher's book as follows:

"A Great and Noble Scheme" is an important book, one that should engender considerable debate and alter the contours of American history, albeit subtly. In it, Faragher argues that the long-overlooked Acadian episode deserves a special black mark in the history of Anglo-American settlement, both because it was the first example of an especially unsavory pattern and because the culture that was wiped out represented such a promising potential example of how Europeans and Native Americans might have coexisted, in peace and (quite literally) brotherhood.

Many French-Canadians who emigrated to Minnesota can trace their ancestry back to Acadians who ended up re-settling in Quebec.

Acadians-Creoles or Cajuns are an ethnic group mainly living in the U.S. state of Louisiana, and consist of the descendants of Acadian exiles (French-speakers from Acadia in what are now The Maritimes). Today, the Acadian Creoles make up a significant portion of south Louisiana's population and have exerted an enormous impact on the state's culture. Since their establishment in Louisiana the Cajuns have developed their own dialect, Cajun French, and developed a vibrant culture including folkways, music, and cuisine.

Cajun Flag (Public Domain)

There are numerous persons in Minnesota who have Acadian roots. My ancestor, Jean Baptiste Guidry dit Labine, was first exiled to Boston and was there from 1755 to 1763. He then went to St. Jacques L'Achigan, Quebec, which is just outside of Montreal to the northeast. (This is the same town that one of Angeline Jolie's ancestors came from.) There were numerous displaced Acadians who settled in St. Jacques, and many of their descendants came to Minnesota in the mass emigration from Canada in the late 1800s.

Cajun music has evolved from its roots in the music of the French-speaking Catholics of Canada. In earlier years, the fiddle was the predominant instrument, but gradually the accordion has come to share the limelight. Cajun music gained national attention in 2007, when the Grammy Award for Best Zydeco or Cajun Music Album category was created. Cajun music and Zydeco is enjoyed by Minnesota residents and is part of the French heritage here in Minnesota.

Cajun cuisine is a style of cooking named for the French-speaking Acadian people and has become a part of the Minnesota restaurant scene. In 2015, some examples of Cajun restaurants in Minnesota included Stella's Fish Café, The Lost Cajun Restaurant, Dixie's on

Grand, J.D. Hoyt's, the Cajun Deli, Bubba Gump Shrimp Company, French Hen Café, Popeyes Louisiana Kitchen, Louisiana Café, Bistro La Roux, Crazy Cajun, among others.

Paul Prudhomme (1940-2015), also known as Gene Autry Prudhomme, was an American celebrity chef whose specialties were Creole and Cajun cuisines. He was the descendant of Claude Prud'homme and Isabelle Alimot who immigrated to Montreal, Quebec before 1650. He was credited with popularizing the Creole and Cajun cuisines all over the United States, including Minnesota. He was the chef proprietor of K-Paul's Louisiana Kitchen in New Orleans, and had previously owned and managed several other restaurants. He developed several culinary products, including hot sauce and seasoning mixes, and wrote a number of cookbooks.

Evangeline, a Tale of Acadie, is a poem written by American Poet Henry Wadsworth Longfellow that was published in 1847. It follows an Acadian girl, Evangeline Bellefontaine, and her search for her lost love, Gabriel Lajeunesse, set during the time of the Acadian Expulsion in 1755. This poem has had a powerful effect defining Acadian history and identity. Today, there are many books and articles written about the Acadians and their Expulsion from present-day Nova Scotia.

Chapter Fifteen
French Huguenots

The term "Huguenot" is used to describe a Protestant religion that existed in France in the 16th and 17th centuries. It was aligned with the theology of John Calvin that arose during the Reformation and flourished in France after 1520. The Huguenot movement had political associations that put it in opposition to the French monarchy. In addition, the Huguenot's Protestant religious beliefs were in direct conflict with the Roman Catholic Church. Religious wars during this time were treacherous and deadly, and there were serious confrontations between the Huguenots and the French Church-State.

During the reigns of Henry II of France (1547-1559) and Francis II (1559-1560), the Huguenots grew in both number and political influence and came to include many prominent members of the French nobility. This increase in strength was looked upon as a threat to both the monarchy and to the Catholic Church and would eventually lead to civil and religious strife that would see many Huguenot families persecuted and driven out of France.

During the reign of Charles IX (1560-1574), the Queen Mother, Catherine de Medici, in alliance with the Catholic Duke of Guise, plotted and carried out what came to be known as the Saint Bartholomew's Day Massacre, which occurred on August 25, 1572. Thousands of Huguenots were killed in and around Paris while they gathered for religious celebration on this important day. Although there were periods of tolerance towards the Huguenots, most notably during the reign of Henry III and the actual establishment of Huguenot religion controlled French cities such as La Rochelle, Huguenot political freedom was eventually eliminated under Louis XIII (1610–1643), and the group's religious freedom was taken away entirely in 1685, when Louis XIV revoked the Edict of Nantes.

The act of Revocation of 1685 took away both the civil and religious liberties of the French Huguenots and ushered in a new wave of Huguenot persecution and discrimination. All Huguenot worship and schooling was forbidden. All Huguenot churches were ordered destroyed or transformed into Catholic churches, and all Huguenot clergymen were ordered to leave France within fourteen days. To further harass the Huguenot population, some 400,000 forced "converts" were ordered to attend mass and participate in the Catholic Eucharist. Many of those who refused were condemned to death or imprisoned. As might be expected, there was a tremendous exodus of Huguenot families from France. Of the 1,500,000 Huguenots living in France in 1660, almost one fourth left the country in the decade following the Revocation. This exodus resulted in the extension of Huguenot family branches into England, Germany, Switzerland, and Holland, and would eventually result in links to the English, German, and Dutch colonies of North America.

It is estimated that 20-30% of the English population have Huguenot ancestors somewhere in their background. Many early English settlers in America had Huguenot French speaking ancestors. A combination of any of the following factors may indicate a Huguenot connection:

1. A French sounding name and/or a family tradition of there being a French connection, possibly aristocratic.
2. Links to the Anglican Church or non-conformist denominations.
3. An ancestor's association with silk weaving or another recognized Huguenot trade such as clock making, silver smithing, furniture making, ironware, or a textile industry trade.
4. Links to known areas of Huguenot settlement, e.g. Spitalfields in the East End of London.

In the Virginia colony, pockets of Huguenot colonists could be found along the James River and in King William Parish. Notable among these settlements is that of Manakintown, where Huguenot surnames may still be found. Other Huguenot enclaves include Berks and Lancaster counties in Pennsylvania and New Rochelle in New York.[295]

---

[295] Baird, Charles W. *History of the Huguenot Emigration to America*, Genealogical Publishing Co, Inc. Baltimore 1973

Bibliography on French Huguenots
(All of these books are available at the Clayton Library
Center for Genealogical Research)[296]

- Bellon, Eugen. Zerstreut in alle Winde [Scattered to all the Winds], 1685-1720. Trans. by Erika Gautschi. West Lafayette, Indiana: Belle Publications, 1983. This is an English translation of historical papers originally published by the German Huguenot Society. Describes the Dauphine French Huguenots' migration into Italy, Switzerland, and Germany. 245 pages. GEN 940.088245 B447 EUR.

- Bennett, Abram Elting. Huguenot Migration: Descendants' Contributions to America. [California: A. B. Bennett], c1984. GEN 973.04944 B471 USA.

- Bernard, Gildas. Les familes protestantes en France: XVIe siecle-1792: Guide des recherches biographiques et genealogiques. Paris: Archives nationales, 1987. Text in French. 699 pages. GEN 944 B518 FRA.

- Beverly, Trevia Wooster, comp. Huguenot Cemetery, St. Augustine, St. John's County, Florida. Houston, Texas: T. W. Beverly, 1992. GEN 975.9 B571 FLA.

- Baird, Charles Washington. History of the Huguenot Emigration to America. 1885. Reprint, Baltimore: Genealogical Publishing Co., 1973. GEN 325.244 B163 USA.

- Cooper, William Durrant, ed. List of Foreign Protestants and Aliens, Resident in England 1618-1688. 1862. Reprint, New York: AMS Press, [1968]. 119 pages. GEN 942 C778 ENG.

- Daniels, George F. The Huguenots in the Nipmuck Country or Oxford Prior to 1713. Boston: Estes & Lauriat, 1880. 168 pages. GEN 974.4 D186 MASS.

- Davis, Harry Alexander. Some Huguenot Families of South Carolina and Georgia.... Washington: H. A. Davis, 1926. Includes information on the families of Peter Lafitte, Andre Verdier, Samuel Montague, Henri Francois Bourquin, Jean Baptiste Bourquin, Peter Papot, and Benjamin Godin. GEN 929.2 D262 USA.

- Douglas, William. The Douglas Register. Edited by W. Mac Jones. Richmond, Virginia: J. W. Ferguson & Sons, 1928. A detailed record of births, marriages, and deaths kept by the Rev. William Douglas between 1750 and 1797; an index to Goochland County (Virginia) wills; and notes on the French Huguenot refugees who lived in Manakintown. 412 pages. GEN 975.5 D737 VA.

- Elliott, Ella Zerbey. Blue Book of Schuylkill County.... Pottsville, Pennsylvania: Pottsville Republican, Joseph Zerbey, proprietor, 1916. Describes eastern Pennsylvania Huguenots and Palatines, their service to England in the French and Indian War, and their involvement in the American Revolution. 456 pages. GEN 974.8 E46 PA.

- Finnell, Arthur Louis, comp. Register of Qualified Huguenot Ancestors of the National Huguenot Society. Bloomington, Minnesota: The National Huguenot Society, 1995. Contains the current compiled list of Huguenot names recognized by the National Huguenot Society. 337 pages. GEN 973 F514 USA.

- Huguenot names recognized by the National Huguenot Society of New England: 1924-1949 Roster of Members and Ancestors. Bloomington, Minnesota: The National Huguenot Society, 1993. 14 pages. GEN 974 F514 USA.

---

[296] The Clayton Library Center for Genealogical Research is located in Houston, Texas and has a large selection of books on Huguenot genealogy.

- Fischer, David, comp. Transactions of the Huguenot Society of South Carolina, Index to Vols. 1-96. Charleston: Huguenot Society of South Carolina, c1994. GEN 975.7 H897 SC.
- Forbes, Allen, and Paul F. Cadman. The Boston French. Cottonport, Louisiana: Polyanthos, 1971. This is a reprint of Boston and Some Noted Émigrés (Boston: 1938). A collection of facts and incidents relating to some well-known citizens of France who found homes in New England. Includes accounts of several visits made by one of the authors to La Rochelle and to the homes of the ancestors of Paul Revere. GEN 974.4 F693 MASS.
- Fosdick, Lucian J. The French Blood in America. New York and Chicago: F. H. Revell Co., [c1906]. 448 pages. GEN 973.04944 F748 USA.
- Franklin, Charles M. Huguenot Genealogical Research. [Indianapolis, Indiana?:] C. M. Franklin, c1985. 58 pages. GEN 929.1072 F831 USA.
- The French Protestant Church in the City of Charleston, South Carolina. Charleston: Press of Walker, Evans & Cogswell Company, 1898. 23 pages. GEN 975.7 C477 SC.
- Gannon, Peter Steven, ed. Huguenot Refugees in the Settling of Colonial America. New York: Huguenot Society of America, c1985. 421 pages. GEN 973.2 H897 USA.
- Gilman, Charles Malcolm Brookfield. The Huguenot Migration in Europe and America: Its Cause. Colts Neck, New Jersey: Arlington Laboratory for Clinical and Historical Research, c1962. Includes index of potential Huguenot ancestors compiled by the National Huguenot Society. 234 pages. GEN 973.04944 G487 USA.
- Goodbar, Richard Loewer, et al, eds. The Huguenots: Their History and Legacy: Biographies of Ancestors of Members of the Huguenot Society of Maryland. [Baltimore:] The Huguenot Society of Maryland, 1993. Published in celebration of the twenty-fifth anniversary of the Huguenot Society of Maryland. 77 pages. GEN 975.2 H891 MD.
- Goree, Langston James, and Janice Curtis Pampell, eds. Master Index to "The Huguenot". Bryan, Texas: Family History Foundation, 1986. Also contains an index to the vestry book of King William Parish, Virginia, 1707-1750. 401 pages. GEN 975.5 H897 VA.
- Gwynn, Robin D. Huguenot Heritage: The History and Contributions of the Huguenots in Britain. London and Boston: Routledge & Kegan Paul, c1985. 220 pages. GEN 942 G994.
- Harrison, Michael, ed. Canada's Huguenot Heritage: Proceedings of Commemorations held in Canada during 1985 of the Tercentenary of the Revocation of the Edict of Nantes. Toronto: Huguenot Society of Canada, 1987. 231 pages. GEN 971 C212.
- Hirsch, Arthur Henry. The Huguenots of Colonial South Carolina. Durham, North Carolina: Duke University Press, 1928. 338 pages. GEN 975.7 H669 SC.
- Holmes, Abiel. A Memoir of the French Protestants who Settled at Oxford in Massachusetts, A.D. MDCLXXXVI. Cambridge: Hilliard and Metcalf, 1826. Bound with the author's The History of Cambridge (Boston: 1801). 84 pages. GEN 974.4 H749 MASS.
- Hovenden, Robert, ed. The Registers of the Wallon or Strangers' Church in Canterbury. Lymington: Huguenot Society of London, 1891-98. Printed from church registers of the Canterbury Cathedral. Contains christenings, 1583-1837; marriages, 1583-1747; baptisms, 1581-1837; deaths, 1581-1715; abstracts of marriage contracts, 1580-1680; abstracts of wills, 1586-1704; and abstracts of miscellaneous documents, 1586-1683. Entries are in French. GEN 942 C229 ENG.
- The Huguenot, vols. 1-30 (1924-83). A publication of The Huguenot Society Founders of Manakin in the Colony of Virginia. GEN 975.5 H897 VA.

- Kelly, Caleb Guyer. French Protestantism, 1559-1562. Baltimore: Johns Hopkins Press, 1918. Originally published in 1916 as a Ph.D. dissertation, Johns Hopkins University. Contains excellent historical background on the Huguenots. 185 pages. GEN 944 K29.
- Koehler, Albert F. The Huguenots, or, The Early French in New Jersey. [New Jersey?:] the Huguenot Society of New Jersey, 1955. Reprint, Baltimore: Clearfield Co., 1992. 51 pages. GEN 974.9 K77 NJ.
- Lart, Charles Edmund. Huguenot Pedigrees. 1925-26. Reprint (2 vols. in 1), Baltimore: Genealogical Publishing Co., 1967. GEN 973.04944 L335 USA, GEN 944 L335 FRA.
- Lavender, Abraham D. French Huguenots: From Mediterranean Catholics to White Anglo-Saxon Protestants. New York: P. Lang, c1990. 264 pages. GEN 944 L399.
- Lawton, Eba Anderson, comp. Family Names of Huguenot Refugees to America. 1901. Reprint, Baltimore: Genealogical Publishing Company, 1963. 20 pages. GEN 929.1 L425 USA.
- MacDowell, Dorothy Kelly, comp. DuBose Genealogy. Columbus, South Carolina: R. L. Bryan Co., 1972. Reprint, Aiken, South Carolina: D. K. MacDowell, 1981. Contains data on the descendants of Isaac Dubose (or Dubois) and wife, Suzanne Couillandeau, French Huguenot refugees who settled on the Santee River in South Carolina about 1689. 533 pages. GEN 929.2 M138 DUBOIS.
- Mann, Florian Alexander. Story of the Huguenots. Los Angeles, California: W. A. Kistler Co., 1912. A narrative set in Florida in the sixteenth century. 198 pages. GEN 975.9 M281 FLA.
- Marmoy, Charles F. A., ed. The Case Book of "La Maison de Charité de Spittlefields," 1739-41. London: Huguenot Society, 1981. Contains genealogical information on Huguenots in London. Entries are in French; the notes and prefatory material are in English. 88 pages. GEN 942 M281 ENG.
- Potter, Elisha Reynolds. Memoir Concerning the French Settlements and French Settlers in the Colony of Rhode Island. 1879. Reprint, Baltimore: Genealogical Publishing Co., 1968. 138 pages. GEN 974.5 P866 RI.
- Publications of the Huguenot Society of London, vols. 1-56 (1887-1985). GEN 942 H897 ENG.
- Ravenel, Daniel. List des Français et Suisses.... 1868. Reprint, Baltimore: Genealogical Publishing Company, 1968. Contains lists, prepared around 1695, of French and Swiss Protestants living in the Charleston, South Carolina area who desired naturalization. Also contains related articles by Daniel Ravenel published in the Southern Intelligencer, 1822. 77 pages. GEN 975.7 R253 SC.
- Reeves, Vera, comp. Register of Qualified Huguenot Ancestors of the National Huguenot Society. 1983. Reprint with corrections, Bloomington Minnesota: The National Huguenot Society, 1993. 117 pages. GEN 369.1 R331 USA.
- Revill, Janie, comp. A Compilation of the Original Lists of Protestant Immigrants to South Carolina, 1763-1773. Columbia, South Carolina: State Co., 1939. Reprint, Baltimore: Genealogical Publishing Co., 1968. 163 pages. GEN 975.7 R454 SC.
- Rosengarten, J. G. French Colonists and Exiles in the United States. 1907. Reprint, Bowie, Maryland: Heritage Books, 1989. 234 pages. GEN 325.44 R813.
- Rupp, I. Daniel. A Collection of Upwards of Thirty Thousand Names of German, Swiss, Dutch, French, and other Immigrants in Pennsylvania from 1727-1776. 1856. Reprint, Baltimore: Genealogical Publishing Co., 1965. Also includes listings of French Huguenots immigrants living in New York. 583 pages. GEN 974.8 R946 PA.
- Scouloudi, Irene, ed. Huguenots in Britain and their French Background, 1550-1800. Basingstoke: Macmillan, 1987. Contributions to the Historical Conference of the Huguenot Society of London, 24-25 September 1985. 296 pages. Includes index. GEN 942 H897 ENG.

- Smiles, Samuel. The Huguenots in France after the Revocation of the Edict of Nantes.... New York: Harper & Brothers, 1874. 430 pages. 944 S641 FRA.
- Stapleton, Ammon. Memorials of the Huguenots in America with Special Reference to their Emigration to Pennsylvania. 1901. Reprint, Baltimore: Genealogical Publishing Co., 1964. 164 pages. GEN 974.8 S794 PA.
- Steedman, Marguerite Couturier. A Short History of the French Protestant Huguenot Church of Charleston, South Carolina. Charleston: French Protestant Church, 1983. 10 pages. GEN 975.7 S813 SC.
- Strati, Patricia Wright, comp. Our Garrigues Ancestors: French Huguenots with Connections to Charlemagne & European Royalty. Baltimore: Gateway Press, 1992. 176 pages. GEN 929.2 S899 GARRIG.
- Stoudt, John Baer. Nicolas Martiau, the Adventurous Huguenot, the Military Engineer, and the Earliest American Ancestor of George Washington. No place or date of publication. Includes photocopies of excerpts from periodicals and other material pertaining to Nicolas Martiau. 103 pages. GEN 929.2 S889 MARTIA.
- Thomas, Theodore Gaillard, pub. A Contribution to the History of the Huguenots of South Carolina.... Columbia, South Carolina: R. L. Bryan, 1972. Consists of pamphlets by Samuel Dubose (reminiscences of St. Stephen's Parish, Craven County) and Frederick A. Porcher (historical and social sketch of Craven County). GEN 975.7 T462 SC.
- Transactions of the Huguenot Society of South Carolina, vols. 1-99. GEN 975.7 H897 SC.
- Vestry Book of King William Parish, Virginia, 1707-1750. [Virginia?:] Huguenot Society of the Founders of Manakin in the Colony of Virginia, 1988. This is a reprint, with new introduction and index, of material originally published in issues of The Virginia Magazine, 1905-06. 167 pages. GEN 975.5 V584 VA.
- Wittmeyer, Alfred Victor, ed. Registers of the Births, Marriages, and Deaths of the "Eglise française á la Nouvelle York" from 1688 to 1804. 1886. Reprint, Baltimore, Genealogical Publishing Co., 1968. 324 pages. GEN 974.7 W832 NY.

Chapter Sixteen
Genealogy Websites and Resources
By Mark Labine
Reviewed and edited by John Schade

People of French-Canadian and Acadian descent have ancestors who are among the best documented people in the world. French-Canadian pedigrees can be constructed on the basis of marriage records and can usually be extended ten to fifteen generations in every line back to the immigrant ancestor. In many cases, the parish or village of origin in France can also easily be found. All that is needed to begin a search are the names of a couple married in Quebec and an approximate date of marriage.

There are a number of books that discuss how to go about researching your French-Canadian genealogy including the following books:

1. Auger, Roland-J. "Tracing Ancestors through the Province of Quebec and Acadia to their place of Origin in France", *French-Canadian and Acadian Genealogical Review, vol. II, no. 4, Winter.*
2. Boudreau, Dennis M. *Beginning Franco-American Genealogy.* Pawtucket, RI: American-French Genealogical Society, 1986. /Gc 020.171 B66b
3. Geyh, Patricia Keeney. *French-Canadian Sources: A Guide for Genealogists.* Orem, UT: Ancestry Publishing, 2002. /Gc 971.4 F887.
4. Normandeau-Jones, Lea. *Finding Your Acadian Ancestors.* Toronto, Ontario: Heritage Productions, 2001. /Gc 971 N789f.

The French-American Heritage Foundation has constructed a website with some useful information on how to research your French-Canadian and French ancestry. Below is a list of places or websites you can go to in order to research your French-Canadian roots.

Acadian History and Genealogies

The French colony of Acadia was founded in 1604 and covered what is now Nova Scotia and parts of New Brunswick, Prince Edward Island and Maine. The territory was a perennial battleground for the French and British, and in 1755, more than 7,000 Acadians were deported to the American colonies. Thousands more were exiled to France. By 1785, many had found refuge in the Spanish colony of Louisiana. Unlike Quebec, Acadian parish registers and notarial records have suffered extensive losses and this could make researching your Acadian ancestors more difficult. Below is a list of some important resources on Acadian genealogy.

Arsenault, Bona. *Histoire et genealogie des Acadiens.* rev. ed. 6 vols. Ottawa: Editions Lemeac Inc., 1978. /Gc 929.171 Ar7hi/ An important work on Acadian genealogy and history to 1755.

Arsenault, Bona. *History of the Acadians*. rev. ed. Ottawa: Editions Lemeac Inc., 1978. /Gc 929.171 Ar7hb/ English translation of vol. 1 above, including a glossary of key French words.

Bergeron, Adrien. *Le Grand Arrangement des Acadiens au Quebec 1625-1925*. 8 vols. Montreal: Editions Elysee, 1981. /Gc 971.4 B45g.

Deville, Winston. *Acadian Church Records 1679-1757*. Mobile, AL: The compiler, 1964. /Gc 971.6 D49a/ Miscellaneous records dating 1679-86 and 1753-57.

Hebert, Donald J. *Index and Key Words to Histoire et Genealogie des Acadiens by Bona Arsenault*. Cecilia, LA: The Author, 1979. /Gc 929.171 Ar7hia.

Jehn, Janet B. *Corrections & Additions to Arsenault's Histoire et Genealogie des Acadiens*. Covington, KY: The Author, 1988. /Gc 929.171 Ar7h suppl.

Morrison, Phoebe Chauvin. *Acadian Church Records Index, with Annotations*. Houma, AL: P. C. Morrison, 2001. /Gc 971 M833a.

Rieder, Milton P., Jr., and Norma Gaudet Rieder, ed. *Acadian Church Records*. Metairie, LA: The editors, 1976-83. /Gc 971.6 D49a/ [For vol. 1 see DeVille] vol. 2 -Beaubassin 1712-1748 vols. 3-5 - Port Royal 1702-1740.

White, Stephen A. *Dictionnaire Genealogique des Familles Acadiennes: premiere partie, 1636 a 1714, en Deux Volumes*. Moncton, NB: Centre d'etudes Acadiennes, Universite de Moncton, 1999. /Gc 971 W585d/ The key work on early Acadian genealogy.

The following contain data useful in connecting the Acadian settlers of Louisiana (1764-85) and other colonies, with those expelled from Acadia (1755-63).

Hebert, Donald J. *Acadians in Exile*. Cecilia, LA: Hebert Publications, 1980. /Gc 929.171 H35a/ Includes: Acadian records in Canada, France and the West Indies; Acadian censuses of 1671, 1686, & 1714; history of the Acadian migrations; and inventory of resources.

Jehn, Janet. *Acadian Exiles in the colonies:* Covington, KY: The author, 1977. /Gc929.171 J38ac/ Includes lists of Acadians in the American colonies, Acadian prisoners at Halifax 1763, and vital records of Acadians in the civil state of Guyana 1763-1792.

Morrison, Phoebe Chauvin. *Early Acadian Census Index, 1671-1714, with Annotations*. Houma, LA: P. C. Morrison, 2001. /Gc 971 M833aa.

Rieder, Milton P., Jr., and Norma Gaudet Rieder, comp. *The Acadian Exiles in the American Colonies 1755-1768*. Metairie, LA: The compilers, 1977. /Gc 929.171 R44a/ Lists for Pennsylvania, New York, Connecticut, S. Carolina, Massachusetts, & Maryland.

Rieder, Milton P., Jr., and Norma Gaudet Rieder. *The Acadians in France*. 3 vols. Metairie, LA: The authors, 1967. /Gc 929.14 R44a/ Rolls of Acadians living in France 1762-1776, and lists of deportees, 1758-63.

Rieder, Milton P., Jr. and Norma Gaudet Rieder. *The Crew and Passenger Registration Lists of the Seven Acadian Expeditions of 1785*. Metairie, LA: The authors, 1965. /Gc 976.3 R44c/ A listing of the Acadians who migrated from France to Spanish Louisiana in 1785.

Robichaux, Albert J., Jr. *The Acadian Exiles in Nantes, 1775-1785*. Harvey, LA: The author, 1978. /Gc 929.171 R55ac.

Robichaux, Albert J., Jr. *The Acadian Exiles in Saint-Malo 1758-1785*. 3 vols. Eunice, LA: Hebert Publications, 1981. /Gc 929.171 R55acs/ The third volume covers marriages in the departments of Cotes-du-Nord, ille-et-Vilaine, Morbihan and Loire-Atlantique, and also supplements the author's book on exiles in Nantes.

Robichaux, Albert J., Jr. *Acadian Marriages in France: Department of Ille-et-Vilaine, 1759-1776*. Harvey, LA: The author, 1976. /Gc 929.171 R55a/ Includes an excellent brief history of the Acadians exiled to France.

Allen County Public Library Genealogy Center

This website provides information on how to research your French-Canadian ancestors and provides information on historical records you can access to assist you in your search. The website address is: http://www.genealogycenter.org/pathfinders/guides/frenchcanadian.aspx.

Acadian and French-Canadian Ancestral Home Website

The Acadian and French-Canadian Ancestral Home Website is full of research materials such as genealogy, historical documents, parish registers, early American newspapers, research aids, and various papers related to our Acadian history as well as French-Canadian, Cajun and French-American ancestry. You will find data relating to the Acadian Deportation, lists of exiles, lists of Prisoners, ships' lists, census records, family genealogies, and mtDNA results. New information is posted on a regular basis. The website address is: http://www.acadian-home.org/frames.html.

American-French Genealogical Society

The American-French Genealogical Society is a non-profit genealogical and **historical** organization devoted to people of French-Canadian extraction. It is a genealogical and historical organization for French-Canadian research. The website states it has a database of over 600,000 listings. Go to http://afgs.org/.

Celebrity Genealogies

In case you want to find out if you are related to a famous person. This website lists celebrity ancestral genealogies. To http://www.geneastar.org/.

Chez Nous

Over a period of twenty-two years, a succession of volunteer editors recorded stories of the heritage and culture of the French and the Midwest in two newsletters, *Chez Nous* and *Nouvelles Villes Jumelles*. Access to these publications is available through the French-American Heritage Foundation (FAHF) website. An index of these 145 newsletters is included on the website. Go to http://fahfminn.org/, click on library tab, click on Chez Nous, click on index for Chez Nous. At page ten of the index are nineteen entries under "Genealogy, general." Complete sets of the newsletters have been provided to the libraries of the Minnesota, North Dakota and Wisconsin Historical Societies, and IF Midwest at the University of North Dakota at Grand Forks. IF Midwest has permission to post the newsletters to the internet.

Cousins et Cousines Genealogy Website

This is the genealogy database website for the Canadian Interest branch of the Minnesota Genealogical Society. The Society began in 1969 as a roundtable with a handful of members. The group met in people's homes and stored the first books of their library collection in the trunks of their cars. There have been a few names to describe the society over the years including the Northwest Territory, Canadian and French Heritage Institute in 1979, the French/Canadian, Metis Genealogical Society in 2001, the Canadian Genealogical & Heritage Society of Minnesota in 2005, and finally the Canadian Interest Group in 2012. The original database was donated in 2006 by Al Dahlquist, past president of the Society. The purpose was to add data from Ruth Charest research of 40+ years and her eight file cabinets filled with folders of French-Canadian families. The address is http://www.mngs2.org/tng/.

Denis Beauregard's French-Canadian Genealogy Resources

Denis Beauregard is a well known genealogist and specialist of records in Quebec, Acadia and France. His first works were made in the 1980s on his ancestral tree and on those of his friends. He later focused on his family, trying to link all the Beauregard to his ancestor. From 1996, he decided to switch to the French immigration to Quebec (and former French colonies of the continent) to better use his recognition by the French genealogists, because he created many resources helping to create that community. At the beginning of the century, he began his masterpiece, the database known as Genealogy of the French in North America. You can google his website with the name "FrancoGene" and his website address is: http://www.francogene.com/index.php.

Dit Names

Many families had "dit" names or aliases reflecting geographic origins, physical appearance, etc., which often replaced the family name. An ancestor's record may be filed under a variant surname.

DNA and Genealogy

Many people searching their family roots are now using DNA tests. A website that has information for genealogists including understanding your DNA results, using third party tools, and other information regarding using DNA tests to trace your family roots is at http://howtodna.com.

FamilySearch

Probably no group is better known for its family history activities than the Church of Latter Day Saints. As part of their faith, the Mormons have cataloged and collected information on millions of individuals. Researchers can access all of this information at LDS Family History Centers located around the world and at their familysearch.org website. Visitors to this fully searchable web site now have online access to the Ancestral File (organized by family and pedigree), the International Genealogical Index (indexing vital records), the Family History Library Catalog, research outlines and guides, and lists of other web sites. With more information being added all the time, this has become the first stop for many family historians. They have a free search engine which can be quite helpful in searching for ancestors. They also have membership services where you can get access to more information, including copies of document, newspapers, and birth, marriage and death records. Their website address is https://www.familysearch.org.

GenoPro

The GenoPro website at http://www.genopro.com/genealogy-links lists genealogy resources in the United States and links to their websites. It also lists genealogy resources in other countries, including France. You can google it at GenoPro Genealogy Links.

Free Name Search

This is a site where you can search for ancestral names via Genealogy.com. The website address is: http://www.genealogy.com/genealogy/allsearch.html.

French Genealogy

If you have ancestors who lived in France, the website called the Guide de Généalogie may be helpful. It is located at the website http://www.guide-genealogie.com. If you don't read French very well, you can use Google Translate to convert most of the web site's pages into English.

French-Canadian and Acadian Genealogy Books

This website has a listing of history and genealogy books available to purchase, including a wide selection of publishers, including Global Heritage Press. You can google by using GlobalGenealogy http://globalgenealogy.com/.

French-Canadian Genealogical Society of Connecticut

The French-Canadian Genealogical Society of Connecticut, located in the Old County Courthouse on the town green in Tolland, Connecticut (Exit 68 on I-84), is dedicated to collecting, preserving and disseminating genealogical and historical information about French-Canadian ancestors who settled in Quebec and Acadia and their descendants. Their focus is on the genealogy of people of French-Canadian and Acadian heritage who settled in Connecticut, Massachusetts, New York, and throughout New England. They also have information about other areas of the United States and Canada. Their website address is: http://www.fcgsc.org/links.html.

French-Canadian Sources

This book titled *French-Canadian Sources, A Guide for Genealogists,* is a six-year collaborative effort of members of the French-Canadian/Acadian Genealogical Society. This book provides detailed explanations about the genealogical sources available to those seeking their French-Canadian ancestors. It was written by Patricia Keeney Geyh, Joyce Soltis Banachowski, Linda K. Boyea, Patricia Sarasin Ustine, Marilyn Holt Bourbonais, Beverly Ploenske LaBelle, Francele Sherburne and Karen Vincent Huniston.

French English Online Dictionary

This website can be helpful when you are trying to interpret historical documents or records that are in French. The website address is: http://www.wordreference.com/enfr/.

GenWeb Project

The goal of the USGenWeb project is to establish non-commercial free family history web sites for every county, in every state, through the work of volunteers. Although web resources vary from area to area, at least some information is available for each state, along with links to official state home pages. USGenWeb also sponsors several ambitious special projects including a national tombstone transcription effort, the transcription of all census data, work on digitizing and making available a variety of maps, and online archives of obituaries from around the country. The WorldGenWeb project hopes to achieve, on an international scale, what the USGenWeb project is aiming for in the United States. In this scheme, the world is hierarchically organized first by region (fifteen total), then by country, then by individual provinces, states, or counties. Presently, more than fifty percent of the world's nations have volunteer hosts working under a regional coordinator. Websites for the USGenWeb project is at http://www.rootsweb.com/~usgenweb/ and the WorldGenWeb project is at http://www.worldgenweb.org/.

Getting Started with Genealogy on the Web

This website is a great resource for anyone wanting to research their family tree on the Internet. The website gives basic instructions on how to search your family history and provides links to a number of websites from around the United States that have useful genealogy information. The website address is: http://www.vodien.com/singapore-community/education/getting-started-genealogy-web.php.

In Search of Your Canadian Roots

In Search of Your Canadian Roots, Tracing Your Family Tree in Canada is a book (3rd Edition) written by Angus Baxter, who some call Canada's leading genealogist. It first discusses the great migrations of Scots, Irish, English, Germans, Huguenots, Ukrainians, and Jews to Canada; describes the national archives in Ottawa, with its holdings of censuses, parish registers, naturalization records, land and homestead records, military records, and passenger lists; summarizes the holdings of the LDS Church relating to Canada; and explores the vast nationwide record sources such as census records and church registers.

Je Me Souviens

This is a publication of the American French Genealogical Society, located at the Franco-American Heritage Center, 78 Earle Street, P.O. Box 830, Woonsocket, Rhode Island 02895 (2015 address). Je Me Souviens publishes stories of interest to people of French-Canadian and Acadian descent and has been publishing these stories since 1978. The American French Genealogical Society accepts requests for ancestral searches. To utilize the AFGS Research Service, print the research request sheet by clicking on the research request form at the bottom of the page at their website located at www.afgs.org, fill in the necessary information, and send via regular mail to the address listed on the form.

Michael Marcotte Genealogy Website

Michael Marcotte has created a website with over 24,000 names of his ancestors and relatives, most of whom are French or French-Canadian. Since most people with French-Canadian ancestors are related, it is very likely you will be able to find an ancestor of yours in his database. The focus of his website is on the Marcotte family, but it includes lineage charts for many French-Canadians, and shows how many celebrities have French-Canadian roots. You can google his website with the word Michael Marcotte Genealogy. His website is at http://michaelmarcotte.com.

Minnesota Genealogical Society

The Minnesota Genealogical Society is located at 1185 Concord Street North, Suite 218, South St. Paul, Minnesota. It is Minnesota's largest and most comprehensive family history research organization. The goal of the Minnesota Genealogical Society and its branches is to provide education on methods of genealogical research, social activities with other individuals with genealogy interests, and a place to research ancestors. Their Library and Research Center provides a wide variety of information covering many countries, articles on vital statistics, military records, immigration, mapping records and numerous other areas of research. Its website address is: http://mngs.org/. There is a large French-Canadian collection on site.

Minnesota Historical Society Genealogical Resources

This website provides resource links to a number of databases and indexes that would assist someone conducting a search on their family history. The following is some of the information included in this website at http://www.mnhs.org/genealogy/family/genweblinks.php.

1. **Minnesota Historical Society Death Certificate Index** at http://people.mnhs.org/dci. This database indexes the official statewide death certificates of the Minnesota Department of Health. The certificates themselves are available on microfilm in the Minnesota Historical Society's Library or through the Library's interlibrary loan service. The web site contains an extensive series of FAQs with additional information on the index. The index currently holds more than 2,600,000 names.

2. **Minnesota Historical Society Birth Certificate Index** is located at http://people.mnhs.org/bci. This database indexes the official statewide birth records of the Minnesota Department of Health. The web site delivers non-certified copies of these records directly over the Internet.

3. **Cyndi's List** at http://www.CyndisList.com/. This site, operated by Cyndi Howells, has grown from a part-time project into one of the most respected and visited family history resources online. Howells offers over 179,000 categorized and cross-referenced links, with more added on a regular basis. Categories are ordered alphabetically on the site's main page, and are dated to indicate currency. Choosing a category reveals further layers of organization and lists of links, some of which

are annotated with brief descriptions. Researchers are further aided by indexes and a search engine.

4. **Online Searchable Death Indexes & Records** at http://www.deathindexes.com

5. **Directory of Online Death Indexes** listed by state, including obituaries, cemetery listings, probate records, and the Social Security Death Index.

6. **National Archives and Records administration**. NARA's Genealogy Page offers guidance to researchers interested in locating and accessing federal records. Detailed information is provided on each of its regional facilities, as well as ordering instructions for NARA publications, including microfilm catalogs. Several research guides are available covering such record types as census, immigration, naturalization, and military. Visitors can also access the Soundex Machine through this site and obtain surname codes for the 1880 through 1930 federal population censuses. The two website addresses are: http://www.archives.gov/research_room/genealogy/index.html   and http://www.archives.gov/research_room/arc/index.html

7. **Archival Research Catalog** (ARC) serves as NARA's online catalog to a limited portion of its nationwide holdings, replacing the older NAIL (National Archives Information Locator) system. As well as providing search access to the collections, it also allows users to view online selected digitized items such as World War II casualty lists.

Nord Pas-de-Calais Website

Nord-Pas de Calais, Nord for short, is one of the twenty-seven regions of France. It consists of the departments of Nord and Pas-de-Calais. This website is a site of GenWeb and provides genealogy information about searching for your ancestors in France. The website address is: http://www.francegenweb.org/~sitesdgw/nord-pdc/.

Nosorigines
Website of Quebec and Acadian Genealogy

Nosorgines is a genealogy database that has thousands of French-Canadian and Acadian names and family ancestral lines. The website is easy to use and allows you to add your family names and information so that the names in the website keep growing. This is an excellent research tool for researching not only your French-Canadian roots, but also your French ones. The website address is: http://www.nosorigines.qc.ca/.

PRDH Database

This genealogy database is at the University of Montreal. PRDH stands for Le Programme de recherche en démographie historique. This research includes an exhaustive reconstruction of the population of Quebec from the beginnings of French colonization in the seventeenth century. http://www.genealogie.umontreal.ca/en/acces.htm.

Quebec Census Records

The Quebec censuses dating from 1666-1901 are also a valuable source for researchers. For a list of published pre-1851 census returns, refer to the periodical *Lost in Canada* vol. 10, no. 3, August 1984, pp. 163-4. The online 1881 Canadian Census found at the FamilySearch website, www.FamilySearch.org, and the 1871 Ontario Census Index, currently provide the only province-wide indexes for the major post-1825 Quebec censuses. Once a specific place of marriage has been discovered, it is fairly easy to search the film for that locality and find the family. Agricultural schedules accompany some censuses, and in 1851 and 1861, wives are listed with their maiden names. The 1901 census gives exact birth dates.

Quebec Notarial Records

Notarial records are a valuable source for researchers. The notary functioned as a general local official in the French colonies, recording civil marriage contracts, inventories, wills, guardianships, land grants, sales, and other transactions. In case of a missing parish register, the marriage contract may supply parents' names. Microfilmed notarial acts are included in the *Drouin Collection* cited earlier.

> Roy, Pierre-Georges. *Inventaire des contrats de mariage du regime francais conserves aux Archives judiciaires de Quebec.* 6 vols. Quebec: Archives de la province de Quebec, 1937-38. /Gc 971.4 Q3in/ An inventory of 17th and 18th century notarial marriage contracts arranged alphabetically by both bride and groom then chronologically within each surname.
>
> Roy, Pierre-Georges, Antoine Roy, et al. *Inventaire des greffes des notaires du regime francais.* 27 vols. Quebec: Archives, 1943-76. /Gc 971.4 R8li/ Chronological item inventories of the records of 81 notaries (1637-1769) which are preserved in the archives of the province of Quebec.

There are name indexes following the records of each notary in volumes 9-27, and a separate cumulative name index for volumes 1-8.

Quebec References

Below are a list of additional reference books that provide information about French-Canadian genealogy and history.

> Bouchette, Joseph. *A Topographical Dictionary of the Province of Lower Canada.* London: Longmans, 1832. /Gc 971.4003 B66t/
>
> *Dictionary of Canadian Biography.* Toronto: University of Toronto Press, 1972-. /Gc 929.17 D561/
>
> Elliot, Noel Montgomery, ed. *The French-Canadians 1600-1900: An Alphabetized Directory of the People, Places and Vital Dates.* 3 vols. Toronto: The Genealogical Research Library, 1992 /Gc 971 F88/ 468,000 references compiled principally from city and town directories, land records, and marriage records.
>
> Gagne, Peter J. *King's Daughters and Founding Mothers: the Filles du Roi, 1663-1673.* Pawtucket, RI: Quintin Publications, 2001. /Gc 971.4 G122k/ Data on women

recruited in France to marry settlers in North America in exchange for a dowry from the king, 1663-73.

Gagne, Peter J. *Before the King's Daughters: The Filles a Marier, 1634-1662*: Quintin Publications, 2002. Between 1634 and 1663, 262 filles à marier or "marriageable girls" emigrated to New France representing one quarter of all the single girls arriving in New France through 1673. They were recruited and chaperoned by religious groups or individuals who had to assure and account for their good conduct. In general, they were poor, although there were some members of the petty nobility among their ranks.

Laforest, Thomas J. *Our French-Canadian Ancestors*. Palm Harbor, FL: LISI Press, 1983-98. 30 vols. /Gc 971.4 L13o/ Documented biographies of immigrant ancestors. Useful appendices in each volume including: bibliographies of sources, maps and a glossary of terms.

List of lands granted by the Crown in the Province of Quebec from 1763 to 31st December 1890. Quebec: C. F. Langlois, printed by order of the legislature, 1891. /Gc 971.4 Q352L/

Répertoire toponymique du Québec, 1987. Québec: Gouvernement du Québec, 1987. /Gc 971.4 R299/ Locates approximately 100,000 place names of all types within a census division.

Thwaites, Reuben Gold, ed. The *Jesuit Relations and Allied Documents: Travels and Explorations of the Jesuit Missionaries in New France, 1610-1791*. 73 vols. Cleveland: Burrows Bros., 1896 1901. Index in v.72-73. /Gc 971 J49/

Quebec Vital Records and Genealogies

The primary source is the Catholic parish register. These records are nearly complete from 1621 to the present, and most are accessible in the publications listed here. Most researchers will begin their search in the marriage index to the Drouin Collection or in the Loiselle Marriage Index, and Rivest Marriage Index all described in the following pages. The Loiselle Marriage Index covers marriages south of the St. Lawrence Seaway, and the Rivest Marriage Index covers marriages north of the St. Lawrence Seaway. Locate an ancestral couple's marriage record and the names of both sets of parents will be given. Then locate the marriage records of those two couples, and so on, until an entire genealogical tree is constructed. If a pre-1755 marriage is not in the Quebec indexes, try the Acadian sources. The French priests used an "8" to indicate a sound in a native language, sometimes translated as "ou." If there is an "8" in the name, you have found an Indian ancestor. Below are publications that contain Quebec vital records:

Bouchard, Leonard. *Morts tragiques et violentes au Canada 17e et 18e siecles*. 2 vols. Les Publications Audiovisuelles, 1982. /Gc 929.17 B66m/ Information on 1,500 people who died a tragic or violent death in Canada during the years 1608-1799, with an appendix on 625 women who died in childbirth.

Brunelle, Claude. *Index for Drouin Microfilm Collection*. Woonsocket, RI: American French Genealogical Society, 2003. /Gc 971.4 P39fa/ A guide to the Drouin Collection listed below.

Drouin Collection. Woonsocket, RI: American French Genealogical Society. /microfilm/ Filmed original parish registers and vital records from all religious denominations in Quebec from their origins until about 1935-42, covering baptisms, marriages, burials, and notarial acts. The collection includes records to mid-1968 for Hull and Gatineau. It also includes records for predominantly French-Canadian areas of Ontario (Ottawa to mid-1968), New Brunswick, Nova Scotia, and the U. S.

Drouin Collection: Repertoire Alphabetique des Mariages des Canadiens-Francaise, 1760-1935. Woonsocket, RI: American French Genealogical Society, 2000. /microfiche/ An index by bride and groom to marriages in the *Drouin Collection*. Names in the *Drouin Collection* marriage index are not always filed in strict alphabetical order.

Charbonneau, Hubert et Jacques Legare, ed *Repertoire des actes de bapteme, mariage, sepulture et des recensements du Quebec ancien*. Montreal: Les Presses de l'Universite de Montreal, 1980-90.47 vols. /Gc 971.4 R29/ A copy of this series is at the Minnesota Historical Society. For an explanatory *Key to the Repertory* in English see /Gc 971.4 R29a/ This comprehensive demographic database extracts almost all information from the parish registers: dates (year-month-day), full names including witnesses and their spouses, sex, age, marital status, occupation, kinship, places of residence and origin, etc., of every person mentioned. Quebec's early nominal censuses are also included. The full range of records covered up to 1765 includes: recantation, baptism, confirmation, hospital sick list, list of migrants, marriage, marriage contract, census, burial and marriage annulment records. All spelling variants must be checked because register entries have been transcribed exactly as recorded.

Denissen, Christian. *Genealogy of the French Families of the Detroit River Region 1701-1936 Revision*. 2 vols. Harold Frederic Powell, ed. Detroit: Detroit Society for Genealogical Research, 1987. /Gc 977.4 D41ga/

Faribault-Beauregard, Marthe. *La population des forts francais d' Amerique: Repertoire des baptemes, mariages et sepultures celebres dans les forts et les establissements francais en Amerique du Nord au XVIIIe siecle*. Montreal: Editions Bergeron, 1982 & 1984. /Gc 929.14 B38p/ 2 vols. Church and census records (1695-1821) from fifteen French outposts on the frontier.

Index des baptemes, marriages, sepultures de protestants de fa region de Quebec ca 1790-1875. Quebec: Archives Nationales du Quebec, 1983. /Microfiche/ Covers the regions of Quebec,

Levis, Lotbiniere and Portneuf. Check the microtext catalog for collections of non-Catholic registers from other areas of the Quebec province.

Institut Genealogique Drouin. *Dictionnaire national des Canadiens francais (1608-1760)* 3 vols. Montreal, 1965 /Gc 929.17 D56/ Dictionary of marriage records often giving the place of origin for the immigrant.

Jette, Rene. *Dictionnaire genealogique des familles du Quebec des origines a 1730*. Montreal: Les Presses de l'Universite de Montreal, 1983 /Gc 971.4 J51d/ Genealogies of families settled in Quebec by 1730. Compiled from Catholic registers, censuses, notarial contracts, etc. An appendix lists surnames and variants. Updates Tanguay, but still contains errors.

Jette, Rene et Micheline Lecuyer. *Repertoire des noms de famille du Quebec des origines a 1825.* Montreal: Institut Genealogique J. L. et Associes Inc, 1988. /Gc 971.4 J51r/

Leboeuf, J. Arthur. *Complement au dictionnaire genealogique Tanguay.* 3 vols. Montreal: Societe Genealogique Canadienne-Francaise, 1957, 1963, 1964. /Gc 929.17 Tl5da/ Corrections to Tanguay's work, with 15,000 additional marriages before 1800.

Loiselle, Antonin. *Loiselle Marriage Index* (1640-1963) and *Supplement.* /Microfilm/ Abstracts of marriages from 460 parishes, indexed by both bride and groom. Entries include: names of bride and groom, parents' names, date (year-day-month) and parish of marriage. Lists of abbreviations and parishes covered are on each reel.

Pepin, Jean-Pierre-Yves. *Inventaire des 2365 microfilms du fonds Drouin.* Longueuil, Québec: Éditions historiques et généalogiques Pepin, 1997?-1998? /Gc 971.4 P39f/

Rivest Marriage Index- The Rivest Marriage Index are microfilms and are supposed to be on permanent library loan at the Church of Latter Day Saints on Douglas Drive in Golden Valley. It covers all the marriages north of the St. Lawrence Seaway.

Tanguay, Cyprien. *Dictionnaire genealogique des familles canadiennes.* Montreal: Eusebe Senecal, 1871-1890. 7 vols. /Gc 929.17 Tl5d/ Genealogies compiled from the archives of 161 parishes. Useful appendices include: 1) a comprehensive list of "dit" names; 2) lists of the 528 parishes founded in Quebec by 1871; 3) an alphabetical list of French villages in 1631; and 4) names of whites married to female natives.

White, Jeanne Sauve. *Guide to Quebec Catholic Parishes and Published Parish Marriage Records.* Baltimore, MD: Genealogical Publishing Company, 1993. /Gc 971.4 W58g/ This work contains a county listing of Quebec parishes to 1900 providing the date of formation and the oldest record available for the parish. In addition, it provides a diocese-by-diocese inventory of the parish covered in *Loiselle,* a listing of organizations that publish parish records, finding aids, background data and other useful research aids.

Marriage "repertoires" are indexed abstracts of all marriages recorded in a particular parish, county or region for a specific time period. Hundreds have been published and some include baptisms and burials. Most are available in the Genealogy Department. Check the online catalog under the name of the town, parish, and county of interest.

Rootsweb

Rootsweb bills itself as "the Internet's oldest and largest genealogy site." Individuals, businesses, and organizations provide financial support for its operation, which focuses on providing online data with search engine access. Rootsweb currently hosts over 3,000 independent web sites. Among the more popular of these are Cyndi's List, the USGenWeb

Project, the WorldGenWeb Project, and the site for the Immigrant Ships Transcribers Guild. Additionally, Rootsweb coordinates over 26,000 mailing lists which fall into such categories as general interest, surname/family, regional, ethnic, and practical advice. The largest family history mailing list is Roots-L, which has been running for more than ten years and currently claims more than 10,000 subscribers. Their website address is: http://www.rootsweb.com/

Societe Genealogique Canadienne-Francaise

French-Canadian Genealogical Society (SGCF) is a nonprofit organization that promotes genealogical science mission. La SGCF administre la Maison de la Généalogie, le plus important centre de recherches concernant l'histoire et la généalogie des Canadiens français d'Amérique du Nord. SGCF administers the House of Genealogy, the most important research center on the history and genealogy of French-Canadians in North America French-Canadian Genealogy. The website address: https://www.sgcf.com.

Chapter Seventeen
French and French-Canadian organizations in Minnesota
By Mark Labine

Afoutayi Dance, Music and Arts Company

Afoutayi's mission is to inspire and engage youth of all ages through dance, percussion, song and storytelling to celebrate the mosaic of Haitian traditional culture. They dream of a world in which the flag of Haitian traditional culture is raised high and flies briskly and freely over Mother Earth and the vibrant and loving community of her creation. Their mission is to extend their vision of delivering a true, creative expression of Haitian culture to the Minnesota community.

Alliance Française

The **mission** of Alliance Française Mpls/St Paul, an independent chapter of a worldwide organization, is to serve the Minnesota community by promoting the use and appreciation of French language and cultures through language classes, cultural programs, social events and information resources. Their **vision** is to build a community of people passionate about Francophone culture in all its global diversity, and hope to become, through high-quality native language instruction along with authentic and exciting cultural activities and social events, the indispensable destination for all things French. Their website is located at http://www.afmsp.org. They are currently located at 113 North First Street Minneapolis, Minnesota 55401-1464 Email: bonjour@afmsp.org.

Association of French-Canadian Pioneers

The Association of French-Canadian Pioneers was formed in Duluth in July, 1911. Its purpose was to bring together old-timers and perpetuate the French-Canadian culture in Duluth.[297]

Belgian Consular Representative

Belgium, a country in Western Europe, is known for its medieval old towns, Flemish Renaissance architecture and international headquarters of the European Union and NATO. The country is divided into two distinctive multilingual regions: Dutch-speaking Flanders to the north and French-speaking Wallonia to the south. The bilingual capital, Brussels, is home to ornate guildhalls at Grand-Place and an art nouveau-influenced European Quarter. The 2015 Belgian Consular Representatives in Minnesota is Ms. Lydie Stassart, Honorary Consul, 238 S. Mississippi River Boulevard, Saint Paul MN 55105: Phone (651) 699-2528: Fax (651) 699-4821: E-mail: St.Paul@diplobel.org.

According to the 2010 census, there are 15,627 Minnesotans who identify themselves as partially or fully of Belgian ancestry. While the first natives of the Southern Netherlands arrived in America in the 17th century, most are descended from immigrants of the 19th and 20th centuries. Many were French Speaking.

---

[297] Echo de l'Quest, July 28, 1911.

Chez Nous

Over a period of twenty-two years, a succession of volunteer editors recorded stories of the heritage and culture of the French and the Midwest in two newsletters, *Chez Nous* and *Nouvelles Villes Jumelles*. Access to these publications is available through the French-American Heritage Foundation (FAHF) website. An index of these 145 newsletters is included on the website. Go to http://fahfminn.org/, click on library tab, click on chez nous, click on index for Chez Nous. At page 10 of the index are nineteen entries under "Genealogy, general." Complete sets of the newsletters have been provided to the libraries of the Minnesota, North Dakota and Wisconsin Historical Societies, and IF Midwest at the University of North Dakota at Grand Forks. IF Midwest has permission to post the newsletters to the internet. Chez Nous was a publication sponsored by La Societe Canadienne Francaise du Minnesota. These newsletters are also available for purchase in a three-volume set online.

Club des Bons-Vivants

A French speaking club said to be open to persons of good nature with smiling faces and happy characters.[298]

Club Democratic Franco Americaine

A club of French-Canadian democrats formed in March 1884.[299]

Consulate General of Canada

Consulate General of Canada Minneapolis is located at 701 Fourth Avenue South, Suite 901, Minneapolis, MN 55415-1899 Tel: (612) 332-7486, Fax: (612) 332-4061 e-mail: mnpls-td@international.gc.ca http://www.dfait-maeci.gc.ca/can-am/minneapolis. At the time of this writing, Jashmed Merchant was the Counsulate General and since Canada is a bi-lingual country, the Consultate General is supportive of French heritage activities and programs, especially when they involve French-Canadian topics.

Concordia Language Villages

The Concordia Language Villages has a French youth and adult immersion program that helps students experience the French language with all their senses. The Lac du Bois program offers instruction in small and large group settings. Les Voyageurs is a French language learning adventure that starts at their basecamp and where students learn the history of the fur trade, practice canoeing skills, create small and big crafts, and live la vie des voyageurs. The basecamp site is in the woods on the Turtle River Lake property of the Language Villages. It has no electricity. The central location of the program is the campfire next to the outdoor kitchen. Students live outdoors the entire session and sleep in shared outfitter-quality tents.

---

[298] Echo de l'Quest, October 19, 1893, February 1, 1895; Le Canadien, March 17, 1887 and September 13, 1888.
[299] "The French-Canadians and the French", by Sarah Rubinstein in book "They Chose Minnesota: A Survey of the State's Ethnic Groups, edited by June D. Holmquist, St. Paul, Minnesota Historical Society Press, 1981. p.49.

Commanderie de Bordeaux

The Commanderie de Bordeaux aux États-Unis d'Amérique was organized in 1957 by a small group of lovers of Bordeaux wines and became a New York corporation in 1959. Since, it has grown to include 30 chapters and approximately 1100 members located in different cities around the United States. It is also affiliated with a worldwide network of 75 Commanderies in 26 countries under the overall patronage of the Bordeaux-based Grand Conseil du Vin de Bordeaux (GCVB). The members ("Commandeurs") of these chapters meet periodically for dinners (called "parlements" from the French verb parler, "to talk" and other events in order to enjoy, discuss and learn more about the wines of the various Bordeaux regions in their different vintages. Through their passion for these wines, the Commandeurs become emissaries of the Bordeaux winemakers to their several localities.

Consulat Général de France à Chicago

Location is at 205 North Michigan Avenue, Suite 3700, Chicago, IL 60601 Tel: 312/327-5200: Fax: 312/327-5201: E-mail: contact@consulfrance-chicago.org and website: http://www.consulfrance-chicago.org.

Dance Revels Moving History

A professional performing ensemble committed to performing the untold stories of our diverse ancestors through the dance, story, and live music of Europe and North America heritage. Two-thirds of their numerous productions have French, French-Canadian, or French Indian themes. These include:

- Bottineau Jig, Untold Tales of Early MN (through the eyes of Pierre Bottineau.)
- A Voyageur's Tale (Voyageurs and Metis origins)
- Versailles to Grand Portage (17th century French fur trade)
- Of Silk and Buckskin (19th century French immigrants)
- Lewis and Clark were Deja Vu (strong French and Metis presence during this famous trip)
- La Peine Si Bonne (17th century music and dance)
- Masquerade at the Palace (a comedy which takes place at Versailles)

Durand Heritage Foundation

The mission of the Durand Heritage Foundation is to preserve the family and cultural heritage of Jean Durand dit La Fortune (1636-1671) family. The Durand Heritage Foundation researches and disseminates genealogical and other information about his ancestors and descendants through the voluntary efforts of its members. Established in 1998, the Durand Heritage Foundation website provides members and the public with access to information about the shared heritage of Jean Durand. Simply google Durand Heritage Foundation to find their website.

Echo de l'Quest

The Echo de l'Quest was a French newspaper printed in Minneapolis, Minnesota from 1883 to 1929. It was founded by Zephirin Demeules, and was carried on by members of the Demeules family until its end. Copies of this newspaper can be found at the Center for Residential Libraries, Newspaper project, Chicago, Illinois; The Institute Canada-American Bibliotheque, Manchester, New Hampshire; The Minnesota Historical Society in St. Paul, Minnesota; and the Union St. Jean Baptiste in Woonsocket, Rhode Island. Its contents included a serialized novel, a directory of French-Canadians engaged in Minneapolis public affairs, a large number of advertisements, news items, commercial reports, and an editorial page listing meetings of French-Canadian organizations.[300]

Franco American Literary Club of Sister Cities

A literary club reported in French language newspapers in the Twin Cities.

French-American Heritage Foundation

In February 2013, a group of people who were involved in a three-day Franco-Fete Festival held in September 2012, formed a non-profit organization that would be called the French-American Heritage Foundation. This Foundation is a 501(c)3 charitable organization with the primary purpose of promoting and cultivating the heritage of French language cultures.

French American Chamber of Commerce

The first French Chambers of Commerce abroad were established in the middle of the 1800's and the very first chapter was in New Orleans in 1876. That chapter died out and was reconstituted in the 1970's. The New York Chapter, established in 1896, was the only other chapter in the United States until that time. The French American Chamber of Minneapolis/St. Paul was officially founded in 1979. The French American Chamber of Minneapolis/St. Paul, an independent and not-for-profit organization, boasts a network of more than one hundred individuals and corporate members, as well as a mailing list nearing 2,000 individuals. In addition, they are part of a national network, FACC (French American Chamber of Commerce), as well as an international network, UCCIFE ("Union des Chambres de Commerce et d'Industrie Française à l'Étranger").

French-Canadian Dramatic Club

A drama club reported in French language newspapers in the Twin Cities.

French Club in Duluth

The French Club was established by the parisheners of the St. Jean the Baptiste Parish in Duluth in the early 1900's. The organization was formed to assist new French and French-Canadian emigrants with the learning of the English language and to help prepare them for citizenship. Their major focus was also on family, and they owned about ten to fifteen acres of land on Lake Elora, just thirty-five miles north of Duluth on Highway 53. The

---

[300] Rubenstein, Sarah, *The French-Canadians and French*, found in Holmquist, June Drenning, *They Chose Minnesota" a Survey of The State's Ethnic Groups*, Minnesota Historical Society Press (1981). p.49.

grounds offered summer activities such as boating, private swimming, a ball field, playground equipment for kids, a sauna and camping areas. There was a large clubhouse with sleeping, cooking and dining facilities.

French Sister Cities

There are two sister cities in Minnesota with French-speaking cities. Fridley's sister city is Foumies, France and Minneapolis is a sister city with Tours, France. Organizations like Sister Cities International foster such relationships, increasing mutual knowledge and understanding between cities and cultures. These collaborations promote trust among citizens and nations, create opportunities for technological and economic innovation and development, and lay the foundation for continued peace and prosperity.

Initiatives in French Midwest

IF Midwest stands for Initiatives in French in the Midwest United States. IFMidwest creates and operates projects which are related to roots and diaspora in the Midwest. Past projects of IF Midwest include:

1. Fieldwork and research into Franco American, Michif, Acadian, African and French cultures in the Midwest.
2. Creation of a special collection of documents, photos, books and other printed material on Franco-American history and culture in the Midwest housed in the Chester Fritz Library at the University of North Dakota.
3. Research, preparation and publication of *Francophone Roots and Diaspora in the Midwest*, a magazine with separate and distinct issues in English & French.
4. Heritage tours focusing on the roots of French North America.
5. Creation of a web site in progress at: www.ifmidwest.org.
6. The annual convention of Initiatives in French.

IF Midwest is a cultural heritage project. Its activities focus on understanding the French presence in the Midwest. Activities consist of information gathering in local communities of French language origin, developing public programs, preparing publications, and offering workshops and courses. IF Midwest's first geographical region of focus is North Dakota and Northwestern Minnesota. IF Midwest's web site is at ifmidwest@und.edu.

International Organization de la Francophonie

The International Organisation of La Francophonie was created in 1970. Its mission is to embody the active solidarity between its eighty member states and governments (fifty-seven members and twenty-three observers), which together represent over one-third of the United Nations' member states and account for a population of over 890 million people, including 220 million French speakers. The 57 member states and governments that belong to this organization are as follows: Albania, Principality of Andorra, Armenia, Kingdom of Belgium, French Community of Belgium, Benin, Bulgaria, Burkina Faso, Burundi,

Cambodia, Cameroon, Canada, Canada-New-Brunswick, Canada-Quebec, Cape Verde, Central African Republic, Chad, Comoros, Congo, Cyprus, Democratic Republic of the Congo, Djibouti, Dominica, Egypt, Equatorial Guinea, France, Gabon, Ghana, Greece, Guinea, Guinea-Bissau, Haiti, Ivory Coast, Laos, Lebanon, Luxembourg, former Yugoslav Republic of Macedonia, Madagascar, Mali, Morocco, Mauritius, Mauritania, Moldova, Monaco, Niger, Qatar, Romania, Rwanda, Saint Lucia, Säo Tomé, Principe, Senegal, Seychelles, Switzerland, Togo, Tunisia, Vanuatu, and Vietnam.

La Société Candienne Française

La Société Candienne Française (LSCF) had an official life span of about 22 Years, from 1979-2001. Like many similar organizations, its beginning and its evolution shared many names and faces. Much of LSCFs history is traced through its newsletters, Chez Nous, and Nouvelles Villes Jumelles, which together and separately chronicled French-Canadian and French heritage from 1980 through 2001. The index of these newsletters are available on file at a number of Midwest historical societies and institutions, and is also available on the website of the French-American Heritage Foundation in the library section.

The following persons served as Presidents of the La Societe Canadienne-Francaise.

1979- John Rivard
1983- Gaston Rheaume
1984- Louis Ritchot
1986- Pierre Girard
1988- Mark Labine
1990- Bruce Bedore
1992- Leroy Dubois
1993- Leo Gouette
1995- Louis Ritchot
1997- Leo Gouette
1998- John Edel
2000- Dick Bernard
2001- Simone Germain

Lafayette-Papineau Republican League of Minneapolis

A political club in the Twin Cities which flourished for a time in Minnesota was the Lafayette-Papineau Republicatin League of Minneapolis.[301] It was formed in 1898. The inclusion of the name Papineau in this political club suggests a strong connection to French Canada.

[301] Rubenstein, Sarah, *The French-Canadians and French*, found in Holmquist, June Drenning, *They Chose Minnesota, a Survey of The State's Ethnic Groups*, Minnesota Historical Society Press (1981) p.49; and Scholberg, Henry, *The French Pioneers of Minnesota/Les Pioniers Francais du Minnesota*, Eau Claire, Wisc.:Northstar, 1996.

La Voix du Lac Newspaper

A paper by this name was published in Duluth in 1892 and also one published in Minneapolis in 1893. The duration of its publication is unknown.[302]

L'Etoile du Nord Newspaper

The first journal published in French in St. Paul was the L'etoile du Nord, an independent weekly paper founded May 15, 1874, by J.B.A. Paradis. The paper was continued until September 1876.[303]

Le Canadien Newspaper

Le Canadien was established by Desire Michaud on August 15, 1877. It was a weekly paper, originally Republican, and then became independent. It was owned by Levaseur and Ledoux. It merged with a Chicago French-Canadian paper in 1903 and ceased publication in 1904. It strongly supported any movement enhancing the French-Canadian heritage as well as urging greater participation in Minnesota politics. The paper regularly campaigned for state conventions of French-Canadians.[304]

Le Citoyen Americain Newspaper

Newspaper available in Minneapolis for a short time in 1884. There also was a newspaper with the same name published in Haverhill Massachusetts in 1911.[305]

Les Amis de la France

Les Amis de la France was organized to promote and help people communicate in the French language. In 2015, Feraidoon Bourbour was the president. Its address is P.O. Box 180, 1043 Grand Avenue #180, Saint Paul, MN 55105. Voice Mail: (651) 310-0425 ext.3 .

Le Courier de Duluth Newspaper

This newspaper was published in Duluth for a short time beginning in 1890.

Le Franco Canadien

This was a weekly Democratic paper, founded by F.C.Carel on August 17, 1877. It was published only for a few weeks.[306]

---

[302] Tetrault, Maximilienne, *Le Role de la Presse dans l"Evolution du people Franco-Americain de la Nouvelle Angleterre*, p. 35,37 (Marseilles, France, 1935).

[303] Rubenstein, *The French-Canadians and the French*.

[304] Rubenstein, Sarah, *The French-Canadians and French*, found in Holmquist, June Drenning, *They Chose Minnesota" a Survey of The State's Ethnic Groups*, Minnesota Historical Society Press (1981). p.49.

[305] "Publications in Foreign Languages: French", *Ayer & Son's American Newspaper Annual*, Philadelphia: N. W. Ayer & Son, 1907

[306] Hennessy, W.B., *Past and Present St. Paul, Minnesota, being a relation of the progressive history of the capital city of Minnesota from the earliest historical times down to the present day*, published 1906 by Chicago, The S.J.Clarke Publishing Company.

Le National Newspaper

Upon the discontinuance of L'etoile due Nord, Le National, an independent weekly paper, was commenced by Dr. L.M.A. Roy, and E.A. Paradis, in October 1876. This paper continued until May 1877.[307]

Les Amis du Theatre

In the early 1970s, Georgette Pfannkuch founded and led a theatre group called Les Amis du Theatre, who performed in French at Hamline University in the 1970s and 1980s. Georgette was born in Paris where she trained for radio performance. She worked at KFAI radio and was the programmer and founder of Bonjour Minnesota.

Les Veillees Canadiennes Newspaper

This was an agricultural newsletter for French-Canadians. They published a book in 1852 titled: Les Veillees Canadiennes Traite Elementaire d'agriculture a l'usage des Habitants Franco-Canadiens Approuve Par la Societe d'agriculture du Bas-Canada de l'instruction-French Edition. Author: Frédéric M. F. Ossaye, Originally published in 1852.

L'Association des Français du Nord

L'Association des Français du Nord, also known as the Association of the French of the North (AFRAN) is an organization whose mission in the Red River Valley of the North is to create an understanding of the world's French heritage through the arts and humanities. Each year, AFRAN sponsors the annual Chautauqua and French Festival to encourage and introduce a historic and multicultural approach to the arts and humanities, while interpreting the role French presence has placed in the Middle West, and, in particular, northwestern Minnesota. This Festival is a four-day celebration of dance, music, food, and art in Huot, Minnesota, at the historic meeting place at Old Crossing and Treaty Park, near Red Lake Falls. The site was used during the era of western exploration by Indian and French traders. Activities also include a French Festival Bake-Off, encampments led by humanities scholars, strolling minstrels, art show, the sale of souvenirs and craft items, and workshops in story-telling, writing, landscape painting, ceramics, puppetry, beadwork, and flute-making.

Le consul honoraire de France - Minnesota

With 937 French registered with the French services of Chicago (September 2014), the presence of France in Minnesota is manifested by the presence of French and Francophone associations, but also by the presence of a Minneapolis Honorary Consul, namely M. Alain Frecon, Frécon & Associates. It is located at 150 South Fifth Street Minneapolis, MN 55402. Tel (612) 338-6868 Fax (612) 338-6878 Mél : afrecon@consulfrance-minnesota.org.

L'Oeil Newspaper

Established in Minneapolis in 1893.

---

[307] Id.

Les Survivants

A group formed in Minnesota and dedicated to French-Canadian culture and language. Their mission statement is 1) To promote the renaissance of the French-Canadian culture by helping, in particular, fellow English-speaking-only French-Canadian Minnesotans rediscover their roots, their heritage language, and their rich culture through educational and social events, 2) To promote a strong mutually rewarding relationship between Minnesota and Quebec as well as other Francophone regions within Canada and 3) To have fun! Website is at www.lessurvivants.org.

Minnesota Chapter of the American Association of Teachers in French (AATF)

The AATF is the only professional association devoted exclusively to the needs of French teachers at all levels. The mission of the AATF is to advance the study of the French language and French-speaking literatures and cultures both in schools and in the general public. Membership is open to anyone interested in the teaching of French who is over the age of 18. Website address is at http://mnaatf.org.

National Huguenot Society

The National Huguenot Society headquarters is located at 9033 Lyndale Avenue South, Suite 108, Bloomington, MN 55420-3535. Huguenots were French Protestants who escaped religious persecution in France in the 17th century. The National Huguenot Society is an organization devoted to: 1) Coordinating activities of member societies, and promoting and supporting fulfillment of their common purposes which include perpetuating the memory and promoting the principles and virtues of the Huguenots; commemorating the great events of Huguenot history and collecting and preserving historical data and relics illustrative of Huguenot life, manners, and customs 2) To give expression to the Huguenot tenets of faith and liberty, and to promote their understanding for the good of the United States and 3) To encourage and foster the organization of new member Societies within states, territories of the United States, and the District of Columbia where none currently exist.

Poulenc Academy

The Académie Francis Poulenc was started in 1997 by François Le Roux with the support of the city of Tours, France, the region where Francis Poulenc made his secondary home. Each August, since inception, the Académie Françis Poulenc has hosted a ten-day series of workshops and performances permitting a limited number of talented young artists to gain further insight into the formalities and nuances of the language and the poetry, along with guidance in musical performance. Le Centre International de la Mélodie Française (CIMF) was founded in the 1990s as a center devoted to the French "chanson" and "mélodie," and shares its website and mission with the Académie Francis Poulenc which has its own membership association, the Association Francis Poulenc. Francis Jean Marcel Poulenc (1899–1963) was a French composer and pianist. His compositions include mélodies, solo piano works, chamber music, choral pieces, operas, ballets, and orchestral concert music. Minnesota artists have participated in these workshops and Poulenc music is sung by choral groups and church choirs in Minnesota. Minnesota is known throughout the United States for its's high level of choral groups.

Québec Delegation, Chicago

The Québec Government office in Chicago represents the Québec government in twelve states across the Midwest. This mandate involves working on a wide range of commercial, economic, political, environmental, and cultural matters of interest to Québec and this region of the United States. The office is located at 444. N. Michigan Avenue, Suite 1900, Chicago, IL 60611 Tel: (312) 645-0392 Fax: (312) 645-0542. Email is qc.chicago@mri.gouv.qc.ca Website address is http://www.mri.gouv.qc.ca.

Saint Vincent de Paul Society

In its 178th year, the Society of St. Vincent de Paul is the largest lay Catholic charitable organization in the world. Founded in 1833 by French college student Frederic Ozanam, the Society today has more than 750,000 members operating in 146 countries. A 501 (c)(3) tax exempt organization, the St. Vincent de Paul Society operates thrift stores and food pantries as well as conducts personal visits to the homes of the poor. The Society's U.S. members annually donate nearly seven million hours of their personal time to aid more than fourteen million of their neighbors in distress and offering services valued at nearly $595 million.

Saint Jean the Baptiste Society

The St. Jean-Baptiste Society (Société Saint-Jean-Baptiste), French-Canadian patriotic association founded 24 June 1834 by journalist Ludger Duvernay, who wanted to stimulate a nationalist spirit among his compatriots and encourage them to defend their linguistic and cultural heritage. Gradually, branches were established throughout Québec and in Francophone communities elsewhere in North America. Placed under the patronage of St John the Baptist, the society has always organized special activities, originally with religious overtones, for June 24th (the Saint's Day), a legal holiday in Québec since 1922. Many French-Canadian communities in Minnesota organized Saint Jean the Baptiste societies.

Société de Bienfaisance Franco-Canadienne de Saint Paul

In 1857, a book titled *The Constitution et reglements de la Société de bienfaisance Franco-Canadienne de Saint Paul* was published by Goodrich & Somers. An organization was formed in St. Paul with this name as a mutual benefit society which financed burials and aided widows and orphans and members who fell ill. [308]

Société des Voyageurs

Orgainzation formed by Pierre Verite and others in 1976, to participate in the bi-centennial celebrations. They sponsored Festival of French Heritage in St. Paul in July 1976.

---

[308] Rubenstein, Sarah, *The French-Canadians and French*, found in Holmquist, June Drenning, *They Chose Minnesota, a Survey of The State's Ethnic Groups* , Minnesota Historical Society Press (1981), pp. 48.

Théâtre de la Jeune Lune

The Theatre de la Jeune Lune was a celebrated theater company based in Minneapolis, Minnesota. The company, in operation from 1978 to 2008, was known for its visually rich, highly physical style of theatre, derived from clown, mime, dance and opera. Theatre de la Jeune Lune (French for Theater of the New Moon) was founded in France in 1978 by Dominique Serrand, Vincent Gracieux and Barbra Berlovitz, who were later joined by Robert Rosen, all graduates of the École Internationale de Théâtre Jacques Lecoq school in Paris.

Théâtre du Monde

Founded by Fawn Wilderson-Legros. While travelling in France, Germany, and Italy in the 1980's, Fawn experienced fantastic theatre, wonderfully written and performed by local artists, often in small town or cities. After spending time as an actress/understudy at the Arena Stage Company, in Washington, DC, and then working with Dawn Renée Jone's Alchemy Theatre, in Minneapolis, she helped organize Théâtre du Monde in Minnesota. Their Mission is to create "Readers Theatre/Radio Drama" presentations that excite, inspire and help foster inter-cultural understanding and appreciation.

Union Francaise

The Union Francaise was a mutual benefit society formed in 1867 which financed burials and aided widows and orphans and members who fell ill. On the Union's 25th anniversary in 1892, they reported cumulative payments over the years of $445 for funerals, $6,491 for members who were sick, and $9,266 for widows and orphans. They had a balance of funds of $4,322.[309]

Union St. Jean Baptiste

The Union of St. Jean Baptiste had lodges in French-Canadian communities throughout the United States. They had lodges in St. Paul, Minneapolis, Duluth, Crookston, Little Canada and other parishes. In Minneapolis and St. Paul they organized in the mid-1870s and by the mid-1890s had been replaced by the Woodmen of the World and the Catholic Order of Foresters. They appear in phone directories between 1870-1900.[310]

Union Catholique de l'Abstenence Totale

The Union Catholique de l'Abstenence Totale was a temperance group formed in 1871 by French-Canadians.[311]

---

[309]Id. pp. 48
[310] Id. pp. 48
[311] Id. p. 48

Chapter Eighteen
French Heritage Sites in Minnesota

Alexander Faribault House

The Alexander Faribault house is located at Twelve 1ˢᵗ Ave NE in Faribault. This home, which dates back to 1853, was the first frame style house built in the county. Alexander Faribault owned the home. He first came to the area in 1826 to trade with the Wahpekute Indians.

Alexander Faribault House

Albert Lea Big Island Rendezvous

This is Minnesota's largest reenactment history event with over 1,000 costumed participants, 250 tents, colonial cuisine, colonial crafts and stage entertainment. French and French-Canadian fur traders and voyageurs perform reenactments during this event. This rendezvous is generally held the first weekend in October in Albert Lea and includes a variety of cultures and historical costumes, including colonial, civil war, pioneer, and other.

Battle Creek Park

Battle Creek Park is named after the Battle of Kaposia which took place on July 8, 1842, and involved local French-Canadian residents. There are several sources of information telling about this battle.[312] One of the accounts of the battle was written in an article in the Northwestern Chronicle titled "A Pioneer's Talk of Pioneer Days."

In this article, Issac Labissoniere recounts his eyewitness version of the battle. Issac was the son of Joesph Labissoniere and Francois Desjarlais. Joesph was a French-Canadian fur trader who worked for the North West Company up in the Red River Valley and Francois was the daughter of a French-Canadian Fur Trader named Antoine Desjarlais and an Ojibwe mother named Pert Won from the Little Snake Tribe in Manitoba. He states that

---

[312] Catholic Historical Society of St. Paul, "Obituary of Issac Labissoniere," in *Acta et Dicta*, Vol. III, No. 1,(July 1911) p.188; Labissoniere, Issac, *A Pioneer's Talk of Pioneer Days.* Northwestern Chronicle; Hennessy, W.B., *Past and Present St. Paul, Minnesota, being a relation of the progressive history of the capital city of Minnesota from the earliest historical times down to the present day,* published 1906 by Chicago, The S.J. Clarke Publishing Company; Military Report of Major Dearborn (Commander of Fort Snelling in 1842); Lass, William E. *History of Minnesota*, W.W. Norton & Company, (2000).

Seth Eastman painting of settler's cabins in 1800s (Public Domain)

at about 10 o'clock in the morning, he was down in the lowlands (near the present-day Fish Hatchery) making hay when he heard a "rattling of guns" and noticed that a large band of

Kaposia Village by Seth Eastman (Public Domain)

Ojibwe had assembled in what is known today at Battle Creek Park. He climbed a tree and observed about eight braves cross the plain to fire on the Dakota Kaposia village across the Mississippi river. These braves fired a volley of shots into the Kaposia village and shouted insults at the Dakota living there.

The Dakota from Kaposia Village then got in their canoes and crossed the river to chase the Ojibwe warriors. The eight Ojibwe braves then began retreating and passed a settler who was married to a Dakota woman. They killed and her son, before continuing their retreat. The Dakota continued their pursuit and were ambushed in the Battle Creek park area, where nineteen of their braves were killed. In the end, nineteen Dakota were killed, ten Ojibwe were killed, plus the Dakota woman and her son.

Beaulieu House

The Captain Charles Beaulieu house is located at the Crow Missions, which is now part of the Crow Wing State Park. A trading post was established at the site in 1823 and a small settlement was established there. Captain Beaulieu (1839–1904) is the son of Colonel Clement Beaulieu, a Métis who ran the American Fur Company's trading post, and later formed a company called Beaulieu and Fairbanks, which became the principal supplier of all Ojibwe Indian posts in the area. When a railroad station opened in Brainerd, the village of Crow Wing vanished, leaving only one house, the Charles Beaulieu house.

Charles Beaulieu House

Bottineau House

The Pierre Bottineau house is located at the Elm Creek Park Reserve, where it will be used to tell the story of Pierre Bottineau, the pioneer guide who helped dignitaries and settlers alike find their way to the region. It is open during scheduled programs and by appointment only.

Built in 1854, the Bottineau House (to the left) was the area's first wood-framed house in Maple Grove Township. It has been moved several times but in 2009, found its permanent home in it's current location. The house today is used as an interpretive space to connect park visitors with the life of Pierre Bottineau. *Address: 12400 James Deane Parkway, Maple Grove. The Elm Creek Park Reserve is located just north of the intersection of Highway 81 and Fernbrook Lane North.*

Bottineau House

Bottineau Gravesite

The gravesite of Pierre Bottineau is located in the St. Joseph's Catholic Cemetery in Red Lake Falls, Minnesota. In 1876, he, and two of his sons, came to what is now Red Lake Falls and staked a claim along the Clearwater River. He encouraged many French-Canadians from St. Paul, Minnesota and the Red River Colony (Winnipeg, Manitoba, Canada) areas to settle here. He died in 1895 and was first buried in the Cyr Cemetery west of Red Lake Falls. In 1978, his remains, and those of four members of his family, were moved to

Pierre Bottineau Memorial at entrance of St. Joseph's Cemetery in Red Lake Falls

the St. Joseph's Cemetery by the Red Lake County Historical Society. In August 2000, a memorial honoring his memory was dedicated at the entrance of the cemetery. Susan Warner, a potter and ceramist of Minneapolis, was awarded the commission, and completed the project that was funded by the Minnesota State Legislature. The structure is six feet in diameter with a slanted face covered with colorful tiles depicting the life of Pierre Bottineau with scenes of early expeditions into territories that brought frontier settlements and industry into Minnesota and the Dakotas.

DlRECTIONS: Take County Road 13 to Highway 32 in Red Lake Falls. Turn left on to Highway 32, go one block, then turn right onto County Road 1. Follow County Road one mile to St. Joseph's cemetery. The Bottineau grave site is near the cemetery entrance.

Cadotte Trading Post Site

The Cadotte Fur Trading Post was located at the junction of the Red Lake and Clearwater Rivers in Red Lake Falls, Minnesota. Jean Baptist Cadotte Jr. was an employee of the Northwest Fur Trading Company. (The actual site is believed to be across the Clearwater River from the Al Buse Sportsman's Park.) Cadotte spent the winter of 1797-98 at this post according to the writings of David Thompson, a geographer and surveyor who found shelter in the cabin during a spring snow storm. Thompson wrote: *"Mr. Baptiste Cadotte was about thirty-five years of age. He was the son of a French gentleman by a native woman, and married to a very handsome native woman, also the daughter of a Frenchman. He has been well educated in Lower Canada and spoke fluently his native French language with Latin, and English."* Cadotte is given credit for opening the region north of the upper Mississippi to the fur traders. For more information scc wcbsite at cadotte.htm.[313]

[313] Benoit, Virgil, "The French- Canadian Presence in the Northwest and the Very Early Beginnings of Red Lake Falls and Red Lake County," in *A History of Red Lake County*, edited by Anne Healy and Sherry Kankel, Taylor Publishing Co., Dallas, 1976.

Jean Baptiste Cadotte was a fur trader who had two sons, Jean Baptiste Jr. and Michel. Each married daughters of prominent Ojibway Indians, and became influential as merchants, interpreters and mediators. Michel Cadotte established the permanent trading post at La Pointe on Madelaine Island and traded on the Chippewa River and tributaries as early as 1787, including Chippewa City, Jim Falls and Cadotte Falls on the Yellow River.

DIRECTIONS: From the courthouse go back to Highway 32, turn north (left) and go one block to Bottineau Avenue. Turn west (left), go one mile then turn left into the Sportsman's Park.

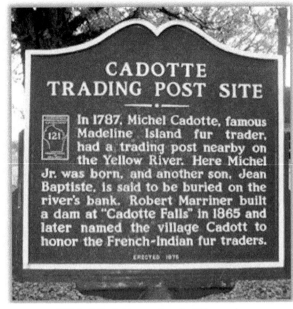

CADOTTE TRADING POST SITE

In 1787, Michel Cadotte, famous Madeline Island fur trader, had a trading post nearby on the Yellow River. Here Michel Jr. was born, and another son, Jean Baptiste, is said to be buried on the river's bank. Robert Marriner built a dam at "Cadotte Falls" in 1865 and later named the village Cadott to honor the French-Indian fur traders.

ERECTED 1975

Michel Cadotte marker in Wisconsin
Michel was brother to Jean Baptiste Jr.

Canal Park at Minnesota Point

Du Lhut landing marker

A stone marker on the grounds of the Lake Superior Maritime Museum and Visitor Center in Duluth's Canal Park marks the site of Little Portage on Minnesota Point where French explorer Daniel de Greysolon, Sieur du Lhut, landed on June 27, 1679.

Alex Coultier House

This single story house was located at 915 2nd Street NE. It is believed, by many, to be the first frame dwelling in the city of Minneapolis. It was built, according to family records, in August 1848 by Alex Coultier, a French-Canadian who came to St. Anthony from Montreal with 60 others to work for the Hudson Bay Company. In this home, Harriet Coultier was born on August 1848, the first white child to be born in the settlement of St. Anthony. It is possible that this house was built several months earlier than the Godfrey house, usually credited as the first dwelling in Minneapolis. The house was torn down.

Euchariste and Louis Carufel House

Louis Francois Carufel (1835–1915) was born in Maskinonge, Quebec. He married Euchariste Marie Marguerite LaRose in 1858, in Faribault, Minnesota. Euchriste was also born in Quebec. Louis operated an evening school teaching the French Language. He was a Daguerreian, which meant he was an expert at using the daguerreotype, the first photographic process that was invented by Frenchman Louis-Jacques Mandé Daguerre (1787-1851). His home is now on the National Register of Historic Places in Minnesota.

Carufel House

Louis is a descendant of Jean Baptiste Sicard de Carufel (1666–1743)and Genevieve Rate (1678–1732). Jean Baptiste Sicard de Carufel, an officer in the Marine Troops in Canada, was awarded a seigneurie in Maskinongé, Quebec by the Govenor, Marquis Philippe de Rigaud de Vaudreuil and the intendant, Francois de Beauharnois in 1705.

Cheese Ripening

The Villaume Box & Lumber Company, founded in 1882 by Eugene Villaume, was a well-known St. Paul business. Eugene was born in St. Michel, France in 1853. This company was one of the nation's leaders in the manufacture of custom millwork, shipping cases and boxes, according to a 1940 promotional brochure. The brochure continued:

Villaume has on its own property, fourteen hillside caves with surface level entrances. Each cave has a ceiling height of twelve feet and is twenty feet wide. The 14 caves contain a total of 50,000 square feet of floor space, usable for manufacturing, storage, or as shelters in event of air raids.

From 1933 to the 1950s, the University of Minnesota rented one of the "V caves," as they were known, and produced a domestic Roquefort cheese—subsequently named "Minnesota Blue." St. Paul was acclaimed "the Blue Cheese Capital of the World" during World War II.[314]

Cheever's Landing

William Cheever established a ferry at this location in 1847. This site was located on Territorial Road from St. Paul and his location was the last safe spot where you could cross the Mississippi before St. Anthony Falls. This is the claimed location where Indians, French fur traders, and French explorers, including Father Hennepin, portaged around the falls of Saint-Antoine or St. Anthony Falls. At this site there is an old portage trail tablet which is a bronze marker on a boulder. This site is now located in the campus of the University of Minnesota.

---

[314] Brick, Greg, *Subterranean Twin Cities*, Minneapolis, MN: University of Minnesota Press (2009).

Coteau des Prairies

The Coteau des Prairies is a plateau approximately 200 miles long and 100 miles wide (320 by 160 km), rising from the prairie flatlands in eastern South Dakota, southwestern Minnesota, and northwestern Iowa in the United States. The southeast portion of the Coteau comprises one of the distinct regions of Minnesota, known as Buffalo Ridge.

The flatiron-shaped plateau was named by early French explorers from New France (Quebec). Coteau means "hill" in French. The general term "coteau" has since been used in English to describe any upland dividing ridge.[315]

George Catlin painting of Coteau des Prairies (Public Domain)

The plateau has numerous small glacial lakes and is drained by the Big Sioux River in South Dakota and the Cottonwood River in Minnesota. Pipestone deposits on the plateau have been quarried for hundreds of years by Native Americans, who use the prized, brownish-red mineral to make their sacred peace pipes. The quarries are located at Pipestone National Monument in the southwest corner of Minnesota and in adjacent Minnehaha County, South Dakota.

Crepeau Nature Reserve

Crepeau Nature Preserve is a beautiful 12.5 acre park with trails located in the southeastern portion of the city off of Harriet Avenue and Benton Way. The land for the reserve was donated by the Hank Crepeau family.

Henry J. Crepeau

Henry J. Crepeau
Henry J. Crépeau (1887–1952) was the son of Albert Crepeau and Rose Anna Fortier who were from Sorel-Tracy, Quebec. In 1920 Crepeau, a member of the Trades and Labor Assembly Executive Board and a leader of Pressmen's

[315] Nord, Mary Ann, *The National Register of Historic Places in Minnesota*. Minnesota Historical Society (2003). ISBN 0-87351-448-3

Local 29, was appointed Chief of Police after labor took several seats on the City Council. The St. Paul Pioneer Press and businessmen raised a storm of protest after Crepeau called scabs "dirty rats" and refused to allow police to break up picket lines. Crepeau was removed from office by Mayor Larry Hodgson, a former newspaper columnist. In 1923 Crepeau and fellow unionist Frank Pampusch bought the Ramaley Printing Co.

Hypolite Dupuis House

The Dupuis house is located at the Sibley House Historic Site in Mendota, Minnesota. Hypolite Dupuis (1804 –1879) was a fur trader with the American Fur Company. He was born in LaPrairie de la Madeleine, near present-day Montreal, Quebec. By 1831 he had moved to what would become the Minnesota Territory to work at Joseph Renville's Lac qui Parle trading post. He moved to Mendota around 1840 and built a house on the property of Henry Hastings Sibley. Dupuis worked as a clerk for Sibley and managed the company store. He married Angelique Renville, daughter of Joseph Renville, and they had eight children. The fur trade had largely died out by the 1850s, and Sibley and Dupuis liquidated their fur trade interests in 1853. In 1854, DuPuis built a home for his family and operated a general store until it closed during the financial panic of 1857. DuPuis was active in the Mendota community, serving as county treasurer in 1854, the justice of the peace in 1855, and as the Mendota postmaster from 1854 to 1863.

Hypolilte Dupuis House (photo by Mark Petty

Alexander Faribault House in Faribault

Alexander Faribault House in Faribault

The Alexander Faribault house was built in 1853 and was the first wood-frame house constructed in Rice County, Minnesota. It was built by Alexander Faribault and is located at 12 First Avenue, Faribault, Minnesota. The house was listed on the National Register of Historic Places in 1970. Alexander Faribault was the son of Jean Baptiste Faribault and served for a time as secretary to Henry Hastings Sibley. He was a fur trader who traded with the Dakota. He was also an owner of a sawmill and a flour mill and donated money for the

Shattuck School, and the local churches in town. He served on the Minnesota Territorial Legislature and was the first postmaster of Faribault.

Jean Baptiste Faribault House in Mendota

Jean-Baptiste Faribault was born in Berthier, Quebec in 1774, one of ten children of Bartholomew Faribault, former Military Secretary to French General Louis-Joseph Montcalm. More information on him is included previously. In June 1839, Faribault signed a contract to have a stone house constructed, "to be furnished in the same manner as the dwelling house built for H. H. Sibley." The house was built of Platteville limestone and sandstone and

Faribault House in Mendota

stood three-stories tall. The project cost Faribault $5000, and construction was completed in June 1840. The house is currently part of the Sibley House Historic Site.

Faribault Heritage Park

Faribault Heritage Park is located in Faribault, Minnesota. A sculpture of Alexander Faribault trading with a Dakota trading partner stands in Faribault's Heritage Park near the Straight River and site of Faribault's trading post. Faribault artist Ivan Whillock created this sculpture which sits atop a fountain known as the Bea Duncan Memorial Fountain.

Sculpture of Faribault trading with Dakota Indian

Father Hennepin Bluffs Park

Father Hennepin Bluffs Park is located in Minneapolis by the stone arch bridge located at the end of historic main street in Minneapolis. The park features paved walking paths and viewpoints of gorgeous downtown Minneapolis and the Mississippi River.

There are large, elder trees scattered throughout the park that shade picnic tables and grills. There is a band shelter and walking paths that

Band Shelter at Father Hennepin Bluffs Park

lead to the Stone Arch Bridge from the historical St. Anthony main waterfront. This park is located near where Father Louis Hennepin first discovered the falls he named St. Anthony Falls.

Father Hennepin State Park

Father Louis Hennepin, a Franciscan priest of the Recollet order, was dispatched to explore western New France in 1680. Hennepin is not thought to have been in the exact location of the park, but the park is named after him because he was the first to write extensively about the Mille Lacs area. He called the area Louisiana in honor of King Louis XIV of France. In the spring of 1680 he and two companions encountered a group of Dakota Indians and were forced to accompany them to a location about 15 miles (24 km) from today's Father Hennepin State Park. Their release was negotiated eight months later by Daniel Greysolon, Sieur du Lhut. Throughout the experience, Father Hennepin kept a journal describing the lakes, rivers, landscapes, and the lifestyle of his hosts, the Mdewakanton Dakota. In 1683, his writings were published in the book titled *Description de la Louisiane*.

**Statute of Hennepin
In front of Bascilica
of St. Mary**

Father Hennepin Statue

A statue of Father Louis Hennepin stands in a small triange in front of the Bascilica of St. Mary, on Hennepin Ave and 16th Street. It was designed by Fred A. Slifer of St. Paul and placed there in 1930 by the Knights of

Columbus to commemorate the 250th anniversary of Hennepin's discover of the Falls of Saint-Antoine or St. Anthongy.

Fort Beauharnois

Fort Beauharnois was a French fort (or fur post) built on the shores of Lake Pepin, on a wide part of the upper Mississippi River, in 1727. The location chosen was on lowlands and the fort was rebuilt in 1730 on higher ground. It was the site of the first Roman Catholic

Fort Beauharnois Replica

chapel in Minnesota, which was dedicated to St. Michael the Archangel. The fort was first named after the Governor of New France at the time, Charles de Beauharnois.[316] The fort was renamed Fort la Jonquière in 1750. It was abandoned in 1756, as the French sent most of their troops to the east to fight the British in the French and Indian War. Today, an Ursuline convent and the Villa Maria Conference Center stand on the site of the old fort, in Florence Township, Goodhue County, Minnesota.

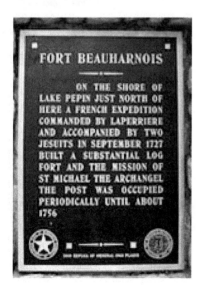

Fort Charlotte

Fort Charlotte was at the inland end of the eight-and-a-half canoe portage called the Grand Portage by French-Canadian voyageurs. It was basically the portage that connected the western interior of Minnesota and Canada with the Great Lakes and great water route of the Northwest Company that led to Montreal.

From 1784 to 1803, the North West Company maintained a year-round presence at Grand Portage, and at least in the summer, many Ojibwe families were present to fish and trade. Today, the historic site of the Grand Portage Bay Depot is occupied by the reconstructed great hall and palisade, and is maintained by the National Park Service as the Grand Portage National Monument.

---

[316] Model of Fort shown above found in 1731 French Historical Documents and published in a Publication of the Florence Township Heritage Preservation Commission in 2007

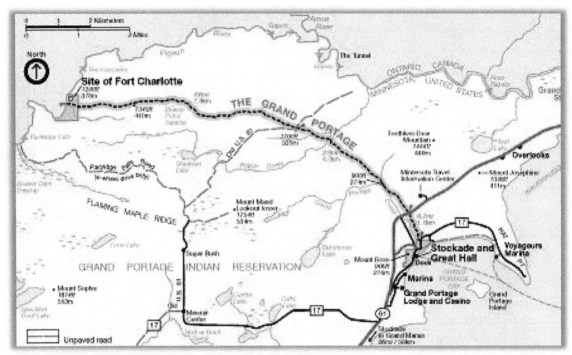

Map of Grand Portage (official U.S. National Monument Map)

Fort Charlotte Reconstruction[317]

---

[317] Picture taken from book: Roberts, Robert B. *Historic Forts, the Military, Pioneer, and Trading Posts of the United States,* Macmillan Publishing Company, New York 1988.

Fort Duquesne

Fort Duquesne was established in 1752, by Joseph Marin de la Malgue, as a French fur trading post along the Mississippi River near the mouth of the Little Elk River near present-day Little Falls, Minnesota. Archeological exploration has revealed a 120 by 80 foot site fronting on the Mississippi River and a number of period French artifacts. Entries in Joseph Marin's journal indicate that the post was abandoned in 1853-1854.

Historic site marker at Fort Duquesne location near Little Falls

Fort L'Huillier

Fort L'Huillier marker near intersection of Blue Earth River and the Minnesota River close to the intersection of Highway 90 and Highway 66

In 1700, Pierre Charles Le Sueur built a fort or post at the intersection of the Blue Earth River and the Minnesota River and used this as his base camp while he explored the area around it. Thomas Hughes of Mankato, historian of the city and county, identified in 1904, the sites of Fort L'Huillier and the mine of blue or green earth, which are described in a paper contributed to the Minnesota Historical Society Collections (vol. XII, pp.283-285).[318] Andre Penicaut's *Relation of Le Suer's expedition* was translated by Alfred J. Hill in the Minnesota Historical Society Collections (vol. III, 1880, pp.1-12) and a map showing the locations of the fort and mine, ascertained by Hughes, was published in 1911 by Newton H. Winchell, *The Aborigines of Minnesota* (1911) p. 493. The name L'Huillier was the name of one of the French King's assayers who secured the royal commission to work the mines in Minnesota based on Le Sueur's description of the area and his description of a bluish green earth that was used by the Sisseton Dakota as a paint pigment. The name Blue Earth River, Blue Earth County, Blue Earth Township, and the city of Blue Earth, all come from the Le Sueur expedition. It should also be noted that the name "Maka" and "to" from which the name Mankato is derived, also refers to the blue earth ("maka"=earth and "to"=blue or green).[319]

[318] Upham, Warren, *Minnesota Place Names, A Geographical Encyclopedia*, Minnesota Historical Society Press; 3rd Revised & Enlarged edition (May 15, 2001) Third Edition, p. 60.
[319] Id, p. 60.

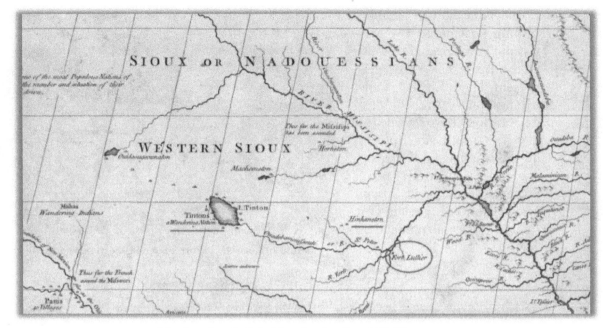

Map based on Delisle Map showing Fort L'Huillier[320]

Fort Snelling

Originally named Fort Saint Antoine or Anthony after Saint Anthony Falls, it was later changed to Fort Snelling. Many early French-Canadian settlers first settled on Fort Snelling's military reservation land until they were evicted in May 1840.

Fort Saint Charles

The first European adventurer credited with seeing Lake of the Woods was Jacques De Noyon of Three Rivers, Quebec, who paddled his way to the mouth of the Rainy River in 1688. Following his arrival, the next known explorer was Pierre La Verendrye. He arrived with a party of more than fifty men in 1732.

Fort Snelling (originally called Fort St. Anthony)
Minnesota Historical Society Collections

---

[320] Guillaume Delisle-Map –Library of Congress Public Domain Site.

Fort St. Charles 1959, Magnusons Island
Minnesota Historical Society Collections

La Verendrye established Fort St. Charles on Magnuson's Island and managed the exploration work which would eventually open up the north and west to a tide of traders who came to gather the rich harvest of furs provided by the forest and lake environment. The post he established was abandoned by 1763. Today a reconstruction of the old fort occupies the exact site on Magnusson's Island. Fort St. Charles is located at the top of the Northwest Angle in Angle Inlet of Lake of the Woods, Minnesota. Infor-

mation on Fort St. Charles can be found at the Lake of the Woods County Historical Society and Museum located in Baudette, Minnesota. The map to the right shows the location of Fort St. Charles. [321] A recreation of the fur trading post at Fort St. Charles is at this museum.

Fort Perrot

The first French establishment in Minnesota was on the west shore of Lake Pepin, a short distance above the entrance. This was a log fort built by Nicholas Perrot, the French explorer. On a map from the year 1700, it was called Fort Bon Secours. Three years later, on a 1703 French

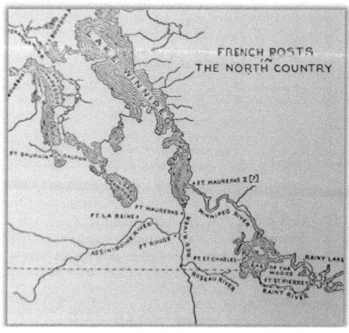
Map showing Fort St. Charles in lower right

map, it was marked Fort Le Sueur. In a much later map, it is correctly called Fort Perrot.[322] On May 8, 1689, Nicholas Perrot formally claimed the territory we now know as Minnesota, for France.[323]

---

[321] Picture from Roberts, Robert B., *Encyclopedia of Historic Forts, the Military, Pioneer, and Trading Posts of the United States,* Macmillan Publishing Company, New York (1988); digitized by University of Michigan 2009).
[322] Information compiled by Pete Payette as part of American Forts Network.
[323] Bunnell, Dr. L.H., *History of Wabasha County* Published Chicago by H.H. Hill, Publishers, 1884, Chapter 1, Aboriginal History.

Guillaume DeLisle's 1702 map showing location of Fort Perrot (called Fort Le Sueur on map) and show location of St. Anthony Falls (calle Saut de St. Antoine de Pade) and the Riviére St. Pierre (now called the Minnesota River). (Public Domain)

Foshay Tower

The Foshay Tower is a skyscraper in Minneapolis, Minnesota. It was completed in 1929, months before the stock market crash in October of that year. It has 32 floors and stands 447 feet (136 m) high, plus an antenna mast that extends the total height of the structure to 607 feet (185 m). The building, which was added to the National Register of Historic Places in 1978, is an example of Art Deco architecture. Its address is 821 Marquette Avenue, although it is set well back from the street and is actually closer to 9th Street than to Marquette.

Wilbur B. Foshay was an American businessman, who built a fortune buying utilities throughout the Midwest in the early 20th century. Foshay had built up three different utility company empires; selling each one in turn to fund the acquisition phase of the next. His second empire included three utility companies that served the Crookston, Bemidji, and Hallock areas in northern Minnesota (all are today served by Otter Tail Power Company). As he worked on his third and largest utility empire, Foshay built the Foshay Tower in

Foshay Tower Phamplet
Minnesota Historical Society Collections

Minneapolis, which opened in August 1929. In 1932, he was convicted of conducting a "pyramid scheme" with shares of his own stock. He was sentenced to fifteen years in prison. President Franklin Roosevelt commuted ten years from Foshay's sentence, but Foshay only actually served three years in Leavenworth because of "good behavior." President Harry Truman granted Foshay a full and unconditional pardon in 1947. Wilbur's paternal ancestor, Joseph Fouchée, was born in France, and accompanied Lafayette on his journey to the United States. Joseph Fouchée's father served as chief of police under Napoleon Bonaparte.

Fountain Cave

Fountain Cave is the site of the residence of Pierre "Pig's Eye" Parrant in the early days of St. Paul. It is located in a West End triangle bound by Randolph Avenue, Drake Street, and Shepard Road. This cave was first described by explorer Major Stephen H. Long in 1817, and named after the spring water flowing from its opening. In 1838,

Pig's Eye, by Robert Perrizo

"Pigs Eye" Parrant stored his liquor in the cave and build a shack at the entrance. Legend has it is that this was the first building constructed in St. Paul and some call Fountain Cave the birthplace of St. Paul. Today, a commemorative plaque marks it location.

Fountain Cave
Minnesota Historical Society Collections

Galtier Plaza

Galtier Plaza is an apartment and condominium development in downtown St. Paul and is named after Father Lucien Galtier. The developer of the site was Robert Boisclair, who has French-Canadian roots. A picture of the complex is to the right. Galtier Plaza as an architectural project was meant to be the centerpiece of Lowertown while "fitting in" with the existing architecture at the turn of the century.

Gervais Grist Mill Site

This historical marker is located near the parking lot entrance to Gervais Mill Park off of Noel Drive. The marker overlooks the property where the first commercial grist mill was built in 1844. Its owner was a French-Canadian by the name of Benjamin Gervais.

Galtier Plaza

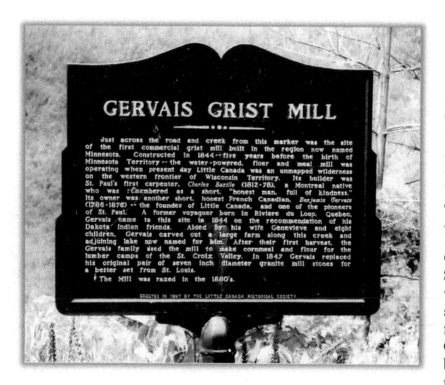

Grand Portage on Lake Superior

Grand Portage, situated along the shores of Lake Superior in the northeast corner on Minnesota, became the hub for a fur trade extending into the middle part of the North American continent. In June 1731 Pierre Gaultier de Varennes, Sieur de la Verendrye, with three of his four sons, brought their flotilla of canoes to Grand Portage. He built a trading post there and between 1731 until about 1805, it was a link in the route between Montreal and the trading posts at Rainy Lake and Lake of the Woods. It is the site of Minnesota's first white settlement. The National Park Service summarizes the post's continuing importance by stating: "Before the United States and Canada existed, the trading of furs, ideas and genes between the

Ojibwe and French and English fur traders flourished." Today, Grand Portage National Monument and Indian Reservation celebrated the heritage of this time.

The eight and a half mile Grand Portage bypassed the unnavigable regions of the lower Pigeon River. Construction on a trading post began in 1768 and by the late 1770s a year-round village in the wilderness had emerged with upwards of 500 people meeting there in the late summers. During the 1780s and 1790s, the North West Company established its headquarters at the Grand Portage and "The Great Carrying Place" reached its most important decades.

The North West Company had the largest presence at the Grand Portage which served as the company headquarters from the mid 1780s to 1803. The 1780s and 1790s proved to be the height of Grand Portage's importance in the fur trade. At its peak, the North West Post consisted of eighteen buildings enclosed by a palisade of 2,000 cedar pickets.

The Grand Hall at Grand Portage
Minnesota Historical Society Collections

Each year the National Park Service re-enacts the rendezvous at Grand Portage in late August. Re-enactors from all over the United States and Canada take part in the activities as interested tourists tour the fort and grounds immersed in the culture. In addition, each year the Ojibwe holds an annual "Rendezvous Days and Powwow Celebration," in which more than 300 Native American dancers participate.

St. Louis River Rapids
Minnesota Historical Society Collections

Grand Portage of the St. Louis River

The Grand Portage of the St. Louis River is located within Jay Cooke State Park, which is located about ten miles southwest of Duluth. The western half of the park contains part of a rocky, thirteen mile (twenty one kilometers) gorge. This was a major barrier to Native Americans and early French fur traders traveling by canoe. They by-passed this river gorge by taking the challenging Grand Portage of the St. Louis River.

Half Breed Tract

When the U.S. government entered into the 1830 Treaty of Prairie du Chien, it specified that a tract of land be set aside for "half-breed" members of the Dakota nation. This tract became known as the "half-breed tract" and is described by the Rev. Edward Neill in his book *History of the Minnesota Valley* as follows:[324]

Map showing Half Breed Tract
off Lake Pepin (Public Domain)

"The Sioux bands in council have earnestly solicited that they might have permission to bestow upon the half-breeds of their nation the tract of land within the following limits, to wit: Beginning at the place called the Barn, below and near the village of the Red Wing chief, and running back fifteen miles; thence, in a parallel line with Lake Pepin and the Mississippi, about 32 miles, to a point opposite the river aforesaid; the United States agree to suffer said half-breeds to occupy said tract of country; they holding by the same title, and in the same manner that other Indian titles are held."

The beneficiaries of this Treaty lived on this land after the treaty until 1852, when the United States government took adverse possession of the land, under the premise of serving as restitution against the Sioux for having violated the terms of an earlier treaty. Two years later, in 1854, Henry Rice, a Minnesota territorial delegate to the U.S. Senate, helped convinced the U.S. Senate to offer the Metis who had lost the right to live on this "half-breed tract," the right to receive up to 640 acres of unsurveyed federal lands by giving up their claim to the Half-Breed Tract. Those eligible would receive "exchanging scrip," certificates that could be used to buy land. This script arrived in Minnesota in the spring of 1857, and was distributed at Wabasha, Red Wing, and other places near the tract. Eligible adults and legal guardians of the qualified received government paper in varying amounts.

Over time, this Half-Breed Tract script would be sold to speculators who used this script to purchase lands that included most of the U.S. controlled lands west of the Mississippi River.[325] For more information on this "Half-Breed Tract" script, read the article written by Frederick L. Johnson located at the MNopedia article "Half-Breed Tract and Scrip," http://www.mnopedia.org/event/half-breed-tract-and-scrip.

[324] Neill, Rev. Edward D., edited by Charles S. Bryant, *History of the Minnesota Valley: Including the Explorers and Pioneers of Minnesota,*, by North Star Publishing Company, Minneapolis, 1882, p 400
[325] Folwell, William Watts, "Sioux Half-Breed Scrip," appendix 11. In *A History of Minnesota*, vol. 1. St. Paul: Minnesota Historical Society, 1956 edition; Curtiss-Wedge, Franklyn. *History of Goodhue County, Minnesota*. Chicago: H.C. Cooper, Jr., 1909; Register of Sioux Half-Breed Scrip, 1857–1861, United States, Red Wing Land District, State Archives Collection, Minnesota Historical Society, St. Paul, Description: An abstract of land entries made in the Red Wing district with Sioux half-breed scrip, issued to mixed-blood Dakota Indians to extinguish their title to land originally reserved to them by the Treaty of Prairie du Chien

Holy Family Church

Holy Family Church

In 1852, Father Francis Xavier Pierz, a missionary from the Austro-Hungarian Empire, established a mission for French-Canadian fur trappers at Belle Prairie on the Mississippi River, north of Little Falls. The mission developed into the Holy Family Parish, the first parish in the Diocese of Saint Cloud. It is the oldest Catholic Church in central Minnesota.

Kaposia

A Dakota village located on the Mississippi River located in present-day South St. Paul. It was also known as "Little Crow's village" after a long line of tribal Chiefs named Little Crow. Today, Kaposia Park is situated where the settlement used to exist. The city of South St. Paul has an annual festival known as Kaposia Days which is held in the last week of June. This village had numerous interactions with early French-Canadian settlers, and was part of the Battle of Kaposia which took place in July, 1842 that involved French-Canadian Settlers located in the Grand Marais area (present-day Pigs Eye) and downtown St. Paul. It is believed Joseph Renville's mother, Miniyuhe, was the daughter of Mdewakanton-Dakota Chief Big Thunder, aka Little Crow, who was from Kaposia Village.[326]

Kaposia Village[327]

[326] Ackermann, Gertrude, *Joseph Renville of Lac qui Parle*, Minnesota History 12 (September 1931) 231-246.
[327] Seth Eastman, Little Crow's Village on the Mississippi, 1846-48, Minnesota Historical Society. (Public Domain)

LaFramboise Gravesite

Joseph Laframboise was a French-Canadian fur trader and interpreter on the upper Minnesota River during the 1830's. He had a fur trading post at the mouth of the Little Rock (Mud) creek, where Joseph Renville, Jr. had a trading station. His gravesite is located at the Fort Ridgely Cemetery in Nicollet County.

Lac qui Parle Mission

The mission was established in 1835 by Dr. Thomas S. Williamson and Joseph Renville. It was located at the southeast end of Lac qui Parle Lake along the Minnesota River. Renville, the son of a French fur trader and Miniyuhe, the daughter of Mdewakanton-Dakota Chief Big Thunder, aka Little Crow, invited missionaries to settle in the area. This historic site is open to the public which includes a self guided tour with interpretive signs. It is located on County Highway 13, eight miles northwest of Montevideo, and three miles west of Highway 59. The wooden chapel was a WPA project that stands on the site of the original mission.

Laframboise Gravesite

Lac Qui Parle Mission

Lake Pepin

Lake Pepin is located on the Minnesota-Wisconsin border and is part of the Mississippi River.[328] There are several different theories about who the lake is named after. The first documentation we have for the Lake being named Pepin is on a map of New France made by Guillaume Delisle in 1703. Father Louis Hennepin, who camped on the shore of the lake in 1680, refers to the Lake in his memoirs as Lac de Pleurs (Lake of Tears), after he observed his Dakota captors weeping near the lake over the death of the chief's son. This name did not stick, however, and was not the name used by Delisle. Andre Joseph Penicaut, in his book "Annals," described the lake as Lac Bon Secours (Lake Good Help). This name was applied by early explorers to the lake.[329] The question is where did Guillaume Delisle get the name Pepin for his map?

Guillaume Delisle 1708 map showing Lake Pepin
(Public Domain)

One belief is that Lake Pepin is named after Guillaume Pépin dit Tranchemontagne (1607–1697) who married Jeanne Meschin or one of his sons, or a combination therof. Guillaume Pépin arrived in Quebec or New France about 1633 and settled in an area that was to become Trois-Rivieres. He was said to be educated and wealthy. According to Tanguay,[330] Guillaume Pépin dit Tranchemontagne was trustee (syndic) of Trois Rivieres, then judge of the seigneury of Champlain. He was established at Trois Rivieres since 1634 on the spot where the community of Ursuline Nuns is found today. On several occasions, he took part in the defense of Trois Rivieres against the repeated attacks of the Iroquois Indians. A great land owner, he was given several concessions, or pieces of land, and he also purchased land in Nicolet, Cap-de-la- Madeleine, Champlain, Lac-Saint-Pierre, and in Trois Rivieres where he resided the major part of his life. It is said that King Louis XIII of France granted a huge concession of land in the Upper Mississippi River Valley to Guillaume Pépin dit Tranchemontagne as a reward for his services.

---

[328] Bunnell, Dr. L.H., *History of Wabasha County* Published Chicago by H.H. Hill, Publishers, 1884, Chapter 1, Aboriginal History Republished Currently by Higginson Books.

[329] Upham, Warren, *Minnesota Place Names, A Geographical Encyclopedia,* Minnesota Historical Society Press; 3rd Revised & Enlarged edition (May 15, 2001) Third Edition p. 10.

[330] Tanguay, Father Cyprien. *Dictionnaire généalogique des Familles Canadiennes depuis la fondation de la colonie jusqu'à nos jours.* First edition. *Eusèbe Senéchal, Imprimeur-Éditeur.* Quebec. 1871, Vol. 1, p.472.

Another theory is that the lake is named after one of Guillaume's sons. According to the English language page of the website *L'Association des Familles de Pepin*, Guillaume's son, Pierre Pépin dit LaForce Sr. (1652-1722), along with his brother Étienne Pepin, took part in the Sieur Du Luht's expedition in 1678 which reached the upper Mississippi.[331] It is also said that Guillaume's son Jean Baptiste Pépin made voyages of discovery into the Midwest and that the Lake could be named after him.[332]

Drawing of Etienne Pépin dit Lafond

Lake Pepin, painted by Seth Eastman (Public Domain)

In Dr. Bunnell's book on the History of Wabasha County, the author speculates that the name was derived from a man with the last name Pepin, Sieur de la Fond, who married the aunt of La Parriere, the builder of an old fort on the north side of the lake, in the fall of 1727.[333]

A historical monument erected in Trois-Rivières, Quebec honors French explorers of the New World, including Jean Nicolet, René-Robert Cavelier, Sieur de La Salle and Pierre Pépin dit Laforce. The fact that there is a historical monument in Trois-Rivières would support the argument that Lake Pepin is, in fact, named after Pierre Pépin dit Laforce. The best conclusion is that the Lake is named after the Guillaume Pépin dit Tranchemontagne family in one way or the other, with perhaps a little truth from all the stories.

---

[331] Jette, Rene, *Dictionnaire genelogique des Families du Qubec ds Origines avant 1730*, Societe de Genealogie de Quebec, 1993, digitized by the University of Wisconsin- Madison, (2008).

[332] Moore, Phillip J., *One Hundred French-Canadian Family Histories*, self published 1994. The research records of Jane Goodrich; Drouin Collection, Quebec, Institut Genealogique Drouin (Ancestry.com Quebec Vital Records) Drouin Collection) 1621-1967 database online; PRDH website, Universite de Montreal (A site that provides access to vital records and the genealogical encyclopedia for Quebec through the year 1799).

[333] Bunnell, Dr. L.H., *History of Wabasha County* Published Chicago by H.H. Hill, Publishers, 1884, Republished Currently by Higginson Books.

Landreville Homestead Cabin

The homestead cabin of Medore Landreville, a French-Canadian from Quebec has been relocated to Settler's Square in Warren Minnesota. Medore was born in 1857 in St. Paul

de Joliette, Quebec and died in 1936 in Argyle, Minnesota. He married Rosalie Forget in 1878 and they have many descendants living today.

LeDuc House

The William G. LeDuc House, located at 1629 Vermillion Street in Hastings, Minnesota, is listed on the National Register of Historic Places. It was built over several years, and completed in 1865, by William G. LeDuc (1823–1917) who came to Minnesota in 1850 from Ohio. He was an attorney who represented a

Medore Landreville Homestead Cabin

party to a suit involving Vermillion Falls, 1,500 feet (457 m) southeast of the homesite. As payment for his services, LeDuc received the land where he built his house. LeDuc was a Civil War veteran and was a Brevet Brigadier General. He served as Chief Quartermaster for the XI and XX Corps. He served as U.S. Commissioner of Agriculture under President Hayes (1877–1881).[334] The name LeDuc is found in Quebec and has known origins in France. It is unknown who William G. LeDuc's ancestors were, although it is believed they were Huguenots.

Little Canada St. John's Cemetery

The St. John's Cemetery in Little Canada is one of the oldest cemeteries in the Twin Cities. In 1851, land for the cemetery was donated by early French-Canadian settler Abraham Lambert. Dedicated in 1855, Saint John's Cemetery is the second oldest cemetery in Minnesota. It is located one block east of the church on Little Canada Road. Over one hundred members of pioneer families (mostly French-Canadian) are buried in the oldest section near the entrance gate.

William LeDuc House

[334] Hiebert, Gareth D., *Little Canada, A Voyageur's Vision*, A compiled history of Little Canada, Minnesota by the Historical Society of Little Canada, Published in 1989 by the Croixside Press, Inc.

Entrance to St. John's Cemetery

Marshall County Courthouse

This courthouse was designed by French-Canadian Architect Charles Napoleon Morin, Architect. Morin was born February 9, 1849, in Quebec. Charles was an architect, contractor and builder in the French-Canadian community of Argyle, Minnesota. He was the second child in a family of fourteen. He was the superintendent of many large buildings with the Marshall County Courthouse in Warren (shown below) perhaps being his most well known. He married Victoria Schiller in 1887 and together had five children.

Massacre Island

The Massacre Island historical marker is located at the Baudette Wayside/Peace Park in Baudette, Minnesota at the Canadian border crossing. The marker tells the story of the murder of Jean-Baptiste La Verendrye, Father Pierre Aulneau and nineteen voyageurs by a Sioux war party on a small rocky island in Lake of the Woods. It was erected by the Minnesota Historic Sites and Markers Commission in 1966. Jean-Baptiste La Verendrye was the son of Pierre La Verendrye.

Marshall County Courthouse

MASSACRE ISLAND

Tradition is woven of fact and fiction. Two islands in the Lake of the Woods are named "Massacre", one on the Canadian, one on the American side of the boundary. The Canadian island, the larger of the two, is heavily wooded. The American island is small, rocky and barren. These islands were so named because of the following events.

In 1732, Pierre Gaultier de Varennes de la Vérendrye, French-Canadian explorer and trader, built Fort St. Charles at Northwest Angle Inlet on Lake of the Woods. From this base he traded with the Cree and Assiniboine for furs to finance explorations for a passage to the Western Sea.

Early in June, 1736, La Vérendrye sent his son, Jean Baptiste, with the priest, Father Pierre Aulneau, and nineteen voyageurs eastward for supplies. At their first campsite, a small rocky island "seven leagues" from the Fort, they were attacked and killed by a Sioux war party. The bodies were decapitated and placed in a row. The heads of the voyageurs were wrapped in beaver pelts and left near the bodies. Those of Jean Baptiste and Father Aulneau may have been carried off as trophies.

Several weeks after the massacre, a party of Chippewa passed a small island and discovered the victims of the massacre. Out of reverence for the priest, and because they could not dig a grave on the rocky island, they raised a stone cairn over his body.

When he learned of the tragedy, the elder La Vérendrye had the remains of the men taken to Fort St. Charles and buried near the chapel. They were found there in 1908 by an archaeological party from St. Boniface College, Manitoba, Canada.

The island where the massacre occurred has never been satisfactorily identified.

Merci Train

The Merci Train, also known as the French Gratitude Train or the Forty and Eight, was presented to the State of Minnesota from the people of France on February 14, 1949. This idea to send railroad cars to the United States was the brainchild of Andre Picard, a French railroad worker and World War II veteran. One train was donated to each of the 48 states that existed at the time, with the remaining train to be shared by the District of Columbia and Hawaii. Each train was filled with "gifts of gratitude," which included dolls, statutes, clothes, ornamental objects, furniture and a Legion of Honour medal which is said to have belonged to Napoleon.

The Minnesota Merci Train is now located at the Minnesota Military Museum located at Camp Ripley National Guard Post located in Little Falls, Minnesota. It was accepted in trust by the Grand Voiture du Minnesota, which was a branch of the national veteran's organization known at "La Societe des Quarante Hommes et Huit Chevaux," also known as the 40 and 8s. This organization had been formed in 1920 by World War I veterans as part of the American Legion.

The Minnesota State Historical Society handled the hundreds and hundreds of gifts that were in the thirty-one crates in the boxcar when it arrived. These contents from the boxcar remained on display at the State Historical Society until July of 1949, when a committee was created by Governor Youngdahl to oversee the distribution of the gifts. Those that were of historical or artistic value remained with the State Historical Society. Those that were educational were given to schools or to public libraries. Items of interest to religious groups were forwarded to them, and the rest was set aside for general distribution to the public.

Merci Train
Fort Ripley, Minnesota

Mushroom Valley

Mushroom Valley, in St. Paul, according to the boast, was the largest mushroom-growing center west of Pennsylvania, or alternatively, west of Chicago. Sometimes it was called the mushroom capital of the Midwest. The name "Mushroom Valley" was the informal name for a several-mile stretch of the Mississippi River gorge, from South Wabasha Street to Pickerel Lake, and on one side of the river only. The original mushroom farmers in St. Paul were Frenchmen who "had seen mushrooms growing in the caves under the sewers of Paris." A French-Canadian named Peltier and his French-Canadian neighbors first discovered mushrooms in the caves in the 1880s. Interviewed on at least two separate occasions by newspaper columnist Gareth Hiebert ("Oliver Towne"), the St. Paul mushroom farmers stated that their predecessors began the local industry in the 1880s.[335] The last cave ceased production in the 1980s during the creation of Lilydale Regional Park.[336]

[335] Hiebert, Gareth, *City of Seven Hills, Columns of Oliver Towne*, Pogo Press, Inc. St. Paul, 1999, p. 177
[336] Brick, Greg, *Subterranean Twin Cities*. Minneapolis, MN: University of Minnesota Press (2009).

North West Company Fur Post
Pine City, MN

North West Company Fur Post (near Pine City, MN) operated for several years beginning in the fall of 1804. Today, it is a historic site maintained by the Minnesota Historical Society.[337]

Photographs at the North West Company Fur Post
Minnesota Historical Society Collections

Old Crossing Treaty State Park

The Old Crossing Treaty State Park is located in Northwest Minnesota near Huot. In the 1800s, this is where the ox cart trains crossed the Red Lake River. A French-Canadian community also settled there. In 1863, the Red Lake and Pembina bands of Chippewa Indians signed a treaty that ceded eleven million acres of land on both sides of the Red River to the U.S. Government. Today, the park offers primitive camping and excellent fishing to the public.

Map of Old Crossing Treaty State Park

Our Lady of Lourdes Church

This French-Canadian congregation is the oldest continuously used church in Minneapolis, Minnesota. A congregation of Catholic French-Canadians acquired the church in 1877 and named it in honor of the Blessed Virgin Mary who Catholics believed had recently appeared to Bernadette Soubirous in France as

---

[337] Photos of the Pine City Fur Post taken by Kurt Kortenhof.

Our Lady of Lourdes. One of many churches throughout the world named for this appearance in Lourdes, Our Lady of Lourdes in Minneapolis was the first in the U.S. with this name. The parish school spoke French until about 1917 when the congregation dwindled, and by 1945, the priests delivered sermons only in English. The church survived extinction when the Minneapolis City Council persuaded bishops of the diocese to stop plans to close and board it up in 1968. Our Lady of Lourdes is now one of 85 contributing properties of the St. Anthony Falls Historic District which is on the National Register of Historic Places.

Our Lady of Lourdes
Church

Our Lady of Victory Chapel

Our Lady of Victory Chapel is located at St. Catherine University in St. Paul, Minnesota. The Chapel was inspired by the Chapel at St. Trophime at Arles, in Provence, France. It is described as architecturally stunning and structurally imposing. The Church of St. Trophime is a Roman Catholic church and former cathedral built between the 12th century and the 15th century in the city of Arles.

Our Lady of Victory Chapel at St. Catherines University

Perrault School

The Perrault School, District #32, was one of six in Lake Pleasant township of Red Lake County. Classes were taught here for 68 years (from 1880 to 1948) when the district was consolidated with that of Red Lake Falls. The school building has served as the Lake Pleasant Town Hall since 1881. The school house has been restored as an interpretive center for early American schools.

Perrault School

The building is locked but the historic insides are visible through the windows. Local teachers bring their students to the Perrault School to spend a day "as it used to be." The Perrault School and the nearby former Perrault Station on the Northern Pacific railroad were named after Charles Perrault, a French-Canadian homestead farmer in the area, who died in 1915. The Perrault School is located on the west (right) side of Highway 32, four miles south of Red Lake Falls.

Rabideau Civilian Conservation Corps Camp

Camp Rabideau

This camp is located near Blackduck, Minnesota. Built in 1935, this CCC (Civilian Conservation Corps) camp is one of the best preserved camps in the United States and is now on the National Register of Historic Places. The camp is named after Lake Rabideau. It is believed that the lake was named after a French-Canadian fur trader who lived in the area. It is run by the U.S. Forest Service. It is located six miles south of Blackduck on County Road 39.

Raspberry Island

This is the island under the present-day Wabasha Bridge where the Minnesota Boat Club House is currently located. This island is part of the French Heritage of St. Paul, because on the evening of July 8, 1842, nineteen French-Canadian families fled to this island to protect themselves from the Dakota warriors who were angry after being ambushed by the Ojibwe in the Battle of Kaposia that took place earlier that day at the location of the present Battle Creek Park.[338]

---

[338] Labissoniere, Issac, *A Pioneer's Talk of Pioneer Days*, Article written in the Northwestern Chronicle about Issac Labissoniere and the Battle of Kaposia. Also see Hennessy, W.B., *Past and Present St. Paul, Minnesota, being a relation of the progressive history of the capital city of Minnesota from the earliest historical times down to the present day*, published 1906 by Chicago, The S.J.Clarke Publishing Company, page 37, which discusses rellocations of Father Ravoux about the French Settlers gathering on Raspberry Island to protect themselves from the Dakota. Also Ravoux, Monsignor V.G., Reminiscences, *Memoirs and Lectures of Monsignor A. Ravoux, V.G.*, Brown, Tracey & Co., Printers and Publishers, 1890, p.7.

St. Paul in 1856 showing Raspberry Island (Public Domain)

The Dakota blamed the French-Canadian settlers because some of them had Ojibwe wives and believed they knew about the ambush. These families spent the night on the island while one of their own, Issac Labissoniere, went up the Mississippi River to Fort Snelling to seek help from the troops stationed there.

Réaume's Trading Post

Joseph Réaume was an independent fur trader who had a fur trading post in present day Wadena County, Minnesota in 1792.[339] He was born at a wintering place on the Mississippi River in 1757 and was the son of Jean-Baptiste Réaume, who was himself a French-Canadian fur trader. Joseph's mother was named Marie Joseph and is believed to be a Native American. Joseph had a good reputation as a trader, and in 1792 went with Jean-Baptiste Cadotte down the Mississippi in search of good land for fur pelts. Cadotte stopped to build a trading post on the Crow Wing River, while Joseph went upstream and set up a winter camp along the Leaf River in what is now Wing River Township. In 2011-2012, students in archaeology from the University of Minnesota did an archaeological research project at this site. The research confirmed a European-style trading post, with up to four collapsed fireplaces lined with stone, wood and daub; at least two buildings; a stockade wall; and two bastions. The spatial distribution of artifacts suggested that one of the buildings was the store or trading house where the trader in charge lived and kept the trade goods, while another building served as the crew's living quarters. Réaume's trading post was listed on the National Register of Historic Places in 1974.

---

[339] Belar, Lina. "Joseph Réaume's Trading Post." Minnesota Historical Society.

Red River Ox Cart Trails

The Red River Trails were a network of ox cart routes connecting the Red River Colony (the "Selkirk Settlement") and Fort Garry (present-day Winnipeg) in British North America with the riverboat landing in St. Paul. These trade routes ran from the location of present-day Winnipeg in the Canadian province of Manitoba across the international border and by a variety of routes across what is now the eastern part of North Dakota and western and central Minnesota to Mendota and Saint Paul, Minnesota on the Mississippi.

Red River Oxcart Trails by Robert Sweeney (1831-1902)
Minnesota Historical Society Collections

The carts used in the trails were two-wheeled wooden carts drawn by horses or oxen. The

Midnight View of an "Ox-train" Camp.

Ox Cart Camp, by Col. Hankins from the book *Dakota Land or the Beauty of St. Paul,* **published by Hankins & Son, 1868. (Public Domain)**

carts were well suited for the open plains, and could travel through difficult conditions caused by shallow water and other obstacles. The carts were fashioned after carts common in Quebec and throughout French Canada, and their design were undoubtedly carried west either by early French traders or by employees of the North West Company.[340]

Travelers began to use the trails by the 1820s, with the heaviest use from the 1840s through the early 1870s, when they were made obsolete by railways. Until then, these cartways provided the most efficient means of transportation between the isolated Red River Colony and the outside world. They gave the Selkirk colonists and their neighbours, the Métis people, an outlet for their furs and pemmican and gave them a source of supplies other than the Hudson's Bay Company. The Hudson's Bay Company had a monopoly since

[340] Gilman, Rhoda R. and Gilman, Carolyn, and Stultz, Deborah, *Red River Trails, Oxcart Routes between St. Paul and the Selkirk Settlement 1820-1870*, Minnesota Historical Society Press.

they took over the Northwest Company, and but for the oxcart trails, would have been the only source for supplies for the Red River colonists.

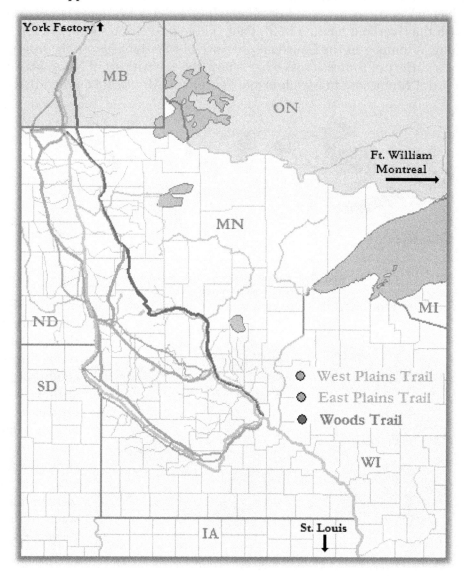

Red River Trails[341]

Free traders, independent of the Hudson's Bay Company and outside its jurisdiction, developed extensive commerce with the United States, making Saint Paul the principal *entrepôt* and link to the outside world for the Selkirk Settlement. The trade contributed to the settlement of Minnesota and North Dakota in the United States, and accelerated the settlement of Canada to the west of the rugged barrier known as the Canadian Shield.

---

[341] "Red River Trails Locator Map cropped" by U.S. Census, Ruhrfisch, Kablammo.

Ox Cart
Minnesota Historical Society Collections

Historical markers identify the location of the trails throughout its length. In the Twin Cities, the trail ran along old Main Street in Northeast Minneapolis and along the current route of freeway 94 down to the St. Paul landing in downtown St. Paul, where the carts were unloaded and their goods put into warehouses where they would eventually be sold. Goods would be loaded into steamboats going to St. Louis and beyond. One of the popular items for trade was pemmican, made by the French Métis from buffalo meat.

Renville City Museum

The Renville City Museum shown below reflects the life and times of French-Canadian and Metis Joseph Renville as well as other examples of pioneer and Dakota life.

Renville City Museum

Rocque's Trading Post

Rocque's Trading Post is located at Read's Landing. This community is located between Lake City and Wabasha along U.S. Highway 61 at its junction with Wabasha County Road 77. This was the site of several trading posts, including Augustin Rocque's (Sr.) Post (1810–1830), Augustin Rocque's (Jr.) Post (1835–1860), Edward Hudson's Post (1840–1845), Charles Read's Post (1847– unknown), and several others from 1840–1860.

Louis Robert Gravesite

This gravesite is located at Calvary Cemetery in St. Paul. Louis Robert was born in St. Louis, Missouri in 1811, the son of Charles and Jeanne (Courtois) Robert. He married Marie Rose Turpin on February 5, 1839, in Missouri. He was a fur trader, an early St. Paul land owner, and a steamboat owner and captain. He died in 1874.

Gravestone for Louis Robert

Saint Cloud Chancery

Saint Cloud Chancery

The Saint Cloud Bishops' residence or Chancery was designed by architect Louis C. Pinault. It is a two-and-a-half story Second Renaissance Revival. The mansard roof gives the house a French emphasis, a hint at the tie between St. Cloud, France and St. Cloud, Minnesota.[342] Louis C. Pinault was born on December 29, 1889, in St. Joseph, Minnesota. His parents were French-Canadians Hubert and Amelia Pinault who were born in Quebec. He attended St. Cloud Normal School, the University of Minnesota and the University of Illinois, where he earned a degree in architecture in 1914. He was a partner in Mann & Pinault, Architects (1915–1922) and beginning in 1922, he was an independent architect based in St. Cloud. Pinault designed many of the secondary schools in central Minnesota and buildings for St. Cloud State University, the city of St. Cloud, Stearns County and the St. Cloud Catholic Diocese. Louis Pinault died on February 19, 1980.

Saint Francis Xavier Church in Benson

Saint Francis Xavier Church

The Saint Francis Xavier Church is located in Benson, Minnesota. This

---

[342] Information obtained on Minnesota Historic Properties Inventory Form.

church was built in 1917 and was designed by the French Architect Emmanuel Masqueray. It was added to the National Register of Historic Places in 1985.

Saint Paul Chapel

The first church built in St. Paul was the log structure named the Saint Paul Chapel by Father Lucien Galtier. This chapel was built on a plot located between Bench and Third Streets and between Minnesota and Cedar Streets. Eight French-Canadian men accepted the job of erecting this building in October 1841. These men were as follows: Pierre Bottineau, Charles Bottineau, Benjamin Gervais and Pierre Gervais,[343] Vetal (Vital) Guerin, Issac Labissoniere, Joseph Labissoniere, and Francois Morin.[344]

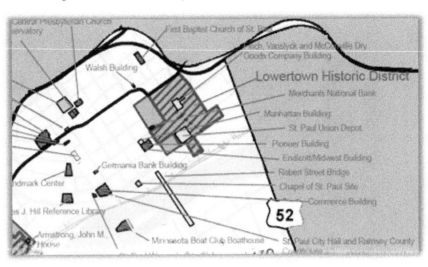

Map showing Chapel site at Kellogg Boulevard and Minnesota Street

St. Paul Chapel (Public Domain)

The chapel was reported to be twenty five feet long, eighteen feet wide, and ten feet high. It had a single window on each side and it faced the river. It was completed in a few days after all the supplies were gathered. The roof slabs came from Stillwater and the men had to work for the lumber mill in order to acquire them. The chapel of Saint Paul was dedicated on the Feast of All Saints Day on November 1, 1841. There is a commemorative display on the site as shown below that names the eight men who built this chapel.

---

[343] The Chapel memorial in St. Paul lists Pierre and Pierre Gervais. Historians who have studied this believe that the two Gervais who built the chapel were brothers. Benjamin Gervais had a brother Pierre and a brother Louis Pierre who was often called Peter. One historian believes that one of the Pierre Gervais was in fact Benjamin. See Scholberg, Henry, *The French Pioneers of Minnesota (Les Pionniers Francais du Minnesota)* Northstar Publications Minnesota, 1995, p. 65.
[344] Catholic Historical Society of St. Paul, "Obituary of Issac Labissoniere," in *Acta et Dicta*, Vol. III, No. 1, (July 1911) p. 188; and Catholic Historical Society of St. Paul, "Monsignor Augustine Ravoux, The Pioneer Missionary of the Northwest," in *Acta et Dicta*, Vol. 1, No. I, (July 1907) p. 66.

Current location of St. Paul Chapel in downtown St. Paul[345]

Sandy Lake Fur Trading Post

In the year 1794, the North West Company built a fur trading post at Sandy Lake, with bastions, and apertures in the angles for musketry.[346] It was enclosed with pickets a foot square and thirteen feet in height. There were three gates at the post. The stockade enclosed two rows of buildings, containing the provision store, workshop, warehouse, room for clerks, and accommodation for the men. On the west and southwest angles of the fort were four acres of ground, enclosed with pickets, and devoted to the culture of the potato."[347] The map to the right shows the location of the post and the drawing below gives you an idea of what the post looked like.

[345] Photo by Mark Petty, member of French-American Heritage Foundation.
[346] Map on this page taken from article written by Hart, Irving Harlow, "*The site of the Northwest Company Post on Sandy Lake*", Iowa State Teachers College, Cedar Falls, IA, property of Minnesota Historical Society.
[347] 1 Wisconsin Historical Society Collections, vol. Iii., Zebulon M. Pike, "Expeditions to the Headwaters of the Minneissippi River" I:138, 139, 281 (Coues edition, New York, 1895).

Drawing of Sandy Lake Trading Post[348] (Public Domain)

Sandy Lake, by Henry Lewis in 1850
Minnesota Historical Society Collections

Savanna Portage

The Savanna Portage is located in the Savanna Portage State Park located north of McGregor, Minnesota. It is 5.4 miles long. It was first used as a portage by the Native Americans and then by the French voyageurs in the mid-1700s. Savanna Portage connects the West Savanna River, which flows south from Big Sandy Lake and on to the Mississippi, and the East Savanna River, which flows east into the Saint Louis River.

---

[348] Drawing from Roberts, Robert B., *Encyclopedia of Historic Forts, the Military, Pioneer, and Trading Posts of the United States*, Macmillan Publishing Company, New York.

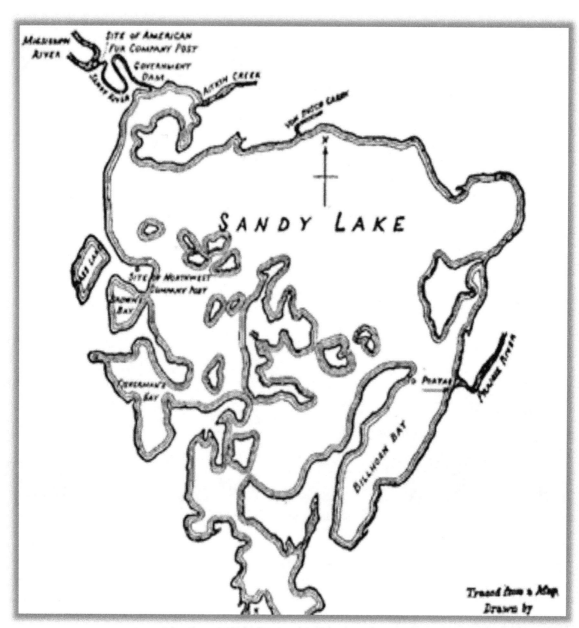

Map showing site of Fur Trading Posts on Sandy Lake
Reprinted with permission from Minnesota Historical Society

Selkirk Colony

In the summer of 1817, Thomas Douglas, the Fifth Earl of Selkirk, recruited the services of two groups of mercenaries to defend his newly founded Red River Colony. The regiments were the De Meurons of Neuchatel and the De Wattevilles of Bern. There were many Swiss among these regiments, the majority of them French speaking. Many of the French speaking Swiss who joined the Selkirk Colony were craftsman such as clockmakers, locksmiths, and carpenters. A few were professionals and many were Huguenots. Abram Perret, later called Abraham Perry, is one of the more well known Swiss colonists of the Selkirk Colony. He became one of the first settlers of St. Paul.[349]

Shrine of the Blessed Virgin

This shrine was built by Father Ernest Bossus, pastor of St. Dorothy's Catholic Church from 1926 to 1935. The roots of St. Dorothy's Parish date back to the Huot area, where Father Pierre Champagne offered mass at the home of Louis Huot as early as 1880. At that time, there were about twenty-five French-Canadian families located in the area. A church, St. Aloysius, was built at Huot in 1883. In 1919, a new

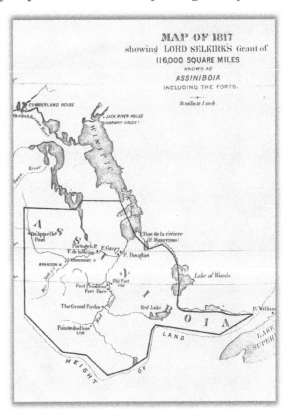

1817 Map of Selkirk Colony (Public Domain)

Shrine of the Blessed Virgin

church was built in the village of Dorothy (five miles north) and the St. Aloysius Church was closed. Father Bossus's sight failed in his last years at Dorothy but his eyesight was successfully restored after a cataract operation. In thanksgiving, he built a shrine in honor of the Blessed Virgin on this knoll across the road from Huot State Park. Dorothy's parishioners still gather annually for services at the Shrine.

---

[349] Holmquist, June Drenning, *They Chose Minnesota" a Survey of The State's Ethnic Groups,* Minnesota Historical Society Press (1981) p.211.

Traverse des Sioux Treaty Site

The Treaty of Traverse des Sioux was a treaty signed on July 23, 1851, between the United States government and Dakota bands in Minnesota Territory by which the Dakota ceded

Traverse des Sioux Park in St. Peter

territory. The negotiations were instigated by Alexander Ramsey, the first governor of Minnesota Territory, and Luke Lea, Commissioner of Indian Affairs in Washington, D.C. The United States wanted the treaty to gain control of agricultural lands for more settlers.

Traverse des Sioux Treaty, by Frank Blackwell Mayer (Public Domain)

Vermilion Interpretive and History Center

The Vermillion Interpretive and History Center houses information about the area around Ely, Minnesota from the time of the voyageurs to present-day. Located in Ely, Minnesota.

Vermilion Interpretive Center

Eugene and Christina Villaume House

The Eugene and Christina Villaume house is located at 123 West Isabel on the West side of St. Paul, Minnesota. The house's prominent round tower, steep roof, and gingerbread ornamentation mark it unmistakably as a Queen Anne architectural style.

Villaume House

Eugene Villaume, born in St. Michel, France, in 1853, came to St. Paul in 1873, following his brother Victor. He started out working as a laborer, notably at a firm called Osgood-Blodgett, a maker of prefabricated houses. After several years he started his own business, expanding over time to lumber and millwork. His company, Villaume Box and Lumber became one of the big employers on the West Side. Directly or indirectly Villaume had 250 employees at his death in 1933. The Villaume firm still exists today, making trusses, pallets, and heavy-duty packaging, and the site of its West Side installation is located along the railroad tracks near Robert Street.

White Oak Fur Post

The White Oak Fur Post is a recreation of the 1798 North West Company Fur and Trading Post. Included at the site are winter quarters for the voyageurs, a smokehouse, quarters for the clerks, a bourgeois and company store. It is located at Deer River, Minnesota. Annual rendezvous occurs during the first full weekend in August. The White Oak Society is a non-profit organization providing living history interpretations of the fur trade era within the Great Lakes region. They operate The White Oak Learning Centre and White Oak Fur Post near Deer River, Minnesota.

Chapter Nineteen
French Place Names in Minnesota

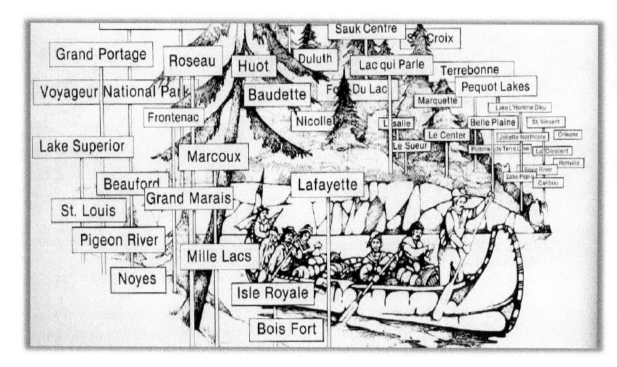

Minnesota's French Heritage is evidenced by place names throughout the state. This chapter lists a number of them and some information about each name. The primary source for information on these place names is the book titled "Minnesota Place Names", a Geographical Encyclopedia, by Warren Upham. Unless another source is cited, the reader should assume the source for the information of the following place names came from Mr. Upham's book.

This list does include some names that were originally French but were later anglicized. This happened not only to place names but to family names.[350] An example of some French names anglicized are as follows:

- Rainy Lake was formerly Lac la Pluie
- Lake of the Woods was formerly Lac du Bois
- Zumbro River was formerly Riviére des Embarras
- Grand Forks was formerly Grande Fourche
- Maple Lake was formerly Lac aux Erables
- Thief River was formerly Riviére Voleuse

---

[350] Lass, William E, *History of Minnesota*, W.W. Norton & Company, (2000) (page 66).

- Sandy Lake was Lac au Sable
- Minnesota River was Riviére St. Pierre
- Red River was formerly Riviére Rouge

Family names were also changed. (**Family Names Changed**) Here are a few examples.[351] There are many more.

- Allard to Lord
- Archambault to Shambo
- Beigue to Beakes
- Boulanger to Baker
- Boisvert to Greenwood
- Boucher to Butcher
- Butolier to Butler
- Clouatre to Coldwater
- Desjardins to Gardner
- Desjarlais to Dejerl
- Decarreaux to Diamond
- Dompierre to Stone
- Dubois to Wood
- Duclos to Nealor
- Fallu to Foley
- Frappier to Foot
- Gouin to Wedge
- Labine to LaBean
- LaFramboise to Rasberry
- La Marche to Walker
- Lamoureux to Love
- Larue to Street
- LeBlanc to White
- Lefebvre to Bean
- Lenoir to Black
- Letourneau to Blackbird
- Levesque to Bishop
- Normandin to Norman
- Monat to Miller
- Ouellette to Wheler
- Pariseau to Perrizo

---

[351] Many of these names I received in letter dated August 1, 1995 from Jean-Marc Charron to Dick Bernard where he discussed French-Canadian and English relationships in Quebec.

- Potvin to Wine
- Roy to King
- Tousignant to Coughin
- Vadeboncoeur changed to Bunker, Goodheart and Hart
- Vadnais to Vanney

Accault Bay

Accault bay is just south of the middle east shore of Lake Mille Lacs. It was named for Frenchman who was with Father Louis Hennepin in 1680.

Argonne

Lakeville includes the Argonne Farms post-World War I settlement project which failed in the early 20th century and was redeveloped in the 21st century into typical suburban retail. Since it was a semi-autonomous village within Lakeville Township before the city's incorporation, it continues to appear today on maps as Argonne. Argonne is the name of a forest in France.

Audubon

Audubon is a city in Becker County, Minnesota. Audubon received its name before it became a town. In August of 1871, an official of the railroad arrived there on an inspection tour with a party of friends accompanying him, including the niece of John J. Audubon. The prairie was bright with wild flowers, birds singing, and water fowl swimming on the lake. Audubon's niece was so impressed by the beauty of the place that she asked if a settlement were ever established here, they name it after her Uncle John J. Audubon, a nature enthusiast. John Audubon (1785-1839) (aka Jean-Jacques Rabin Audubon) was born in Les Cayes in the French Colony of Saint-Domingue (now known as Haiti). He was an American ornithologist, naturalist, and painter. He was known for his expansive studies to document all types of American birds and for his detailed illustrations that depicted the birds in their natural habitats. His major work, a color-plate book entitled *The Birds of America* (1827–1839), is considered one of the finest ornithological works ever completed. Audubon identified twenty-five new species The National Audubon Society was named in his honor.

**John Audubon
(Public Domain)**

Bain

In 1901, a French speaking man by the name of William Bain came to settle in this area. His homestead was located just west of what became the village of Bain. William was a French-Canadian from Quebec who had a Scottish name with Scottish family connections. William born in 1861 in Montreal and died in 1952 in St. Cloud, Minnesota.

Battle Creek

Battle Creek is named for the Battle of Kaposia which occurred in 1842 between the Ojibwe and Dakota tribes. This battle involved early French-Canadian settlers and Metis. It contains a large ravine called Pine Cooley, which is from the French word "coulee," meaning a ravine or run.

Baudette

Thomas Cathcart came to the border area in 1891. Working at the Beaver Mill in Rainy River, Ontario, he soon became attracted to the unsettled American side of the river. He moved to the south bank, settling at the mouth of the Beaudette River which, like the Rainy, had received its name during the earlier fur trade days. The town assumed the Beaudette name as well although the initial "e" was eventually dropped. In 1893, Cathcart's family arrived from eastern Canada via Kenora aboard the Shamrock to become Baudette's first family. Spooner, the village on the east bank of the Baudette River, was incorporated in 1906, the same year as Baudette.

Baudette River

Originally called the Beaudette River, the assumption is that this river was named after the city in Quebec Canada called Riviere-Beaudette by a French-Canadian fur trader. It is a short tributary of the Rainy River in northern Minnesota and the town Baudette is named after the river.

Beauford Township

Beauford is located in Blue Earth County, Minnesota.

Beaulieu

Beaulieu is an unincorporated community located in Mahnomen County, Minnesota. It is also the name of the local township. It is named for Henry and John Beaulieu, who served in the Civil War and afterward owned farms there. They were descendants of a French fur trader named Bazille Beaulieu and his Ojibwe wife, Queen of the Skies.

Beaudry

Beaudry was a post office in Lake Pleasant Township of Red Lake County from 1882-94. Named after John T. Beaudry, postmaster.

Bejou

Bejou Township is located in Mahnomen County, Minnesota. It was incorporated as a village in 1921 and was created by the Minneapolis, St. Paul, and Sault Ste. Marie Railroad (Soo Line) in 1904 as a railroad village. It is named after the French words Bon Jour which means "Good Day" used by former French fur traders and trappers.

Belgium Township

Belgium Township is located in Polk County, Minnesota. The population was 111 at the 2000 census. It is part of the Grand Forks-ND-MN Metropolitan Statistical Area. Belgium is a Francophone country where French is one of their official languages. Many of the early Belgium immigrants to North America were French speaking.

Bellaire

Bellaire is an unincorporated community in White Bear Township, Ramsey County, Minnesota. The community is located on the south shore of White Bear Lake, and is completely surrounded by the cities of White Bear Lake and Birchwood Village.

Belle Fontaine

A post office with a French name was located in Scott County from 1857 to 1865. The current location is unknown.

Belle Plaine

Minnesota Territorial Supreme Court Judge Andrew G. Chatfield selected the townsite of Belle Plaine in 1853, while traveling from Mendota to Traverse des Sioux to hold court, as it was a halfway point on his usual path of travel. Judge Chatfield chose to name the townsite Belle Plaine, which is French for "Beautiful Prairie." Even today, the city has select areas of protected, natural prairie grasses. It is located on highway 169, southwest of the Twin Cities.

Belle Plaine Township

Belle Plaine is located in Scott County. It was named by the Honorable Andrew G. Chatfield, an associate justice of the Supreme Court of Minnesota Territory, who settled there in 1854. It is a French name, meaning "Beautiful Prairie."

Belle Prairie Township

Located in Morrison County. First settled in 1849. Adopted name meaning beautiful praire from French fur traders and voyageurs, for its tract of grassland five miles long and averaging about a mile in width, nearly adjoining the Mississippi River. Frederick Ayer had a mission for Indian and Caucasian children near a small settlement of Métis farms which Ayer called Belle Prairie about two miles north of the present town of Belle Prairie.[352]

Belle River

This river flows from the Eastern Township in Otter Tail County into Douglas County, where there is Belle River Township.

Bellevue Township

Settled in 1852 and adopted a French name meaning "beautiful view," in reference to the outlook from its prairie beside the Mississippi.

---

[352] Gilman, Rhoda R. and Gilman, Carolyn, and Stultz, Deborah, *Red River Trails, Oxcart Routes between St. Paul and the Selkirk Settlement 1820-1870*, Minnesota Historical Society Press. P.67

Belview

City located in Redwood County. Incorporated in 1893 and derived from French words meaning a "beautiful view."

Benoit

A village in section 22 of Kertsonville Township in Polk County. Named after Frederick Benoit who was postmaster of the Lawton post office from 1899-1903.

Bernadotte Township

Located in Nicollet County and organized in 1869. It was named for a French General, Jean Baptiste Jules Bernadotte (1764-1844), who was elected crown prince of Sweden in 1810 and became the Swedish king in 1818, with the title King Charles XIV.

Big Cherry and Little Cherry Portage

Located in Cook County. Translated from French names used by Mackenzie in his book. [353]

Big La Salle Lake

Located in Clearwater and Hubbard County. It is next to the smaller La Salle Lake and is connected by the La Salle River. The river was named by Captain Willard Glazier in 1881.

Birch Coulee Township

Located in Renville County. Named for small stream in township originally called La Croix Creek. Later renamed Birch Coulee. Coulee is a French word meaning the bed of the stream, even if dry, when deep and having inclinded sides. On September 2, 1862, the Battle of Birch Coulee took place in Renville County, resulting in thirteen dead, 47 wounded and 90 horses killed. It was the most deadly battle for the United States forces in the Dakota War of 1862. The Birch Coulee Battlefield is a State Historic Site.

Attack on New Ulm during Dakota War of 1862
Artist: Anton Gag (1859-1908)
Minnesota Historical Society Collections

Blanchard

Located in Morrison County. Near the Blanchard Rapids Dam, which was built in 1924. Seven miles south of Little Falls on the Mississippi. Blanchard is a French family name. It is also used as a given name. It is derived from the Old French word *blanchart* which meant "whitish, bordering upon white." It is also an obsolete term for a white horse.

---

[353] Mackenzie, Alexander, *Voyages from Montreal*, published in 1801.

Boisberg

Located in Traverse County, Minnesota. Platted in 1901 in section 3 of West Monson Township. Named after the Bois de Sioux River and from the large granite boulder (berg) on the opposite or South Dakota side of this river. The city was never incorporated.

Bois de Sioux River

Located in Traverse County, Minnesota, the Bois de Sioux River drains Lake Traverse, the southernmost body of water in the Hudson Bay watershed of North America. It is a tributary of the Red River of the North and defines part of the western border of Minnesota, and the eastern borders of North Dakota and South Dakota. It is about 41 miles (66 km) in length.

Bois de Sioux River about 1853[354] (Public Domain)

Bois Forte

A post office located in the Bois Forte Indian Reservation in Koochiching County.

Bois Forte Indian Reservation

Bois Forte Indian Reservation is an Indian reservation in Northern Minnesota formed for the Bois Forte Band of Ojibwe.

---

[354] Drawings by John Mix Stanley, in Stevens, Issac I. *Narrative ...of Explorations for a Route for A Pacific Railroad...from St. Paul to Puget Sound*, plates 3,4,5 in 36 Congress, 1 session, House Executive Documents no. 56 (serial 1054).

Bois Franc Creek

A creek located on the Minnesota Valley Ox Cart Trail near Blakeley, Minnesota. It is now called Robert Creek, after French-Canadian fur trader Louis Robert.

Brule River

Little and Large Brule River are located in Cook County. They flow through Elephant Lake, more commonly known by people in the region as Northern Light Lake. Little Brule River is tributary to Lake Superior about a mile west of the large Brule River. Named after Etienne Brule, who is credited with being the first white person to see Lake Superior.

Brule Mountain

Brule Mountain is the summit of the highland located just south of Lower Trout Lake on the Brule River.

Burdette

Located in Lime Township in Blue Earth County on the Chicago and Northwestern Railway.

Burau

Located in Wilkin County in section 35 of Akron Township. Was a post office from 1887 to 1905, with August Burau as its first postmaster. This is an ancient French name that you find in England. It is said to have arrived in England after the Norman Conquest of 1066.

Cannon River

This name comes from the French name Riviére aux Canots, meaning Canoe River, which alluded to canoes frequently left in concealment near its mouth by Indians and French traders, especially when going on the hunt for buffalo in the adjoining prairie country. The name was incorrectly Anglicized by narratives of Zebulon Pike's expedition in 1805-06 and by Long's expeditions in 1817 and 1823. Pike used both Canoe River and Cannon River in his narratives.

Caribou Lakes

There are two Caribou Lakes in Cook County which comes from the French name for the American reindeer. Named derived by the French from the Micmac Indians who used the term kalibu meaning "pawer or scratcher." Deer were noted for shoveling snow with their forelegs to look for food. There is also a Caribou Lake in St. Louis County on west side of Canosia Township.

Chateau Theatre

Located in Rochester on 15 First Street SW. This was an elaborate theatre built in the early 1900's. Has French village decor complete with balconies and turrets, then remodeled into a Barnes and Noble store.

Chaudiere Falls and Portage

Located between Lake Namekan and Rainy Lake in St. Louis County. This is a French name meaning "a great boiling kettle."

Cloquet

Cloquet, Minnesota, is named after the Cloquet River which is a tributary of the St. Louis River. The exact origin of the name is uncertain. The word "Cloquet" first appeared on a map of the area by Joseph N. Nicollet in 1843, which named the Cloquet River, a tributary of the Saint Louis River, and the Cloquet Rapids to the north. "Cloquet" is a French surname but historians researching the name of the river and city have found no direct link to a person and are reduced to speculations. One of which is that the river might have been named after 19th century French scientists, the Cloquet brothers Hipployte and Jules, with the settlement later being named after the river. The name is also applied to an island of the Mississippi in section 10, Dayton Township, Hennepin County.

Cloquet River

Located in St. Louis County. See explanation above for origin of name.

Cloutier's Island

Cloutier's Island is an island in Ramsey Township located on the Mississippi River opposite the town of Ramsey. It was used as a campsite in 1849 by John R. Bean and John Simpson.

Coteau des Prairies

The Coteau des Prairies is a highland in Lincoln County which extends north-northwest through the southwestern part of the county. The Coteau des Prairies is a plateau approximately 200 miles in length and 100 miles in width (320 by 160 km), rising from the prairie flatlands in eastern South Dakota, southwestern Minnesota, and northwestern Iowa in the United States. The southeast portion of the Coteau comprises one of the distinct regions of Minnesota, known as Buffalo Ridge. The flatiron-shaped plateau was named by early French explorers from New France (Quebec), coteau meaning "hill" in French.[355]

Cottonwood County

This county derived its name from the Cottonwood River. The French-Canadian fur traders gave the cottonwood the name Liard, meaning "a farthing." This is probably because the lumber from cottonwood was nearly worthless for building and so was not worth much. Early records of this river refer to it as the "Riviére aux Liards" which was translated to the Cottonwood River.

Crooked Lake

Located in St. Louis County adjoining to the northwest corner of Lake County. This is translated from the old French name Croche, which means "crooked, bent." This name was given by the early voyageurs and traders for the irregular path of lake.

---

[355] Oxford English Dictionary.

Crow Wing River

Zebulon Pike in 1805 and Henry R. Schoolcraft[356] in 1820 used the French name for this river, "de Corbeau" in their expedition writings and notes. The complete name given to this river by early French fur traders was "rivière á l'Aile de Corbeau" meaning "river of the Raven." The river was incorrectly translated to Crow Wing as noted by Schoolcraft in his writing. The word for crow in French is corneille, not corbeau.

Dalles of the Saint Croix

The Upper Dalles of the Saint Croix are located near Taylor's Falls. The lower Dalles are located two miles farther south. The name Dalles, applied by the early French voyageurs to rock-walled gorges of the Wisconsin River, the St. Croix and St. Louis rivers in Minnesota, and the Columbia River on the boundary between Oregon and Washington. It comes from the French word "Dalle," meaning a "flagstone or slab or rack."

Dalles of the Saint Louis

The Dalles of the Saint Louis River are located from Thompson and Carlton almost to Fond du Lac.

Deer River

Named Rivière aux Chevreull by French fur traders. Later anglicized to Deer River.[357]

De Forest

Located in section 35 and 36 of Nichols Township in St. Louis County. It is not clear where the name comes from although it appears to be a French name.

Delorme

A village in Lake Pleasant Township in Red Lake County and named for Ambrose Delorme, a homestead French-Canadian farmer.

Demarest

Demarest was a post office in Ramsey Township in Anoka County from 1897-1902. Named by Daniel M. Demarest, postmaster, for his father Franklin Demarest. Demarest is French-Canadian name, also spelled Demarais, Desmarais, among other spellings.

Des Moines River Township

Located in Murray County and organized in 1878. The Des Moines River crosses this township. The French fur traders called this river "Rivière des Moines," meaning either "River of the Monks" or "River of the Mounds" named after trappist monks who lived

---

[356] Schoolcraft, Henry R., *Summary Narrative of an Exploratory Expedition to the Sources of the Mississippi River in 1820*, Published in 1855.

[357] Perreault, Jean Baptiste, *Narrative of the Travels and Adventures of a Merchant Voyageur in the Savage Territories of Northern America," Leaving Montreal the 28th Day of May, 1783 to 1820*. Written in 1830, (Found in Schoolcraft Manuscripts in the Smithsonian Institute in Washington, D.C.)

nearby or the Indian word *"Moingona"* which referred to burial mounds located near this river"[358]

Demontreville Lake

Located in Washington County and named after Dr. Clarence de Montreville, a dentist from St. Paul, who had a country home on this lake. His father was born in France.

Detroit Lakes

Detroit Lakes was incorporated as a village in 1880 and as a city in 1900. It is located on Detroit Lake and the Pelican River in Becker County. The name Detroit Lake was given by a French traveler who was a Catholic missionary. The story goes he camped on the north shore of the lake in full view of the long bar that stretches nearly across it and leaves a strait (Detroit, in French) between its two parts. He therefore applied that name to the lake which appears on state maps in 1860. The city was named after the lake.

Detroit Township

Derived its name from Detroit Lake. Located in Becker County.

Desnoyer

Desnoyer Park and Desnoyer Avenue in St. Paul are named after Stephen Desnoyer (1805–1877), who managed a half-way house for stagecoach travelers between St. Paul and Minneapolis, located at approximately Fairview Avenue and Interstate 94. He was a French-Canadian born in St. Jean d'Iberville, Quebec. He was a farmer in New York state, a clothier in St. Louis and a lumber merchant in Dubuque, Iowa before coming to Minnesota where he purchased 320 acres between what is today Cleveland Avenue and the

Desnoyer Stagecoach Station
Minnesota Historical Society Collections

Mississippi River. Desnoyer Park is located at Pelham Boulevand and Doane Avenue, and the Desnoyer Park neighborhood is on the western end of the city bounded by Marshall and Cretin Avenue, the Mississippi River and Interstate 94. A picture of his Stagecoach station in St. Paul is shown to the right. [359]

Dorothy

A village located in Louisville Township in Red Lake County named after St. Dorothy's Catholic Church, which was built in 1919 for the French-Canadian families in the area.

---

[358] Upham, Warren, *Minnesota Place Names, A Geographical Encyclopedia*, Minnesota Historical Society Press; 3rd Revised & Enlarged edition (May 15, 2001) Third Edition.
[359] B.J. Sturtevant, photographer, from book Gilman, Rhoda R. and Gilman, Carolyn, and Stultz, Deborah, *Red River Trails, Oxcart Routes between St. Paul and the Selkirk Settlement 1820-1870*, Minnesota Historical Society Press, p.86.

Du Forte Lake

Located in White Earth Township in Becker County.

Duluth

Located in St. Louis County and named after Daniel Greysolon, sieur Du Luth (found spelled in records as Du Lhut, Du Lhud and Du Lud). He was born in St. Germain Laval near Roanne, France and died in his home in Montreal in 1710.

Duluth Township

Located in St. Louis County on east boundary of county, including the former sites of Buchanan and Clifton.

Dumont

Located in Traverse County in Croke Township. Named by the officers of the Chicago, Milwaukee and St. Paul Railroad company, perhaps for a local French hunter who supplied food to the railroad men.[360] Dumont is a French surname and generally means "from the mount." Jean-François-Benjamin Dumont de Montigny, or Dumont de Montigny was a French explorer and author (1696-1760) who wrote about French colony in Louisiana. Gabriel Dumont was a metis buffalo hunter in the 1800s and it is possible he may also have a connection to this name.

Duquette

Located in Pine County in section 24 of Kerrick Township. First settlers of this village were French-Canadians, among them Frank Duquette, who built a sawmill and store here. Built on the site of former Indian village.

Durand Township

Located in Beltrami County. Named in honor of Charles Durand, a homesteader on the northeast side of Lake Puposky.

Emard Township

Located in Red Lake County. Named after Pierre Emard, who was born in Longueuil, Quebec, which is near Montreal. He was born in 1835 and came to Minnesota in 1878.

Embarrass Township

Located in St. Louis County. The name comes from French explorers, who used the term "embarrass" for river obstacles, blockages, and difficulties relating to logjams and the like.

---

[360] Upham, Warren, *Minnesota Place Names, A Geographical Encyclopedia*, Minnesota Historical Society Press; 3rd Revised & Enlarged edition (May 15, 2001) Third Edition, p.597.

Embarrass River

Located in St. Louis County. The name comes from French explorers, who used the term "embarrass" for river obstacles, blockages, and difficulties relating to logjams and the like. The Embarrass River is a 50.5 mile long tributary of the Saint Louis River. It rises just west of the city of Babbitt and flows southwest, between the Embarrass Mountains to the east and the Mesabi Range to the west. The river flows into the Saint Louis River southeast of Eveleth. During the fur-trading days and the era of exploration, the river was part of a historic trade route from Lower Canada via Lake Superior, across the Height of Land, and down the Rainy River to Lake Winnipeg to the pays d'en haut—the fur-bearing regions of the Canadian northwest.

Faribault

The city of Faribault is located in Rice County in Cannon City Township. This is the county seat of the county. Named in honor of Alexander Faribault, the eldest son of Jean Baptiste Faribault. Alexander was born in Prairie du Chien, Wisconsin in 1806 and died in 1882. He was a fur trader and established fur trading posts at Waterville in Le Sueur County and Morristown in Rice County. Alexander was the first postmaster of the city in 1853.

Flacon Portage

Located in St. Louis County near Crooked Lake. This refers to the French word "flagon" or "decanter." The English translation is "bottle." This portage leads to the Lake of La Croix.

Flandreau

Flandreau was a post office in Nicollet County from 1894-97. It was named in honor of Charles Eugene Flandrau, a judge in the territory and state of Minnesota, who is credited with saving the community of New Ulm, Minnesota, from destruction during conflict with the Dakota in 1862. He was a descendant of Jacques Flandreau, a French Huguenot who came to New Rochelle, New York in the 1690s.[361]

Flandreau Creek

Located in Pipestone County in Fountain Prairie and Altona Townships. This creek also named in honor of Judge Charles Flandrau. Note the spelling has been changed.

Flandreau Street

Located in the city of St. Paul. Flandrau place is a southern extension of the street near Battle Creek Park. This street is also named in honor of Judge Charles Flandrau.

---

[361] For information on Charles Flandrau, see Shutter, Marion Daniel, & McLain, John Scudder (1897). *Progressive men of Minnesota. Biographical sketches and portraits of the leaders in business, politics and the professions; together with an historical and descriptive sketch of the state.* Minneapolis: Minneapolis Journal., p. 121-2.

Folles Avoines

Folles Avoines was the French name used for the upper stretches of the St. Croix River.[362] The term was used to describe the land lying between the highlands southwest from Lake Superior and the Mississippi River, which included part of Minnesota. This term comes from the word that French traders and voyageurs used to describe wild rice. They called it "folles avoines," which means *"fool oat or false oat."* There is currently a Fort Folle Avione Historical Park located near Danbury, Wisconsin. Minnesota Wild Rice has been called Manoomin (good berry or good seed) or Riz Sauvage (Wild Rice) or Folles Avoines (wild oats).

Fond du Lac

The name Fond du Lac, meaning the "farther end" or "head of the lake," was applied by the early French traders and voyageurs to their trading post on the north side of the St. Louis River. The name was also given to this river called R. du Fond du Lac on Jean Baptiste Louis Franquelin's map in 1688, renamed the St. Louis River by Gilles Robert de Vaugondy's map in 1755. Fond du Lac in St. Louis County was a fur trading post of the North West Company in 1792, located on the south of Wisconsin shore of the St. Louis River where it comes to the still water level of Lake Superior. Later the American Fur Company operated a trading post on the opposite side of the river. The site is now a suburban area of Duluth.

Fond du Lac Dam

Located on the St. Louis River located down stream from Jay Cooke State Park.

Fond du Lac Indian Reservation

The Fond du Lac Indian reservation was established by a treaty of La Pointe, Wisconsin in September 30, 1854 for the Fond du Lac band of the Lake Superior Ojibwe. The name Fond du Lac, meaning the "farther end" or "head of the lake," was applied by the early French traders and voyageurs to the trading post on the north side of the St. Louis River.

Fortier Township

Located in Yellow Medicine County. The name Le Roy was first given to it, but later changed to Fortier in honor of Joseph Fortier. He was a French-Canadian born in Napier, Quebec, came to Minnesota in 1854, was employed at the Upper Sioux Agency, was in the Battle of New Ulm, the defense of Fort Ridgely, and the Battle of Weed Lake. Also served in Henry Sibley's and Alfred Sully's expeditions in 1863 and 1864 and later was the sheriff of Yellow Medicine County.

Fremont

Fremont was a post office in McLeod County Minnesota from 1856-61. First established in Hennepin County and later transferred to McLeod County in 1859. Named for John C. Frémont, an assistant with Joseph N. Nicollet in his expedition through the region in 1838. John C. Frémont was the son of Louis Rene Frémon, born 1768 in Quebec, a French-Canadian immigrant to the United States.

---

[362] Wisconsin Historical Collections 20:398.

Fremont Avenue

A street located in St. Paul between White Bear Avenue and Hazel Street, between Third and Fifth Streets. Named for John C. Frémont.

Fremont Township

A township in Winona County. Named in honor of Frenchman John Charles Frémont (1813-1890), who assisted Joseph N. Nicollet in his expedition through southwestern Minnesota in 1838 and was the first Republican candidate for President of the United States.

French

A village located in Otter Tail County in Carlisle Township, six miles west of Fergus Falls. It is sometimes called the French Stub.

French Creek

A small stream which runs into Lake Itasca. Also name of a creek in Wright County flowing out of French Lake. There is also a French Creek in Rochester.

French Lake

Located in Wright County. Named for French-Canadians who settled in this area. There is also a French Lake in Rice County.

French Lake Township

Located in Wright County. Organized in June 1865, it bears the name of its largest lake and the outflowing creek, given in compliment of French-Canadians who settled in this area.

French Lick

This name was located on a map in 1916 in Duluth Township in St. Louis County. Not identified in 1930 map.

French River

French River "R des Francais" as noted in Owen's geological report in 1852. This river is also called Angwassago Zibi in the Ojibwe language, meaning "Floodwood River." This is also a community located on the shore of Lake Superior, in sections 17 and 18 of Duluth Township

Frenchmans Bar

Name of locality around 1867 in the bend of the Mississippi River, just below the mouth of the Minnesota River.

Frenchy Corner

A village in Anoka Township, section 4, south of Crooked Lake.

Frontenac

Frontenac is an unincorporated community in Florence Township, Goodhue County, Minnesota, on the Mississippi River.

French River Rapids, by Paul Kane, 1845 (Public Domain)

The name was changed to Frontenac in 1860 by the Garrard brothers after Frenchman, Louis de Buade de Frontenac, who was born in 1622. He was the French Colonial Governor of Canada in 1672–82 and 1689–98. He died in Quebec, Canada on November 28, 1698. There is not a record of him actually traveling to the Mississippi River.

Frontenac State Park

Frontenac State Park is a Minnesota State Park, located on the Mississippi River ten miles southeast of Red Wing.

Gentilly and Gentilly Township

Located in Polk County. The township was organized in 1879 and is named after a village on the St. Lawrence River in the province of Quebec, which was named for the town of Gentilly in France, which is a southern suburb of Paris. The village of Gentilly was a French Catholic settlement that began as a rest stop for the stage line. Joseph Beaudette settled a claim there in 1876 and is credited with naming the place.

Gervais Lake

Gervais Lake commemorates Benjamin Gervais, a pioneer French-Canadian farmer, who was born at Riviére du Loup, Canada in 1786 and died in Minnesota in 1876. He settled on the Red River in the Selkirk Colony in 1812, came to Fort Snelling in 1827, and after being ordered to leave the Fort Snelling military reservation, he started a farm in St. Paul in 1838. He moved to Lake Gervais in 1844.

Gervais Township

Located in Red Lake County. Named in honor of French-Canadian Isaac Gervais, who was born at Fort Garry (now Winnipeg) in 1831 and settled in Red Lake Falls in 1876.

Girard Township

A township organized in 1882. Was named in honor of Stephen Girard. Stephen Girard (May 20, 1750–December 26, 1831; born Étienne Girard) was a French-born, naturalized American, philanthropist and banker. He personally saved the U.S. government from financial collapse during the War of 1812, and became one of the wealthiest people in America, estimated to have been the fourth richest American of all time, based on the ratio of his fortune to contemporary GDP. Childless, he devoted much of his fortune to philanthropy, particularly the education and welfare of orphans. His legacy is still felt in his adopted home of Philadelphia.

Goodin Island

An island located near downtown Dayton, Minnesota. Named after Paul Goodin, who was born in France in 1810 and considered the first settler of Dayton. He had established a trading post there.

Gooseberry River

In 1775 a stream in Cook County was called the "Riviére Aux Groseilles" by French fur traders. It has since been translated to "Gooseberry River."

Grand Côte

This was the name for a steep two hundred foot hill on Minnesota Valley Oxcart Trail north of LeSueur, Minnesota. It was said that after climbing this hill the oxcart drivers were rewarded with one of the grandest scenes in all Minnesota.[363]

Grand Marais

Grand Marais and Grand Marais Township are located in Cook County. The name is derived from the French word meaning "a great marsh." The area around Pig's Eye Lake near downtown St. Paul used to be called Grand Marais in the early years.

Grand Marais Creek

A small stream in Polk County which joins the Red River just north of East Grand Forks. Named by early French-Canadian fur traders and trappers.

Grand Portage Bay

Bay in North Shore on Lake Superior in Minnesota.

Grand Portage Island

Island located in Grand Portage Bay in North Shore on Lake Superior in Minnesota.

---

[363] Gilman, Rhoda R. and Gilman, Carolyn, and Stultz, Deborah, *Red River Trails, Oxcart Routes between St. Paul and the Selkirk Settlement 1820-1870*, Minnesota Historical Society Press.p.53.

Gratiot Lake

Joseph P. Nicollet gave the name of a lake a mile east of Jenkins Village in Crow Wing County in honor of General Charles Gratiot, the son of Charles Gratiot, a French-Canadian Fur Trader, and Victoire Chouteau. He served in the War of 1812. The name of this lake was later changed to Upper Hay Lake.

Groseilliers and Radisson Lakes

Located in Clearwater County. Located south of Whipple Lake. Named after Frenchmen Groseilliers and Radisson.

Henriette

Located in Pine County in section 17 of Pokegama Township. Was named for a local sawmill of the same name. The origin of this name is uncertain although it is most certainly French.

Huot

A village on the Red Lake River in Red Lake County. Named for Louis Huot, a French-Canadian homesteader who came to the area in 1876. Louis Huot was the first postmaster of the village.

Isle

Located in Mille Lacs County. Isle is also used in Isle Harbor Township. Isle is the city and port on Lake Mille Lacs and is noted for its excellent harbor. "Isle" is French word for "Island."

Isle Royale

Isle Royale is an island of the Great Lakes, located in the northwest of Lake Superior, and part of the U.S. state of Michigan. It's name comes from the early French fur traders and voyageurs. The island and the 450 surrounding smaller islands and waters make up Isle Royale National Park. Isle Royale is within about fifteen miles of the Canadian and Minnesotan shores of the lake, (near the city of Thunder Bay, Ontario), and is fifty six miles from the Michigan shore, on the Keweenaw Peninsula. There are seasonal passenger ferry services to the island from Grand Portage, Minnesota; Copper Harbor, Michigan; and Houghton, Michigan.

Jessenland Township

A township near Henderson, Minnesota said to be named after Hyacinth "Jesse" Cameriand (Cameron), a French-Canadian who was one of the first settlers there in 1852. It was known for a time as Jesse's Land which later became Jessenland.[364] There is another explanation that this name was named by Bishop Cretin on a trip there after the land of Gessen in the Bible.

---

[364] Neill, Rev. Edward D., edited by Charles S. Bryant, *History of the Minnesota Valley: Including the Explorers and Pioneers of Minnesota*, by North Star Publishing Company, Minneapolis, (1882).

Kettle River

Rivière la Chaudière, today anglicized as "Kettle River," is a stream in Carlton County that empties into the St. Croix River a little above the mouth of the Snake River.

Joseph LaBathe Island

The Joseph LaBathe Island is located in Cottage Grove and is located next to Grey Cloud Island. It is named after a French-Canadian pioneer who worked at a trading post and ferry in Prescott, Wisconsin in the 1840s. He later settled on a farm on Grey Cloud Island.

Labine School

A country school that was located on the northeast quarter of section 11 in Bloomer Township in Marshall County. Named for French-Canadian Labine families located nearby.

LaBine School House -- District #11
[Back] Lawrence King, Rolland Fournier, Oliver LaBine, Paul Parent
[Second row] Adeline Stoltman, Rita Parent, Isabel Riopelle, Margaret LaBine, Helen LaBine, Mae Riopelle, Richard Poitras, LeRoy Dufault
[Third Row] Harry Stoltman, Ella Mae Loranger, Wally Loranger, Tom LaBine, Rudolph Parent, Rita LaBine
[Front] Leonard Riopelle, Ethel Poitras, Robert Loranger, Clarion Stoltman, Marie Poitras, Cliff LaBine, Olive Poitras, Richard Riopelle, and Ludger Parent

Lac qui Parle

A place name in Yellow Medicine County in Norman Township. It was a small village located on Lac qui Parle Creek. Lac qui Parle is a French translation of the native Dakota name, meaning "lake which speaks."

Lac qui Parle County

Lac qui Parle County is a county located in Minnesota. As of the 2010 census, the population was 7,259. Its county seat is Madison. The name of the county is French for "lake which speaks."

Lac qui Parle Resevoir

Lac qui Parle is a reservoir located in western Minnesota, which was formed by the damming of the Minnesota River. The dam was built by the Works Progress Administration (WPA) in 1939. It was reconstructed in 1996. Lac qui Parle is a French translation of the native Dakota name, meaning "lake which speaks." The northernmost point of the lake is about three miles southeast of the city of Appleton. The lake flows ten miles southeast to the dam, which is about four miles to the west of the town of Watson.

Lac qui Parle River

The Lac qui Parle River is a tributary of the Minnesota River, 118 miles long, in southwestern Minnesota. A number of tributaries of the river, including its largest, the West Branch Lac qui Parle River, also flow in eastern South Dakota. Lac qui parle means "the lake which speaks" in the French language, and was a translation of the Sioux name for Lac qui Parle, a lake on the Minnesota River upstream of the mouth of the Lac qui Parle River.

Lac qui Parle State Park

Lac qui Parle State Park is located on the southern portion of the lake. Lac qui Parle serves as a temporary home of thousands of migratory Canada geese and other waterfowl.

La Crescent

La Crescent is a city in Houston and Winona counties in Minnesota. The French name was given to the town because its early founders wanted a romantic sounding name for the town to attract settlers. They came up with "La Crescent," after the bend or "crescent" shape of the Mississippi River around the town. La Crescent was incorporated in 1857.

Lacrosse Avenue

Street in St. Paul named after Lacrosse, Wisconsin. The name originated from the game with sticks that resembled a bishop's crozier or la crosse in French, which was played by Native Americans there.

Lafayette

The word Lafayette is found in several places in Minnesota. Lafayette Park is a neighborhood in St. Paul within a few blocks of Lafayette Square. Lafayette Road was established in St. Paul in 1872. The name is in honor of the Marquis de Lafayette (1757-1834), a French Statesman and soldier who fought with George Washington during the Revolutionary War.[365]

Lafayette

A village located in Clay County, Minnesota, named for the French General, the Marquis de Lafayette (1757-1834), who came to America and greatly aided Washington in the Revolutionary War.

Lafayette Township

A township located in Nicollet County named for the French General, the Marquis de Lafayette (1757-1834) who came to America and greatly aided Washington in the Revolutionary War.

La Fleche Prairie

Name of prairie view used by oxcart trail travelers once they arrived at the top of the Grande Côte on the Minnesota Valley Trail. This name is no longer used and is no longer on the map.[366]

---

[365] Empson, Donald L., *The Street where you Live, A guide to the place Names of St. Paul.* Published 2006 University of Minnesota Press, P.153

[366] Gilman, Rhoda R. and Gilman, Carolyn, and Stultz, Deborah, *Red River Trails, Oxcart Routes between St. Paul and the Selkirk Settlement 1820-1870*, Minnesota Historical Society Press.p.53.

L'Etoile du Nord

The Minnesota state motto, "L'Etoile du Nord" (the Star of the North) shows the strong influence of the French explorers and voyageurs that lived and worked in the Western Great Lakes region and vast prairie lands spreading to the Rocky Mountains.

Lafond Avenue

Lafond Avenue in the Frogtown area of St. Paul is named after French-Canadian Benjamin Lafond who was an early settler there. In addition, he was instrumental in naming the streets Edmund, Charles and Thomas after relatives, and Blair after a young lady friend.[367]

Lafontaine

Located in Lake Pleasant Township of Polk County. It had a post office from 1881 to 1883.

Lambert Township

Located in Red Lake County. Named for Francois Lambert, who was born in St. Ursule, Quebec in 1847 and came to Minnesota in 1881.

Lamoille

Village in Winona County in section 7 of Richmond Township. Platted in 1860. Has the name of a river and county in northern Vermont. It had a post office from 1858 to 1975. The Lamoille River is a river which runs through northern Vermont and drains into Lake Champlain. It is about 85 miles in length,and has a drainage area of around 706 square miles (1,830 km2). The river generally flows southwest, and then northwest, from the water divide of the Green Mountains, and is the namesake of Lamoille County, Vermont. The river's valley also gave its name to the now-defunct Lamoille Valley Railroad Company, successor to the St. Johnsbury and Lamoille County Railroad.

Legend has it that early French settlers named the river "La Mouette" meaning "The Seagull." However, a cartographer subsequently forgot to cross the t's, which led people to begin calling it "La Moulle" Over time, this became "Lamoille."

La Grande Prairie

From a river bluff on the north side at the Ox Cart Trail Old Crossing of the Red Lake River, the drovers or oxcart drivers called the view "La Grande Prairie" because at the top

[367] Hiebert, Gareth, *City of Seven Hills, Columns of Oliver Towne*, Pogo Press, Inc. St. Paul, 1999, p. 132.

of this hill you had a beautiful view of the stream and the treeless prairie stretching out over a long distance.[368]

La Prairie

"Prairie" is the French word for "meadow." La Prairie, located in Clearwater County, was named for Scotty La Prairie, a leader among the Ojibwe. There is also a LaPrairie just east of Grand Rapids.

Lake Antoinette

Located in section 28, Rice Lake Township of St. Louis County.

Lake Fremont Township

Located in Martin County. Named for John C. Frémont, an assistant with Joseph N. Nicollet in his expedition through the region in 1838. John C. Frémont was the son of Louis Rene Frémon, born 1768 in Quebec, a French-Canadian immigrant to the United States.

Lake Fremont

Located in Murray County near the northeast end of Lake Shetek. Named for John C. Frémont, an assistant with Joseph N. Nicollet in his expedition through Minnesota in 1838. John C. Frémont was the son of Louis Rene Frémon, b. 1768 in Quebec, a French-Canadian immigrant to the United States. There is also a Lake Fremont village located in Sherburne County which adjoins Lake Fremont. Named for John C. Frémont.

Lake Gervais

Located in Ramsey County. Named after early French-Canadian settler Benjamin Gervais who lived on the lake. In 1844, French-Canadian settler Benjamin Gervais moved north from Saint Paul to claim land in order to build the first grist mill in Minnesota that was independent from the government. Today, the large lake on the east side of Little Canada bears his name (Lake Gervais). The grist mill was converted into a park, which is recognized as the birthplace of the city.[369]

Lake LaBelle

Located in Becker County in Lake Park Township.

Lake Marquette

Located in Clearwater County, just south of Bemidji. Named by Nicollet in his map.

---

[368] Gilman, Rhoda R. and Gilman, Carolyn, and Stultz, Deborah, *Red River Trails, Oxcart Routes between St. Paul and the Selkirk Settlement 1820-1870*, Minnesota Historical Society Press. P.59.
[369] Hiebert, Gareth D., *Little Canada, A Voyageur's Vision*, A compiled history of Little Canada, Minnesota by the Historical Society of Little Canada, Published in 1989 by the Croixside Press, Inc.

Lake Pepin

Lake Pepin was first named in a map of New France made by Guillaume Delisle at the request of Louis XIV of France in 1703. The lake was named for the Pepin family. According to the English language page of L'Association des Familles de Pepin, Pierre Pepin, Sr., dit LaForce (1652–1722), along with his brother Etienne Pepin, took part in the Duluth expedition in 1678 which reached the upper Mississippi. On the Wisconsin-Minnesota border there is an enlargement of the Mississippi River which many historians believed was named Lake Pepin in honor of these two Pepin brothers. Pierre Pepin's nickname, "LaForce," is said to come from his co-discovery of the Mississippi River. However, it is not certain if the lake is, in fact, named after Pierre, or if it is named after his father, Guillaume Pépin dit Tranchemontagne, who was granted large tracts of land by the King of France.

Lake Saint Croix

Located in St. Louis County. French meaning is "Lake of the Cross" and is named from it's shape by the early voyageurs and fur traders.

Lake Superior

Étienne Brûlé is credited with the European discovery of Lake Superior before 1620. Named "Lac Supérieur" by Claude Dablon, Claude-Jean Allouez and Jacques Marquette after their navigation of Lake Superior in 1668. Their map shows the name of the lake to be Lake Tracy or Superior. The name Superior stuck. The name Tracy was in honor of the Marquis Alexandre de Prouville de Tracy (1596a–1670) who was the Lieutenant General of the Carignan-Salieres Regiment that was sent to Quebec to fight the easterly tribe of the Iroquois Confederacy, resulting in a military victory.

A Dakota village and platform for the dead near Columbia Fur Company post at Lake Traverse in 1823[370]

---

[370] Drawings by John Mix Stanley, in Stevens, Issac I. *Narrative …of Explorations for a Route for A Pacific Railroad…from St. Paul to Puget Sound*, plates 3,4,5 in 36 Congress, 1 session, House Executive Documents no. 56 (serial 1054). (Public Domain)

Lake Traverse

Lake Traverse is the southernmost body of water in the Hudson Bay watershed of North America. It lies along the border between the states of Minnesota and South Dakota. Lake Traverse is an Anglicization of "Lac Traverse," a French name meaning "across the lake." [371] It is located in Traverse County in Minnesota and the county is named after the lake.

Lake Vadnais

Named after Jean Vadnais, a French-Canadian who settled on its southeast shore in 1846, just north of the first settler on record, Paul Bibeau, in 1845.

Lake Vermilion

Lake Vermilion is a freshwater lake in northeastern Minnesota. The Ojibwe originally called the lake "Onamuni," which means "Lake of the Sunset Glow." French fur traders translated this to the Latin word Vermilion, which is a red pigment. There are several lakes with the Vermilion name, including Big and Little Vermilion, the Upper Vermilion Lakes, all located in Cass County.

Larpenteur

There are a number of place names in St. Paul that use the name Larpenteur, including Larpenteur Avenue. There are also business and real estate developments that use the name. The name comes from Auguste Larpenteur, an early settler of St. Paul.

La Salle

Located in Watonwan County. Incorporated in 1921. Named after French explorer Robert Cavelier, sieur de la Salle (1643–87). The Younger brothers (part of Jesse James gang) were one mile south of La Salle on September 21, 1876, following their holdup of the Northfield bank.

La Salle is also given to names of streets in both St. Paul and Minneapolis.

Le Center

Le Center located in Le Sueur County. Originally called "Le Sueur Center," the name changed in 1931 to Le Center.

Leech Lake

Named "Lac de la Sansue" by French fur traders. Later anglicized to Leech Lake.[372]

---

[371] Gannett, Henry (1905). *The Origin of Certain Place Names in the United States.* Government Printing Office. p. 178

[372] Perreault, Jean Baptiste, *Narrative of the Travels and Adventures of a Merchant Voyageur in the Savage Territories of Northern America," Leaving Montreal the 28th Day of May, 1783 to 1820.* Written in 1830, (Found in Schoolcraft Manuscripts in the Smithsonian Institute in Washington, D.C.).

Le Homme Dieu Lake

Located in Douglas County near Alexandria. It is said the lake was named for an early settler who was a friend of Gleny King. Generally spelled l'homme-Dieu in French, it translates to man of God, and was used to describe Jesus Christ.

Lemond Township

Located in Steele County. Settled in 1856. Lemond is a known French surname.

Lemond Lake

Located in Steele County. Lemond is a known French surname. The Lake and the Township are probably named after same person.

Le Sauk Township

Settled in 1854, in Stearns County. Received its French name meaning "The Sauk" from the same derivation as Sauk Rapids, the Sauk River, Sauk Centre and Lake Osakis.

Le Claire

Le Claire, a small community, grew around two fisheries at Oak Point on the east end of Curry's Island on Four Mile Bay. This was the first truly American settlement in the county and the site of the first post office and customs house.

Le Roy Township

Located in Mower County and organized in 1858. It is not clear where this French name comes from.

Le Sueur County

Named after Frenchman Pierre Charles Le Sueur. More information on Le Sueur is printed in the chapter on early French Explorers in Minnesota.

Le Sueur River

Located in Le Sueur County and also Waseca County. Named after Frenchman Pierre Charles Le Sueur.

Little Canada

Located in Ramsey County and named after French-Canadian settlers who settled there. The first settler was French-Canadian farmer, voyageur, and trader Benjamin Gervais, who came in 1844. He was the postmaster from 1852 to 1854.[373]

[373] Hiebert, Gareth D., *Little Canada, A Voyageur's Vision,* A compiled history of Little Canada, Minnesota by the Historical Society of Little Canada, Published in 1989 by the Croixside Press, Inc.

Little Marais

A village located in Cramer Township in Lake County. Named by early French-Canadian voyageurs for its little marsh located nearby.

Lorain Township

Located in Nobles County. Named after ancient large district of Lorraine in France and Germany.

Louisville Township

Located in Scott County. It is said to be named after Louisville, Kentucky, the previous home of H.H. Spencer, who settled there in 1853. Louisville, Kentucky was named after King Louis XVI of France by George Rogers Clark. Another story says it was named after Louis Robert, who had fur trading posts in the area. The Minneapolis Journal on June 6, 1937 said the following about Louisville: "Started as a trading post by Louis LaCroix, a Frenchman, on the Minnesota River in 1850. Louisville flourished with the times, became a settlement of some 30 homes, a few stores, two saw mills, a schoolhouse, a grist mill, a post office, then fell into decay and all but vanished in a decade…" This town site was located just across the river from present day Carver. It is said LaCroix sold his interest in a trading post he established there to Louis Robert. The township plat, dated 1856, shows a "LaCroix Ferry" across the Minnesota River in Section 32.[374]

Louisville Township

Located in Red Lake County. Named for Louis Huot, a French-Canadian homesteader who came to the area in 1876.

Maine Township

Located in Otter Tail County and organized in 1871. Named after the State of Maine. There is no definitive explanation for the origin of the name "Maine." However, the state legislature of Maine in 2001, adopted a resolution establishing Franco-American Day, which stated that the state was named after the former French province of Maine. The province of Maine in France is an old traditional province, with its capital city being Le Mans.

Maine Prairie Township

Located in Stearns County and organized in 1858. Named after the state of Maine from a pioneer from Maine.

---

[374] Neill, Rev. Edward D., edited by Charles S. Bryant, *History of the Minnesota Valley, Including the Explorers and Pioneers of Minnesota*, by North Star Publishing Company, Minneapolis (1858).

Marcoux/Marcoux Corner

A former restaurant and motel located at intersection of Highways 2 and 32 in Lake Pleasant Township in Red Lake County. Named after Edward Marcoux, who moved to California from Minnesota in 1936.

Marillac Lane

Located in the city of St. Paul. Named for Saint Louis DeMarillac (1591–1660), who was born in Paris and who helped establish an order called the Sisters of Charity of St. Vincent de Paul. Louis DeMarillac was canonized in 1934 and declared the patron saint of social workers in 1960.[375]

Marine on St. Croix

Located in Washington County on the St. Croix River. Both the name Marine and St. Croix have their origins in France. Marine has an ancient Latin origin and generally means "from the sea."

Mille Lacs Lake

This lake is located in Mille Lacs County. This term was given to the lake and area by French voyageurs and traders, translating the Indian name referring to "land of many lakes." The terms translated from French means "a thousand lakes." In the Ojibwe language the lake is called "Misi-zaaga'igan" ("grand lake").

Mille Lacs

A post office located in Pine County from 1856-59. Location uncertain.

Montcalm Place

Street name in St. Paul and a part of Lexington Park. Named after the Marquis Louis Joseph de Montcalm de Saint-Veran (1712–1759), a French General killed in the French and Indian War when the British captured Quebec in 1759. Montcalm Court, Montcalm Hill and Montcalm Estate Road all take their names from this source.

New Canada Township

Located in Ramsey County. Named for its French-Canadian settlers. Organized in 1858.

Neville

Located in Winona County. Named for Jepe P. Neville who was postmaster, but was not French or French-Canadian, but believed to be from New England. This surname is of

---

[375] Empson, Donald L. (2006). *The Street Where You Live: A Guide to the Place Names of Saint Paul.* Published 2006 by University of Minnesota Press. p.174.

Norman origin, introduced into England after the Conquest of 1066. It is a French locational name from "Neuville" in Calvados or "Neville" in Seine-Maritime, Normandy, both so called from the Old French "neu(f)" new, with "ville," a settlement.

Nicollet Lake
Located in Clearwater County just to the south of Lake Itasca.

Nicollet County
Established in 1853, the county was named in honor of Joseph Nicolas Nicollet, geographer and explorer, who prepared a map and report of the region that now comprises Minnesota and the eastern parts of North and South Dakota.

Nicollet Lower, Middle and Upper Lakes
Located in Clearwater County. Noted by Nicollet in his map of 1836.

Orleans
Located in Kittson County on the east edge of Clow Township. Named by officers of the Soo Railway. Derived from the city of Orleans, France.

Otter Tail Point
Referred to as "La Quen de Loutre" by French fur traders. Name later anglicized to Otter Tail Point.[376]

Pape de Terre
Was a post office in Stevens County where current city of Morris is located. The city website makes reference to the post office moving from John B. Folsom's farm at Pape de Terre where it was located from 1870-71.

Parent Lake
Located in northern district of Lake County. Origin of name unknown although Parent is a French-Canadian name.

Pelland
A hamlet at the mouth of the Little Fork in Koochiching County. Was named for Joseph Pellard, a French-Canadian farmer, who also was its postmaster.

---

[376] Perreault, Jean Baptiste, *Narrative of the Travels and Adventures of a Merchant Voyageur in the Savage Territories of Northern America,"* *Leaving Montreal the 28th Day of May, 1783 to 1820.* Written in 1830, (Found in Schoolcraft Manuscripts in the Smithsonian Institute in Washington, D.C.).

Perrault

A Northern Pacific station near the center of Lake Pleasant Township in Red Lake County. Named after Charles Perrault, a French-Canadian homestead farmer.

Peltier Lake

Peltier Lake was named for early settlers Charles, Paul and Oliver Peltier, the first of whom built a sawmill. It is located in Lino Lakes, Minnesota.

Pettit

A Duluth, Missabe and Iron Range Railroad Station in section 25 of Missabe Mountain Township. This is a French name, but it is not clear where the name comes from.

Picard Lakes

Located in Clearwater County. These lakes were named for Antoine Auguelle Picard du Gay, (also referred to as Anthony Auguelle) who was a companion of Father Louis Hennepin. They are located south of Whipple Lake.

Pig's Eye

Pig's Eye is located in Ramsey County opposite the nineteenth century village of Kaposia. It was also known as "Weldsville" and "LeClaire's settlement" in the early days. The name is also given to a lake, an island, a road, a sandbar and a lighthouse. All named for Pig's Eye Parrant, a French-Canadian.

Pine River

Called "Riviére au Pins" by French fur traders. Name later anglicized to Pine River. Located in Cass County, Minnesota.[377]

Plantagenet Lake

Located in Hubbard County just to the southwest of Bemidji. Named for the French speaking Plantagenet Kings who ruled over England and parts of France.

Platte River

Located in Morrison County. "Platte" was a name used by early French-Canadian fur traders meaning "dull, flat, shallow."

---

[377] Perreault, Jean Baptiste, *Narrative of the Travels and Adventures of a Merchant Voyageur in the Savage Territories of Northern America," Leaving Montreal the 28ᵗʰ Day of May, 1783 to 1820.* Written in 1830, (Found in Schoolcraft Manuscripts in the Smithsonian Institute in Washington, D.C.)

Platte Township

Located in Morrison County. Platte Township organized in 1899 and named for the Platte River, which crosses it. This stream comes from Platte Lake on the north line of the county. "Platte" was a name used by early French-Canadian fur traders meaning "dull, flat, shallow." In Morrison County you also find the Platte River and Platte Lake

Pomerleau Lake

Located in Hennepin County and consists of twenty-six acres. It is believed all Pomerleaus are direct descendants of Paul Vachon, who was born in the village of La Copechagniere in the parish of La Roche-sur-Yon, Diocese of Lucon, in Poitou (now Vendee) France in 1630. Paul Vachon's second son was Noel Vachon dit Pomerleau. He married Monique Giroux. Their descendants eventually became Vachon or Pomerleau.[378]

Pomme de Terre Fort

The U.S. Army hastily put up a fort around the stage station at Pomme de Terre immediately after the U.S.-Dakota War of 1862. The goal was to provide back up support to Fort Abercrombie farther west in Dakota Territory. Fort Pomme de Terre was a small garrison consisting of troops marched in from Fort Ripley in Morrison County to the east.[379]

Pomme de Terre River

Located in Swift County and in Otter Tail County and Grant County. The Pomme de Terre River is a 125 mile long (201 km) tributary of the Minnesota River in western Minnesota. Via the Minnesota River, it is part of the watershed of the Mississippi River. The name Pomme de Terre is French and means literally "soil apple," usually meaning "potato." In this case, the river was named by early French explorers for a different root vegetable, the potato-like prairie turnip (Psoralea esculenta), which was commonly eaten by the Dakota.[380]

Pomme de Terre Lake

Located in Stevens County in Swan Lake Township. Lake just to the west of the Highway 94 and Highway 78 intersection.

Portage de Rideau

Located in St. Louis County. It means "curtain portage."

Portage River

Located on eastern branch of Moose River in Carlton County.

---

[378] Info obtained from "Pomerleau Family History and Genealogy."

[379] Nord, Mary Ann, *The National Register* of *Historic Places in Minnesota, a Guide.* Minnesota Historical Society Press; 1 edition (May 5, 2003)

[380] Waters, Thomas F. (2006). "*The Minnesota: Corridor West*". *The Streams and Rivers of Minnesota.* Minneapolis: Published 2006 University of Minnesota Press. pp. 304–323. ISBN 0-8166-0960-8.

Portage Lake

Located in Cass County.

Portage Township

Located in St. Louis County. Township 65N, Range 17W.

Poupore

A post office in Arrowhead Township in St. Louis County. Poupore is noted to be an Americanized spelling of the French name "Poupard." This is a French-Canadian name found in Quebec.

Prairie

"Prairie" is the French word for "meadow," but the ultimate root is the Latin "partum" (same meaning). According to Theodore Roosevelt: "We have taken into our language the word prairie, because when our backwoodsmen first reached the land in the Midwest and saw the great natural meadows of long grass, sights unknown to the gloomy forests wherein they had always dwelt. They knew not what to call them, and borrowed the term already in use among the French inhabitants."[381] "Prairie" is a commonly used word in Minnesota place names and elsewhere in the United States.

Prairie Island

Located near Red Wing, this name was translated from its early French name Isle Pelee, visited by Radisson and Groseilliers in 1655-56. In 1695, Pierre Charles LeSueur built a fort on this island.[382]

Prairie Portage

A village located in Lake County near site of a portage bearing the same name. Named by early French-Canadian voyageurs.

Rabideau Lake

Located in the Chippewa National Forest near Birch, Minnesota. Located in Beltrami County 8 miles south of Blackduck. Named after early settler who is assumed to be French-Canadian.

Racine Township

Located in Mower County and organized in 1858. Racine is a French name meaning "root."

---

[381] Roosevelt, Theodore (1889). *The Winning of the West: Volume I.* New York and London: G. P. Putnam's Sons. p. 34
[382] See H.S.M. Collection, Vol. X, part II, pp. 449-594, with maps. Also see Mikesell, Marie-Reine, L'Etoile du Nord, Notes on French Influence in the History of Minnesota, self published 1980.

Radisson Bay

Located on Lake Mille Lacs. Named for Pierre E. Radisson, writer of travels in Minnesota, who came with Medard Chouart, sieur de Groseilliers to Prairie Island in 1655 and region of Kanabec County, not far southeast of Mille Lace, in midwinter of 1659-1660.

Rainy Lake and River

Named by Jacques de Noyon, a French-Canadian voyageur who traveled in this area in 1688. He named the river "Lac de la Pluie" (Lake of the Rain) which was later translated to Rainy Lake. Zacherie Roboutel, Sieur de la Noue, occupied the trading post at Rainy Lake from about 1717 to 1720. Later, Joseph la France described this lake in his book titled "An Account of the Countries Adjoining Hudson's Bay," published by Arthur Dobbs in London in 1744. This lake is located in Koochiching County.

Ravoux Street

Street in St. Paul named after Father Augustin Ravoux (1815-1906), a Roman Catholic Priest at the time this street was named in 1871. Father Ravoux was born in France, traveled to this country in 1836, was ordained in 1840, and embarked on missionary work among the Dakota's in 1841. From the departure of Father Galtier in 1844, to the arrival of Bishop Cretin in 1851, Father Ravoux was in charge of the entire Catholic Church in the St. Paul area.[383]

Red Lake

Called "Lac Rouge" by French fur traders. Later anglicized to "Red Lake."[384]

Red River

The first European explorer to reach the Red River Valley was the French voyageur, Pierre Gaultier de Varennes, Sieur de La Verendrye. He reached the Rivière Rouge in 1732 and established a series of posts in the area, including Fort Rouge on the present site of Winnipeg. He called it the Rivière Rouge because of the reddish-brown silt it carries. The name was later anglicized to the Red River.

Renville

City located in sections 5 and 8 of Emmet Township in Renville County named after Joseph Renville, a "bois brule" whose father was French and mother Dakota. A post office was established here in 1862.

Renville County

Established in 1855 and named for Joseph Renville, a "bois brule" whose father was French and mother Dakota.

---

[383] Empson, Donald L. (2006). *The Street Where You Live: A Guide to the Place Names of Saint Paul.* Published 2006 by University of Minnesota Press. P.226

[384] Perreault, Jean Baptiste, *Narrative of the Travels and Adventures of a Merchant Voyageur in the Savage Territories of Northern America,"* *Leaving Montreal the 28th Day of May, 1783 to 1820.*

Revere

City in sections 23-26 of North Hero Township in Redwood County. Incorporated in 1900. Named in honor of Paul Revere, a French Huguenot patriot in the American Revolution.

Rice Lake

Rice Lake is an English translation of the word "Lac du Siens" which was used by the French to describe the grain grown in shallow water and marshes in northern Minnesota. A writer named La France used the term "Lake du Siens" described as a kind of wild oat, of the nature of rice, the outward husk is black, and the grain within is white and clear like rice. The Indians used it for food.[385]

Robert Creek

Located in Scott County. Named for Captain Louis Robert of St. Paul, a notable French-Canadian river boat captain, businessman and early settler of Saint Paul, Minnesota, who established a trading post on this creek in 1852.

Rochert

Located in Holmesville Township of Becker County.

Rondo Neighborhood

Most of the original Rondo Avenue and much of the historic Rondo neighborhood were destroyed when Interstate 94 was built. The street was named for an early settler, Joseph Rondeau. Part of the original street is now the frontage road near the Best Western Kelly Inn. Joseph Rondeau was born in Canada, worked as a voyageur, and later took up farming near Fort Snelling until he was forced out of the military reservation. In 1862, he purchased a large amount of land northeast of the Cathedral of St. Paul, which was a swamp at the time. Louis Street in St. Paul is named after his son, Louis (1835–1913).[386]

[385] Hubbard, Lucius F.; Murray, William Pitt, Baker, James H., Upham, Warren, Holcombe, R.I. and Holmes, Frank R., *Minnesota in Three Centuries 1655-1908*, published1908 by The Publishing Society of Minnesota, vol. 1, pp. 299-302)
[386] Empson, Donald L. (2006). *The Street Where You Live: A Guide to the Place Names of Saint Paul.* Published 2006 by University of Minnesota Press. p.226.

Rolette

Located in Norman County. A former Great Northern Railway village. Was superseded by Lockhart village. Name commemorates Frenchman Joe Rolette (1820–1871), shown to the right.

Roseau

The name Roseau appears on the La Verendrye map of 1737 for a river and is assumed to be the French name of a plant. The English translation of Roseau is "reed." This includes various moist soil plants that are hollow and rigid, more or less woody. The city and county of Roseau in Northwestern Minnesota are named after the Roseau River.

Roseau County

This county was established December 31, 1894, and received an addition from Beltrami County on February 10, 1896. It is named from the Roseau Lake and river, of which the former appears, with this name, on Verendrye's map (1737). The river is shown on Thompson's map (1814), with

Joe Rolette
Minn Historical Society

the name Reed River, translated from this French name, which is in turn a translation of the Ojibway name. Gilfillan wrote it, "Ga-shashagunushkokawi-sibi or the-place-of-rushes-river, or briefly, Rush River." It is more accurately called "Reed-grass River" on Long's map (1823) and on Pope's map (1849). The very coarse grass, or reed, referred to as "Phragmites communis," is common or frequent in the shallow edges of lakes throughout the prairie region of Minnesota and Manitoba. During a canoe trip around all the shore of Red Lake in September 1885, this species was observed in great abundance at many places, growing eight to twelve feet in height.

Information of the origins and meanings of geographic names has been received from Syver G. Bertilrud, county auditor, interviewed at Roseau, the county seat, during a visit there in September, 1909; and from him a second time, also from D. H. Benson, dealer in real estate, and J. W. Durham, janitor of the High School, each of Roseau, interviewed there in September, 1916.

Sacred Heart Township

Organized in 1869. One explanation for the name of this township given by Louis G. Brisbois who said the name came from a French missionary priest who gave name of his mission Sacred Heart. The mission was established for French Metis and Indians.[387]

[387] Curtiss-Wedge, Franklyn, *History of Renville County,* assisted by Renville County Pioneer Association Committee, published 1916, H.C. Cooper Jr. & Co., page 1332.

Sauk Centre

When the community was voting on names for the town, the name Sauk Centre was suggested by Alexander Moore. The town was located on Sauk Lake with the roads centering around the lake. Therefore, the town was named Sauk Centre.

The name Sauk comes from the French (Sac) and English (Sauk) name for a Native American tribe that originally were located along the St. Lawrence River. They were driven west by the Iroquois.

The Minnesota origins for this name refers to the historical paper written by Judge Loren W. Collins who said that five Sacs, refugees from their own tribe on account of murder they had committed, made their way to the Lake Osakis area and settled near the outlet on the east side of the lake. Later, there were all discovered killed, supposedly by the Dakota.[388]

Saint Anthony and Saint Anthony Park

The city of St. Anthony is a city within Hennepin County. St. Anthony Park is the most northwestern part of St. Paul. Both come from the name St. Anthony Falls, named by Father Louis Hennepin who named them after his patron saint, Anthony of Padua.

Saint Anthony Falls

In 1680, these falls became known to the Western world when they were observed and published in a journal by Father Louis Hennepin, a French speaking Catholic friar of Belgian birth, who also first published about Niagara Falls to the world's attention. Hennepin named them the "Chutes de Saint-Antoine" or the Falls of Saint Anthony after his patron saint, Anthony of Padua.

Saint Clair

Saint Clair lake is in Detroit Township in Becker County. It has its origin in France and today you find the name in France, England and Australia, as well as the United States. The name Sinclair is a contraction of St. Clair. In Spanish and Portuguese it is called Santa Clara. There is also a St. Clair village located east of Chisholm, in St. Louis County.

Saint Cloud

Minnesota was organized as a territory in 1849. The St. Cloud area was opened up to settlers in 1851, after treaty negotiations with the Winnebago (Ho-Chunk) tribe in 1851 and 1852. John Wilson, a Maine native with French Huguenot ancestry and an interest in Napoleon, named the settlement St. Cloud after Saint-Cloud, the Paris suburb where Napoleon had his favorite palace.

---

[388] Mitchell, William Bell, *History of Stearns County, Minnesota*, published by Chicago H.C. Cooper Jr. & Co 1915, (vol. 1, p.24).

Saint Croix River

Father Louis Hennepin wrote in 1683, from information probably provided by Daniel Greysolon, Sieur du Lhut: "There is another river which falls ... into the Meschasipi ... We named it The River of the Grave, or Mausoleum, because the Savages buried there one of their Men who was bitten by a Rattlesnake." In the original French, this is translated as "Rivière Tombeaux."

Jean-Baptiste-Louis Franquelin's 1688 map recorded a "Fort St. Croix" on the upper reaches of the river.[389] The name "Rivière de Sainte-Croix" was applied to the river sometime in 1688 or 1689, and this name supplanted Father Hennepin's earlier designation. On *Map of the Territories of Michigan and Ouisconsin* (1830) by John Farmer, the St. Croix River is shown as the "Chippewa River." However, by 1843, Joseph Nicollet's Hydrographical Basin of the Upper Mississippi River reinforced the name provided by Franquelin's 1688 map. It was said by the early French that the name comes from a fur trader with the last name St. Croix who was shipwrecked at the place where the Saint Croix meets the Mississippi.[390]

Saint Croix State Park

Located in Pine County.

Saint Francis

St. Francis Township settled in 1855 and was organized in 1857. It bears the name given by Father Louis Hennepin in 1680 to the Rum River. The name is in commemoration of St. Francis of Assisi of Italy, who was born around 1181, and died in 1226, founder of the Franciscan order to which Hennepin belonged.

Saint Hilaire

Located in Pennington County, on the west side of the Red Lake River. It was incorporated as a village in 1883. There are three versions of where the name came from. First, a Frenchman named St. Hilaire lived there, selling items like gunpowder and tobacco. Second, a Frenchman named Arthur Yvernault bought land there and named it for his hometown in France. Third, it was named by Honorable Frank Ives for the French statesman and author Jules Barthelemy-Saint-Hilaire, who was born in Paris in 1805 and died in 1895.

Saint Lawrence Township

Saint Lawrence Township first settled in 1854 and is locatd in Scott County. Its name is derived from the St. Lawrence River and the Gulf of St. Lawrence in Quebec. The name was first applied by Jacques Cartier on August 10, 1536, this being the feast day of St. Lawrence, who suffered martyrdom on August 10, 258.

---

[389] Franquelin, Jean-Baptiste *Service historique de la Marine*, Vincennes, France; McMahon, Eileen M. and Karamanski, Theodore J. *Time and the River: A History of the Saint Croix*, Midwest Regional office, National Park Service, United States Department of Interior, Omaha, Nebraska (2002).

[390] Neill, Edward Duffield, Secretary of the Minnesota Historical Society, T*he History of Minnesota from the earliest French Explorations to the Present Time*, Philadelphia: J. B. Lippincott & co. (1858).

Saint Louis County

Saint Louis County is named after the Saint Louis River. See below.

Saint Louis River

The Saint Louis River is the largest entering Lake Superior. The river was named by Pierre Gaultier de Varennes, Sieur de la Verendrye (1685–1749). The king of France in 1749 conferred on Verendrye the "Cross of St. Louis" as a recognition of the importance of his discoveries. It is believed that is where the name of the river came from. On Jean Baptiste Louis Franquelin's map (1688), and Philippe Buache's map (1745), it is called the Riviére du Fond du Lac, and the map by Gilles Robert de Vaugondy (1755), and Jonathan Carver's map (1778), are the earliest to give the name St. Louis River.

Saint Louis is used to refer to King Louis IX of France. He was born in Poissy, France in 1215, and died near Tunis, Africa in 1270. He died of an illness in his second crusade to the Holy Land. He is also commemorated by the city of St. Louis in Missouri. The state of Louisiana is named for King Louis XIV, who was king from 1643 to 1715.

Saint Louis Township

Saint Louis Township is located in St. Louis County and is named after the Saint Louis River.

Saint Paul

Saint Paul is named after the Chapel of Saint Paul that was built by French-Canadian settlers in 1841. Father Lucian Galtier was the missionary priest who suggested the name, probably in conjunction with the church of St. Peter which he had helped establish just up the river at present-day Mendota.[391] An 1849 view of Saint Paul is shown below.[392]

Saint Peter

Located in Nicollet County. First settled in the fall of 1853. It was named for the St. Pierre or St. Peter River, as the river was called by the early French explorers. The name of the river was later changed to the Minnesota River. There are at least three explanations as to

---

[391] Catholic Historical Society, "A collection of historical data regarding the origin and growth of the Catholic Church in the Northwest," in *Acta Et Dicta*, Vol II, No. 1 (July 1911).
[392] St. Paul, Minnesota, Drawn by Henry Lewis, Printed by C.H. Muller, Aachen, Published by Arnz & Co., Dusseldorf, 1857, Lithograph

the origins of the name St. Peter River. One explanation is that it was named in honor of Pierre Charles Le Sueur. Another explanation is that it was named after the commander of Fort Beauharnois, named Jacques Legardeur de Saint Pierre, located at the site where the Villa Maria School was located south of Red Wing.[393] The third explanation is that early French explorers named the river "sans Pierre" because the river was silty and had few rocks. "Pierre" is the French word for rock. This is the explanation given on the Historical Marker in Mendota. It is unclear where this explanation came from. Early Mendota was also called St. Peter at the time of the Dodge Treaty of 1837.

1849 Lithograph of St. Paul by Henry Lewis (Public Domain)

Saint Vincent Township

Located in Kittson County. Organized March 19, 1880. Its name had been given to a French-Canadian fur trading post located there. Named after French native St. Vincent de Paul, founder of missions and hospitals in Paris, France.

Saint Vincent de Paul Society

The St. Vincent de Paul Society is named after Vincent de Paul, who was born in Pouy, Gascony, France, around 1580, and died in Paris in 1660. He was a priest of the Catholic Church who dedicated himself to serving the poor. The Society of Saint Vincent de Paul, a charitable organization dedicated to the service of the poor, was established by French university students in 1833, led by the Blessed Frederic Ozanam.

---

[393] Neill, Edward Duffield, Secretary of the Minnesota Historical Society, *The History of Minnesota from the earliest French Explorations to the Present Time,* Philadelphia: J. B. Lippincott & co. 1858.

Saulteurs

Word used by the French to describe the Ojibwe who, at one time, were living in large numbers around Sault Ste. Marie.[394]

Snake River

Located in Marshall County in Northwestern Minnesota. Called the La Rivière Serpent by the early French Fur Traders. There is also a Snake River called Rivière Serpent by the French that enters the St. Croix not many miles below the Yellow River (called Rivière Jaune by the French).

Terrebonne Township

Terrebonne Township is located in Red Lake County. It is named after a French-Canadian town in the province of Quebec. The village had a post office from 1881–1915. It means "good land."

Tetagouche State Park

Located on the North Shore. The word Tetagouche is found in Quebec and the Eastern Provinces of Canada. It was used by the French and believed to have its source to the Mi'kmaq Indians. It first appears on Franquelin-DeMeulles map of 1686 as "Toutegouch" or "Tout-gouch."[395]

Thief River

Thief River was formerly called Riviére Voleuse by the early French fur traders.[396] The name comes from a Dakota who, for years, lurked in the marshes, robbing and scalping his foes as they would pass alone. Later the name was anglicized to Thief River.

Traverse County

County on western edge of Minnesota established in 1862. It received its name from Lake Traverse (Lac Travers in French).

Traverse des Sioux

Village with French name in Traverse Township, County of Nicollet. It had a post office from 1853–1873.

[394] Upham, Warren, *Minnesota Place Names, A Geographical Encyclopedia*, Minnesota Historical Society Press; 3rd Revised & Enlarged edition (May 15, 2001) Third Edition, p. 105.

[395] Hamilton, William Baillie, *Place names of Atlantic Canada*, published 1996 by University of Toronto Press, p. 142.

[396] Perreault, Jean Baptiste, *Narrative of the Travels and Adventures of a Merchant Voyageur in the Savage Territories of Northern America," Leaving Montreal the 28th Day of May, 1783 to 1820*. Written in 1830, (Found in Schoolcraft Manuscripts in the Smithsonian Institute in Washington, D.C.)

Sisseton Lodges, Traverse des Sioux, 1851
Frank Blackwell Mayer (1827-1899) (Public Domain)

Vadnais Heights

Named after Lake Vadnais, a lake named for Jean Vadnais, a French-Canadian who settled on its southeast shore in 1846, just north of the first settler of record, Paul Bibeau, in 1845.

Vermilion

There are two Vermilion Rivers in Minnesota. One is located in Cass County. A tributary of the Mississippi that flows from the Vermilion Lakes.

A second Vermillion (spelled with two l's) flows through Lakeville. Its headwaters are just west of the city limits in Credit River Township, and it flows eastward across Dakota County until it empties into the Mississippi River at the Wisconsin border. The Vermillion River has been designated as a trout stream by the Minnesota Department of Natural Resources.

The word "Vermilion" is used to name Vermilion Dam, Vermilion Lake, Vermilion Lake Township, and Vermilion Grove. All located in St. Louis County. The word vermillion came from the old French word "vermeillon," which was derived from "vermeil," from the latin "vermiculus," diminutive of the Latin word "vermis," or worm. It has the same origin as the English word "vermin." The name originated because it had a similar color to the natural red dye made from an insect, the Kermes vermilio, which was widely used in Europe.[397]

---

[397] Eastaugh, Nicholas (2004). *Pigment Compendium: A Dictionary of Historical Pigments.* Butterworth-Heinemann. ISBN 0-7506-5749-9, p.211.

Vermilion Dam

A Post office from 1920-27 on the Vermilion River where it runs into Vermilion Lake. Exact location uncertain.

Vermilion Grove

This was a proposed village site for summer homes on the south side of Frazer Bay of Vermilion Lake. It was never built.[398]

Vermilion Lake

A post office from 1867-71 and a Duluth, Missabe and Iron Range Railroad station. Location uncertain.

Vermilion Township

Located in St. Louis County.

Voyageurs National Park

Located in St. Louis County. Named for the French canoe men of the fur trade, it contains about 55 miles of the old fur trade route between the Great Lakes and the continent's interior. It was established in 1975.[399]

Wyandotte Township

This township named for an aboriginal name of a confederation of four Iroquoian tribes, called Hurons by the French, who lived in Canada southwest of Lake Huron and the Georgian Bay. In the year 1655, Huron exiles accompanied Medard Chouart, sieur de Groseilliers, and Pierre E. Radisson.

Zumbro Falls

This city is at the falls of the Zumbro River in section 31 of Gillford Township. It was incorporated in 1898. It is named after the Zumbro River, derived from the early French name, "Rivière des Embarras."

Zumbro River

The name Zumbro River is derived from the early French name, "Rivière des Embarras," meaning "river of difficulties or encumbrances," or a stream by which canoeing was hindered by driftwood.

---

[398] Upham, Warren, *Minnesota Place Names, A Geographical Encyclopedia*, Minnesota Historical Society Press; 3rd Revised & Enlarged edition (May 15, 2001) Third Edition, p.538
[399] Id, p.548

Zumbro Township

This township named for Zumbro River and is derived from the early French name, "Rivière des Embarras."

Summary

This book was written about French heritage in Minnesota. Not everyone feels a connection with their cultural heritage, especially their French cultural heritage, but many people do. For some, exploring cultural ancestry and family history gives them a connection to certain social values, beliefs, religions and customs. It allows them to identify with others of similar heritage and backgrounds. It can provide an automatic sense of unity and belonging within a group and allows us to better understand previous generations and the history from whence we came.

The Heritage Cycle[400] as formulated by Simon Thurley helps explain the process of finding and incorporating heritage and culture into our lives. It begins with understanding the culture. Only then may we begin to value it. From there, we can learn to care for a culture and eventually enjoy it. With more enjoyment, we will want to learn and understand more, and so the circle goes.

- By understanding (cultural heritage), people value it
- By valuing it, people want to care for it
- By caring for it, it will help people enjoy it
- From enjoying it, comes a thirst to understand
- By understanding it, people will have a higher value for it, etc.

---

[400] Thurley, Simon, *Into the future. Our stategy for 2005-2010.* In: Conservation Bulletin [English Heritage], 2005 (49).

The French Heritage in Minnesota is rich and an important part of our state's history. It has many different faces and influences and the immigration of French speaking emigrants to Minnesota continues to this day. It should not be forgotton. It should be understood, valued and enjoyed.

Heritage is something all of us have, and it is our inheritance. Heritage helps determine our physical characteristics, but even more important, it helps to explain our culture and the intangible attributes of our society. Minnesota has a French accent, and the influences of our French speaking past lurks in the background of our state. Our state motto, the names of our rivers and streams and lakes, the educational influence of the French speaking religious orders, and the contribution and influence of the many French speaking Catholic congregations and their hard-working parishioners have helped make Minnesota into the wonderful place it is today.

French-American Heritage Foundation of Minnesota

Appendix A
French-American Heritage Foundation

The French-American Heritage Foundation is a 501(c)3 charitable non-profit organization with the primary purpose of promoting and sponsoring French Heritage events in Minnesota. The Mission Statement for the Foundation is as follows:

To preserve and promote the French-American Heritage in Minnesota through education and community events.

French language cultures have played an important role in the history of Minnesota and Minnesota's connections to French language cultures continues to this day. It is important and proper that these French connections should be celebrated and remembered, both through education and public programming.

Organizational Information

The French-American Heritage Foundation is run by a Board of Directors who meet monthly. The current members of the Board are shown below:

FAHF Board of Directors

1. Mark Labine,
President

2. Dick Bernard,
Vice President

3. Mark Dillon
Secretary

4. Jerry Foley, Treasurer

5. Pierre Girard

6. Donald Marier

7. Dustin DuFault

8. Mark Petty

9. Brian Caldwell

10. Marie Trepanier

11. Jane Skinner Peck

12. Corey LeVasseur

13. Robert Hughes Perrizo

14. Patricia Ruffing

15. Samantha Katafiasz

16. Gregory Cash

17. Virgil Benoit

French-American Heritage Foundation of Minnesota

P.O. Box 25384, Woodbury, MN 55125

President
Mark Labine

Vice President
Dick Bernard

Treasurer
Jerry Foley

Secretary
Mark Dillon

Directors

Virgil Benoit
Brian Caldwell
Gregory Cash
Dustin Dufault
Pierre Girard
Samantha Katafiasz
Donald Marier
Jane Peck
Mark Petty
Robert Perrizo
Patricia Ruffing
Marie Trepanier
MaryEllen Weller

Website
www.fahfminn.org

Mission Statement:

To preserve and promote the French-American Heritage in Minnesota through education and community events.

French-American Heritage Foundation Letterhead 2016

FAHF Advisory Committee

At the present time, the French-American Heritage Foundation Advisory Committee consists of twenty-four members, as shown below. Members of the Advisory Committee support the mission of the French-American Heritage Foundation and provide advice and counsel to the Foundation when requested regarding their area of expertise.

1. **Beth Helle,** *Director of Tourism City of Minneapolis*
2. **Jerry Landreville***Food Service and Liquor Sales Former owner of Champps, Gallivans, Showboat, North End Depot, Chain Link, Gabes by the Park and Ol'Mexico. Has French-Canadian Heritage*
3. **Richard Martin Guidry,** *Expertise in Cajun/Acadians foods, music, genealogy, and organization of festivals or events.*
4. **Kerith Iverson,** *Public & Cultural Affairs Officer Québec Délégation Government Office in Chicago*
5. **Barbara Redmond,** *Design Publisher, A Woman's Paris Communications/advertising/Promotion expertise*
6. **Steve Madson,** *SRO Productions, Inc. Productions and Promotion Company. Creates and Produces Festivals and Events*
7. **Jacqueline Regis,** *District Court Judge, former Assistant Attorney General, and President of Minnesota Women's Lawyers. Born and raised in Les Cayes Haiti. Strong Francophone interests and member of Alliance Francaise*
8. **Dr. Fatima Lawson,** *Principal, L'Etoile du Nord Immersion School*
9. **Rev. Jules Omalanga,** *Pastor St. Boniface Catholic Church, Francophone African Chaplaincy*
10. **Annie Muske,** *French Teacher since 1995. Currently French Teacher at Lakeville South High School. Coordinator, A Vous la Parole Minnesota AATF*
11. **François Fouquerel,** *Dean of French Voyageur Program for Concordia Language Villages. Native of Normandy, France.*
12. **Christine LOYS,** *Author, Director and Producer of "En Avant" which is a film about French Heritage in Minnesota*
13. **John Schade, Librarian,** *Minnesota Genealogical Library. Former President of Minnesota Genealogical Society. Expert in French-Canadian Genealogical Research.*
14. **Joëlle Vitiello,** *Associate Professor Department of French and Francophone Studies, Macalester College*
15. **Guy Vadeboncoeur,** *Professional museologist and Vice-President, Museology for the Musée McCord-Stewart Museum in Montreal, Quebec*
16. **Professor Daniel Brewer,** *Professor, Department of French and Italian, University of Minnesota*
17. **Rev. Ronald G. DesRosiers,** *S.M., Assistant Professor (ret.), Department of Religious Studies & Philosophy, Madonna University, Livonia, Michigan, Church of St. Louis King of France*
18. **Carrie Heuing,** *Owner of Carrie-On-Travel. Advisor on travel accommodations for out of town entertainers, guests of Franco-Fete Festival.*
19. **Simeon A. Morbey, Esq.** *Legal Counsel for Foundation Attorney at Law Former resident of Ottawa, Canada is both Canadian and U.S. citizen. Proficient in French Language. French Ancestry.*
20. **Jordi Teillard,** *Dean/Site Manager, Academic Programs French Program Coordinator, Lac du Bois, Stillwater, Concordia Language Villages at The Forest*
21. **Michael Rainville,** *Partnership Marketing Manager, Meet Minneapolis Convention and Visitors Association*
22. **Christina Selander Bouzouina,** *Executive Director, Alliance Francaise*
23. **Thierry Ajas,** *Former President, French-American Chamber of Commerce*
24. **Diane Kruger,** *Associate Dean, Finance and Operations, College of Education, Leadership and Counseling (CELC) St. Thomas University.*

Charitable Foundation

On June 26, 2014, the Internal Revenue Service granted the French-American Heritage Foundation full tax exempt status as shown in the letter below:

INTERNAL REVENUE SERVICE   DEPARTMENT OF THE TREASURY
P. O. BOX 2508
CINCINNATI, OH 45201

Date: JUN 26 2014

FRENCH-AMERICAN HERITAGE FOUNDATION
C/O MARK LABINE
1887 BECKMAN AVE
ARDEN HILLS, MN 55112

Employer Identification Number:
  36-4760955
DLN:
  17053148332003
Contact Person:
  CUSTOMER SERVICE   ID# 31954
Contact Telephone Number:
  (877) 829-5500
Accounting Period Ending:
  December 31
Public Charity Status:
  170(b)(1)(A)(vi)
Form 990 Required:
  yes
Effective Date of Exemption:
  March 21, 2013
Contribution Deductibility:
  Yes
Addendum Applies:
  No

Dear Applicant:

We are pleased to inform you that upon review of your application for tax exempt status we have determined that you are exempt from Federal income tax under section 501(c)(3) of the Internal Revenue Code. Contributions to you are deductible under section 170 of the Code. You are also qualified to receive tax deductible bequests, devises, transfers or gifts under section 2055, 2106 or 2522 of the Code. Because this letter could help resolve any questions regarding your exempt status, you should keep it in your permanent records.

Organizations exempt under section 501(c)(3) of the Code are further classified as either public charities or private foundations. We determined that you are a public charity under the Code section(s) listed in the heading of this letter.

Please see enclosed Publication 4221-PC, Compliance Guide for 501(c)(3) Public Charities, for some helpful information about your responsibilities as an exempt organization.

Sincerely,

Tamera Ripperda

Director, Exempt Organizations

Enclosure: Publication 4221-PC

Letter 947

Membership Structure

Membership of the French-American Heritage Foundation was established as a means to raise funds to finance and support its mission statement. A membership structure based on the calendar year was set up as a way to solicit donations for the Foundation. Three membership categories were established.

Supporting Member: $25
Sustaining Member: $100
Sponsor: $500 and above

The membership was structured so that 100% of the membership payment is tax deductible. IRS rules state that membership payments are fully deductible where there are no services given to members. The hope is that people will become members on an annual basis because they support the mission statement of the French-American Heritage Foundation.

Although no services, per se, will be given members, members will be given notice of activities, receive news by email, and will be given an annual report each year. It is also anticipated that members will make contributions to the website in the form of articles on French American Heritage, information about their genealogy and family history, and list any websites they know about that deal with French American Heritage. Of course, it is also hoped that members will be willing to volunteer to assist in activities the Foundation sponsors in years to come, such as the Franco Fete French Festival.

Appendix B
Americans with French Descent

John P. DuLong is a writer who has written numerous articles on French-Canadian genealogy projects. He has categorized persons in North America he classifies as "North American French." These are persons who have French ancestry or who had ancestors who spoke French. Below is a list of these categories which he has agreed we could include in this book, written in his words:

French-Canadians

Descendants of predominately French settlers in the St. Lawrence River valley (especially Québec), the Great Lakes, and the northern Mississippi River valley. This area includes the states and provinces of Illinois, Indiana, Manitoba, Michigan, Minnesota, Ohio, Ontario, Québec, and Wisconsin. Historically, these people were known as Canadiens or Canadiens-Français. The Francophones now living in Québec usually refer to themselves Québécois. French-Canadians living in Ontario are often referred to as Franco Ontariens, while those in Manitoba are called Franco Manitobains. Those living in the United States were known as Franco-Américains, but now generally go by French-Canadians. For our purposes all these people are considered French-Canadians, because they share a common ancestral stock, whether they still live in Québec, in another Canadian province, or in the United States.

Acadians

Acadiens were French inhabitants of the Canadian Maritime provinces of Nova Scotia, New Brunswick, and Prince Edward Island. The British exiled them in 1755, and scattered them to the British American colonies, the Caribbean, England, France, and even the remote Falkland Islands. Some hid in the Maritimes and eventually resurfaced there. Others escaped to Québec. Many migrated back to the Maritimes after the period of persecution. There are now thriving Acadian communities in the Maritimes, especially in New Brunswick. Some of the dispersed Acadians eventually resettled in Louisiana at the invitation of the Spanish; they are now known as Cajuns. The Cajuns have their own culture that has emerged in their Louisiana homeland. Also, some families of non-Acadian background have become accepted as Cajun. The Cajuns remain close to their Acadian cousins because of the common ancestry and history they share. Many people throughout the United States have Acadian ancestors.

Creoles

The Créoles are descendants of French-speaking colonists in the southern Mississippi River Valley, that is, Alabama, Arkansas, Louisiana, Mississippi, and Missouri. In addition to these states, Illinois was also considered administratively to be a part of colonial Louisiana. Illinois and Missouri, in particular, became the meeting ground for Creoles and French-Canadians. This group includes both white and black (or Afro-Creole) people of French ancestry in these areas. Although there are many challenges to doing Afro-Creole genealogical research, prejudice and the legacy of slavery often taints records, it is still possible for some to trace their Afro-Creole ancestors back to the colonial period using French records.

French Métis

In Canada, people of mixed European and Native people ancestry have become known as Métis. The Métis are products of the fur trade that bound together French voyageurs, British businessmen, and Native trappers in a common life style. Originally this term, meaning "mixed," was applied towards the offspring of French and Native People parents. However, the term is now becoming generally accepted to mean anyone of mixed Native People and Scottish, Irish, English, or other ethnicity. In the past, these non-French Métis were often called country born, mixed breeds, or half breeds. In the United States, the term Métis has not been widely used. Many, but certainly not all, Métis have Cree or Ojibwa ancestry. Given the ongoing evolution of this term, for our purposes, I will be referring mostly to French Métis only, that is, people of predominately mixed French and Native People ancestry. Nevertheless, given their common origins in the life of the fur trade, it is often necessary to discuss the other Métis as well. Note that some scholars differentiate between Métis used for the mixed bloods of the Red River and western Canada versus métis used for all other mixed bloods.

Huguenots

Huguenots were French Protestants settled in the British and Dutch American colonies before the American Revolution. Most Huguenots fled France in 1685, when persecution renewed in earnest. They scattered to Great Britain, Germany, the Netherlands, Switzerland, and even South Africa. Many of those who came to America did not come directly from France but filtered through one of these refuges first. Many people who can trace their ancestry back to the colonial period in North America will find several Huguenot ancestors.

Foreign French

These are immigrants from French-speaking lands to the United States after the colonial period. I refer to them as the Foreign French because to the Creoles, Acadians, and French-Canadians--who were living here for generations—these newcomers were indeed strangers with different ways. This term for them is less awkward and confusing than saying the French from France. I will concede that is an artificial catch-all term. Nevertheless, it is convenient. Obviously, the Foreign French do not have an ethnic identity as do the other groups we will examine. Besides immigrants from France, this group also includes any other French speakers. The diversity of this group is amazing. It covers people of French ancestry from the following areas:

- France, including non-French speaking Alsatians and Basques.
- The Caribbean (especially the islands of St-Domingue [now Haiti], Martinique, and Guadeloupe) and French Guiana.
- Walloons from the French-speaking provinces of Belgium (Hainault, Namur, Liège, Luxembourg, and part of Brabant).
- People from the French-speaking cantons of Switzerland (Geneva, Neuchâtel, Vaud, and parts of Berne, Fribourg, and Valais).

- French-speaking immigrants from the French colonies and mandates of the late eighteenth and early twentieth century, including, Algeria, Morocco, Tunisia, Lebanon, Syria, French West Africa, French Equatorial Africa, Madagascar, Réunion (formerly Île Bourbon), French India (Pondicherry), Indochina, French Polynesia, and even Mexico.

Appendix C
French Words in the English Language

According to an estimate by the Global Language Monitor on January 1, 2014, there are 1,025,109 words in the English language. Webster's Third New International Dictionary lists 450,000 words, and the Oxford English Dictionary has 615,000. Technical and scientific terms would add many more.[401] The Second Edition of the 20-volume *Oxford English Dictionary* contains full entries for 171,476 words in current use, and 47,156 obsolete words. This suggests that there are, at the very least, a quarter of a million distinct English words, excluding inflections, and words from technical and regional vocabulary not covered by the *Oxford English Dictionary*, or words not yet added to the published dictionary. To this may be added around 9,500 derivative words included as subentries. In summary, it is a reasonable estimate that 200,000 English words are in common use.

The English language is an amazing language, and is really a combination of many different languages. It was born out of the dialects of three German tribes (Angles, Jutes, and Saxons), influenced by Latin, who settled in Britain about 450 A.D. This group of dialects forms what linguists refer to as Anglo-Saxon. After adding in a mix of Scandinavian, a language developed into what we know as Old English. Old English was the primary language of Britain when the French Normans invaded in the year 1066.

When William the Conqueror became King of England in the year 1066, French took over as the language of the court, administration, and culture, and stayed there for 300 years. It was not until 1399, when Henry IV took the throne, that the English had a king whose mother tongue was English.[402] During the Norman occupation, about 10,000 French words were adopted into English, some three-fourths of which are still in use today.[403]

After the Norman conquest, the majority of the population of England continued to use their Anglo-Saxon language, but it was influenced by the language of the ruling elite. The French influence tended to focus on matters of court, government, fashion, and high living. Meanwhile, the common man continued to use English. An example of this is illustrated by Bill Bryson in his book:

> *The more humble trades tended to have Anglo-Saxon names (baker, miller, shoemaker) while the more skilled trades adopted French names (mason, painter, tailor). At the same time, animals in the field usually were called by English names (sheep, cow, ox) but once cooked and brought to the table, they were generally given French names (beef, mutton, veal, bacon).*[404]

The use of different words to describe the same thing is also known as "doublets" and is found often in the English language as a result of the French influence. Examples are:

---

[401] "The Mother Tongue: English and How it Got That Way" by Bill Bryson.
[402] Id.
[403] Id.
[404] Id

beef/ox, mutton/sheep, veal/calf, pork/pig, or pairs of words pertaining to different registers of language: commence/start, continue/go on, disengage/withdraw, encounter/meet, vend/sell, purchase/buy.

After the rise of Frenchman Henry Plantagenet to the throne of England, other forms of dialectal French may have gained in influence to the detriment of Norman French, notably the variants of Anjou in France where the House of Plantagenet came from, and possibly Poitevin, the tongue of Eleanor of Aquitaine. With the English claim to the throne of France, the influence of the language in use at the royal court of France in Paris increased. The cultural influence of France remained strong in the following centuries and from the Renaissance onward borrowings were mainly made from Parisian French, which became the de facto standard language of France.

One thing is indisputable, however, about the English language. It contains a lot of French words and Minnesota's French heritage must include our English language. French language origins in our English language can be classified into at least the following categories: French language origins, Middle French origins, Old French origins, Old Northern French origins, Anglo-Norman language origins, Norman language origins, Canadian French origins, Louisiana Cajun French origins and Louisiana Creole French origins. The influence of French West Africa and Haiti must also be added to this list.

Here are a few examples of French words used in our English language.[405]

Feudalism

Chivalry (homage, liege, peasant, government, seigniorage, suzerain, vassal, villain) and other institutions (bailiff, chancellor, council, government, mayor, minister, parliament), the organization of religion (abbey, clergy, cloister, diocese, friar, mass, parish, prayer, preach, priest, sacristy, vestment, vestry, vicar), the nobility (baron, count, dame, duke, marquis, prince, sir), and the art of war (armour, baldric, dungeon, hauberk, mail, portcullis, surcoat). Many of these words related to the feudal system or medieval warfare have a Germanic origin (mainly through Old Frankish) (see also French words of Germanic origin). The Norman origin of the British monarchy is still visible in expressions like Prince Regent, heir apparent, Princess Royal where the adjective is placed after the noun, like in French.

Heraldry

The vocabulary of heraldry has been heavily influenced by French (blazon, or, argent, sable, gules, passant), for more details see tinctures, attitudes, and charges of heraldry. Sometimes used in heraldry, some mythological beasts (cockatrice, dragon, griffin, hippogriff, phoenix) or exotic animals (lion, leopard, antelope, gazelle, giraffe, camel, zebu, elephant, baboon, dolphin, ocelot, ostrich, chameleon) draw their name from French. It is also the case of some animals native of Europe (via Anglo-Norman: eagle, buzzard, falcon, squirrel, coney, rabbit, leveret, lizard, marten, ferret, salmon, viper).

---

[405] Rignon, John C., *French and English Cognates, Over 8,000 Words Which are the Same in French and English*, Creatspace Independent Publishing Platform (2017).

Military

The vocabulary of warfare and the military include many words of French origin (battalion, dragoon, soldier, marine, guard, officer, infantry, cavalry, army, artillery, corvette, musketeer, carabineer, pistol, fusilier, squad, squadron, platoon, brigade, corps, sortie, reconnaissance/reconnoitre, surveillance, rendezvous, espionage, volley, siege, terrain, troop, camouflage, logistics, accoutrements, bivouac, aide-de-camp, legionnaire, morale, esprit de corps. See also military ranks: sergeant, lieutenant, captain, colonel, general, admiral). Many fencing terms are also from French.

Politics and Economics

The political/economic lexicon include many words of French origin like money, treasury, exchequer, commerce, finance, tax, liberalism, capitalism, materialism, nationalism, plebiscite, coup d'état, regime, sovereignty, state, administration, federal, bureaucracy, constitution, jurisdiction, district.

Law

The judicial lexicon has also been heavily influenced by French (justice, judge, jury, attorney, court, case).

Diplomacy

Attaché, chargé d'affaires, envoy, embassy, chancery, diplomacy, démarche, communiqué, aide-mémoire, détente, entente, rapprochement, accord, treaty, alliance, passport, protocol.

Arts

Surrealism, impressionism, fauvism, cubism, symbolism, art nouveau, gouache, aquarelle, collage, grisaille.

Architecture

Aisle, arcade, arch, vault, belfry, arc-boutant, buttress, bay, estrade, facade, balustrade, terrace, lunette, niche, pavilion, pilaster, porte cochère.

Aviation and Automobile Engineering

France played a pioneering role in the fields of aviation (nacelle, empennage, fuselage, aileron, altimeter, canard, decalage, monocoque, turbine) and automobile engineering or design (chassis, piston, arbor, grille, tonneau, berline, sedan, limousine, cabriolet, coupé, convertible.

Cuisine

Veal, beef, pork, mutton, petit four, soufflé, mille-feuille, croissant, pastry, gateau, baba au rhum, cream, caramel, custard, fondant, fondue, marmalade, meringue, clafoutis, flognarde, beef bourguignon, cassoulet, casserole, confit, gratin, mustard, mayonnaise, sauce, pâté, foie gras, terrine, navarin.

Wine

For hundreds of years, France has had the reputation of being the world's greatest producer of wines. This ancient French reputation and tradition has now become a part of the Minnesota Wine industry. The first vineyard in Minnesota was started by a descendant of one of the first French-Canadian traders, Alexis Bailey, who is discussed earlier in this book. The Alexis Bailly Vineyard in Hastings was started in 1973. Many of the grape varieties that grow in Minnesota and which the growing number of wineries use to make their wine have French names, such as Chardonnay, Frontenac, Frontenac Blanc, Frontenac Gris, La Crescent, Marquette, Petit Ami, Seyval Blanc, and Vidal Blanc. One of the first cold-hardy grapes grown in Minnesota, called the Maréchal Foch, was developed in Alsace, France.

Colours

Other influences include colour names (ecru, mauve, beige, carmine, maroon, blue, orange, violet, vermilion, turquoise, lilac, perse, scarlet, cerise); vegetables or fruits (courgette, aubergine, cabbage, carrot, cherry, chestnut, nutmeg, quince, spinach, lemon, orange, apricot); months of the year (January, March, May, July, November, December).

Terms coined by French people

Some of the French words that made their way into the English language were coined by French inventors, discoverers or pioneers, or scientists: cinema, television, helicopter, parachute, harmonium, bathyscaphe, lactose, lecithin, bacteriophage, chlorophyll, mastodon, pterodactyl, oxygen, hydrogen, carbon, photography, stethoscope, thermometer, stratosphere, troposphere.

Named after French people

Some French words were named after French people (from their family name), especially in the fields of science (ampere, baud, becquerel, coulomb, curie, daguerreotype, pascal, pasteurise, vernier), botany and mineralogy (begonia, bougainvillea, clementine, magnolia, dolomite, nicotine), fashion and style or any other cultural aspect (lavalier, leotard, recamier, mansard, chauvinism, kir, praline, saxophone, silhouette).

Placenames

There are many cities in non-francophone regions or countries with French spelled names, such as (Ypres, Bruges, Turin, Milan, Venice, Plaisance, Florence, Rome, Naples, Syracuse, Vienna, Prague, Munich, Cologne, Aix-la-Chapelle, Seville, Constantinople, The Hague).

Other Names

Arbitrage, ambiance, Aplomb, armoire, barrage, bateau, bourgeoisie, brochure, budget, bureau, café, challenge, collage, critique, debris, décor, dossier, élite, ennui, entourage, entrepreneur, espionage, expertise, financier, fuel, garage, gay, genre, gin, glacier, gourmet, hotel, humour, interview, intrigue, liaison, lingerie, machine, mirage, management, mess, montage, panache, pedigree, penchant, plaque, record, repertoire, sport, squat, standard, suspense, tennis, terrain, ticket, toast, toboggan, tranche, tunnel, and vintage.

Here is a list of other sources that discuss the influence of French in the English language"

1. *"The Mother Tongue: English and How it Got this Way," by Bill Bryson.*
2. *"French is Not a "Foreign Language," American Assoicaiton of Teachers in French.*
3. *The American Heritage Dictionary of the English Language, ed. Houghton Mifflin Company.*
4. *"French Inside Out: The French Language Past and Present," by Henirette Walter.*
5. *"Honni Soit Qui Maly y Pense: L'incoryable histoire d'amour entre le francais et l'anglais," by Henriette Walter.*
6. *"The Languages of the World," by Kenneth Katzner.*
7. *"Made in America: An Informal History of the English Language in the United States," by Bill Bryson.*

Tours, France

Tours, France is a Sister City to Minneapolis, MN. This association was established in 1991. Since then many exchanges including local government officials, student exchanges and tourist groups have happened. Cultural events in both cities have led to a greater understanding and interest in what our two cities can learn from each other.

Picture of L'hôtel de ville in Tours, France (Public Domain)

Bibliography

Bibliography

Aby, Anne J., *The North Star State*, Minnesota Historical Society Press, St. Paul, (2002).

Ackermann, Gertrude, *Joseph Renville of Lac qui Parle*, Minnesota History 12 (September 1931).

Ahern, Reverend Patrick H., *Catholic Heritage in Minnesota, North Dakota and South Dakota*, published by the Most Reverend Archbishop and Bishops of the Province of Saint Paul 1964

Amato, Joseph, *Jacob's Well: A Case for Rethinking Family History*, Minnesota Historical Society Press, St. Paul, (2008).

American Association of French Teachers Advocacy, *Minnesota Francophone Connection*, August 2006.

Andreas, A.T., *An Illustrated Historical Atlas of the State of Minnesota*, published by A.T.Andreas, (1874).

Anonymous, *Compendium of History and Biography of Central and Northern Minnesota*, G. A. Ogle & Company: (1904).

Babcock, Willoughby M., *Louis Provencalle, Fur Trader*, published by the Minnesota Historical Society in St. Paul.

Bachman, Walt, *Northern Slave Black Dakota, The Life and Times of Joseph Godfrey*, Pond Dakota Press 2013.

Baird, Charles W. *History of the Huguenot Emigration to America*, Genealogical Publishing Co, Inc. Baltimore 1973.

Belanger, Damien-Claude, *French-Canadian Emigration to the United States, 1840-1930*, Department d'histoire, Universite de Montreal, and Department of History, Marianopolis College, last revised August 23, 2000.

Belar, Lina. "Joseph Réaume's Trading Post." MNopedia, Minnesota Historical Society. http://www.mnopedia.org/place/joseph-r-aumes-trading-post.

Belliveau, Walter, *The Life of Alexis Bailly, Minnesota Pioneer*, Dictionary of Canadian Biography, (1928).

Benoit, Virgil, "The French- Canadian Presence in the Northwest and the Very Early Beginnings of Red Lake Falls and Red Lake County," in *A History of Red Lake County*, edited by Anne Healy and Sherry Kankel, Taylor Publishing Co., Dallas, (1976).

Birk, D.A. and J. Poseley, *The French at Lake Pepin: An Archaeological Survey for Fort Beauharnois, Goodhue County, Minnesota*, Minnesota Historical Society, St. Paul (1978).

Blegen, Therodore C. *Five Fur Traders of the Northwest*, and edited by Charles M. Gates, Minnesota Historical Society, St. Paul, (1965).

Blegen, Therodore C., *The Land Lies Open*, D.C. Heath and Company, Boston (1938).

Borneman, Walter R., *1812, The War that Forged a Nation*, Harper Collins Publishers, New York (2004).

Boutros, David, "Confluence of People and Place: The Choteau Posts on the Missouri and Kansas Rivers," *Missouri Historical Review*, Vol. 97, No. 1 (October 2002).

Bray, M.C., Joseph Nicolas Nicollet, Geologist, *Proceedings of the American Philosophical Society* 114 (1970).

Breckenridge, W.C., Early gunpowder making in Missouri, *Missouri Historical Review* 20 (1925).

Brick, Greg, Le Sueur's Saltpeter Caves at Lake Pepin, Minnesota, and Wilderness Gunpowder Manufacture, *Minnesota Archaeologist* 71 (2012).

Brick, Greg, "What Happened to Fountain Cave—The Real Birthplace of St. Paul?" *Ramsey County History* 29 (1995).

Brick, Greg, *Subterranean Twin Cities*, Minneapolis, MN: University of Minnesota Press (2009).

Broden, Holly, *French Immigrants and the Catholic Church in Centerville*, published in History Center News, a Newsletter of the Anoka County Historical Society. Vol 39, No.3 (May-June 2009).

Brooks, Rev. David, *History of Dayton* (early 1900's).

Bunnell, Dr. L.H., *History of Wabasha County* Published Chicago by H.H. Hill, Publishers, (1884).

Burke-Gaffney, M. W. . Dictionary of Canadian Biography, vol. 2, University of Toronto/Université Laval, (2003).

Cailleux, A., "The Geological Map of North America (1752)" of J.E. Guettard, in C.J. Schneer (editor), *Two Hundred Years of Geology in America* (Hanover, NH: The University Press of New England, 1979).

Camarota, Steven, *Fact Sheet on Immigrants in the United States*, Center for Immigration Studies (January 2010).

Campeau, Lucien, *Jean-Pierre Aulneau*, Dictionary of Canadian Biography, (2000).

Catholic Encylopedia, *Jacques Marquette*. New York: Robert Appleton Company, (1913).

Catholic Historical Society of St. Paul, "Obituary of Issac Labissoniere," in *Acta et Dicta*, Vol. III, No. 1, (July 1911).

Catholic Historical Society of St. Paul, "Monsignor Augustine Ravoux, The Pioneer Missionary of the Northwest," in *Acta et Dicta*, Vol. 1, No. I, (July 1907).

Catholic Historical Society, "A collection of historical data regarding the origin and growth of the Catholic Church in the Northwest," in *Acta Et Dicta*, Vol II, No.1 (July 1911).

Castle, Henry A. History of St. Paul and Vicinity, Volume I, The Lewis Publishing Company, Chicago and New York, 1912.

Chabot, Marie-Emmanuel, O.S.U., *Guyart, Marie, dite Marie de l'Incarnation*, Dictionary of Canadian Biography, University of Toronto/Universite Laval (2015).

Chaput, Donald, *Jacques Legardeur de Saint Pierre*, Dictionary of Canadian Biograph, University of Toronto/Universite Laval (2015).

Chiamaka Nwosu, Jeanne Batalova, *Haitian Immigrants in the United States*, Migration Information Source (May 29, 2014).

Chouteau, Francois and Chouteau, Berenice and Marra, Dorothy, *Cher Oncle, Cher Papa: The Letters of Francois and Berenice Chouteau*, University of Missouri Western Historical (2001).

Clayton Andrew R.L. and Sisson, Richard and Zacher, Chris, *The American Midwest: An Interpretive Encyclopedia*, Indiana University Press, (2007).

Conrad, G.R. (editor), *The Historical Journal of the Establishment of the French in Louisiana.* by Jean-Baptiste Benard de La Harpe. Translation by J. Cain and V. Koenig, Lafayette: University of Southwestern Louisiana (1971).

Coen, Rena Neumann. *Alexis Jean Fournier, the Last American Barbizon*. St. Paul: Minnesota Historical Society Press, 1985.

Curtiss-Wedge, Franklyn, *History of Wright County, Minnesota* (Volume I, Chicago, H.C. Cooper Jr. & Co. (1915).

Curtiss-Wedge, Franklyn, *History of Goodhue County, Minnesota.* Chicago: H.C. Cooper, Jr., (1909).

Curtiss-Wedge, Franklyn, *History of Renville County,* published H.C. Cooper Jr. & Co. (1916). Assisted by Renville County Pioneer Association Committee.

Danborn, David B., *"Flour Power" The Significance of Flour Milling at the Falls,* Minnesota History 58(5).

Dansereau, Antoinio, *LeSueur, Pierre,* Biography at the Dictionary of Canadian Biography, Univeristy of Toronto/Universite Laval.

DeVoto, Bernard. *The Journals of Lewis and Clark,* Appendix II. Note names of interpreters and boatmen. Mariner Books, NYC, NY. (1997).

Dierkins, Tony and Norton, Maryanne, *Lost Duluth, Landmarks, Industries, Buildings, Homes and the Neighborhoods in Which they Stood,* Zenith City Press, Duluth, Minnesota, (2012).

Dobbs, Arthur, *An account of the countries adjoining to Hudson's Bay in the north-west part of America* (London, 1744; reprinted New York, (1967).

Dulong, John P., *French-Canadians in Michigan,* Michigan State University Press, (2001).

DuLong, John P. *North American French,* published online at http://habitant.org/franco.htm (1995).

Eastaugh, Nicholas *Pigment Compendium: A Dictionary of Historical Pigments.* Butterworth-Heinemann. ISBN 0-7506-5749-9 (2004).

Edwards, Owen, *A Larger Than Life Toussaint Louverture,* Smithsonian Magazine, www.Smithsonian.com, (May 2011).

Empson, Donald L. (2006). *The Street Where You Live: A Guide to the Place Names of Saint Paul.* Published by University of Minnesota Press, (2006).

Eyles, N. and Miall, A., *Canada Rocks: The Geologic Journey* (Markham, Ontario: Fitzhenry and Whiteside, 2007).

Faust, B., "Saltpetre Mining Tools Used in Caves," *National Speleological Society Bulletin* 17 (1955).

Feard, Rev. John R.,D.D., *Toussaint L'Overture of Hayti,* James Redpath, Publisher (1863).

Ferguson, Will, *Canadian History For Dummies,* 2nd Edition, John Wiley and Sons, Mississauga, Ontario, (2005).

Fisher, David Hackett, *Champlain's Dream*, Vintage Canada, (2009).

Flandrau, Charles, *The History of Minnesota and Tales of the Frontier*, CreateSpace Independent Publishing Platform, (2015).

Fletcher, J. Williams, "Memoir of William W. Warren," in William W. Warren, *History of the Ojibway People*, Minnesota Historical Society, (1885).

Fletcher, J. Williams, *The History of the City of Saint Paul and the County of Ramsey, Minnesota*, Minnesota Historical Society Press, St. Paul, (1983).

Fleury, Norman. *Michif Dictionary 2013*. Gabriel Dupont Institute, Saskatoon, Saskatchewan. (2013).

Folwell, William Watts, "Sioux Half-Breed Scrip," appendix 11. In *A History of Minnesota*, vol. 1. St. Paul: Minnesota Historical Society, 1956 edition.

Franquelin, Jean-Baptiste, *Service historique de la Marine* 1688, copies available in National Archives of Quebec, Canada.

Friesen, Gerald, *Gabriel Franchere*, The Dictionary of Canadian Biography, University of Toronto/Universite Laval. (1974-2015).

Gannett, Henry, *The Origin of Certain Place Names in the United States*, U.S. Government Printing Office. (1905).

Gitlin, Jay, *The Bourgeois Frontier: French Towns, French Traders, and American Expansion*, Yale University Press (2010).

Gilman, Rhoda R. and Gilman, Carolyn, and Stultz, Deborah, *Red River Trails, Oxcart Routes between St. Paul and the Selkirk Settlement 1820-1870*, Minnesota Historical Society Press (1979).

Goodrich, Albert M., *History of Anoka County and the Towns of Champlin and Dayton in Hennepin County, Minnesota*, (Minneapolis, 1905).

Green, William D. *A Peculiar Imbalance: The Fall and Rise of Racial Equality in Early Minnesota*, Minnesota Historical Society Press, (2007).

Hafen, LeRoy R, "Auguste Pierre Chouteau," in *French Fur Traders and Voyageurs in the American West*, ed. Spokane, Wash; Arthur H. Clark, (1995).

Hamelin, Jean, *Nicollet, Jean*, Dictionary of Canadian Biography, University of Toronto/Universite Laval, (2015).

Hamilton, William Baillie, *Place names of Atlantic Canada*, University of Toronto Press, (1996).

Hamre, John, *The Minnesota to St. Jerome Connection*, Let's Play Hockey, October 16, 2014.

Hankins, Col. *Dakota Land or the Beauty of St. Paul, an Original, Illustrated, Historic and Romantic Work*, published by Hankins & Son, New York, 1868.
Hart, Irving Harlow, *"The site of the Northwest Company Post on Sandy Lake"*, Iowa State Teachers College, Cedar Falls, IA, property of Minnesota Historical Society.

Hatle, Elizabeth Dorsey, and Vaillancourt, "One Flag, One School, One Language, Minnesota's Ku Klux Klan in the 1920s," *Minnesota History*, 61/8, Winter 2009-10.

Hazel, Reverend Robert, *Notre Dame de Minneapolis"*, *The French-Canadian Catholics*, (Second Printing 2003).

Hennepin, Louis, *Carte de la Nouvelle France et de la Louisiane* (Paris:Sebastien Hure, 1683) Minnesota Historical Society.

Hennessy, W.B., *Past and Present St. Paul, Minnesota, being a relation of the progressive history of the capital city of Minnesota from the earliest historical times down to the present day*, published by Chicago, The S.J. Clarke Publishing Company (1906).

Hiebert, Gareth D., *Little Canada, A Voyageur's Vision*, A compiled history of Little Canada, Minnesota by the Historical Society of Little Canada, Published by the Croixside Press, Inc. (1989).

Hiebert, Gareth, *City of Seven Hills, Columns of Oliver Towne*, Pogo Press, Inc. St. Paul, (1999).

Hill, C.A., "Origin of cave saltpeter," *National Speleological Society Bulletin* 43 (1981).

Hill, C.A. and P. Forti, *Cave Minerals of the World*, second edition (Huntsville, AL: National Speleological Society, 1997).

"History of the Red River Valley : past and present, including an account of the counties, cities, towns, and villages of the Valley from the time of their first settlement and formation. Written by various writers, published by C.F. Cooper & Company, Chicago, (1909).

Holcombe, I. and Bingham, William H, *Compendium of History and Biography of Polk County, Minnesota*, 30-33 (Minneapolis, 1916).

Holmquist, June Drenning, *They Chose Minnesota, a Survey of The State's Ethnic Group*, Minnesota Historical Society Press (1981).

Houlihan, Jesse, *Minnetonka Cabin on the Move*, Lakeshore Weekly News, October 20, 2008.

Hubbard, Lucius F.; Murray, William Pitt, Baker, James H., Upham, Warren, Holcombe, R.I. and Holmes, Frank R., *Minnesota in Three Centuries 1655-1908*, published 1908 by The Publishing Society of Minnesota, vol. 1, pp. 299-302).

Jette, Rene, *Dictionnaire genelogique des Families du Qubec ds Origines avant 1730*, Societe de Genealogie de Quebec, 1993, digitized by the University of Wisconsin- Madison, (2008).

Jillson, W.R., "Early mineral explorations in the Mississippi Valley (1540-1840)," *Transactions of the Illinois State Historical Society* (1924).

Keating, William H., *Narrative of an Expedition to the Source of St. Peter's River...under the Command of Stephen H. Long* (Philadelphia, 1824)

Labissoniere, Issac, *A Pioneer's Talk of Pioneer Days*, Article written in the Northwestern Chronicle about Issac Labissoniere and the Battle of Kaposia (published prior to 1910).

Lakem, Neoma, *History of Wilkin County, Minnesota*, (2015).

Lamarre, Jean, *French-Canadians of Michigan*, Wayne State Community Press, (2003).

Lamontagne, R., "La participation canadienne a l'oeuvre mineralogique de Guettard," *Revue d'histoire des sciences et de leurs applications* 18 (1965).

Lass, William E, *History of Minnesota*, 2nd edition, W.W. Norton & Company, (2000).

Lavender, David, *Winner Take All, The Trans-Canada Canoe Trail*, McGraw-Hill Book Company, New York, (1977).

Leger, Ellen Nelles, *Letters to George*, self published in Minneapolis, Minnesota, 2005.

Leger, Jacques Nicolas, *Haiti, Her History and Her Detractors*, New York, Neale, (1907).

Levine, Ben, *Waking Up French...! Réveil*, documentary presented at Universite de La Sorbonne, Paris, France (January 30, 2006).

Lynch, John, *"Simon Bolivar: a Life,"* Yale University Press (July 5, 2007).

Mackenzie, Alexander, *Voyages from Montreal*, published (1801).

Macleod, Roderick C., *Gabriel Dumont*, Dictionary of Canadian Biography, Volume XIII (1910-1910), University of Toronto/Universite Laval (2015).

McMahon, Eileen M. and Karamanski, Theodore J., *Time and the River: A History of the Saint Croix*, Midwest Regional office, National Park Service, United States Department of Interior, Omaha, Nebraska (2002).

Mikesell, Marie-Reine, L'Etoile du Nord, Notes on French Influence in the History of Minnesota, self published 1980.

Mitchell, William Bell, *History of Stearns County, Minnesota*, published by Chicago H.C. Cooper Jr. & Co (1915).

Martin, Horace T., *Modifications of the Beaver Hat, Castorologia, or the History and Traditions of the Canadien Beaver* (Montreal: W. Drysdale, 1892), reprinted by Minnesota Historical Society.

Merrill, G.P., *The First One Hundred Years of American Geology*, New York and London: Hafner Publishing Company, (1969).

Mitchell, Peter, *Peoples and Cultures of Africa, West Africa*, Chelsea House Publishers (2006).

Minnesota Historical Society Handout, *People of the Fur Trade: on the backs of men, in the hands of women*, Northwest Company Fur Post.

Moore, Phillip J., *One Hundred French-Canadian Family Histories*, Self published, (1994).

Morin, Gail. *First Metis Families of Quebec*, 5 volumes. Clearfield Company, Baltimore, Maryland. 2012-2015.

Morton, A.S., "La Verendrye: commandant, fur-trader, and explorer," *Canadian Historical Review* 9 (1928).

Neering, Rosemary. *Louis Riel*, Fitzhenry and Whiteside, Ontario, Canada (1999).

Neill, Edward Duffield, Secretary of the Minnesota Historical Society, *The History of Minnesota from the earliest French Explorations to the Present Time*, Philadelphia: J. B. Lippincott & co. (1858).

Neill, Rev. Edward D., edited by Charles S. Bryant, *History of the Minnesota Valley: Including the Explorers and Pioneers of Minnesota*, by North Star Publishing Company, Minneapolis, (1882).

Nelson, Loren, *Voice of the Tourney*, Minnesota Hockey Hub News, March 8, (2011).

Newson, T.M. St. Paul, *Minnesota and Biographical Sketches of Old Settlers, from the Earliest Settlement of the City, up to and including the year 1857*, published by the author in St. Paul, Minnesota in 1886.

Nicollet, Joseph, *Joseph N. Nicollet on the plains and prairies: the expeditions of 1838-39* (reprinted St. Paul: Minnesota Historical Society (1976).

Nicollet, J.N. *Hydrographical Basin of the Upper Mississippi River* (Washington, 1843).

Nord, Mary Ann *The National Register of Historic Places in Minnesota.* Minnesota Historical Society (2003). ISBN 0-87351-448-3.

Nute, Grace Lee, *The Voyageur* (Minnesota Historical Society, St. Paul, 1955).

Nute, Grace Lee, *Posts in the Minnesota Fur-Trade area, 1660-1855,* Minnesota History, Vol. 11, No. 4 (December 1930).

Nute, Grace Lee, *Rainy River Country* in Minnesota History, Minnesota History Press (1959).

Nute, Grace Lee, *Red River Trails* in Minnesota History, 6:278-82 (September, 1925).

O'Hehir, Andrew, *America's Forgotten Atrocity,* published in Salon Media Group, Inc. Tuesday, March 1, 2005.

O'Leary, Johanna, *A Historical Sketch of the Parish of the Immaculate Conception, Faribault, Minnesota,* Faribault Journal Press (1938).

O'Neill, Arthur Barry, *Congregation of the Holy Cross,* The Catholic Encyclopedia. Vol. 7. New York: Robert Appleton Company, 1910. (10 Sept. 2015).

Parkman, Francis, *La Salle and the Discovery of the Great West,* France and England in North America, vol. 3 (Boston: Little, Brown, 1869).

Park G.B., *Report from the Select committee on the Hudson's Bay Company, Together with the Proceedings of the Committee,* Order by the House of Commons, to be printed, 31 July and 11 August, 1857.

Perreault, Jean Baptiste, *Narrative of the Travels and Adventures of a Merchant Voyageur in the Savage Territories of Northern America,"* Leaving Montreal the 28th *Day of May, 1783 to 1820.* Written in 1830, (Found in Schoolcraft Manuscripts in the Smithsonian Institute in Washington, D.C.).

Perrot, Nicolas, *Mémoire sur les mœurs, coustumes et relligion des sauvages de l Amérique septentrionale,* éd. Jules Tailhan (Leipzig et Paris, 1864; Canadiana avant 1867, Toronto, 1968).

Peterson, Chris, *Birchbark Brigade; A Fur Trade History,* Calkins Creek, Honesdale, Pennsylvania, (2009).

Peterson, Jacqueline and Brown, Jennifer. *The New Peoples*, Edmund, R. David, "Unacquainted with the laws of the Civilized World…", Minnesota Historical Society Press, St. Paul, Minnesota. 2001.

Petto, Christine Marie, *When France was King of Cartography: The Patronage and Production of Maps in Early Modern France*, Lanham: Lexington Books, (2007).

Pamphile, Leon D., *Haitians and African Americans: A Heritage of Tragedy and Hope*, University Press of Florida, 1st Edition (December 30, 2001).

Raiche, Annabell CSJ, and Biermaier, Ann Marie OSB, *"They Came to Teach" the Story of Sisters who Taught in Parochial Schools and Their Contribution to Elementary Education in Minnesota*. North Star Press of St. Cloud, Inc. (1994).

Ramsey, Walter Reeve, *The Selkirk Colony of the Red River of the North…and its profound influence on early development of the Twin Cities; a factual research*, originally published before 1923, reprinted Nabu Press (2011).

Ravoux, Monsignor V.G., Reminiscences, *Memoirs and Lectures of Monsignor A. Ravoux, V.G.*, Brown, Tracey & Co., Printers and Publishers, 1890.

Rife, Clarence W., *Norman W. Kittson: A Fur Trader at Pembina* in Minnesota History 6:246-48 (September 1925).

Register of Sioux Half-Breed Scrip, 1857–1861, United States, Red Wing Land District, State Archives Collection, Minnesota Historical Society.

Rife, Clarence W., *Norman W. Kittson, A Fur Trader at Pembina*, Dictionary of Canadian Biography, University of Toronto/Universite Laval (2015).

Roberts, Robert B., *Encyclopedia of Historic Forts, the Military, Pioneer, and Trading Posts of the United States*, Macmillan Publishing Company, New York (1988); digitized by University of Michigan 2009).

Roby, Ives, *The Franco-americans of New England: Dreams and Realities* Mcgill Queens Univ Pr (May 16, 2005).

Rolle, Andrew F. John Charles Fremont: Character as Destiny. University of Oklahoma Press (1991).

Roosevelt, Theodore, *The Winning of the West: Volume I.* New York and London: G. P. Putnam's Sons, (1889).

Rubenstein, Sarah, "The French-Canadians and French," found in Holmquist, June Drenning, *They Chose Minnesota" a Survey of The State's Ethnic Groups*, Minnesota Historical Society Press (1981).

Rubertus, Donald, *History of the Holy Redeemer Catholic Church, 1869-1916, Marshall*, typescript, 1956, in Southwest Minnesota Historical Center, Marshall.

Russ, C.J., *Jacques de Noyon*, Dictionary of Canadian Biography, University of Toronto/Universite Laval. (1974-2015).

St. Genevieve Council of Catholic Women, *Heritage Recipes and Historical Notes from Centerville and Hugo, Minnesota, a Collection of Recipes and Remembrances*, published 2013 by Morris Press Cookbooks.

Savage, Sister Mary Lucida PhD, *The Congregation of Saint Joseph of Carondolet*, Second Edition, Published by B. Herder Book Co. (1927).

Scherer, Bill, *History of Medina*, published in Western Hennepin County Pioneers Association, Volume 158, (Spring 2013).

Scholberg, Henry, *The French Pioneers of Minnesota (Les Pionniers Francais du Minnesota)* Northstar Publications Minnesota, 1995.

Schoolcraft, Henry R., *Summary Narrative of an Exploratory Expedition to the Sources of the Mississippi River in 1820*, (Published in 1855).

Shaw, T.R., *History of Cave Science: The Exploration and Study of Limestone Caves, to 1900*, second edition (New South Wales, Australia Sydney Speleological Society, 1992).

Sherman, William C. and Thorson, Playford V. editors, Plains Folk, North Dakota's Ethnic History, part of North Dakota Centennial Heritage Series, published by The North Dakota Institute for Regional Studies at North Dakota State University, 1986.

Shin, Hyon B. and Bruno, Rosalind, *Language Use and English-Speaking Ability*, 2000 U.S. Census (October 2003).

Shutter, Marion Daniel, & McLain, John Scudder, *Progressive men of Minnesota. Biographical sketches and portraits of the leaders in business, politics and the professions; together with an historical and descriptive sketch of the state.* Minneapolis: Minneapolis Journal, (1897).

Sibley, Henry Hastings, *The Unfinished Autobiography of Henry Hastings Sibley,"* page 336, Found in the Henry Hastings Sibley Papers of the Minnesota Historical Society's Manuscript Collection.

Sibley County Historical Society *Henderson Then and Now, in the Minnesota River Valley 1852-1994, 3rd edition*, published by the Sibley County Historical Society, 2005.

Siggins, Maggie, *Riel, A Life of Revolution*: Toronto, HarperCollinsPublisherLtd, 1994.

Skinner, Claiborne, *The Upper Country, French Enterprise in the Colonial Great Lakes*, The John Hopkins University Press, 2008.

Snee, Mike, *NCAA men's hockey: Minnesota the capital of hockey nation*, ESPN Sports Online, April 5, 2011.

Snodgrass, Mary Ellen, *Settlers of the American West, The Lives of 231 Notable Pioneers*, published 2015.

Somerset, Wisconsin: 125 pioneer families and Canadian connection: 125th year, from The State of Wisconsin Digital Collection (1984).

Stepick, Alex and C.D. Stepick.*) Haitian Boat People: A Study in the Conflicting Forces Shaping U.S. Immigration Policy. Law and Contemporary Problems*. Duke University Law Journal 45/2 (spring 1982).

Stevens, Issac I., *Narrative Final Report of Explorations for a Route for A Pacific Railroad, near the Forty-Seventh and Forty-Ninth Parallels of North Latitufe from St. Paul to Puget Sound*, plates 3,4,5 in 36 Congress, 1 session, House Executive Documents no. 56 (serial 1054).

Stevens, Hiram Fairchild, *History of the Bench and Bar of Minnesota, Volume 2*, Minneapolis and St. Paul Legal Publishing and Engraving Company, J. Clyde Lindsey, Manager, 1904.

Stotz, Charles Morse, *Outposts Of The War For Empire: The French And English In Western Pennsylvania: Their Armies, Their Forts, Their People 1749-1764*. Pittsburgh: University of Pittsburgh Press. ISBN 0-8229-4262-3 (2005).

Tanguay, Father Cyprien. *Dictionnaire généalogique des Familles Canadiennes depuis la fondation de la colonie jusqu'à nos jours*. First edition. *Eusèbe Senéchal, Imprimeur-Éditeur*. Quebec. 1871, Vol. 1.

Taylor, K.L, "American geological investigations and the French, 1750-1850," *Earth Sciences History* 9 (1990).

The Catholic Encyclopedia: *An International Work of Reference on the Constitution, Doctrine, Discipline, and History of the Catholic Church*, (1911).

The monthly South Dakotan, *Joseph LaFramboise, First Settler*, in Watertown South Dakota Library Collection, March 1901, No. 11, Third Year.

Tetrault, Maximilienne, *Le Role de la Presse dans l'Evolution du people Franco-Americain de la Nouvelle Angleterre*, p. 35,37 (Marseilles, France, 1935).

Thein, Duane, *Father Joesph Goiffon: A Tale of a French Missionary*, White Bear Stereoptics Company, (2005).

Thurley, Simon, *Into the future. Our strategy for 2005-2010*. In: Conservation Bulletin [English Heritage], (2005).

Trap, Paul, *Biography of Jean Baptiste Faribault*, Dictionary of Canadian Biography, University of Toronto/Universite Laval (1974-2015).

Trewartha, G.T., "A second epoch of destructive occupance in the Driftless Hill Land," *Annals of the Association of American Geographers 30* (1940).

Trimble, Steve, *Historic Photos of St. Paul*, Text and Captions by Steve Trimble, published by Turner Publishing company (2008).

Trudel, M., *Introduction to New France* (Toronto and Montreal: Holt, Rinehart and Winston of Canada, Limited, 1968).

Upham, Warren, *Minnesota Place Names, A Geographical Encyclopedia*, Minnesota Historical Society Press; 3rd Revised & Enlarged edition (May 15, 2001) Third Edition.

Van Kirk, Sylvia's *"Many Tender Ties," Women in Fur-Trade Society in Western Canada, 1670 -1870*, Watson and Dwyer Publishing Ltd, (1980).

Waters, Thomas F., "*The Minnesota: Corridor West". The Streams and Rivers of Minnesota*, University of Minnesota Press (2006).

Wedel, M.M., "Le Sueur and the Dakota Sioux," in Johnson, E. (editor), *Aspects of Upper Great Lakes Anthropology: Papers in Honor of Lloyd A. Wilford*. Minnesota Prehistoric Archaeology Series (St. Paul: Minnesota Historical Society, (1974).

Watterworth, Heather, *Hockey Culture*, Canadian Living, February 15, 2011.

Wells, J.W., "Notes on the earliest geological maps of the United States, 1756-1832," *Journal of the Washington Academy of Sciences* 49 (1959).

West, Nathaniel, *The ancestry, life, and times of Hon. Henry Hastings Sibley*, Pioneer Press Publishing Company, Saint Paul, (1880).

Williams, J. Fletcher, *The History of the City of Saint Paul and the County of Ramsey, Minnesota*, Minnesota Historical Society Press, St. Paul, (1983).

Winchell, N.H., "Historical Sketch of Explorations and Surveys in Minnesota," In *The Final Report, Geology of Minnesota*, Minneapolis: Johnson, Smith & Harrison, (1884).

Winchell, N.H., "*The Aborigines of Minnesota*" St. Paul: Minnesota Historical Society, (1911).

Wingerd, Mary Lethert, *North Country, the Making of Minnesota*, Illustrations complied and annotated by Kirsten Delegard, University of Minnesota Press, Minneapolis, (2010).

Winsor, J., *Cartier to Frontenac: Geographical Discovery in the Interior of North America in its Historical Relations 1534-1700*, Boston and New York: Houghton, Mifflin and Company, (1894).

Wood, W. Raymond, "An Atlas of Early Maps of the American Midwest: Part II," *Illinois State Museum Scientific Papers* XXIX (2001).

Wood, W.R. and D.A. Birk, "Pierre-Charles Le Sueur's 1702 Map of the Mississippi River," *Minnesota Archaeologist* 60 (2001).

Index

CPSIA information can be obtained
at www.ICGtesting.com
Printed in the USA
BVHW012147220921
617383BV00011B/236